NORTHERN LIGHTS

The Stories of Minnesota's Past

www.mnhs.org/mhspress

Cover: *Fiery Sunset over the Island River,* Superior National Forest, by photographer Raymond Gehman, 1996. Used with permission.

Library of Congress Cataloging-in-Publication Data

Kenney, Dave, 1961–
Northern lights : the stories of Minnesota's past / Dave Kenney ; investigations by
    Hillary Wackman and Nancy O'Brien Wagner.—2nd ed.
        p. cm.
Includes index.
Summary: Surveys the history of Minnesota from the Ice Age through the end of
    the twentieth century, with "Investigations" that encourage the examination of
    primary source documents and use of proper historical methods.
ISBN 0-87351-440-8 (alk. paper) 1. Minnesota—History—Juvenile literature.
    2. Minnesota—History—Sources—Juvenile literature. 3. Minnesota—History—
    Study and teaching—Juvenile literature. [1. Minnesota—History.] I. Wackman,
    Hillary, 1965– II. Wagner, Nancy O'Brien, 1973– III. Title.
F606.3.K46 2003
977.6—dc21   2002044381

Manufactured in the United States of America

10 9 8 7 6 5 4 3 2 1

International Standard Book Number 0-87351-440-8

NORTHERN LIGHTS

The Stories of Minnesota's Past

SECOND  EDITION

Dave Kenney

Investigations by Hillary Wackman and Nancy O'Brien Wagner

MINNESOTA HISTORICAL SOCIETY PRESS

BENEFACTORS

Generous financial support for the development and publication of the second edition of *Northern Lights: The Stories of Minnesota's Past* was provided by the following:

Whitney and Betty MacMillan

Deluxe Corporation Foundation

Edwards Memorial Trust

George A. MacPherson Fund

The McKnight Foundation

In-kind support for the two-chapter pilot project was provided by West Group.

ADVISORY COMMITTEE

Annette Atkins
Professor of History, St. John's University and the College of Saint Benedict

Patricia G. Avery
Associate Professor, Department of Curriculum and Instruction, University of Minnesota

Marjorie Bingham
Former Co-Director of the Upper Midwest Women's History Center

Michael F. Graves
Professor of Literary Education and the Guy Bond Fellow in Reading, University of Minnesota

John Fraser Hart
Professor of Geography, University of Minnesota

Deborah L. Miller
Minnesota Historical Society

Marcia M. Olson
Teacher, Wayzata Public Schools

Leslie Greaves Radloff
Librarian, Rondo, IRC, St. Paul Public Schools

David Vassar Taylor
Historian and Dean of the General College, University of Minnesota

Marium Toure
Teacher, Minneapolis Public Schools

NORTHERN LIGHTS
The Stories of Minnesota's Past

CONTENTS

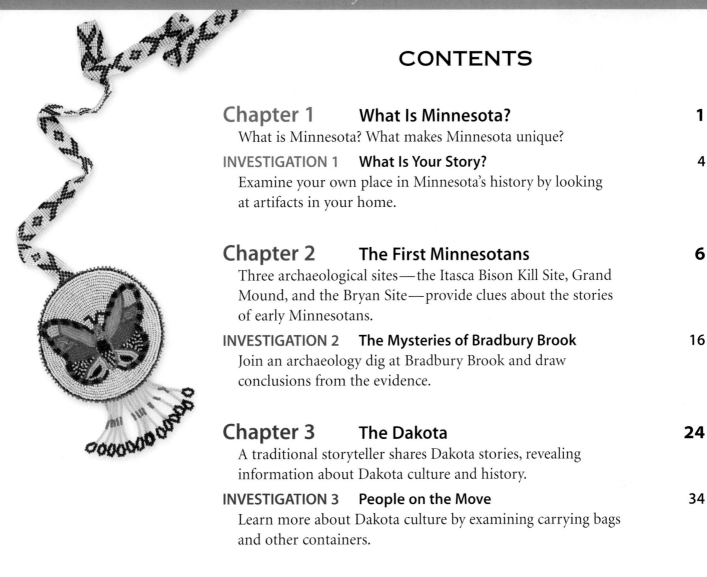

Chapter 1   **What Is Minnesota?**   **1**
What is Minnesota? What makes Minnesota unique?

INVESTIGATION 1   **What Is Your Story?**   **4**
Examine your own place in Minnesota's history by looking
at artifacts in your home.

Chapter 2   **The First Minnesotans**   **6**
Three archaeological sites—the Itasca Bison Kill Site, Grand
Mound, and the Bryan Site—provide clues about the stories
of early Minnesotans.

INVESTIGATION 2   **The Mysteries of Bradbury Brook**   **16**
Join an archaeology dig at Bradbury Brook and draw
conclusions from the evidence.

Chapter 3   **The Dakota**   **24**
A traditional storyteller shares Dakota stories, revealing
information about Dakota culture and history.

INVESTIGATION 3   **People on the Move**   **34**
Learn more about Dakota culture by examining carrying bags
and other containers.

Chapter 4   **The Ojibwe**   **40**
The Ojibwe migrate west through the Great Lakes region, into
the homelands of the Dakota. Fur traders follow, continuing
their trade with the Ojibwe and establishing trade with the
Dakota.

INVESTIGATION 4   **What My Grandmother Taught Me**   **50**
Study the stories of Maude Kegg, an Ojibwe elder who lived
from 1904 to 1996, to understand the importance of
oral tradition.

Chapter 5   The Fur Trade   56

The roles and relationships of the people of the fur trade are revealed through the journals of Michel Curot, a clerk and trader in the region.

INVESTIGATION 5   Trading Places with a Voyageur   66

Read primary sources describing the life of a voyageur and then write a diary of an imaginary voyageur.

Chapter 6   The Land Changes Hands   74

Through treaties with Minnesota's Dakota and Ojibwe, the U.S. government acquires vast tracts of land for settlement by European Americans.

INVESTIGATION 6   In Their Own Words   84

Discover the importance of perspective by reading the opinions of both Dakota and newcomers about the treaties.

Chapter 7   Minnesota's Newcomers   90

The stories of an early Swedish immigrant and St. Paul's first schoolteacher show how immigrants to Minnesota influenced the state during the territorial years.

INVESTIGATION 7   Writing Home, Writing Minnesota   100

Explore point of view by studying advertisements used to entice immigrants to Minnesota and stories told by immigrants themselves.

Chapter 8   The Civil War   106

The experiences of three Minnesotans—two African American slaves and a soldier in the First Minnesota Regiment—illustrate the Civil War's impact on the state.

INVESTIGATION 8   Missionary Ridge, the "Soldier's Battle" 116

Examine a Civil War painting to analyze its value as history and as art.

Chapter 9   **Minnesota's Civil War**   **122**

In the summer of 1862, a complex mix of factors led to the
Dakota War, a deadly conflict with devastating consequences.

INVESTIGATION 9   **Untold Stories of the Dakota War**   134

Encounter a little-known perspective on the Dakota War
by reading personal accounts of survivors.

Chapter 10   **Sodbusters**   **140**

A young family builds a farm in southwestern Minnesota
during the era of sodbusting and railroad expansion across
the state.

INVESTIGATION 10   **Small Town Life**   150

Plan and develop your own frontier town to examine the
factors that affected a town's success or failure.

Chapter 11   **Flour, Lumber, and Iron**   **156**

Industrialists and laborers work together—and often against
each other—while building the successful milling, lumbering,
and mining industries of Minnesota.

INVESTIGATION 11   **Picturing Working Life**   168

Analyze early photos of Minnesota workers to draw
conclusions about work life between 1880 and 1920.

Chapter 12   **Bigger, Taller, Faster**   **174**

A small-town state legislator living in St. Paul reflects on the
urban boom at the turn of the twentieth century.

INVESTIGATION 12   **Blueprints of Our Past**   186

Compare Victorian and Prairie School architecture to
consider how home design reflects family lifestyle.

Chapter 13   The Common Good   **192**

During the Progressive Era, Minnesotans campaign for reforms to solve government, corporate, and social problems.

INVESTIGATION 13   Why is Miss R. Sick?   204

Explore public health issues at the turn of the twentieth century.

Chapter 14   The Good Life   **212**

The experiences of three Minnesota children show how new goods and new conveniences altered the lifestyles of people in the cities, small towns, and rural areas.

INVESTIGATION 14   Capturing Leisure in Scrapbooks and Diaries   224

Study scrapbooks to uncover how people in Minnesota spent leisure time around the turn of the twentieth century.

Chapter 15   Boom and Bust   **230**

The dramatic stories of a young jazz musician and a farm family illustrate the contrast between the Twenties and the Great Depression.

INVESTIGATION 15   St. Paul's Gangster Era   240

Investigate the effects of Prohibition on crime by attempting to solve a kidnapping case.

Chapter 16   World War II   **248**

With the country at war, Minnesotans work for the war effort in the armed forces, at home, and on the job.

INVESTIGATION 16   Virginia Mae Hope: WWII Pilot   258

Explore letters and photographs of pilot Virginia Mae Hope to learn about women's contributions to the war effort.

Chapter 17   Cold War, Warm Kitchens   **264**

After the war, a major Minnesota company develops new products in response to the issues and values of Cold War America.

INVESTIGATION 17   Playing with History   274

Analyze games and toys to discover how themes of the Cold War, the space race, and domesticity are reflected in them.

Women in the war

WE CAN'T WIN WITHOUT THEM

Chapter 18   Taking a Stand   **280**

In the 1960s and 1970s, Minnesotans join with others to fight for equal rights for African Americans, American Indians, and women.

INVESTIGATION 18   Singing Out for Social Change   292

Study lyrics of protest songs to explore how music can raise awareness of social and political issues.

Chapter 19   Transforming the Land   **298**

In the second half of the twentieth century, Minnesotans change their landscape with extended suburbs, fewer but larger farms, and the protection of wilderness areas.

INVESTIGATION 19   The Transformation of Duluth's Canal Park   308

Examine the changes of Duluth's Canal Park over two centuries.

Chapter 20   New Minnesotans   **314**

At the end of the twentieth century, new immigrant groups such as Somalis, Hmong, and Mexican Americans make Minnesota their home.

INVESTIGATION 20   Welcome to Minnesota   324

Welcome a newcomer by creating a gift basket of objects that tell Minnesota's stories.

Index   326

Credits   332

Acknowledgments   334

Creating *Northern Lights*   335

Population Statistics   336

ATLAS

Elevation, Rivers, and Lakes   337

Cities, Counties, Parks, and Reservations 338

Transportation Systems   339

Environment, Around 1850   340

Environment, Around 2000   341

Major Industries   342

Greetings from MINNESO[TA]

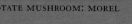

State mushroom: morel

State flag

State bird: loon

W hat is Minnesota?

At first glance this might look like a simple question, but actually it is more complicated than it appears. Think of all the possible answers. You could say that Minnesota is a lake-studded chunk of land bordered by Canada, Lake Superior, Wisconsin, Iowa, and North and South Dakota. Or you could say that it's a great hodgepodge of people—some who were born here and some who were not. Maybe you like to think of Minnesota as an idea—a mind picture that portrays everything from hot-dish dinners, to microprocessors, to hockey pucks slapped off the ice. Or then again, maybe you prefer a simpler answer:

Minnesota is your home.

Over the centuries, millions of people have called this place home— even if they didn't always call it Minnesota. Some were born here. Some died here. But *all* of them lived here at least part of their lives. And many of those lives remain with us today in the form of stories. Happy stories. Sad stories. Inspiring stories.

LOOK FOR

◆ What do you think Minnesota is?
◆ What sets Minnesotans apart as a people?
◆ How do we know about our past?

KEY TERMS

shared history

STATE TREE: RED PINE

STATE BUTTERFLY: MONARCH

STATE FISH: WALLEYE

STATE FLOWER: PINK LADY SLIPPER

1

Even a few boring ones. We can learn a lot about Minnesota by reading and listening to those stories.

The stories of Minnesota's people pop up in all sorts of likely and unlikely places. They're carved into rock walls rising above northern lakes and on rocky ridges in the southwestern prairies. They pass from generation to generation through the mouths of talented storytellers. They jump from the pages of diaries, journals, and written histories. They hide in the things of everyday life—clothes, buildings, tools, toys.

Spend enough time rooting around in this great collection of stories and you'll discover that Minnesotans are a complicated bunch. It's hard to put labels on them. Not that we haven't tried. Over the years, people have made plenty of blanket statements about Minnesotans. They're tough. They're independent. They're politically progressive. They do quirky things and then make fun of themselves for doing them. And above all, they're nice—as in "Minnesota nice." But statements like those can be misleading. Sure, there may be a certain amount of truth to them, but do they accurately describe every Minnesotan you know? Of course not. Minnesotans come in a dizzying variety of colors and styles. Not everyone who lives here is nice. In fact, a few are even downright mean.

So what is it about Minnesotans—beyond geography—that binds them together as a people and makes them different from Iowans, Californians, and Vermonters? Certainly it's not a shared ancestral heritage. Minnesotans come from a wide variety of ethnic and racial backgrounds. It's not their political beliefs, either. Minnesotans identify themselves as conservatives, liberals, and everything in between. They don't all talk the same, dress the same, cheer for the same sports teams, or laugh at the same jokes. So what is it? What sets Minnesotans apart as a people?

Maybe the answer lies in those stories that the people of Minnesota

PAUL BUNYAN
AND BABE,
THE BLUE
OX

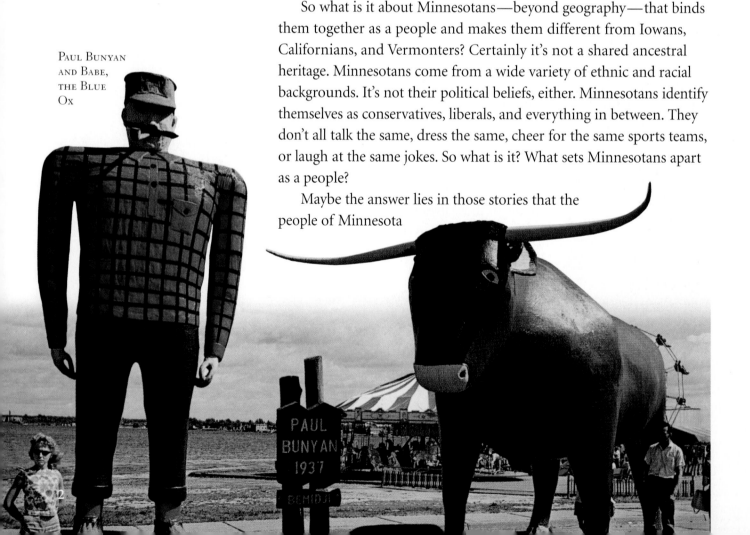

are always leaving behind. Bundle all those stories together and you wind up with a package of experiences—a **shared history** that can help all Minnesotans understand how their home state got to be the way it is today. That's not to say that all Minnesota stories reflect the experiences of all Minnesotans. The stories that you find most interesting may not appeal to a student living in another part of the state. You may even find it hard to understand the importance of a story that has great meaning to the classmate sitting next to you. But that package of experiences that forms the history of Minnesota is something you and every other person who lives in this state can share and contribute to.

Now you are about to unwrap that big package of Minnesota experiences. Inside you will find the stories of dozens of people who made Minnesota what it is today. Some of them were famous in their time. Some remain well known today. But most of them were people, like yourself, who went about their lives completely unaware that they were making history. They didn't realize that people would continue to tell their stories decades, and even centuries, after they were gone.

MINNESOTA POSTCARD QUILT, 1979

Most of these stories will take you back in time. As you become familiar with them, try to keep in mind the many different ways that stories stay alive over the years. The most recent stories often come from a variety of artifacts including written documents, recordings, and photographs. Many of the older stories have passed down to us through the voices of our ancestors. But the oldest stories we tell about Minnesota are often the hardest to piece together. They're the ones that are written in stone and earth. They require the most detective work.

They are the first stories—the first chapters of a centuries-old tale called the history of Minnesota.

What Is Your Story?

The next time you visit your grandparents, or other relatives or friends, take a close look around their home. Chances are you will find an interesting photograph or unusual souvenir—something that has a story behind it, something that tells you about their past.

PRIMARY SOURCES: PIECES OF THE PAST

To investigate stories from the past, historians examine primary sources. Primary sources are first-hand, original objects such as letters, photographs, baby books, diaries, and official documents like birth certificates. Primary sources can also be items like clothing, toys, and sports equipment. People are also primary sources. Historians use primary sources as evidence of past events, just as detectives use clues to solve a crime.

POINT OF VIEW: WHAT PEOPLE SEE AND UNDERSTAND

Historians keep in mind that primary sources reflect a certain point of view. For example, if your grandmother and her brother both wrote in their diaries about the same family event, the diary entries would be different. This is because each person has a unique point of view. Point of view—how you see and understand the world— is formed by education, beliefs, and life experiences. Culture, time period, and the place where you live also shape your point of view.

Family photographs give clues to that family's history. **How far back in time do these photographs seem to go?**

INTERPRETATION: TELLING A STORY BASED ON EVIDENCE

When historians study the past, they begin by gathering a wide variety of sources. They try to make sure that these sources represent many points of view. Using this information, historians try to explain what the primary sources say about the past. This explanation is called historical interpretation. Often, historians know only a small part of what happened. They know that if a new primary source is discovered, they might have to revise their original interpretation.

INVESTIGATIONS: YOUR CHANCE TO BE A HISTORIAN

The Investigations in this book give you a chance to be a historian. Each Investigation has images of actual primary sources for you to explore. As you read each Investigation, look for the small magnifying lenses like this: ⚲. They give you something exciting to do with the information you uncover.

When you get home tonight, look at your home through the eyes of a historian. What evidence in your home connects you to the past, and to Minnesota? What stories do your photographs and objects tell? After all—like the people you will read about in this book—you, too, are part of Minnesota's history.

⚲ **Brainstorm a list of primary sources you might find in your home. Which documents, photographs, and objects tell something about you?**

The top of someone's dresser is a good place to find items the person values or uses every day.

Historians use primary sources to piece together the stories of the past. **What can you tell about this family by looking at the outside of their refrigerator?**

5

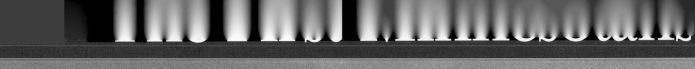

Ancient American Indian people carved more than 30 types of images in this rocky ridge near Jeffers, Minnesota.

16,000 B.C.	**10,000** B.C.	**8000** B.C.	**7000** B.C.	**5000** B.C.	**4000** B.C.	**3100** B.C.
Glaciers cover much of what is now Minnesota, except the southeastern part of the state.	Glaciers have almost completely melted from Minnesota. Earliest known stone tools in North America date from this period.	Farming develops in central Asia in Mesopotamia.	Evidence of human activity in Brown's Valley, in western Minnesota, dates from this period.	People hunt bison at Itasca, in central Minnesota.	Evidence of humans living near Pelican Rapids, in central Minnesota, dates from this period.	Writing developed by Sumerians in southwest Asia.

About halfway between the towns of Jeffers and Comfrey, in what is today southwestern Minnesota, is a place where history is written in stone. Over thousands of years, people came to this spot and carved images in the long, rocky ridge that rises above the prairie. Sometimes they carved images of hunters carrying weapons called atlatls (A-tuh-LA-tuhls). Sometimes they carved figures representing bison and other animals that the hunters were trying to kill. These carvings, called petroglyphs (PEH-troh-glifs), are among the most important examples of ancient rock art in North America. But they're not the only things you'll find carved in the stone here.

At several places on this ridge, it looks as if a giant has scratched the rock with its fingernails. And in fact, the rock *has* been scratched, but not by a giant. The scratches were caused by moving sheets of ice called **glaciers.**

LOOK FOR

- ◆ How has Minnesota's landscape changed over the last 12,000 years?
- ◆ What cultures developed in Minnesota before the year 1700?
- ◆ How did early people adapt to life in what is now Minnesota?
- ◆ What tools did they develop?
- ◆ How do historians and archaeologists study the past?

KEY TERMS

glacier
evidence
migration
artifact
archaeologist

glacier: a large body of ice that can grow or shrink depending on the climate

3000 B.C.	**2600** B.C.	**1000** B.C.	**800–300** B.C.	**509** B.C.–A.D. **476**	A.D. **300–900**	A.D. **1100**
People begin carving petrogylphs in rock near Jeffers.	Egyptians begin building pyramids at Giza around this time.	Burial Mounds, including Grand Mound near International Falls, are built in Minnesota.	Ancient Greek civilization flourishes around eastern Mediterranean Sea.	Ancient Roman civilization flourishes in Europe, western Asia, and northern Africa.	Maya civilization flourishes in Meso-America (Central America).	Cahokian culture flourishes near present-day St. Louis, Missouri. Early farming communities develop near present-day Red Wing.

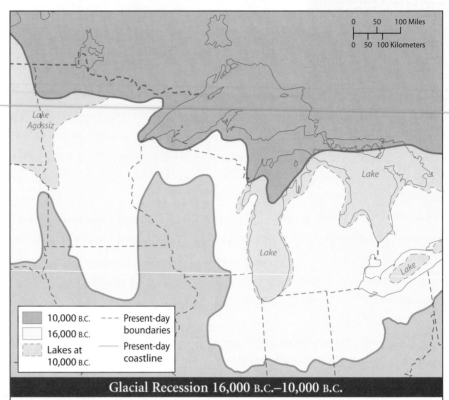

░ 10,000 B.C.	- - - Present-day boundaries
▫ 16,000 B.C.	
▒ Lakes at 10,000 B.C.	—— Present-day coastline

Glacial Recession 16,000 B.C.–10,000 B.C.

The glaciers that covered the Minnesota area around 16,000 B.C. extended south into what is now north central Iowa. By 10,000 B.C., the glaciers were receding and deep pits remained where the glaciers had dragged boulders. Gradually, the pits filled with water as the glaciers melted and created many of the thousands of lakes Minnesota has today.

Living on the Edge of the Glaciers

Glaciers have covered what is now Minnesota many times. The ice last moved southward into this region about 18,000 years ago. By 12,000 years ago the ice was melting, but northern Minnesota was still partly covered. As the ice turned to water, it made foaming rivers and lakes. One called Lake Agassiz (AG-uh-see) was hundreds of miles wide. The climate was cooler and drier than it is today, and on the shores of the lakes and along the edges of the ice grew dark forests, mostly of spruce. Moss covered the forest floors. Few flowers blossomed, and not many birds sang. But in the open places grass grew, and herds of large animals roamed. There were mammoths and mastodons, which were like huge elephants with shaggy hair and long, curving tusks. There were giant bison, twice the size of the buffalo we know today. There also were smaller animals, such as caribou and arctic hare.

One day, about 10,000 years ago, a band of human hunters came, probably following a herd of animals from the south. These were the ancestors of the people we now call American Indians. We know very little about these earliest Minnesotans. The only obvious traces that have been found here are a few stone spear points.

We know a little more about the people who came after them.

Sometime around 12,000 years ago, someone living in what is now Yellow Medicine County chipped or flaked stone into this point. It is called a Clovis point because archaeologists first found points like this at Clovis, New Mexico.

Game Hunters in a Warming Climate

Between 6000 and 5000 B.C., the climate in the region was becoming warmer and drier. Many of the large animals that had moved in as the glaciers melted could not adapt to the warmer climate. Their numbers began shrinking until, eventually, there were none left. The dense spruce forests that had grown up following the glacial retreat also began to retreat northward.

But as those animals and plants vanished, new ones appeared. Bears, elk, deer, beavers, and other smaller animals entered the region. Open grasslands grew in the areas that had once been spruce forests. Pines and leafy trees such as oaks and elms began thriving as the weather turned milder. Plants bearing nuts and fruit became more common. As the natural surroundings of Minnesota changed, so did the people who lived here. They began eating new kinds of food.

One of the places they looked for food was on the southern shore of what we now call Lake Itasca (eye-TAS-kuh).

Archaeologists imagine that mammoth hunts looked something like this. Most of the animal was used: meat for food, hides for clothes and shelters, and tusks for tools.

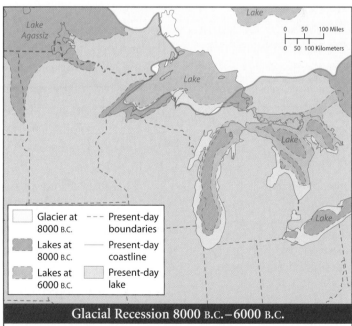

Glacier at 8000 B.C.
Lakes at 8000 B.C.
Lakes at 6000 B.C.
Present-day boundaries
Present-day coastline
Present-day lake

Lake Agassiz

Glacial Recession 8000 B.C.–6000 B.C.

By 8000 B.C., the glaciers had receded north of the present borders of Minnesota. Around 6000 B.C., Lake Agassiz began to drain southward. As it gushed, the water created what became the Minnesota River valley.

Itasca Bison
Kill Site

LAKE ITASCA
7,000 YEARS AGO

A strong north wind pushes whitecaps across the big lake and into the shallow inlet. The bison don't seem to notice. They're interested only in moving east, toward the wooded areas that provide shelter during the winter. But it's slow going here. The bottom of the inlet is soft and mucky. It's easy to get stuck. Suddenly, something strikes one of the cows in her right flank. It's a spear. The cow bellows in pain and stumbles into the water. Her calf remains at her side. Within minutes, both the mother and her calf are dead. So are 14 other members of the herd. Four men are standing over the fallen animals.

The men butcher the bison, using sharp stone knives. They haul the heavy cuts of meat up a slope to a ridge where their families have been waiting. Here they hang the meat over fires for smoking and drying. The women begin scraping and tanning the skins. The children run after the dogs, trying to keep them from stealing the meat. Then the families celebrate the successful hunt. They feast not only on bison meat but on other foods as well. Fish, turtle, acorns, and hazelnuts all are available here.

The families don't stay long. They need to find shelter from the snow and cold. They cross the inlet and head east. Their dogs run ahead, pulling sleds loaded with food and skins.

THE ITASCA BISON KILL SITE 7,000 YEARS AGO

In 1937, some workers were building a bridge over a creek just south of Lake Itasca when they discovered some large bones. A team of archaeologists traveled to the site and uncovered even more bones. The scientists determined that many of the bones came from an extinct species of very large bison. Others came from a variety of smaller mammals, birds, fishes, and turtles. There was even a dog skull. Over the years, on a hill overlooking the creek, archaeologists found many stone artifacts made by humans. Other evidence showed that fruits and nuts were common in the area at this time. All these things, when taken together, tell us that the people who hunted here probably ate many different foods.

evidence: the material on which a judgment or conclusion may be based. Artifacts, documents, photos, paintings, interviews, and rock carvings are all forms of historical evidence.

migration: seasonal movement from one region to another

This story about a bison hunt at Lake Itasca is based on **evidence** found at what we now call the Itasca Bison Kill Site. Much of the evidence tells us what sorts of things the people who lived in this area ate. And it appears that they ate many kinds of foods—not just bison. We can guess that the changes in their diet affected other parts of their lives, too. They probably organized their lives according to when food was available in certain places. Fish would be easiest to catch during the spring. Bison were easiest to find during their spring and fall **migrations,** as were many birds. Wild fruits ripened during the summer. Nuts were ready for eating in the fall.

New Tools in a Cooling Climate

By about 3,000 years ago, Minnesota's climate had cooled down a bit, and the weather had settled into patterns that were more like those we know today. The plants and animals living then also would have been familiar to us. It was at about this time that the people in the region started changing the way they lived. This time, the changes were the result of new methods of doing everyday things. At least two of these methods had been developed by people who lived in lands to the south.

Around this time, people began using clay to make pottery for cooking and storing food. Previously, the people who lived in the area had cooked many of their foods by placing them in baskets or skin bags with fire-heated stones. But with clay pots, they could heat food close to a fire. It was a much more efficient way to cook. Food stored in clay pots was also less likely to spoil.

A new religious practice also took hold during this time. Up to that point, the people in the region had buried their dead in individual graves. But now many people began burying bodies in mounds of earth. Most of the mounds were small and round. Some were long and low. A few were animal-shaped. They were almost always located on high points of land. Over the centuries, the people in the region built thousands of such mounds.

One of those mounds arose near what we now call the Rainy River in northern Minnesota.

Archaeologists can learn much about early people's diets by examining the remains of food left inside pots.

About 1000 B.C., people created burial mounds like these located near Pine City in east central Minnesota. As many as 10,000 of these burial mounds may have been built throughout the state.

Grand Mound Site

RAINY RIVER
2,000 YEARS AGO

The people are gathered at the base of a huge mound of dirt that is taller than three men standing on each other's shoulders. At the top of the hill, an old man is chanting. At his feet are many bundles of bones. The bones belong to relatives who died during the past year. When the elder has finished, the people at the bottom of the hill scrape up baskets of dirt from the ground and carry them to the top of the mound. There they cover the bones and make the monument even taller than it was. For as long as anyone can remember, people have been coming to this place and doing this.

When the ceremony is complete, the people return to their camps. Clay pots brimming with bubbling fish stews nestle in the coals of small campfires. Families who haven't seen each other for many months gather together to share food, goods, and stories. Soon, many of the families will leave the woods and head south and west toward their prairie hunting grounds. They'll return next spring to bury their dead and renew friendships.

GRAND MOUND 2,000 YEARS AGO

Grand Mound, at the northern border of the state, is the largest burial mound in Minnesota. It is 25 feet tall and more than 100 feet wide at its base. It contains almost 5,000 tons of earth. No one is allowed to dig here now, but we know from previous excavations that the mound has many separate soil layers containing stone tools, clay pots, and bundles of human bones. One of the first things archaeologists noticed when they started excavating the areas where people lived near the mound was the large number of sturgeon bones and scales. The lake sturgeon is a fish that can grow 8 feet long and weigh up to 250 pounds. During the spring, sturgeon swim upstream into rivers such as the Rainy and the Big Fork to lay their eggs. Archaeologists believe that the people who gathered at Grand Mound went there during the spring so they could feast on the big fish at a time when they were especially easy to catch. Excavations have turned up two types of bone harpoon points that were probably used for fishing. Most of the other tools found near Grand Mound also were used for catching or preparing sturgeon.

This story about mound-building people in northern Minnesota is based on evidence found at a place we now call Grand Mound. The mound itself, and the **artifacts** buried inside it, help us understand how people lived 3,000 years ago. Evidence from areas around the mound, where people camped and lived, provide clues about what the people did and what they ate while they stayed here.

New Foods, New Relationships

About 1,000 years ago, something was happening hundreds of miles down the Mississippi River that seems to have had a big impact on many of the people who lived in Minnesota. A large city had developed across the river from where St. Louis, Missouri, is today. We call this city Cahokia (kuh-HOH-kee-uh). At its largest, Cahokia may have been home to at least 20,000 people. The residents there built huge mounds and used them for worship. They also planted and harvested crops such as corn, beans, and squash in the rich soil alongside the Mississippi.

The Cahokians traveled widely. It's very likely that, at some point, they made their way to Minnesota by traveling up the Mississippi River. No one knows for sure, but the people who lived here probably learned many things from their neighbors to the south. One thing we do know is that the people of Minnesota started growing more kinds of food plants at about this time. Some of those plants may have come from the Cahokians.

The growing season here was short 1,000 years ago, just as it is today. Only in southern Minnesota could people grow the kinds of crops raised at Cahokia, such as corn, beans, squash, and sunflowers. Some of the biggest farming communities in Minnesota developed along the Mississippi and Cannon rivers near present-day Red Wing.

One of these communities was located on a high gravel terrace overlooking the Cannon River in southeastern Minnesota.

CANNON RIVER 1,000 YEARS AGO

Two young women climb up a well-worn path, using their wooden digging sticks and hoes for support. They don't say much to each other. They're too tired. They've spent most of the day breaking soil in the bottomlands near the river. Tomorrow they'll begin planting corn and beans.

Artifacts such as this hoe made from the shoulder blade of a bison are important clues about past cultures. **How does this artifact suggest that these people were both hunters and farmers?**

Finally, they reach the top of the bluff. Before them are the imposing log walls that surround and protect their village. They walk through the entrance and join a bustle of activity. In the open area at the center of the village, children have gathered around a pair of boys who are rolling around on the ground in a wrestling match. A hunter walks by carrying three dead rabbits by the ears. A woman kneels over a campfire and stirs a pot of boiling soup.

As the two women arrive at their dwelling, a boy and a girl wearing big smiles run up to them and grab them around the knees. The women set down their farming tools and hug their children.

This story about a farming community on the Cannon River is based on evidence found at a place we now call the Bryan Site. Many of the artifacts uncovered there indicate that the people who lived there grew much of their own food. Other evidence suggests that they were used to meeting people from other places and other cultures. One thing that evidence has not been able to tell us yet is what happened to this

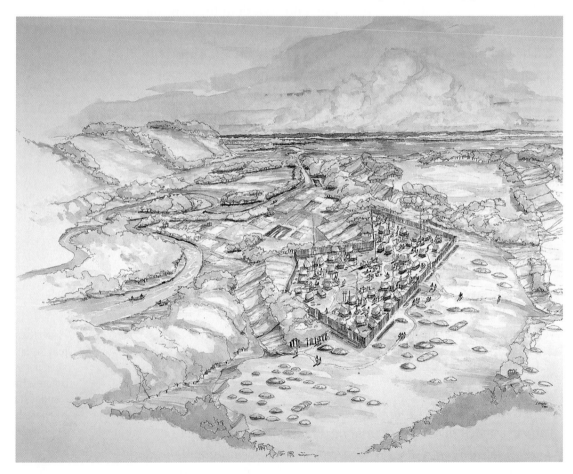

This painting represents an archaeologist's idea of what the Bryan Site looked like about 1,000 years ago.

In 1885, a man named T. H. Lewis drew a series of maps showing the locations of many human-made mounds in the Red Wing area. One cluster of more than 160 mounds was located on a high gravel terrace overlooking the Cannon River. This place became known as the Bryan Site. Over the years, archaeologists have uncovered many clues about the people who once lived and farmed here.

Hoes made from the shoulder blades of bison are among the many farming tools that have been discovered. The many bell-shaped storage pits found at the site suggest that the people here stored food for future use. Other evidence found at the site provides important information. For example, the pottery discovered here is not all one kind. Some of it is similar to pottery produced by the Cahokians.

Other pieces are typical of pots produced to the west in the region now called the Great Plains. This suggests that the people who lived in the Red Wing area traded with people from other cultures. The evidence of a palisade, or wall, surrounding the Bryan Site village may mean that the people here were in conflict with other groups or that they were trying to keep out animals.

community. People lived at the Bryan Site for only about 300 years, a short time in archaeological terms. Why they left is a mystery.

This chapter began with a quick description of the rock carvings in southwestern Minnesota. One thing not mentioned was how mysterious those carvings can be. Some of them, such as the carvings of hunters and bison, are fairly easy to understand. But many are much more difficult to figure out. This is an important point to keep in mind. Much of what we know about the early Minnesotans is based on evidence that's been collected and explained by **archaeologists** (ahr-kee-AHL-uh-jists). The evidence includes clues that were left behind by the people who once lived here—things such as stone tools and weapons, pieces of pottery, and earth mounds. It also includes clues of nature, such as animal bones and plants. But remember: this kind of evidence can be confusing or incomplete. It does not always give us clear or full answers to the questions we have about history.

Sometimes we have to turn to other kinds of evidence—like the stories that people pass down from generation to generation.

Bryan Site

archaeologist: a scientist who studies past human life and activities by examining physical evidence such as tools, fire pits, and ruins from dwellings

THE MYSTERIES OF BRADBURY BROOK

AN UNEXPECTED DISCOVERY

On a cold day in October 1989, archaeologists Mike Magner and Leroy Gonsior and their team gathered in the field between the edge of Highway 169 and Bradbury Brook, near Mille Lacs. The state Department of Transportation had hired them to study the area where a stretch of Highway 169 would be widened. A light snow began falling as they formed a line and walked carefully, side by side, across the field, searching the surface for any evidence of ancient people. Suddenly, a team member called out, "I found something!"

Magner and Gonsior stooped over the cold ground to study the discovery—small, slate-gray rocks with a whitish coating on them and sharp edges. They knew immediately that these rocks were ancient artifacts, but what were they, exactly? Who had made them? Magner and Gonsior gathered up some of the artifacts, then went home to spend a long winter wondering what lay below the snow by Bradbury Brook.

This photo was taken near the end of the excavation. Notice the road construction trucks in the background.

From June to September 1990, archaeologists found more than 125,000 artifacts at the Bradbury Brook Site. Note the man on the right using a metersquare grid to help map the location of the artifacts. **What other activities and tools do you see?**

THE DIG BEGINS

In early June 1990, Magner, Gonsior, and their team returned to Bradbury Brook to begin the "dig"—the process of uncovering artifacts and studying them. The Department of Transportation had agreed to delay the construction on the highway, but only for a few months. The archaeologists would have to work fast. But there was an even bigger problem: the site was a mess. Years of plowing had mixed up the soil and scattered the artifacts.

During an archaeological dig, it is very important to keep the artifacts undisturbed until their locations are mapped. The exact spots where items are found can be the best clues about what happened long ago. Since the Bradbury Brook Site had been plowed for decades, the archaeologists knew that many artifacts and clues had probably been destroyed.

This image shows the edge of the excavation. Note the lighter-colored layer of earth that is the plowzone. Archaeologists were excited when they reached the layers below the plowzone, which hadn't been disturbed by the plows or tractors.

The team spent the first few days of the dig making a careful map of the site. The work was slow. Whenever they found an artifact, they drew its location, recorded its type, collected it, and labeled it for the lab. Once the team had collected all the artifacts they could find on the surface, they began the excavation. As they dug through the plowzone, the layer of earth that had been mixed up by the tractors, they were pleased to discover thousands of artifacts. They collected and labeled these, too.

On August 1, 1990, workers at the site reached the layer of earth below the plowzone. What they saw amazed them. Artifacts lay where they had rested for thousands of years. "Seeing them was like peering directly back into time," Gonsior said. "No other site like this had ever been found in Minnesota." The archaeology team was excited, but the unexpected find meant they would have to work extra hard. For the next seven weeks, the men and women hurried to map, record, and collect as many artifacts as they could. On September 20, the archaeologists moved out and the bulldozers moved in. Whatever artifacts they did not collect are now buried under the expanded highway.

BACK AT THE LAB

As archaeologists like to say, "It's not what we find. It's what we find out." For archaeologists, the work at the dig is only the beginning. Once the artifacts and the information are brought back to the lab, a whole new type of work begins. Imagine having to judge a trial in which there are more than 125,000 pieces of evidence, but having no idea what event or "crime" occurred or who was involved. What would you do? The first thing archaeologists do is observe, or carefully look at and make notes about what they see. The second thing they do is infer, or make educated assumptions about what they observe.

Now it's your turn to think like an archaeologist. Look over their shoulders as the archaeologists investigate Bradbury Brook. Keep track of what you discover on your Investigation Guide, then make a drawing that shows what might have happened there long ago.

The objects on pages 19–21 are some of the Bradbury Brook artifacts.

WHAT WERE THE ARTIFACTS?

Back at the lab, archaeologists Kent Bakken and Riaz Malik began the process of observing the Bradbury Brook artifacts. They carefully weighed, measured, described, identified, and counted each one. When they were finished, they organized the items into groups and noticed some connections between the types of artifacts.

Look at the table of the artifacts from Bradbury Brook. What types of artifacts do you see? How are the artifacts related?

Artifacts from the Bradbury Brook Site	
Artifact Categories and Descriptions	**Number**
Anvilstones: large rocks used to hold cores during the process of making stone tools. Strong blows to the core caused some anvilstones to be damaged or split.	17
Cores: rocks that were broken up into smaller pieces and shaped into tools	732
Hammerstones: rocks used to strike cores in order to break them and form them into tools. Most of the ends of these hammerstones were damaged.	115
Semifinished tools: roughly formed tools	68
Completed tools: adzes, points, knives, scrapers, and blades	47
Flakes, fragments, and residuals: pieces of rock that are broken off a core	124,066
Other nonchipped stones: field stones that archaeologists collected accidentally	580
Modern bones: animal bone pieces that archaeologists collected accidentally	4
Charcoal: burned wood	1
Total	125,630

This image shows the Bradbury Brook dig from above. Compare it to the map made of the site. **What features are easier to see in the photo? On the map on page 21?**

WHAT WERE THE PEOPLE DOING?

Once Malik and Bakken had identified the artifacts, they tried to infer what the early people had done with them. Malik and Bakken found important clues in the map that the field archaeologists had made at the site. For example, Malik and Bakken noticed a pattern in how the anvilstones were laid out. They wondered why people might have arranged them as they did.

○ Study the artifact location map on the opposite page. How were the anvilstones laid out? How might the ancient people at Bradbury Brook have used the tools shown on the map?

WHEN WERE THEY HERE?

In archaeology it is often difficult to know exactly when an artifact was made or used. In most cases, the whitish coating found on the Bradbury Brook artifacts is a sign that they have been buried for thousands of years. To get a clearer sense of when people were at Bradbury Brook, Bakken and Malik had to use a method called radiocarbon dating.

Radiocarbon dating works only on items that are organic—items that were once living—such as bones or charcoal, which is burned wood. The test compares the amount of Carbon-12 and Carbon-14 found in the item. The more Carbon-12, the older the item is. But because these test results are never exact, a time range is often given. Items that have been tested this way also are dated "before present," or "B.P.," which means before 1950, the year when radiocarbon dating was invented. The notation "250–240 B.P." means "250 to 240 years before 1950" (or 1700–1710).

Just one ancient organic item was found at the Bradbury Brook Site: a piece of charcoal.

That charcoal was radiocarbon dated to 9295–9145 B.P. What years are those in B.C. notation?

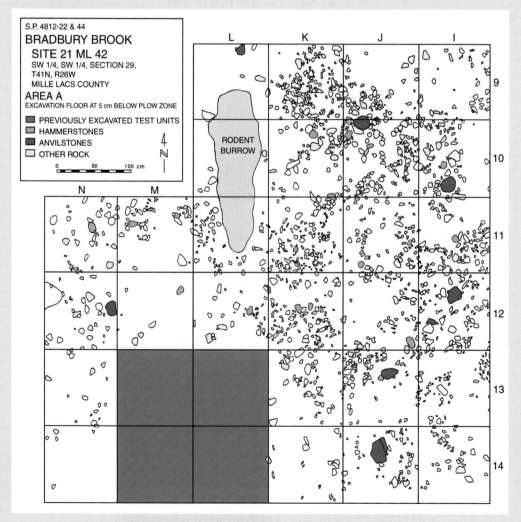

S.P. 4812-22 & 44
BRADBURY BROOK
SITE 21 ML 42
SW 1/4, SW 1/4, SECTION 29,
T41N, R26W
MILLE LACS COUNTY
AREA A
EXCAVATION FLOOR AT 5 cm BELOW PLOW ZONE

■ PREVIOUSLY EXCAVATED TEST UNITS
▨ HAMMERSTONES
■ ANVILSTONES
□ OTHER ROCK

0   50   100 cm

N

RODENT BURROW

L   K   J   I

N   M

9
10
11
12
13
14

Each section of this map was made at the site, using metersquare grids to help the archaeologists draw the artifacts in the right places. Later, the individual maps were put together to form this one.

WHO MADE THE ARTIFACTS?

Bakken and Malik found some unusual pieces among the artifacts. One was the bottom half of an arrow or spear point. What had happened to the top half? The two men knew they couldn't answer that question, but they could guess who had made the point.

One way archaeologists identify ancient cultures is by the types of tools made by people in those cultures. Think about finding a pair of chopsticks or a fork. Both tools are used for the same purpose, but you could see a difference between them and recognize that they are tools used by different cultures.

Archaeologists can see differences between point shapes and recognize which cultures made them.

Bakken and Malik compared the broken point to similar points and narrowed their comparison down to two well-known types of points, Alberta points and Scottsbluff points.

Some archaeologists think the Bradbury Brook point looks like an Alberta point, and some think it looks like a Scottsbluff point.

Known Scottsbluff point

Known Alberta point

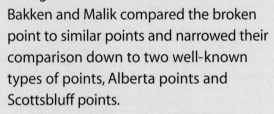

Broken Bradbury Brook point

Compare the Bradbury Brook point to the two other points. Which one do you think it matches? Why?

WHAT WERE THE PEOPLE LIKE?

Knowing that the Bradbury Brook point was either an Alberta point or a Scottsbluff point, Bakken and Malik researched those two cultures. Both cultures existed in what is now Minnesota about 9,200 years ago. The people in both cultures lived in small groups that migrated and hunted animals. But there were differences between them, too. The Alberta culture began in an earlier period, and its people lived mainly in the grasslands, where they hunted large animals. The Scottsbluff culture continued longer, and its people lived mainly in the woodlands, where they probably began making and using more wooden tools, as well as hunting smaller forest animals.

Broken point found at the Bradbury Brook Site

To help decide which of these two cultures the Bradbury Brook people most likely belonged to, Malik and Bakken studied the location of Alberta and Scottsbluff sites in Minnesota. They looked to see which sites were closer, or which sites had a similar environment.

Which culture do you think the Bradbury Brook people were from? Were they mainly a grassland or a woodland culture?

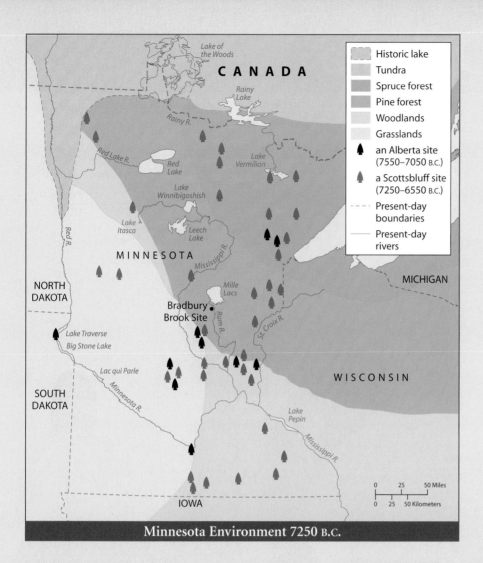

Minnesota Environment 7250 B.C.

Historic lake
Tundra
Spruce forest
Pine forest
Woodlands
Grasslands
an Alberta site
(7550–7050 B.C.)
a Scottsbluff site
(7250–6550 B.C.)
Present-day
boundaries
Present-day
rivers

⊙ Now it is time for you to make a drawing showing what you think the Bradbury Brook Site looked like when these early people were there. Before you begin drawing, use your Investigation Guide to think about what you do know about the Bradbury Brook Site, as well as what you don't know. Like an archaeologist, you will have to use your imagination to fill in what you don't know or can't know. But make sure your drawing is as truthful as possible—based on what you have observed and inferred—and doesn't mislead your readers.

A Dakota elder teaches children using stories. American Indian artist Oscar Howe painted this watercolor in 1951.

1492	1519	1603	Early 1600s	1659–1660	1660s
Christopher Columbus sails to the New World.	Spaniards under Hernando Cortez attack the Aztecs in Mexico. These Spaniards bring cattle and horses to North America.	French explorer Samuel de Champlain sails up the St. Lawrence River, the future route of Minnesota's fur trade.	Ojibwe start migration from near Atlantic coast toward Great Lakes area.	Radisson and Groseilliers are the first known white explorers to winter with Dakota in the Mille Lacs region.	Ojibwe and Dakota fight in several wars in the upper Great Lakes region.

Oscar Howe

O f all the people who live in Minnesota, the Dakota have lived here the longest. Their history in this place goes back hundreds, some believe even thousands of years, to the time when wooly mammoths and giant bison roamed the land. Any history of Minnesotans must begin with the Dakota many years ago. But how can we understand what life was like for people who lived so long ago?

We can start by listening to their stories.

For centuries, the Dakota have kept their history alive through a process called **oral tradition,** the purposeful repeating of stories. Sometimes these stories tell of events that actually happened long ago. Sometimes they are legends that teach lessons or explain why things are the way they are. Sometimes the stories tell what will happen in the future if you don't listen to your elders. They connect the Dakota people to each other and to their past.

All Dakota are familiar with at least some of these oral traditions. A few have a special talent for making

LOOK FOR

- ◆ How do the Dakota use oral tradition?
- ◆ How does the Dakota story explain what causes storms?
- ◆ How did Dakota life change with the seasons?
- ◆ What did the Dakota do for food in each season?
- ◆ In what ways did the Dakota show respect for one another?
- ◆ How do the Dakota view the past?

KEY TERMS

oral tradition
elder
tipi
sugar camp
bark house
oḣanwaśte
tiyośpaye
wohoda

oral tradition: the custom of telling stories about the histories and legends of a group in order to teach about that culture

1673
Louis Joliet and Jacques Marquette canoe down the Wisconsin River and explore the Mississippi River.

1679
Daniel Greysolon, Sieur du Luth, explores the area from the head of Lake Superior to Mille Lacs.

1680
A Dakota hunting party takes Father Louis Hennepin and his French companions to Mille Lacs.

1740s
The Dakota move south from central Minnesota.

1750s
One group of the Dakota, the Tetons, moves across the Red River to the western plains.

1770s
Horses are introduced into Dakota culture.

ORAL TRADITIONS RECORDED

Although the Dakota traditionally have used the spoken word to keep their history alive, some have written down their oral traditions. They've done this mainly to teach other people about the Dakota. Their written accounts provide much of the information included in this chapter.

Several of these accounts were written by Ohiyesa (oh-HEE-yay-sah). Born to a Dakota woman in 1858, he spent his childhood among the Dakota. But when he was 15, his father took him to live among white people and gave him a new name: Charles Eastman. Ohiyesa went to college and became a respected doctor. He also wrote 10 books about the Dakota, most of which contain oral traditions that had never been written down before. The stories about the Thunderbird and the Water Spirit and about the North Wind and Star Boy come from his book *Indian Boyhood*, which was published in 1902.

Ohiyesa's name means "the victor" in Dakota. He is shown here in 1920.

elder: an older member of the tribe who is respected for his or her knowledge and wisdom

tipi: a cone-shaped house made by stretching animal skins over a frame of wooden poles

the stories come alive. It is the job of these expert storytellers to make sure the oral traditions of the Dakota do not fade from memory. Storytellers are living books. Their minds are libraries of Dakota traditions and history.

In this chapter we will imagine that we've gone back in time about 500 years to visit a Dakota **elder** in her **tipi** near the shore of a frozen Minnesota lake. As we do this, we should respect the ways of our host. Everyone remains silent until the storyteller has finished her tale.

A Visit with the Storyteller

It is the middle of winter, the time of year that the Dakota call Witeĥiwi (wee-TAY-hee-wee)—the Hard Moon. It is very cold. The snow is deep. The ice on the lake shifts, thunders, and echoes. But it's warm and cozy inside the storyteller's tipi. A fire of large logs is burning in the middle. It provides warmth and light. The smoke escapes through an opening at the top of the tipi.

Five children in deerskin robes have gathered around the fire. They have brought gifts of food. Now they are eagerly waiting to hear from the storyteller, who is both a teacher and an entertainer. The stories she tells are exciting. On this cold evening, she will treat the children to a warm-weather tale about Wakiŋyaŋ (wah-KEE-yah), the Thunderbird, and Uŋkteĥi (oonk-TAY-hee), the Water Spirit.

WAKIŊYAŊ AND UŊKTEĤI

Warm yourselves, children, with this story of Wakiŋyaŋ, the great storm-maker who cleans the earth and sky. Sometimes he makes life hard for us. But usually his work is good.

Long ago, Wakiŋyaŋ was always at

war with his enemy, Uŋkteḣi, the Water Spirit. All would be calm as Wakiŋyaŋ approached. But then he would attack. He breathed the storm wind. On his drum, he beat the rhythm of thunder. He threw tomahawks of lightning. Uŋkteḣi responded to these attacks by churning up the surfaces of the lakes and rivers. Line after line of white-capped warriors would roll over the water and crash on the shore. The fish of the water, the birds of the air, and all the creatures of the land would hide to escape the terrible battle.

But then came the great peacemaker, the Sun.

The Sun held a rainbow in his hand to signal that the war between Wakiŋyaŋ and Uŋkteḣi should finally come to an end. Gentle winds came down from the sky and played with the tiny waves that danced upon the water.

Even now, the Sun watches over Wakiŋyaŋ and Uŋkteḣi to make sure that whatever battles they may still have end quickly. This allows all the living creatures to work and play without too much fear in the warmth of spring and summer.

The Dakota used spears to hunt muskrats in the winter. The Dakota considered the muskrat to be better tasting during winter and early spring than during warm weather.

Spring

With the first thaw, each Dakota village split up to begin the springtime work. While the men went off to hunt for muskrat, beaver, and ducks, the women and children trekked through the snow and slush to get to the **sugar camp** where the maple trees grew. This was where the Dakota would begin the annual work of turning sap from the maples into sugar and syrup.

sugar camp: village location during spring, when Dakota made sugar from maple sap

The sugar-makers often returned to the same sugar camp each year. The first few weeks were for making preparations. The women cleaned and repaired the **bark houses** and the sugarhouse, which was used to store the sugaring equipment during the off-season when they were away. They also made wood and bark containers for holding the maple sap. The children were expected to help with these chores, but often they had plenty of spare time to play in the woods.

bark house: a rectangular house made with poles and covered with large overlapping strips of bark

By April, when the snow began melting, it was time to see if the maples were ready to give up their sap. In the words of the Dakota writer Ohiyesa, "The trees, like people, have their individual characters;

What different steps of sugaring are shown in this painting? Seth Eastman, a U.S. Army officer stationed at Fort Snelling, painted this scene in the early 1850s.

some were ready to yield up their life-blood, while others were more reluctant." The women tested the trees by striking them with an ax. If sap appeared, the harvest could begin.

The women then pounded wood chips into the cuts they had made. The sap trickled drop by drop from the corners of the chips into little birch-bark dishes. Then came the hard part. All the sap was collected and poured into specially prepared wooden troughs or clay pots. The containers were placed over hot fires. The sap boiled down and turned into syrup and sugar.

OCETI ŠAKOWIŊ

Each Dakota belonged to one of seven distinct bands within the Oyate (oh-YAH-tay), or Dakota nation. The Dakota called these bands Oceti Šakowiŋ (oh-CHAY-tee shah-KOH-wee)—the Seven Council Fires. Each council fire was named for the place where its people lived.

Six of the seven council fires still exist today as organized groups. (Only a few Dakota now claim to be Waȟpekute.)

But these days, the members of each council fire live in many different places. The Dakota inhabit four communities in Minnesota and several others in North Dakota, South Dakota, Nebraska, and Manitoba, Canada. They also live in towns and cities throughout Minnesota and the Upper Midwest. Even though the Dakota have moved, or have been forced to move, frequently over the past 200 years, they have carried the traditions of the council fires with them wherever they have gone.

Dakota	Common Usage	Translation
Mdewakantoŋwaŋ	Mdewakanton	Spirit Lake people
Waȟpetoŋwaŋ	Wahpeton	Dwellers in the leaves
Waȟpekute	Wahpekute	Shooters in the leaves
Sisitoŋwaŋ	Sisseton	Dwellers of the marsh
Ihaŋktoŋwaŋna	Yanktonai	Little end-village dwellers
Ihaŋktoŋwaŋ	Yankton	End-village dwellers
Titoŋwaŋ	Teton	Prairie dwellers

Summer

Summer was a time of planting, cultivating, and harvesting for the Dakota. Families gathered back together at summer villages of bark houses along rivers where the soil was soft and sandy. The women planted and tended crops, such as corn, squash, and beans. The men fished and

In the 1850s, Robert Sweeny, an artist who lived in St. Paul, sketched this Dakota village in the summertime. The Dakota had kept dogs for centuries, but did not acquire horses until the late 1770s.

hunted small animals. Once the corn was harvested, the Dakota turned their attention to harvesting another important food: wild rice.

Wild rice is a tall grass that grows in the shallow waters of northern ponds and lakes. The seeds, or grain, from wild rice plants were among the Dakota's favorite foods and the focus of their lives during the days of late summer.

The Dakota prepared for the wild rice harvest by celebrating the bounty that nature had given them. They held feasts of fish, duck, and venison. They made offerings to Uŋkteȟi in hopes that there would be no drownings during the harvest. They picked blueberries and cranberries.

Then the rice harvest began.

The families launched their canoes and went to work. First they tied the stalks of grain into bundles and let them stand there to dry for a

Which step in harvesting wild rice is shown in this painting? Many of Seth Eastman's American Indian paintings were shown in the East, where they gave many people their first view of Dakota life.

few days. Then they returned and struck the bundles with a rod so that the rice fell into the bottom of the canoe. The rice was brought to shore and placed on mats to dry in the sun. Then it was roasted over a fire and poured into a pit lined with a hide. There, boys wearing clean moccasins would grind the husks off the grains by stepping lightly on them. Finally, the husks were removed from the grains by shaking the rice so that the wind would blow away the chaff, the outer coverings of the grain.

All the work was done by September, but the Dakota had little time to rest: autumn and winter were coming, and they had to get ready.

Autumn

Preparing for winter meant, above all, hunting animals for food, clothing, and shelter. If the hunters did not kill enough large animals—deer, bison, or bear—people might starve or freeze during the long, cold winter.

The autumn hunt began when the rice harvest was done and the weather had begun to cool. The villagers, who had spent most of the summer in one place, now became a community on the move. Each family packed up its belongings and headed to the hunting grounds that the chief had chosen. At each new destination, they built fires and set up tipis. The women worked to prepare, cook, and preserve food for the winter, while the men did the hunting.

All hunters were expected to follow certain rules. In the morning, they gathered at a large bonfire to learn the boundaries for the day's hunting area. This was important. They knew that if they strayed outside the designated hunting grounds, they and their families would

Dakota bows were powerful and convenient weapons. They were made from hardwood such as hickory or ash, which made them strong.

The Dakota were skilled horsemen and could kill a bison with one arrow shot into the animal's rib cage.

be punished, possibly by having their hunting weapons broken. By setting new boundaries each day, the village made sure that no area was overhunted.

Oȟanwaśte (oh-HAHN-wahsh-tay), or generosity toward everyone, was an important part of the Dakota hunter's life. The one who killed the first animal of the day would announce the news throughout the forest. He then would share the meat with his fellow hunters. Those who killed the most animals were respected and admired.

oȟanwaśte: Dakota word meaning generosity

Another Visit with the Storyteller

The harsh winds of Witeȟiwi are howling outside as the children gather again in the storyteller's tipi. It's the perfect time to retell one of the many stories about the Dakota hero Wicaŋȟpi Hokśidaŋ (wee-CHAHNK-pee hohk-SHEE-dah)—Star Boy. The children all know about Wicaŋȟpi Hokśidaŋ, who is the son of a woman and a star. He travels the earth, protecting the weak from the strong. This evening's story tells of his struggle with one of the Dakota's strongest enemies—Tate Waziyata (tah-TAY wah-ZEE-yah-tah), the North Wind.

TATE WAZIYATA AND WICAŊȞPI HOKŚIDAŊ

One day, when the earth was still young, Wicaŋȟpi Hokśidaŋ traveled far to the north—to a cold land where the snow was deep, and the ice sounded like thunder when it moved. There he found a nation of people in great distress. They were hungry and cold and afraid. Tate Waziyata, the North Wind, had driven away the bison that provided the meat these people needed to survive. Wicaŋȟpi Hokśidaŋ offered to help the people.

"Come," he said. "Let's hunt some bison."

Wicaŋȟpi Hokśidaŋ led a small group of men to the open plain where the bison had fled. And it was there that Tate Waziyata appeared, howling in anger at the small band of hunters. The men were afraid, but Wicaŋȟpi Hokśidaŋ was not. Tate Waziyata saw this and challenged Wicaŋȟpi Hokśidaŋ to a fight.

It was a great battle. At first, Wicaŋȟpi Hokśidaŋ seemed to be winning. Then Tate Waziyata slammed him to the ground and left him for dead. But Wicaŋȟpi Hokśidaŋ did not give up. He rose to his feet and continued to fight. The battle went on for some time until both Wicaŋȟpi Hokśidaŋ and Tate Waziyata were too tired to continue. They sat down on a snowbank to rest.

Dakota women shouted and made noises to keep birds away from the corn crop when it was ripening.

31

Wicaŋħpi Hokṡidaŋ began fanning himself with a large plume of eagle feathers. This created a warm breeze that quickly melted the snow. Tate Waziyata saw this and knew he was defeated. He made a treaty with Wicaŋħpi Hokṡidaŋ. From then on, Tate Waziyata and the cold weather he brought would visit the earth for only half of the year. The other half of the year would be a time of warm weather.

This is how the seasons came to be. Wicaŋħpi Hokṡidaŋ's fan of eagle feathers ushers in the warmth of spring and summer. Tate Waziyata arrives in the autumn and gives the people enough time to prepare for the hard days of winter that are to come.

Winter

The autumn hunt often lasted until January. Then it was time to settle down for the cold season. The Dakota set up tipi villages deep in the sheltering woods, near rivers or lakes. At the center of each village stood the council tipi. This was where village leaders discussed issues and made decisions. Men were free to come and go as they pleased. Women usually entered only to bring the men food. Forming a circle around the large council tipi were many smaller tipis in which the village families lived.

Life in the winter village often seemed relaxed compared to the busy activity at other times of the year. The men rested, went ice fishing, and visited with each other. The women tanned hides and sewed clothing. For food, they dug up their stores of corn and rice and relied on dried meat from the autumn hunts. The children played in the snow and ice

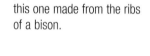

In winter, Dakota children played with sleds like this one made from the ribs of a bison.

THE CIRCLE OF HISTORY

The Dakota believe that time and events occur in a circle, and for a reason. Elden Lawrence, a Dakota elder and the president of the Sisseton-Wahpeton Community College in Sisseton, South Dakota, explains:

"The way we look at history is different from the way that non-Indians look at history. We think of history as a circle, not a line. Some people say about Indians, 'Just get on with life. When are you Indians ever going to forget that and get on with life?' But the Dakota view history as a circle—things keep coming back. If you don't heal that wound, it's going to come back

again. A few years down the road, maybe twenty years down the road, it's going to happen again because it was never corrected. In Indian society, we know that if we did something wrong, sooner or later, it's going to come back on us. What happened once will happen again.

"An elder once told me, 'We don't have a history.' Our way is we take a young person and we say to them, 'I am the past. You are the present. We are the future.' So you're bringing the living past up to the present. That young person is learning from you and together you're going to move into the future. That's the

way the history continues. That's the way your past life continues.

"When you look at history in a linear fashion, you're just going along the line. You're preserving things as you go along, preserving memories and stuff, but that's not enough to change the course of life. But when events keep coming back around, there's a reason for that. You can do something about it. You can change. You can do something that could change the course of the future without blindly repeating the past."

on sleds made of bison ribs. They skated on moccasins with tree-bark soles. And they learned stories from elders.

But winter was not just a time for resting and playing. It was a hard season, full of dangers. Deep snow and bitter cold often made it difficult to gather firewood and hunt for food. Blizzards blew down tipis. In the worst winters, hundreds of people died. Many others suffered frostbite.

Family life was especially important during the hard winter months. Mothers, fathers, children, and members of their *tiyośpaye* (tee-YOHSH-pah-yay), or extended family, all lived together in the family tipi. It was often crowded inside, and family members were expected to show each other *wohoda* (WOH-hoh-dah)—respect and courtesy. They learned to honor each other's privacy by keeping their eyes lowered. When children talked to their elders, they knew they should speak with respect. If their uncle's name was Swift Cloud, they would always call him "my uncle Swift Cloud"—never "Swift Cloud."

tiyośpaye: Dakota word meaning extended families, including cousins, aunts, and uncles

wohoda: Dakota word meaning respect and courtesy

But this emphasis on family life extended well beyond the family tipi. Most Dakota believed that it was important to include everyone in what they called a great "ring of relatives." One saying, passed down through generations, put it this way: "Be related, somehow, to everyone you know. Make him important to you. He is also a man."

Eventually the snow would begin melting, the sap from the maple trees would begin running, and the Dakota would begin a new year. They knew that some things would stay the same from year to year. Spring meant sugaring. Summer meant planting and harvesting. Autumn meant the big hunt and preparations for the long winter. But that didn't mean *everything* stayed the same. Babies were born. People got older and died. New ways of doing things were discovered. And sometimes, new people—strangers—would enter their lives. Some of these strangers would come and go without leaving much of a trace. But others would eventually bring changes that would forever alter the lives of Dakota people.

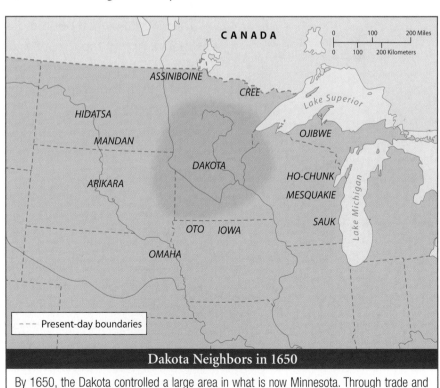

Dakota Neighbors in 1650

By 1650, the Dakota controlled a large area in what is now Minnesota. Through trade and other contacts, the Dakota met many other Indian groups living near them.

People on the Move

… Life was well organized there [in the tipi], with a definite place for everybody. The members of the family had their own spaces where they habitually sat, ate, slept, and worked. Everyone kept his personal things in skin containers, which were always ornamented, sometimes handsomely. These were secured only as far as tying strings could make them so. There were no locks and keys, but they were not missed. A good relative did not open another's things. Even small children were gently but firmly warned to leave things alone.

These words were written in 1944 by Ella Deloria, a Yankton Dakota, in her book *Speaking of Indians*.

The Dakota were a people on the move. In springtime they went to sugar camps to tap maple trees and make sugar. They returned to permanent villages in the summer to grow crops. At the summer's end they traveled to lakes to harvest rice, and throughout the fall they were on the move hunting deer and bison. Even in the deepest snows of winter, the Dakota sometimes moved camp to be closer to the wild animals they hunted in order to survive.

So what was it like to live a life on the move? How did the Dakota move camp and bring home heavy loads of meat? What did they use to store and carry things? On the next few pages are examples of containers, bags, and carrying packs made by Dakota within the last 200 years. You will also find accounts written by Dakota people and people who witnessed the traditional Dakota way of life. As you investigate these primary source objects, paintings, and descriptions, try to imagine what it would be like to live among the Dakota centuries ago.

Dakota containers were made in all shapes and sizes and were often beautifully decorated.

How many storage containers can you find inside this Dakota tipi?

If you had to carry everything you owned from place to place, what would you keep? What would you give up? Study the containers and bags on the next few pages, and think about something that you own that is important enough to carry from one home to another. What size and shape of container would best protect your most valuable possession?

The Dakota used the travois (trah-VOY) to carry their possessions. They made the travois by stretching an animal skin between long poles, often the same poles used to support their tipi.

MOVING CAMP

In order to live close to food resources such as maple forests or ricing lakes, the Dakota had to pack and move their whole household. Since Dakota women owned the tipis and everything in them, packing and moving was usually women's work. Moving camp was hard, especially during the winter. Starting at daybreak, women and children packed and carried heavy bundles through snow and icy water, if the streams were not frozen. The missionary Samuel Pond, who traveled with the Dakota in the early 1800s, never forgot what it was like to set up camp in winter after a long day of moving:

Worn over the shoulder, this type of bag often held essential items like the flint and steel needed to start a fire.

> Fourteen tepee poles were to be found and dragged often a considerable distance through the snow, making two or three heavy loads for a strong woman. The tent was then erected, and dry grass cut up from some swamp was brought and put all around the tent or tepee on the outside, for the Indian women would not bank their tents with snow lest it should melt and injure the tent. Hay was also strewn inside to spread the beds on, for the frozen ground was hard and cold. Then wood was brought for the fire, very dry for they burn no other. Last of all water was brought and hung over the fire to warm or cook the supper, which by this time was well earned if ever suppers are.

AFTER THE HUNT

While carrying the tipi was women's work, hunting was men's work. Dakota men traveled great distances to find game, and wounded animals frequently led hunters even farther. But it was after the hunt that the heavy work began. Once game was killed it was cut up and carried back to camp, often many miles. Hunters sometimes slipped and fell while carrying their heavy loads through forests or swamps. If a hunter was injured or killed while hunting, his companions carried him home, no matter how far.

Ohiyesa (oh-HEE-yay-sah), or Charles Eastman, was raised in a traditional Dakota manner in the 1870s and 1880s. He recalled the extra challenges that hunters faced during the winter. After the village men hunted bison in the snow, they cut them up and carried the meat home on sleds pulled by dogs:

> No ponies could be used [to hunt the bison]. ... Sleds were made of [bison] ribs and hickory saplings, the runners bound with rawhide with the hard side down. These slipped smoothly over the icy crust. Only the small men rode on the sleds. ... The men had their bows and arrows, and a few had guns. The huge animals could not run fast in the deep snow. [The bison] all followed a leader, trampling out a narrow path. The dogs with their drivers soon caught up with [the bison] on each side, and the hunters brought many of them down. I remember when the party returned, late in the night. The men came in single file, well loaded, and each dog followed his master with an equally heavy load. Both men and animals were white with frost.

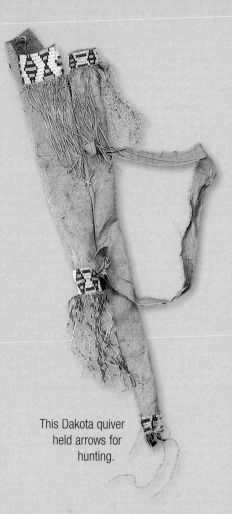

This Dakota quiver held arrows for hunting.

This painting shows only part of the story. If a hunter was lucky and killed an animal, he had to transport it back to camp. **How do you think Dakota hunters carried a bison back to camp?**

PRECIOUS CARGO

Of all the things the Dakota carried, the most precious cargo were their babies. "Infants were very tenderly cared for," recalled missionary Samuel Pond.

Dakota infants were kept on a wooden cradleboard for most of their first year. They were wrapped in blankets and secured to their upright cradles by strips of cloth or hide. A wooden bow protected the infant's face in case of an accidental fall and was also used to hang toys and small objects to entertain the baby. According to Pond, "Nothing better than this cradle could have been contrived for the comfort and safety of the infants. There was no other way in which they could be carried on the frequent journeys with safety."

DAKOTA CONTAINERS

The Dakota made many specialized containers, like the cradleboard, to make packing and travel easier. Storage containers were made from materials available in the natural world, and different materials had different benefits. Bark containers were lightweight and held up well in wet and humid weather. Bags woven from reeds were easy to pack and could be dyed beautiful colors. Animal hides were readily available and made strong, waterproof containers.

One special kind of hide container was called a parfleche (PAHR-flesh). Parfleche containers were made from folded and painted rawhide, which was stiff and very strong. Parfleches were made in four basic shapes: an envelope style, a flat case, a cylinder, and a box.

The painted hide on this cradleboard covers the wooden frame beneath. **Look inside the magnifying glass on page 34 to see how the baby was carried.**

PARFLECHE BOX

photograph, a Dakota woman makes two large parfleches out of a single hide. The hide was painted before the containers were cut and folded.

To make a parfleche, a Dakota woman began with a fresh hide from a bison, elk, or moose. She removed the fur and then scraped or "fleshed" the inside of the skin to remove the tissue and fat. The skin was then washed, staked down, and painted in geometric designs using colors such as red, black, yellow, and green.

Now it's your turn. What important possession would you carry with you everywhere? Follow the instructions in the Investigation Guide to make a Dakota parfleche for your valuable item. Look at the containers in this investigation for ideas on how to decorate your parfleche with traditional Dakota designs.

PARFLECHE CYLINDER

PARFLECHE ENVELOPE

PARFLECHE FLAT CASE

In the 1970s, Ojibwe artist Carl Gawboy created this painting of an Ojibwe storyteller.

1500s	1607	1620	1620s	1659–1660	1660s	1670
The Ojibwe, Potawatomi, and Ottawa live north of Lake Huron.	English colonists establish Jamestown in Virginia.	Pilgrims establish a colony at Plymouth in Massachusetts.	The Ojibwe live at Sault Sainte Marie.	Radisson and Groseilliers are the first known white explorers to winter with Dakota in the Mille Lac region.	The Ojibwe and the Dakota begin conflict over control of the upper Great Lakes region.	The Ojibwe become the main suppliers of fur to the French in the western Great Lakes region.

The Dakota knew they were not alone in the world. In all directions they were surrounded by neighbors. To the north were the Assiniboine (uh-SI-nuh-boin) and the Cree. To the east were the Ho-Chunk and the Mesquakie (meh-SKWAH-kee). The Iowa lived to the south. The Mandan and Hidatsa made their homes to the west. Besides these immediate neighbors were other Indian nations far beyond the lands that the Dakota knew. Every once in a while, they would see and hear evidence of these faraway people and lands. They would receive colorful seashells in trade. Or nearby tribes would tell them stories of more distant tribes with different customs.

One day, around the year 1500, word arrived among the Dakota that some new people had settled at the eastern edge of the lands that the Dakota called home. Dakota territory extended eastward along the southern shore of Lake Superior all the way to the waterfalls that spill into Lake Huron. In many ways, these people were much like the Dakota. They lived in the forests and moved with the seasons. They hunted game, harvested wild rice, and made sugar and

LOOK FOR

◆ Where did the Ojibwe first come from?
◆ How did the fur trade change the Ojibwe?
◆ What caused conflicts between Indian groups in the Great Lakes area?
◆ What happened when the Ojibwe entered Dakota territory?
◆ Why did the French encourage peace between the Ojibwe and Dakota?
◆ What were some Ojibwe fishing methods?

KEY TERMS

wigwam
oral tradition
pelts
alliance

1679	1680	1689	1693	1740s	1745	1763
Daniel Greysolon, Sieur du Luth, explores northern Minnesota and helps negotiate an alliance between the Ojibwe and the Dakota.	Father Hennepin is first European to record existence of St. Anthony Falls.	At Fort St. Antoine on Lake Pepin's Wisconsin shore, explorer Nicolas Perrot claims the surrounding area for France.	French build a fort, which becomes an important fur trading center, on Madeline Island near the Ojibwe village at Chequamegon Bay.	The Ojibwe have settled into northern Minnesota, and the Dakota have moved farther south.	The Ojibwe are living around Mille Lacs. Dakota settlements are on Elk River south of Mille Lacs.	Britain defeats France in the French and Indian War and wins all French territory east of the Mississippi River.

wigwam: a round dwelling made out of poles and saplings and covered with sheets of birchbark or woven mats

syrup from maple sap. But they were also different. During much of the year, they lived in **wigwams**—rounded frames made of poles or saplings that were covered with sheets of birchbark or woven mats, unlike the Dakota's bark houses and hide tipis. Their canoes were formed out of birchbark, not from hollowed-out logs like those made by the Dakota. And they spoke a different language.

The Dakota may have first become aware of these new neighbors when the newcomers began gathering in villages near the waterfalls. The Dakota started calling them the Ḣaḣatoŋwaŋ (hah-HAH-too-wah), or People of the Falls. But not all of them stayed put in this place, which is now called Sault Sainte Marie (soo saynt muh-REE), Michigan. Some of them moved north and west along the northern shore of Lake Superior. Many of them moved west along the southern shore of Lake Superior. The Dakota did not want these people to get too close, and battles broke out between them. Finally, some of the strangers settled along Chequamegon (shih-KWAH-mih-gehn) Bay, near the western edge of Lake Superior. Here the Dakota and their new neighbors watched each other from a distance and tried to guess what the other was doing. Both peoples were about to enter a time of tremendous change.

Western Great Lakes

The Dakota first met the Ojibwe at the waterfalls in a place now called Sault Sainte Marie, Michigan. Later the Ojibwe moved west to Chequamegon Bay.

A People on the Move

The new neighbors called themselves Anishinaabe (uh-nih-shih-NAH-BAY)—the People. But others called them the Ojibwe (oh-jib-WAY), a name that may have referred to the puckered moccasins they wore.

FISHING

The Ojibwe have always lived in the lands of forests and lakes, so it makes sense that fishing has long been an important part of their culture. The fishing skills that they developed during their migration across the Great Lakes served them well as they began to settle in the lake regions of central and northern Minnesota.

During the warm months of the year, Ojibwe women did most of the fishing. Usually, they used weighted nets that hung straight down in the water. The women set their nets at night and hauled in their catches early in the morning. Sometimes they used other fishing tools such as spears, traps, and hooks. The Ojibwe either cooked and ate the fish fresh or dried it for eating during the winter.

During the cold months, men did much of the fishing. They cut holes in the ice and tried to attract fish using decoys made of wood and birchbark. A fisherman would lie flat on the ice with his face over the opening. When a fish came close to the hole, the fisherman speared it.

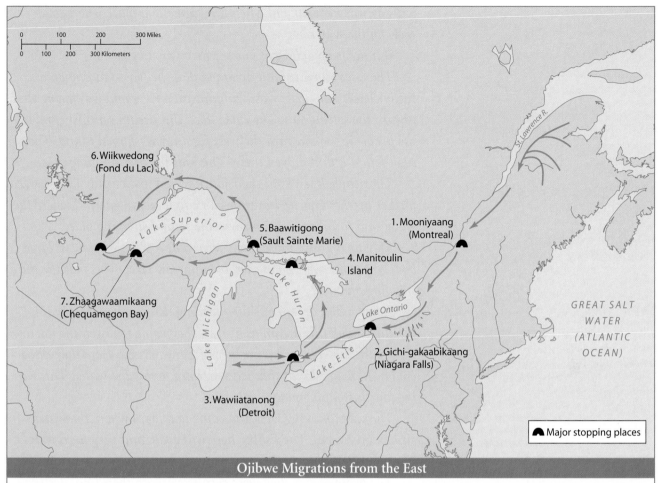

Ojibwe Migrations from the East

The Ojibwe migrated from the East Coast, traveling along the St. Lawrence River and around the Great Lakes. At Lake Superior they split up, with some continuing along the southern shore and settling at Chequamegon Bay. Others moved north into what would become Canada.

Like the Dakota, the Ojibwe were woodland people who felt at home in the area surrounding the Great Lakes. But unlike the Dakota, the Ojibwe had come from lands far to the east. In many ways, their history is a story of migration.

Oral tradition is just as important to the Ojibwe as it is to the Dakota. Through the telling and retelling of stories, they keep their history alive. One of the most important Ojibwe stories is about their migration from the shores of the Atlantic Ocean to the shores of Lake Superior. Young Ojibwe learn this story from their grandmothers and grandfathers. It goes something like this:

> *Many strings of lives ago, our ancestors lived far to the east near the great salt water. One day, seven prophets appeared and made predictions about the people's future. One of the prophets predicted that they would leave their homes beside the ocean and travel to a far-off land. He said they would make seven stops on their journey. The first one would be on a turtle-shaped island. Their last stop would be on another turtle-shaped island. They would know their*

oral tradition: the custom of telling stories about the histories and legends of a group in order to teach about that culture

journey was near an end when they came to a place where food grew on the water.

But the people did not know which way to go.

Then, a young woman dreamed that she was standing on a turtle's back. The turtle was swimming in a river and was facing west, toward the setting sun. The elders took this dream seriously and told the people to look toward the west for a turtle-shaped island. They soon found it and moved there. This was the first stopping place.

The people knew that their journey had just begun. They moved farther up the river and in time came to a great waterfall where the water and thunder met. This was the second stopping place.

Moving on once more, they arrived at a place where two large bodies of water were connected by a narrow river. This was the third stopping place.

A boy had a dream of stones leading across the water. Again, the elders took this dream as a sign. The people followed the narrow river until they reached a northern freshwater sea. Here they discovered a chain of islands that led westward across the water. This was the fourth stopping place.

They kept moving west and came to a place where the water rushed over rocks. The fishing here was good, and they lived well. This was the fifth stopping place.

The people knew they were getting closer to their final destination. One group set off along the southern shore of a great lake. The other moved along the northern shore. With time, the northern group arrived at the far western edge of the lake. Here they found wild rice, the food that grew on the water. This was the sixth stopping place.

Finally, the northern group reunited with the southern group at an island, off a long point of land that was shaped like a turtle. This was the seventh, and final, stopping place.

The Ojibwe used winnowing baskets made of birchbark, like the one shown here, during the wild rice harvest to shake the husks off the rice kernels.

The oral traditions of the Ojibwe provided many other details about their migration across the Great Lakes. They told of how the Ojibwe, the Potawatomi (pah-tuh-WAH-tuh-mee), and the Ottawa (AH-tuh-wuh) separated from each other after having been a single people. They told of great wars with other Indian nations in the east, such as the Iroquois (IR-uh-kwoi). Over time, the oral traditions of the Ojibwe began including stories of a new way of life that was transforming their world.

A New Way of Life

In the early 1600s, Ottawa and other Indians from farther east began arriving in the Ojibwe's new land near Chequamegon Bay, Wisconsin, carrying all sorts of things the Ojibwe had never seen before. For the first time, Ojibwe saw blankets and clothes made of woven fabric, pots and tools made of hard metal, and powerful weapons that shot deadly lead balls through the air. The Ottawa said they had gotten these things from strangers who had come from across the great saltwater ocean—from lands called France, England, and Holland. The strangers had light skin, pale eyes, and hairy faces, the eastern neighbors reported. And they were willing to trade their goods for animal furs. The Ottawa asked the Ojibwe if they would be interested in exchanging furs for these new kinds of goods. Some of the Ojibwe said they would.

Changes came quickly after that, and not all of the changes were good. The European traders brought diseases with them. Many Indians, including many Ojibwe, died because their bodies couldn't fight off the unfamiliar diseases. Sometimes the traders cheated the Indians by trading poor-quality goods.

Still, the Ojibwe prized many of the items that the Europeans brought. Tools such as the metal ax chopped hours and even days off the time needed to build a dwelling, make a canoe, or gather firewood. Guns made hunting easier. Women wore blouses and skirts made of soft, woven cloth. Men wrapped themselves in blankets or coats of heavy wool. Brass and tin kettles replaced clay pots. Many Ojibwe liked these new things, and they wanted more of them. At the same time, the white-skinned strangers wanted more furs. They wanted to ship the **pelts**—stretched skins with the fur still on them—across the ocean, where they would be turned into hats prized by wealthy Europeans.

Many Ojibwe began devoting more and more time to providing pelts for the Europeans. Men hunted, and women cleaned and cured the hides. Traditional activities, such as pottery making and basket weaving, became less important than they once had been.

Guns like this were called trade guns because they were specifically made to trade with the Indians.

pelts: animal skins that have been cleaned, stretched, and dried

The Ojibwe wanted to acquire metal kettles because they were more durable and easier to cook with than baskets or pottery.

Beaver skins were valuable trade items.

This foot-long spear, made of iron, was used to hunt muskrats. **What material might the Ojibwe have used for their spears before trading for these iron ones?**

After a few decades, the Chequamegon Bay Ojibwe noticed that the fur-bearing animals they were seeking were becoming harder to find. They started hunting and trapping farther and farther west just to keep the fur supply flowing. This often led them into the hunting grounds of their Dakota neighbors, where they were not always welcome.

Conflict in the Great Lakes Fur Trade

alliance: an agreement made between two or more different groups to join forces to achieve a common goal; the participating groups are called allies

The Ojibwe were not the only Indians moving into their neighbors' territory in search of new hunting grounds. By the mid-1600s, the Great Lakes region was an area of frequent skirmishes. Almost every Indian nation in the region had formed an **alliance** with either the French or the British. These white people represented the European nations that were struggling to control the Great Lakes fur trade. The Indians' European allies encouraged warfare among the Indians whenever they believed it would help them get more furs. But when the fighting

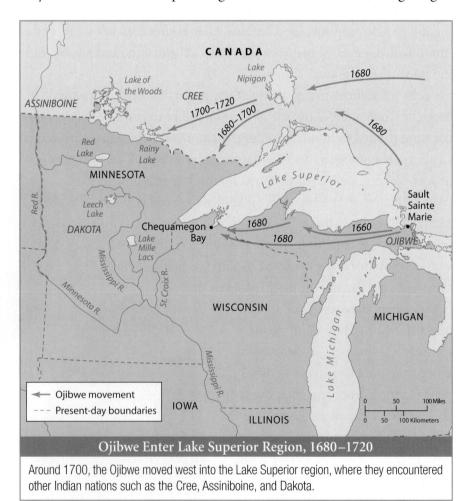

Ojibwe Enter Lake Superior Region, 1680–1720

Around 1700, the Ojibwe moved west into the Lake Superior region, where they encountered other Indian nations such as the Cree, Assiniboine, and Dakota.

threatened to cut off trade routes, the Europeans pressured the Indians to make peace.

In 1670 the Ojibwe became the main suppliers of furs to the French. With French encouragement, the Ojibwe began expanding west along both shores of Lake Superior. On the southern shore, where tensions were already high between the Ojibwe and the Dakota, the struggle for hunting grounds only made matters worse.

War and Peace between the Dakota and the Ojibwe

By the 1670s, the Dakota knew all about the French and how badly they wanted more furs. The Dakota had already pushed out another Indian nation, the Huron, who had recently intruded on Dakota lands and had been hunting and trapping for the French around Lake Pepin, on the Mississippi River. Now the Dakota turned their attention to Lake Superior and the Ojibwe. It wasn't long before the two groups were at war.

The center of the hostilities was the Ojibwe village on Madeline Island in Chequamegon Bay. The Ojibwe had moved there from the mainland to protect themselves from attacks, but the Dakota were determined fighters. Traditional Ojibwe stories tell of how Dakota warriors ambushed Ojibwe hunters who left the island in search of food. Ojibwe warriors then rushed to the rescue, and large battles broke out on land and water. Many people died. The warriors on both sides retreated, knowing that more battles would come.

The fighting continued, off and on, during the 1670s. The Ojibwe continued to push west into Dakota territory. But

OJIBWE NAMES

Ojibwe is a complex language with more than 6,000 verb forms. The language is descriptive, but it does not always translate exactly into English. That is why many Ojibwe believe that, to truly understand Ojibwe history and culture, you must learn the language. Like those in many American Indian tribes, elders know the language and traditions best. Many people fear that as the elders die, the language and traditions will be lost. Language programs have been set up to give young people the chance to learn from the elders.

The chart below identifies some Ojibwe names for places in Minnesota.

Ojibwe name	Meaning	English name
Gichi-ziibi (gih-chih-ZEE-bih)	great river	Mississippi
Bimijigamaag (bih-mih-jih-guh-MAHG)	lake where current flows directly across the water	Bemidji
Wiinibiigozhish (WEE-nih-BEE-go-zhihsh)	dirty water	Winnibigoshish
Gichigami (gih-CHIH-guh-mih)	great lake	Lake Superior
Manoomin (muh-NOH-mihn)	wild rice	Mahnomen

eventually, the Dakota and the Ojibwe got tired of war. With the help of the French, they began negotiating for peace. In the fall of 1679, at a gathering near present-day Duluth, they finally agreed to stop fighting and cooperate.

It was an important meeting for everyone involved—including the French. The French representative to the gathering, Daniel Greysolon, Sieur du Luth, had pushed for peace because he knew that warfare threatened the French fur supply. The Ojibwe were happy with the agreement because it gave them permission to collect furs farther west,

DANIEL GREYSOLON SIEUR DULHUT
AT THE HEAD OF THE LAKES — 1679

Daniel Greysolon, Sieur du Luth, was a French military officer, explorer, and fur trader in the Lake Superior region from 1678 to 1687. The city of Duluth is named for him.

in the heart of the Dakota's homeland. And the Dakota were pleased because it gave them access to the same European tools, cloth, and weapons that the Ojibwe and other Indians to the east of them already had.

After nearly 200 years as wary and warring neighbors, the Dakota and Ojibwe were again at peace. Occasional skirmishes broke out as the Ojibwe pushed into central Minnesota, but usually they got along. Years later, the Ojibwe writer William Warren would describe the relationship this way:

William Warren, son of an English father and a French-Ojibwe mother, wrote the first book on the history and culture of the Ojibwe people.

> Good-will existed between the two tribes, and the roads to their villages were clear and unobstructed. Peace-parties of the Dakotas visited the wigwams of the Ojibwe, and the Ojibwe, in like manner, visited the Tepees and earthen lodges of the Dakota. The good feeling existing between them was such, that intermarriages even took place between them.

They learned from each other, too. The Ojibwe taught the Dakota how to build birchbark canoes, which were lighter and faster than the Dakota's hollowed-out canoes. The Dakota taught the Ojibwe how to hunt bison.

Despite their occasional clashes, the alliance between the Ojibwe and the Dakota held. Furs continued to flow across the Great Lakes and on to Europe. At this point, the European fur traders were only occasional visitors to the lands of the Dakota and the Ojibwe. But that was about to change.

What My Grandmother Taught Me

Maple Sugar Taffy

A long time ago my grandmother and I used to boil maple sap. When she sugared off, I stood there. I dipped in that little carved paddle called neyakokwaanens (nay-yuh-ku-KWAH-naynhs).

When the sugar started to get done, she'd say, "Get the ice!" So I took off running down to the shore where the ice piles up to get some.

She recognized just what the sugar looked like when it was about to finish cooking. She used a wooden ladle to scoop it out. She scooped it up when it sugared. Then she poured it on the ice. My, I was really happy making that maple sugar taffy and eating it.

Maude's great-granddaughter Lindsey makes maple sugar taffy on ice just as Maude did years before.

Although Ojibwe artist and storyteller Maude Kegg lived not so long ago, she grew up practicing centuries-old Ojibwe customs. Maude's grandmother taught her how to make maple sugar and taffy, how to construct a wigwam, and how to find the best berries. She showed Maude how to cure a deer hide and decorate it with beads.

Maude's grandmother also told her stories about the history and culture of the Ojibwe people. She spoke to Maude in Anishinaabemowin (uh-nih-shih-NAH-BAY-moo-wihn), the Ojibwe language, and she always called Maude by her Ojibwe name Naawakamigookwe (NAH-wuh-kuh-mih-GOO-KWAY), which means Middle of the Earth Woman.

When Maude grew up, she told stories to her children and grandchildren. She often told her stories in the Ojibwe language. Later, she translated them into English and published the stories in two books. Some stories teach practical skills, while others are entertaining tales of her childhood. But all of Maude's stories teach something about the right and wrong way to behave.

Can you discover the lesson that each story teaches?

Maude Kegg is pictured here in 1946 in front of her home. **As you read more of Maude's childhood stories, ask yourself, "What is she trying to teach?"**

LEARNING RIGHT FROM WRONG

Each spring, Maude and her family made maple sugar. Men, women and children all worked together to tap trees, boil sap, and make the sugar. During sugaring, the old and young worked together, but they still had fun. Maude remembered one spring at the sugar camp when she was a little girl:

The Sugaring Trough

When I was small, my grandmother used to come over here to boil sap. I was a naughty little girl. Sometimes while they were sleeping or maybe while they were hauling sap, I'd steal the sugaring trough. Long ago there was a puddle there with lots of water in it, so I stole the sugaring trough. I must not have been very big.

The trough wasn't very big. I used to get in that trough and paddle it around in the puddle. Then when I heard them boiling sap down and wondering where they had misplaced it, I'd hide. Sometimes I got a licking when it was found out that I'd stolen the sugar trough for paddling around in the mud puddle.

Today, instead of using a wooden trough, Maude's youngest daughter Loretta Kegg Kalk (Lindsey's grandmother) makes sugar using a metal bowl.

Gathering wild rice in the fall was another complex process that Maude learned by watching her grandmother, father, uncles, and aunts. Maude remembered one wild rice harvest when her mischievous nature got the best of her:

A Big Handful

Sometimes they had a feast when they first got the rice. Then they were in a hurry. After my namesake, my uncle, finished tramping the rice, his wife winnowed it, winnowed the rice.

The fine broken rice flew out when the rice was winnowed. I was always grabbing and eating it. I was always eating it. Then the lady, Dookisin (DOH-kih-sihn) she was called, said, "Naawakamigook (NAH-wuh-kuh-mih-GOOK), don't eat it. Don't do that! You'll get bloated."

I'd always steal a great big handful of rice and eat it. One night I really got sick, I really felt bad after they finished the ceremony. My, was grandmother ever scared about my condition. There wasn't any Indian doctor around there. I was very sick and kept vomiting hard, but it was only rice, only the broken stuff.

"Oh, goodness gracious, she's just bloated," she said, and so she wasn't scared anymore.

LEARNING FROM LEGENDS

Stories are not only fun to listen to—they teach important lessons. Ojibwe children like Maude learned the history of their ancestors from stories. They learned the teachings of their religion from stories. Some stories were ancient legends that came with a warning:

Don't Make Snowmen

Then again not long ago I remembered about the time we were making snowmen. The old lady got mad, "Don't, go break it up quick!"

You can see why the youthful Maude thought the sugaring trough and neyakokwaanens looked like a small canoe and paddle.

Ojibwe children played with games and toys such as these dolls made by Maude.

"But why, why?" I said to her.

"Long ago some children were making snowmen. Then it got very cold. A snowman became a wiindigoo (WEEN-dih-GOO). They used to tell us, 'Don't make snowmen!'"

Today children are still told not to make an image from snow. It could stand up, so the story goes, become a wiindigoo, and eat them.

According to Ojibwe legend, a *wiindigoo* was a man-eating beast with a core of ice. In past times, a stranger who came to the wigwams was closely watched to see if he might be a wiindigoo.

LEARNING ABOUT GENEROSITY

Through her grandmother, Maude learned about many customs of the past. At first, the custom of *zaagido* (ZAH-gih-du) did not make sense to her. As you read this story, see if you can figure out what the zaagido custom meant:

"I'm Poor, I'm Poor in Beads"

I barely remember about long ago when I was little and they used to come here to the point for the Midewiwin (mih-DAY-wih-wihn) [a large ceremonial gathering].

Sometimes when the women took a break, they cooked. They sat around the fire. They did bead work embroidery.

I sat there too. I used to take the beads away from them. "Naawakamigook," said one of my aunts, "why don't you go around and zaagido there at the wigwams."

She taught me what to say. "You'll be given beads. This is what they used to do long ago." I was hesitant. I was foolish. I was small. But I wanted the beads badly, so she covered me with a shawl. "Go there to wigwams. Go around and say, 'I'm poor, I'm poor in beads.'"

So I bravely took off. I stood there by the doorway, as they lived in wigwams. Long ago when the Indians got together for Midewiwin they lived in wigwams. They weren't in houses when they gathered there but in wigwams. They came from different places.

I stood there [singing], "I'm poor, I'm poor in beads." I stood there. I almost ran away. After a while a lady appeared. She had some beads on her hand and came and put them in my shawl.

Maude Kegg learned beading from her grandmother. She worked on this bandolier bag on and off for five years. Bags such as this were used as a symbol of status and leadership and were given to their owners to wear for special occasions.

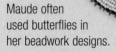

So I went on to another wigwam, "I'm poor, I'm poor in beads." I stood there a while and another old lady appeared. She threw quite a few beads to me, laughing just hard at me.

And so I went on around and kept saying the same thing. I went to about five wigwams. Then I had lots of beads. They were all different colors. "Well, that's how many I want," I thought, so I ran home.

As I came in, my goodness, they were laughing hard at me. As they looked at my beads, I asked them, "Why am I doing this?"

"Long ago," began my grandmother, "the Indians did that when they were short of anything, maybe maple sugar or whatever they were short of. Back then, a person said zaagido. *They went around asking when they were short of something."*

The old lady told that when anyone was hungry, he went around to the lodges and asked, and so was given lots of food. That's it.

Zaagido was an ancient custom that is no longer practiced today. It was a special and accepted way to ask for something that you really needed. Because most families could spare a little bit of rice, or meat, or sugar, zaagido involved going from wigwam to wigwam to ask for what could be spared. As Maude's daughter Loretta Kegg Kalk explained, "We didn't have old age homes and orphanages. The village took care of everyone. Nobody needed anything."

Maude often used butterflies in her beadwork designs.

PASSING ON STORIES

As an elder, Maude Kegg worked to keep her stories alive. She taught them to her eleven children and had the stories published. She also taught her children to speak the Ojibwe language and worked with language scholars to write an Ojibwe dictionary. Maude shared and taught Ojibwe traditions to family, friends, and anyone who visited the Mille Lacs Indian Museum where she worked.

In 1986, Governor Rudy Perpich proclaimed August 24 Maude Kegg Day, and in 1990 she was flown to Washington, D.C., to receive a National Heritage Award for her work to preserve Ojibwe culture.

Before she died in 1996, Maude wrote down her advice to young people everywhere:

Five generations of women in the Kegg family: Maude holds great-great-granddaughter Desiree. In the back from left to right are Maude's great-granddaughter Kristine Verkennes, her granddaughter Victoria Verkennes, and her oldest daughter Betty Kegg.

A Final Message

My advice would be first of all to thank the Almighty Creator for each and every blessing. I was taught and I have always taught my children and grandchildren to respect elders. Stop, look, and listen. Stop what you are doing and look them straight in the eye and listen intently to what they have to say. If you see or hear of anyone needing help in any way, do so right away.

Sometimes you may have more of something or other that someone needs. Be sure to share with them. Be honest—lies have a way of catching up with the liar. Don't cheat. Better to lose than to win by cheating. Don't abuse the body that the Almighty Creator has given you with drugs and booze. Teach your children from early childhood right from wrong.

5 The Fur Trade

Voyageurs paddle a canoe through rapids, one of the most dangerous parts of the fur trade.

1659	**1670**	**1680**	**1756–1763**	**1768**	**1776**	**1781**
Radisson and Groseilliers build a trading post at Chequamegon Bay.	King Charles II of England issues a charter to Hudson's Bay Company.	Father Louis Hennepin travels up the Mississippi River to present-day Minnesota.	British defeat French in French and Indian War, ending French control in Canada.	Construction begins on a fur trading post at Grand Portage.	U.S. Declaration of Independence is issued.	Colonists defeat British at Battle of Yorktown, the final battle of the American Revolution.

The oral traditions of the Ojibwe tell of the first meeting between a wise Ojibwe man and a group of mysterious white-skinned strangers. The story hints at the tremendous changes that swept over North America once the Ojibwe and other Indians began trading furs for European manufactured goods.

One night long ago, an elder named Meziwepige (MAY-zih-WAY-pih-GAY) dreamed that he had traveled east, toward the rising sun, and met a group of spirits in human form. The spirits had white skin. Their heads were covered. They smiled and approached him with outstretched arms.

Meziwepige woke up and decided to try to find the white spirits.

After many days of paddling eastward, Meziwepige came across a hut with smoke rising from its top. Inside were the white spirits he had seen in his dream. They greeted him with handshakes. They welcomed him into their home. When it was time for Meziwepige to leave, the white spirits gave him a steel ax, a knife,

LOOK FOR

◆ How did the fur trade begin?

◆ Who was involved in the fur trade?

◆ How did the fur trade work?

◆ What was life like at a fur trading post?

◆ What were some common sources of conflict at a fur trading post?

◆ Why did missionaries and explorers come to Minnesota?

KEY TERMS

trader
social status
clerk
voyageur
portage
rendezvous

1784	Around 1798	1803	1804	1808	1812	1815
Fur traders in Montreal form the North West Company to compete with the Hudson's Bay Company.	Traders form the XY Company to compete with the Hudson's Bay Company.	The United States purchases Louisiana Territory from France. Fur trade clerk Michel Curot builds fur post near St. Croix River.	Lewis and Clark expedition begins.	U.S. businessman John Jacob Astor forms the American Fur Company.	War of 1812 between the United States and Great Britain disrupts trade throughout North America.	United States wins War of 1812 and forbids foreign traders on U.S. soil. British cannot trade in Minnesota without becoming U.S. citizens.

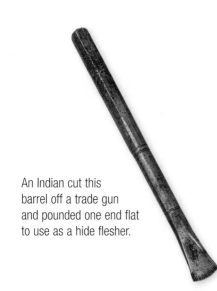

Iron axheads were popular trade items. Wooden handles were added later by the new owners.

beads, and a small strip of scarlet cloth. He put these gifts in his bag and returned to his village.

The following spring, Meziwepige and many of his fellow villagers made another journey to the home of the white spirits. This time, they loaded their canoes with many beaver skins. The white spirits welcomed Meziwepige and his friends. They thanked the Ojibwe for bringing the beaver skins and gave the Ojibwe many goods in exchange. Meziwepige and the other villagers returned home in the fall, their canoes filled with the white spirits' goods.

Two Worlds Meet

The North American fur trade began in the early 1600s, when French explorers first encountered American Indians along the valley of the St. Lawrence River, in what is now eastern Canada. In exchange for the furs of beaver, mink, and other animals, the Frenchmen gave the Indians blankets, jewelry, and metal goods such as knives, kettles, and guns. The Indians thought they were getting a bargain. So did the French.

Then other explorers and traders began arriving, along with missionaries seeking to convert Indians to Christianity. Before long, that early exchange of goods along the St. Lawrence had grown into the biggest business North America had ever seen.

By the 1700s, traders from France, Great Britain, and Holland were exchanging tons of manufactured goods each year for thousands of furs collected by the Indians. The traders began organizing themselves into businesses, and some of them became extremely wealthy. As they moved west, the traders founded settlements and gave them European names. Quebec and Montreal were among the first and largest of these settlements. Almost all the furs collected in the fur trade passed through these settlements before being shipped off to Europe.

An Indian cut this barrel off a trade gun and pounded one end flat to use as a hide flesher.

EUROPEAN EXPLORERS AND MISSIONARIES

Many of the first Europeans to venture into Minnesota were fur traders—but not all of them were. Some were explorers in search of fame and adventure. Others were missionaries who wanted Indians to give up their religions in favor of Christianity. Explorers Radisson (rah-dee-SOHN) and Groselliers (groh-zeh-YAY) were among the first to arrive in this region. They probably ventured into the region we now call Minnesota during the 1650s. In 1680 two Frenchmen and a Belgian Catholic priest named Louis Hennepin traveled up the Mississippi River into the lands of the Dakota. Hennepin later wrote a book about his adventures. His wildly embellished accounts made him famous and sparked Europeans' curiosity about the Upper Mississippi Valley.

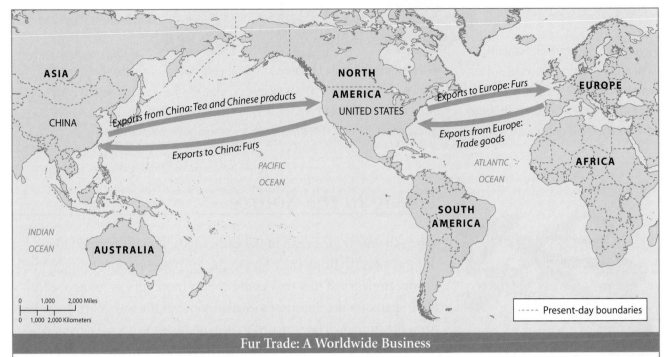

Fur Trade: A Worldwide Business

The fur trade stretched across the Northern Hemisphere. Furs from North America left from cities such as Montreal, New York, St. Louis, and outposts on the Pacific Coast. Trade goods came from European cities such as London, Paris, Milan, and Asian cities such as Canton (now known as Guangzhou).

I Want, You Want

The fur trade thrived because the Europeans wanted things that the Indians had, and the Indians wanted things that the Europeans had.

The Europeans wanted furs, especially beaver furs. Felt hats made with beaver fur were considered symbols of the rich and powerful in Europe. People there were willing to pay a lot of money for them. But by the 1600s, the beaver was almost extinct in Europe. Hatmakers and fur traders had to find a new source of fur in order to make more beaver hats. They found that new source in North America. Their suppliers were the Indians.

The Indians wanted European goods. Clothes made of woven fabric were more comfortable and easier to clean than the animal-skin and bark-fiber clothing that the Indians were used to wearing. Colorful glass beads provided a new way to decorate leather moccasins and bags. Brass and tin kettles were fireproof, easy to carry, and almost unbreakable. The Indians found that these and other goods, such as metal tools and guns, seemed to make life easier.

These glass beads date from the 1600s, before machines made them exactly the same in shape and size.

BEAVER HATS

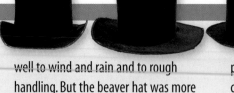

From about 1550 to 1850, it was the fashion of European gentlemen to wear felt hats. The finest and most expensive felt hats were made of beaver fur. Beaver fur is both soft and durable. It stands up well to wind and rain and to rough handling. But the beaver hat was more than a useful head protector. It was a symbol of social status. Wealthy and powerful men from the European ruling classes wore these hats almost everywhere they went. Working-class men could not afford such finery.

Iron traps snapped shut on one of the beaver's legs, leaving the pelt undamaged.

trader: a wealthy man in charge of a trading post

social status: position or rank of a person in society

clerk: a man who usually managed the day-to-day business at a fur trading post

voyageur: a workman who performed the physical labor of the fur trade

Montreal canoes were the semi-trucks of the fur trade. Voyageurs served as the boat's engine, paddling about 40 times per minute for hours at a time.

Going to the Source

When the fur trade began in the early 1600s, Indians traveled long distances east to bring their furs to the Europeans. Soon, though, the Europeans learned that they could collect more furs by going west to the Indians. So the Europeans learned some of the ways of the new land from the Indians. They learned to use birchbark canoes. They made snowshoes and toboggans for winter travel. They traced the routes that the Indian traders followed. And they spent their winters in trading posts, among the Indians who provided the furs. The Europeans who traveled to the lands of the Ojibwe and the Dakota were of three social classes:

The **trader** was in charge of one or more trading posts. The more furs he collected, the more money he made. The trader could read and write and often came from a wealthy family. He was considered a gentleman whose high social position gave him privileges that no one else at the trading post had. Traders often brought along belongings that showed their **social status**—items such as fine china and silverware and stores of tea, coffee, chocolate, and brandy.

The **clerk** worked under the trader. Sometimes he was put in charge of an entire trading post. Sometimes he just managed the day-to-day business at the post—keeping journals, supervising trade, and packing pelts. Like the trader, the clerk could read and write, but he didn't hold the same high social position as the trader. Clerks were often young men who dreamed of becoming traders themselves.

The **voyageur** (voy-uh-ZHOOR) was the ordinary workman of the fur trade. He paddled canoes and hauled heavy loads on his back for low pay. Each canoe was usually paddled by two or more voyageurs. Most voyageurs were the sons of French farmers and workers in eastern Canada. Few could read or write. Their opportunities were limited. They could stay at home and do hard work, or they could become voyageurs and do their work somewhere else.

The traders, clerks, and voyageurs, along with their Indian suppliers, all belonged to a vast trading network that took only a few decades to develop. Indians caught the animals, prepared the furs, and offered them in trade to the Europeans. The traders and clerks negotiated with the Indians and collected as many pelts as they could. The voyageurs paddled hundreds of miles, carrying trade goods and pelts back and forth between the trading posts and the big settlements, such as Montreal.

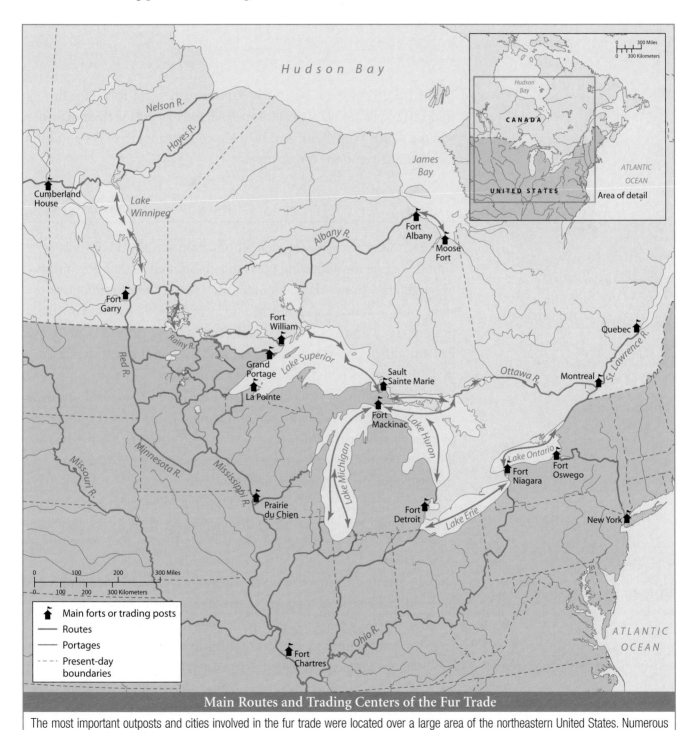

Main Routes and Trading Centers of the Fur Trade

The most important outposts and cities involved in the fur trade were located over a large area of the northeastern United States. Numerous rivers and lakes made traveling across a vast region fairly easy. Some of the important portages are also shown.

Have you noticed how the stories about the fur trade seldom include accounts of individual women? There's a reason for that. The men who wrote about their experiences in the fur trade rarely mentioned the women they dealt with by name, so we don't know who those women were. That's unfortunate, because Indian women were very important to the fur trade. In addition to cleaning the pelts, women were the ones who provided many of the resources that kept the trade going—things such as wild rice, maple sugar, and materials to make and repair canoes. They served as translators. And they provided an important link between European and Indian communities by marrying traders. These marriages formed family bonds that helped the traders in their business dealings with the Indians. They also made it more likely that the traders would continue providing goods to the communities their wives belonged to.

The soft undercoat of a beaver's fur was used to make felt for fashionable hats.

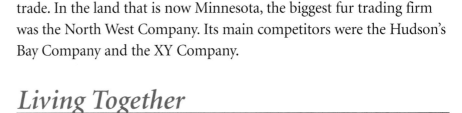

By the end of the 1700s, a few big companies controlled the fur trade. In the land that is now Minnesota, the biggest fur trading firm was the North West Company. Its main competitors were the Hudson's Bay Company and the XY Company.

Living Together

Late each summer, crews of men set out from the central fur post at Grand Portage for wintering posts throughout areas that now make up northern Minnesota and Wisconsin. One of their destinations was a lush, wooded area near the St. Croix (KROY) River, along the present-day Minnesota-Wisconsin border. The North West Company had a trading post there. The Ojibwe who lived in the area were used to doing business with the North West Company.

In the autumn of 1803, the Ojibwe near the St. Croix had someone new to trade with. A clerk for the XY Company had arrived with a crew of men and made it known that he wanted to trade for Ojibwe furs. For seven months, the North West Company and the XY Company competed for the business of the Ojibwe.

The things that happened in the St. Croix River valley during that trading season can tell us a lot about how the fur trade actually worked.

AUTUMN

Ojibwe elder **Giishkiman** (GEESH-kih-muhn), or Sharpened Stone, and his band had traveled a long way to get to this place. Usually they lived around Waaswaaganing (WAH-SWAH-guh-nihng), later called by the French Lac du Flambeau, about 120 miles to the east. But the wild rice harvest there had been the worst in memory. It appeared that there wouldn't be enough food to keep everyone alive through the winter. So Giishkiman and the other elders decided to lead their people here, to the St. Croix. The hunting was usually good, and the white men who wintered here were always eager to trade for the Ojibwe's furs, food, and supplies.

Michel Curot (mee-SHEHL kyer-OH) was new to the fur trading business. The XY Company had sent him as a clerk to this place to compete with the powerful North West Company. His duties were to be similar to those of a trader, but as a clerk, he had very little authority in the XY Company itself. Curot's first job was to set up his own trading post and convince the Ojibwe who wintered near the St. Croix to trade with him instead of with the North West Company. It wasn't easy. For a while, he had to live and work out of a tent because his voyageurs wouldn't help him build a log house.

Toussaint Savoyard (too-SAHNT SAH-voy-YAHRD), a voyageur for the XY Company, knew this area well. He had come here in previous years as a voyageur for the North West Company. Now he was working for the competition. Curot was his boss. Savoyard and the other voyageurs had left Grand Portage in late July, their canoes stuffed with trade goods. They had paddled along the shore of Lake Superior until they arrived at the river that would lead them to the St. Croix. The trip up the river was always hard. Savoyard had to carry 90-pound bales over **portages** (PORT-ij-uhs) and haul his heavy canoe through shallow waters and around rapids. The first thing Savoyard did when he arrived at the final destination on the St. Croix was to take a gift to his mother-in-law. Savoyard was married to an Ojibwe woman who lived year-round in this area.

John Sayer (SAY-er), the trader, arrived with his Ojibwe wife and their two children in early November 1803. Sayer was a partner in the North West Company. He had been a fur trader for many years in this region and had become quite wealthy. Sayer had left one of his clerks here during the summer to watch over the company's trading post. Now he was back, and he was in charge.

WINTER

Giishkiman's family and all the other Ojibwe families spread out through the forest. Each one camped and hunted in a certain area. But the winter was hard. Food started running out. Giishkiman's wife stayed in the family's camp while her husband hunted deer and elk and trapped beavers. She cleaned the furs that he brought back and traded them directly to the white men.

Michel Curot was not enjoying winter near the St. Croix River. Food was scarce, and supplies were running low. The Ojibwe continued to visit his post, but they were coming less often. Soon Curot was making

The fur companies set prices for furs and goods, but the traders and Indians always bargained for the best deal they could get. **What trade goods do you see in this trading post?**

portage: the place where boats or goods are carried overland from one stretch of water to another

most of his trades for food, not furs. When an Ojibwe hunter brought him "two geese, nine ducks, a fisher, an otter, and two skins full of wild rice," Curot gave the hunter's wife five feet of cloth.

Toussaint Savoyard was getting fed up with his boss, Michel Curot. When Curot tried to cut Savoyard's ration of wild rice to one pint a day, Savoyard exploded. He punched Curot in the face. Curot punched back. The two men fought to a draw. Savoyard soon left the post to stay with his Ojibwe family. But food was scarce there, too. Savoyard asked Curot whether he and the other men could return to the post. Curot replied that "they could come back if they chose, but they would stand a pretty good chance of starving," along with him, as well.

John Sayer knew that food was running low, so he, too, cut back his men's rations. In February 1804, Sayer had something new to worry about. Dakota scouts were spotted in the area. The Dakota did not want him to trade with their rivals, the Ojibwe. He expected an attack. Sayer was confident that his fortlike trading post could withstand an attack by the Dakota. He wasn't so sure about Curot in his little log cabin. He invited Curot to move into the North West Company's headquarters. Curot accepted. The Dakota never attacked.

SPRING

Giishkiman and the other Ojibwe continued bringing their furs to the two trading posts, even as the traders were preparing to return to Grand Portage. Many of the Ojibwe were trying to pay back debts that they had taken on during the fall. In June, the Ojibwe began preparing to make the long journey back to their homeland at Waaswaaganing.

Curot counted the pelts he had collected since arriving last autumn. Altogether he had nine packs. About one-third of them were beaver furs, the most valuable of all. He asked an Ojibwe woman to prepare some gum—a sticky substance made from pine-tree sap—so that he could repair his leaky canoes. In return, Curot gave the woman a large blanket that normally would have fetched him three or four beaver pelts.

THE MÉTIS

Some of the European men who married Indian women eventually returned to the East, leaving their Indian families behind. But many traders and voyageurs stayed in the West with their wives and children. As the years passed, these mixed—or Métis (may-TEE)—families gathered into communities. The daughters usually married Métis men or, sometimes, white traders and missionaries. A few of the sons became farmers. Some were hunters or guides. But most worked in the fur trade. By the early 1800s some of the leading Métis families had been in the trading business for more than three generations. This Métis coat combines features from both Indian and white cultures.

Toussaint Savoyard had returned to Curot's post after his wife left for the maple-sugar camps. But he still refused to follow any of Curot's orders, whether it was drying fish, pressing pelts into packs, or fetching hidden containers of rum. In mid-May, Savoyard set out with Curot and the rest of his men. They arrived at Grand Portage about a month later.

John Sayer had managed to collect more than twice as many pelts as Curot. In April, Sayer and some of his men had met some Ojibwe and made plans to build a new trading post for the following winter. Sayer, his family, and his voyageurs arrived in Grand Portage at about the same time Curot did.

Springtime in the Canadian city of Montreal was always a busy time. These canoes, full of voyageurs, clerks, and traders are preparing to head west to fur trading posts.

SUMMER

Summer in Grand Portage was, in part, a time to relax. It was where the **rendezvous** (RAHN-day-voo) took place, a yearly gathering of people involved in the fur trade. John Sayer dined, drank brandy, rum, and wine, and talked about business with his North West Company partners. Michel Curot spent much of his time drinking and gossiping with other young clerks like himself. Toussaint Savoyard and his fellow voyageurs laughed, fought, and rested their sore muscles in a tent village outside the towering log walls of the North West Company's headquarters. In a camp not far away, Ojibwe families enjoyed meals of Lake Superior fish and made frequent visits to the post to visit friends and trade for goods.

But Grand Portage was more than a vacation resort. Hundreds of traders, clerks, and voyageurs arrived at Grand Portage each June, bringing with them tons of furs that Indians had trapped and cleaned. At the same time, huge canoes arrived from Montreal, carrying tons of manufactured goods. During the weeks that followed, pelts were counted, repacked, and loaded for the long trip back to Montreal. From there, the pelts would be carried by sailing ship across the Atlantic Ocean to London, Paris, and other European cities. Meanwhile, the trade goods were parceled out according to each trader's wishes. Before long, they were packed up and readied for the journey to the wintering posts, where the cycle of trading would begin again.

By 1804 the fur trade was entering its final decades. In a few years, the newly formed American Fur Company would take control of the fur trade in this region. If the British and French wanted to keep trading here, they would have to become U.S. citizens. After the War of 1812, only U.S. citizens were allowed to trade in this area. It was one of the first signs that this new nation, which had formed in lands to the east, was now looking west to a place that would later be called Minnesota.

rendezvous: an annual summer meeting of traders, clerks, voyaguers, and Indians

Trading Places with a Voyageur

DUTIES OF THE VOYAGEUR

Return trip from Montreal to Fort William; Pass by [Mackinac] and go to Rainy River, if requested; Six days of [regular labor]; Make two portages from Fort William to Portage de la Montagne; Or, instead of the above, to give six days of other labor; Assist in carrying the 3-man canoes on land; To exercise due care to deliver the merchandise, livestock, pelts, utensils, and other necessaries to the destination; To promptly and honestly serve, obey, and faithfully execute all that the [traders] demand… To promote their profitable advantage, prevent harm, and warn them of things that come to their attention; To abstain from private trading, absenteeism, or quitting, under pain of law and loss of wages

Voyageurs were the workmen who carried the weight of the fur trade on their backs. But who were these men? What was it like to be a voyageur? Unfortunately, few voyageurs could read or write, so they left no diaries that describe their experiences. Yet there are documents that other people left, including employment contracts, diaries, songs, letters, and other accounts. Through these, you can begin to understand what the life of a voyageur was like.

In this Investigation, you will study documents, images, and captions to begin to uncover what a voyageur's life was really like. Then, using your imagination and the Investigation Guide, you will write a diary that describes what it would be like to trade places with a young voyageur.

JUST SIGN HERE

From the 1650s to the 1850s, Montreal, Canada, was a bustling center of the fur trade and the place where most voyageurs were hired. Fur companies were always looking for new men, and they attracted them with advance pay. All a man had to do was sign a contract and he would receive one-third of his salary, plus equipment such as a blanket, a shirt, a pair of trousers, some handkerchiefs, and tobacco. There was a catch, though: the voyageur might sign up for one to three years, but he would probably build up debts to the company, which would force him to work even longer.

Although few voyageurs could read, the contracts they signed bound them to perform very specific duties. Look at the tasks detailed in the 1811 contract (on the opposite page) between the voyageur Louis Mallette and the McTavish, McGillivrays fur company.

○ **Diary Entry 1: Write a diary entry that describes your background and why you chose to become a voyageur.**

The fur trade was a year-round business. **Can you tell what happened in each season?**

THE RHYTHM OF THE PADDLE

The fur trading season began each year in early May, when the ice broke on the St. Lawrence River. Voyageurs started their work by loading up canoes bound for western Great Lakes posts, such as Grand Portage, Mackinac (MAK-uh-nah), or Fort William. Once everything was loaded, groups of canoes (called brigades) pushed off from the wharves and headed west. As the men paddled upstream, they often started singing. Their songs, sometimes nostalgic, sometimes bawdy, helped the men keep the rhythm of the stroke and pass the time.

In my birch-bark, canoeing, in the cool of the evening I ride
Where I have braved every tempest of St. Lawrence's rolling tide.

My canoe's of bark, light as a feather
That is stripped from silvery birch;
And the seams with roots sewn together,
The paddles made of white birch. ...

It's when I come on the portage, I take my canoe on my back
Set it on my head topsy-turvy; it's my cabin too for the night ...

— You are my voyageur companion! —
I'll gladly die within my canoe.
And on the grave beside the canyon
You'll overturn my canoe.

His cart is beloved of the [farmer], the hunter loves his gun, his hound;
The musician is a music lover — to my canoe I'm bound.

Diary Entry 2: Describe the sights and sounds as your brigade departs from Montreal. Consider what this song reveals about the life and values of the voyageurs. As a new voyageur, do you share these values?

Montreal canoes were almost 36 feet long and could carry up to 8,000 pounds of trade goods, provisions, and equipment, plus seven to twelve people and their belongings. Canoes also transported passengers, such as traders and clerks, who sat in the middle and did not paddle.

INTO THE FRONTIER

After leaving Montreal, the brigades would often stop at St. Anne's, a Catholic church on the edge of the settled territory. Peter Pond, an early explorer and trader, visited St. Anne's in 1773 and noted in his diary what most travelers did there, even those who weren't Catholic:

> This Church is Dedacated to St. Ann who protects all Voigers. Heare is a small Box with a Hole in the top for ye Reseption of a Little Money for the Hole father or to say a small Mass for those Who Put a small Sum in the Box. Scars a Voiger but stops hear and Puts in his mite and By that Meanes they Suppose thay are Protected.

Diary Entry 3: Consider why the voyageurs might leave a donation at the church. How do you feel as you paddle away from this outpost toward an unfamiliar land?

Paddling started early—before dawn. Breakfast was a mixture of peas, corn, fat, and perhaps a little pork or bacon. Since this food was available only to men traveling from Montreal, new voyageurs were teased by other voyageurs and called "pork-eaters." **What are the men in this painting doing?**

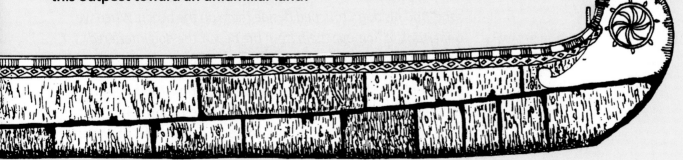

ACROSS THE INLAND SEA

For voyageurs, the trip across the vast waters of the Great Lakes could be dangerous. Strong winds and waves could dash the canoes into the rocky shorelines, tip the canoes into the cold water, or even tear the boats apart.

In the summer of 1789, the trader Jean Perrault (ZHAWN per-OH) waited out a windy day along the western shore of Lake Huron, near the town of Mackinac. He and some other men were playing cards when they saw a canoe with a sail coming through the whitecaps. When the canoe arrived, the trader Paterson boasted that he would continue, despite the bad weather.

An old voyageur named Laporte, who was traveling with Paterson, warned against continuing. He pointed out that the canoe was overloaded—there were eleven people in the canoe, including the Indian woman accompanying Paterson, plus a large white dog. Paterson ordered Laporte to get back in the canoe, and they set off.

For twenty minutes, Perrault and the others watched the canoe as it bounced between the waves. When they could no longer see the sail, someone rushed to find a telescope. Through the telescope, Perrault saw "some debris of the canoe on The water, moved by the waves, which Confirmed our belief that they Had perished."

Later, Perrault and the others canoed to the shoreline near the site of the accident.

We discovered The Casks and the bales, and the men that the waves had cast here and there Along the beach. We disembarked As soon as we arrived, and our first care was to draw in the Bodies which were rolling in the waves…

Mr. patersonne Was the Farthest away, holding [the Indian woman] by his hand, both half buried in the sand, and his dog Crouched beside them on the beach. When we undertook to Remove them from the beach, the dog interfered. It was necessary to strike him, in order to approach them.

Voyageurs were choosy about their paddles. The steersman, who stood, needed a paddle such as this one, which is 6 feet 4 inches tall.

◯ **Diary Entry 4: Even in the calm summer months, the journey across the Great Lakes was sure to have some rough days. Imagine that you are trying to get across a rough area of water in bad conditions, similar to the ones Perrault wrote about. Describe what goes through your mind and what your leader decides to do.**

RENDEZVOUS

In June, after weeks and sometimes months of travel, traders, clerks, and voyageurs met at the rendezvous—the summer meeting at Grand Portage. Those who arrived from Montreal brought news of friends and family. The men who came from the interior posts, called winterers, told stories of the long months in the wilderness. In his written recollections, George Nelson, a clerk for the XY Company, described some of the other activities in Grand Portage in 1802:

> At last [the brigades] began to come in, [and] all was business. Receiving goods, corn, flour, pork, etc. from Montreal & Mackinac, & furs from the different wintering posts—Gambling, feasting, dancing, drinking & fighting. After a couple of weeks to rest, for the Winterers to give in their returns & accounts, & to make up their outfits, they begin to return again, to run over the same ground, toils, labors, and dangers.

Diary Entry 5: As a young voyageur, describe the activities at Grand Portage that interest you most and tell what makes them interesting.

Some Indian women married traders or voyageurs to help build ties between their families and the trade companies. Carefully examine this 1857 painting of four Ojibwe women at Grand Portage. **Do you notice any trade goods in the picture?**

CARRY ON

West of Grand Portage, voyageurs faced a challenging series of lakes and portages. Finding a portage was difficult, but missing a portage was worse, since it could mean an unwanted trip through the stretch of water that the portage bypassed—down a rapids or over a waterfall. The portages themselves were often slick or muddy, and the combination of poor footing and heavy loads was dangerous. Wretched blisters, twisted ankles, tender bruises, strained muscles, broken limbs, and even death were common. Most men could handle this type of work only for a few years. The missionary William T. Boutwell described the agonies of portaging in his diary in 1832:

> The musketoes came in hords and threatened to carry a man alive, [or] devour him [before] they could get him away. ...
> [The rain] has [made] the portage almost impassable for man or beast. The mud, for the greater part of the way, will average ankle deep and from that upwards. In spots, it is difficult to find bottom—a perfect quagmire. Our men looked like renegades, covered with mud from head to foot, some have lost one leg of the pantaloons, others both. Their shirts and mocasins are of a piece full of [holes] and mud. Face, hands and necks, look like men scarred with the small pox.

Many voyageurs died while canoeing through rapids or while portaging. When a voyageur died, his friends erected a cross nearby. It was not unusual to see clusters of a dozen or more such crosses at the especially difficult portages.

Diary Entry 6: Describe a scene in which a brigade reaches some rapids and has to choose between running the rapids or portaging. What do you want to do? What does the trader who is with you want to do? What happens?

Winter travel by snowshoe or dogsled could be a welcome break from the normal routine—even when the travelers had to face snow blindness or freezing temperatures.

THE WINTERERS

At an interior trading post, voyageurs spent their days performing various tasks: building and repairing the shelters, gathering firewood, hunting for and preparing food, and following the orders of the clerks and traders. When not working, the voyageurs faced brutal boredom. Since most voyageurs couldn't read, their only distractions were religious holidays, feasts, and parties, during which they could drink, dance, and sing.

Deep in winter, boredom might bring about crankiness, depression, and self-doubt. As early as January, some men started dreaming of next summer's rendezvous. The trader Alexander Mackenzie described his emotions in a 1794 letter:

> I am fully bent on going down [to Grand Portage]. I am more anxious now than ever. For I think it unpardonable in any man to remain in this country who can afford to leave it. What a pretty situation I am in this winter. Starving and alone, without the power of doing myself or any body else any Service.

Final Diary Entry: After a winter of hard work and boredom, you return to Grand Portage. There, some men learn that they owe debts to their company and will either have to keep working or run off. Others choose between returning to Montreal or staying in Minnesota. As a young voyageur, just finished with your first season, what choice do you make? Why?

The Land Changes Hands

On July 23, 1851, the U.S. government and the Dakota signed a land treaty at Traverse des Sioux on the Minnesota River.

1776

Thirteen colonies in North America declare independence from Great Britain.

1787

Northwest Territory is created by United States.

1803

Louisiana Purchase adds 908,380 square miles to the United States.

1805

Lt. Zebulon Pike buys land near present-day Fort Snelling from the Dakota.

1812–1815

United States and Great Britain fight War of 1812.

1819

United States begins construction of the future Fort Snelling, near the junction of Mississippi and Minnesota rivers.

1830–1860

Each year, Métis trappers drive hundreds of oxcarts loaded with furs through the Red River valley, traveling between Winnipeg, Canada and St. Paul.

For nearly 150 years, fur traders and European travelers had come and gone from the land we now call Minnesota. Most of them were not interested in changing the ways of Indians or in owning the land. Some of them wrote reports and drew maps of what they saw. The Upper Mississippi valley and the area west of Lake Superior began to appear on charts of the world.

Far away in Europe, people gave names to the lakes and rivers and drew boundaries on paper. Different countries claimed Minnesota. At one time it appeared on maps as part of New France. Later it was divided between England and Spain, then among England, Spain, and a new country called the United States of America. Finally, the United States claimed all of it.

By the early 1800s, thousands of white settlers were pushing west toward Minnesota and were pressuring the U.S. government to make land available to them. The U.S. government supported this **westward expansion** by acquiring land from the Indians who lived on it. The

LOOK FOR

◆ Why did the United States establish Fort Snelling?

◆ Why did government officials, fur traders, and missionaries want to make treaties?

◆ Why did the Ojibwe and Dakota agree to make treaties?

◆ What happened during the treaty negotiations at Traverse des Sioux?

◆ What concerns did the Dakota have at Traverse des Sioux?

KEY TERMS

westward expansion

treaty

sovereign

military base

territory

delegation

negotiation

westward expansion: the nineteenth-century movement of settlers and immigrants from the eastern United States to the Midwest and West

1832	1836	1837	1841	1849	1851	1855
Explorer Henry Schoolcraft identifies the source of the Mississippi River at Lake Itasca in northwestern Minnesota.	U.S. government sends Joseph Nicollet to explore and map the Upper Mississippi River valley.	United States signs land treaties with the Ojibwe and the Dakota to gain land in western Wisconsin and eastern Minnesota.	The village of Pig's Eye is renamed St. Paul.	Minnesota becomes a territory. James Goodhue publishes Minnesota's first newspaper in St. Paul.	U.S. government and the Dakota sign land treaties at Traverse des Sioux and at Mendota.	U.S. government and the Ojibwe sign land treaty at Washington, D.C.

treaty: a written agreement between two or more nations

sovereign: self-ruling and independent

government made written agreements, or **treaties,** with the Indians to buy land for cash and goods.

The making of treaties was—and still is today—a familiar practice among countries considering each other **sovereign** (SAH-vruhn) nations with the power to control their own affairs. But the treaty-making process between the Indians and the U.S. government was different. The United States treated Indian groups as sovereign nations *and* as groups of people who needed the government's protection. This complicated approach to sovereignty led to confusing agreements that often became still more confusing as time went on.

As western expansion continued during the early 1800s, the U.S. government began turning its attention to the lands west of the Mississippi River. In Minnesota, the land that the government wanted was home to the Dakota and Ojibwe.

The First Land Deal

In 1805, a young U.S. army officer named Zebulon (ZEH-byoo-lahn) Pike traveled with 20 soldiers up the Mississippi River. He camped on a flat, sandy island where the Minnesota River joined the Mississippi. There, the Dakota bands met for a council with him. Pike told their leaders that he had been sent by the United States to find a good place for a fort. He gave gifts to the tribe. Then he asked whether they would let the U.S. government have some land.

The Dakota thought it over and said a small amount of land would be all right. They signed a document granting the United States two pieces of land. One was at the mouth of the St. Croix River, where it joined the Mississippi River. The other ran along both sides of the Mississippi from the mouth of the Minnesota River to the Falls of St. Anthony. In exchange, the U.S. government promised to pay the Dakota $2,000 in cash or goods. It was the first time that the United States acquired land from Indians in Minnesota.

Fourteen years passed before the U.S. government finally sent soldiers to build a fort on the Mississippi land that Zebulon Pike had bought from the Dakota. The United States believed that the fort would help protect the U.S. fur trade from the British and would help keep peace

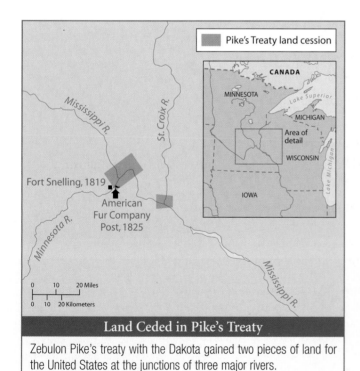

Land Ceded in Pike's Treaty

Zebulon Pike's treaty with the Dakota gained two pieces of land for the United States at the junctions of three major rivers.

among the Indians. Warfare between tribes made travel dangerous for traders and kept Indian hunters from gathering furs. Construction on the fort began in 1819. It would eventually be called Fort Snelling.

Fort Snelling overlooks the junction of the Mississippi and Minnesota rivers. The steamboats and stone houses in this 1844 painting hint at the changes coming for the Dakota and whites.

A Place to Gather

Fort Snelling was a **military base,** but its soldiers were not there to fight. They were there to enforce U.S. laws related to the fur trade. Their worst enemies were loneliness, boredom, bitter cold, and hard work.

The Dakota lived in five communities near Fort Snelling. They gathered there—as they had for centuries—for celebrations and trading where the Minnesota and Mississippi rivers joined in the valley below the fort's walls. Sometimes Ojibwe came down the Mississippi from their country to the north. They and the Dakota usually met in peace, but now and then old conflicts flared up. When trouble arose, the officers at the fort often took it upon themselves to punish those who started it.

Just west of the fort stood the home and headquarters of Lawrence Taliaferro (TAHL-i-ver). Taliaferro was what the U.S. government called an Indian agent. He oversaw the government's relations with the Indians and tried to resolve disputes between Indians and fur traders. Taliaferro welcomed the Indians to the agency day and night. He talked and conducted business with them in the agency's council house.

A large American Fur Company trading post stood just across the river from Fort Snelling at a place called Mendota ("where rivers meet"). It was one of the busiest and most successful trading centers in the region. The private home that stood on the trading post grounds often served as a guest house for travelers.

As the people living in and around Fort Snelling looked around them, they saw different things.

To the newcomers, Minnesota looked like a land of riches—property to be bought and sold and fenced. The dark, rich soil was capable of supporting an abundance of crops. The forests could produce riches in timber. The rivers could serve as both transportation routes and power sources.

military base: a central location where an armed force keeps its supplies and organizes its operations

As the Indian agent at Fort Snelling, Lawrence Taliaferro helped the Dakota and Ojibwe avoid dealing with dishonest traders.

To the Indians, Minnesota was something else. It was home. They believed that it belonged to the people who lived there, just as the people belonged to it. The land held the graves of their ancestors and the places of their sacred traditions and way of life. No one could own it and no one could sell it.

Making Treaties

The Dakota, the Ojibwe, and the United States signed the first major Minnesota land treaty in 1837. The treaty covered a large part of western Wisconsin as well as a large part of Minnesota land east of the Mississippi. The Ojibwe and Dakota had not yet been paid when lumbermen rushed into the pine forests along the St. Croix River. The Indians heard the thud of axes and the crash of falling trees. They saw mills built and settlements grow up at places like Marine on St. Croix, Taylors Falls, and Stillwater.

Around 1838, another settlement began to grow a few miles down the Mississippi from Fort Snelling. It was called Pig's Eye Landing, for a one-eyed man who opened a tavern there. Later settlers decided to rename their town St. Paul, after a little log church built by a missionary. Down the river from St. Paul stood a much older settlement. It was the Dakota community of Kaposia (kah-POH-zhah). The people of Kaposia anxiously watched the changes on the east side of the Mississippi. The Dakota had seen other Indians pushed from their lands. Soon, the Dakota feared, they would be forced to leave, too.

Initially, St. Paul was known as Pig's Eye Landing. When Father Lucien Galtier built the Chapel of St. Paul, he persuaded the residents to change the village's name to honor the new chapel. When this painting was made in 1845, there was not much to the settlement.

INTERPRETERS

Language barriers often posed serious problems during the making of a treaty. Most of the government's treaty negotiators did not speak the languages of their Indian counterparts. Most Indians could speak only a little English. So how did they communicate with each other? They relied on interpreters—men and women who were familiar with the languages and customs of both Indians and white people.

Often the interpreters were fur traders whom the Indians knew. Sometimes missionaries who had lived among Indians were also called on to translate from one language to another.

One of the more famous interpreters during this period was a fur trader named George Bonga. Bonga was the son of an African American fur trader and an Ojibwe woman. His father's parents had both been slaves. Bonga spoke three languages—English, Ojibwe, and French. When the government began making treaties with the Ojibwe in Minnesota, Bonga was called upon to be an interpreter. His signature appears on an 1867 treaty between the Ojibwe and the United States.

Many Motives

In 1849, Minnesota became a **territory** of the United States. Suddenly it seemed as though everyone was talking about treaties.

Although many Indians believed it was no more possible to sell their land than the air they breathed, others felt the time was right. Already, more than 5,000 white settlers were living in Minnesota Territory. Some Indians argued that they really had no choice—that the whites were going to take over their lands no matter what. The Dakota believed that through treaties they could keep at least some of their land and control their own future. Others argued that times were hard, and that the Dakota might help themselves by trading land for food and money. The Dakota elder Iŋyaŋgmani (EE-yahng-mah-nee), known to the Americans as Running Walker, described how the lives of his people had changed in recent years:

> *The Great Spirit does not smile. He growls at us. Something does not suit him. Our corn fields, where are they? Our young men cannot hunt. The powder in our rifles is wet. It will not burn. We kill no game. Nothing.*

The Americans also had their own reasons for wanting to make a treaty. Three groups in particular were especially eager to do so.

territory: a part of the United States that is not within a state but is organized with its own governing leaders

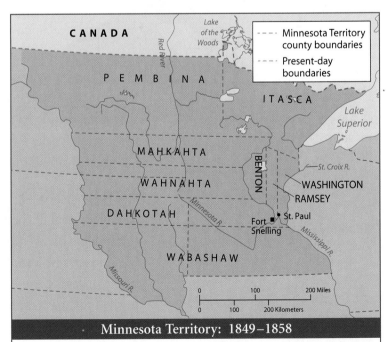

Minnesota Territory: 1849–1858

Minnesota Territory extended west to the Missouri River and north to Canada and had nine counties. Compare the size of Minnesota Territory with the actual state.

Alexander Ramsey was the first territorial governor and the second state governor.

GOVERNMENT OFFICIALS

Many people in the United States believed their nation would become great only if it expanded across North America. They considered Minnesota an important part of that expansion. But Minnesota still belonged to the Indians, even though it was now also a U.S. territory. American settlers could not legally move in unless the Indians sold it. So U.S. officials appointed a governor to represent its interests in Minnesota and convince the Indians to give up their land. The governor's name was Alexander Ramsey. In an early speech to the territorial legislature, Ramsey proclaimed that Minnesota was destined to become the land of white settlers. "I feel a conviction," he said, "that this country, once thrown open for settlement, would be peopled with a rapidity exceeding anything in the history of western civilization."

FUR TRADERS

By the time Minnesota became a U.S. territory in 1849, the fur trade in the region was entering its final years. Fur traders knew

Fur trader, politician, and territorial representative, Henry Hastings Sibley played a major role in Minnesota's economic and political development.

that they could make more money in new businesses like lumbering and selling land, once a treaty opened the Indians' land to white settlement. A treaty was also important to the traders for another reason. Many of them had extended credit to the Indians, giving them goods they needed with the understanding that the Indians would pay them back later with the money they would gain when they signed a treaty to give up land. Henry Sibley was Minnesota's most powerful fur trader and served as Minnesota's territorial representative in Washington. He would play a major role in the treaty-making process. "The Indians are prepared to make a treaty when we tell them to do so," he wrote. "No treaty can be made without our claims being first secured."

Missionary Stephen Riggs acted as a translator and witness at the treaty negotiations.

MISSIONARIES

The main goal of the missionaries in Minnesota was to persuade the Indians to give up their own religion and accept Christianity. Missionaries believed that treaties could help them achieve this goal by encouraging the Indians to give up their traditional ways. They pushed for the treaties to include plans for manual-labor schools, where children would be separated from their families and taught to farm like the white newcomers. "Disintegrate them," the missionary Stephen Riggs wrote of the Dakota's close-knit communities. "Encourage them to be thrifty farmers rather than poor villagers."

The Treaty of Traverse des Sioux

In the summer of 1851, the steamboat *Excelsior* carried a group of Americans—including Alexander Ramsey and Henry Sibley—up the Minnesota River to a place called Traverse des Sioux (tra-VERSE day SOO). There they were met by hundreds of Dakota who had traveled from different places on the Minnesota plains, and by a handful of missionaries—including Stephen Riggs—who lived in the area. They had all come to make a treaty.

July 18, 1851

The treaty-making council officially gets down to business. Alexander Ramsey leads the U.S. **delegation.** He welcomes the gathered elders of the Dakota nation's Sisseton and Wahpeton bands. He tells them that the U.S. president has sent him, and that the president has heard that the Dakota are poor and hungry. He says the president "is anxious that something should be done to mend your condition." He proposes that the Dakota accept money and goods for some of their land. The Dakota elders do not speak or ask questions. The council adjourns for the day.

delegation: one or more persons chosen to represent others

negotiation: the process of discussing a question or conflict in order to settle it

July 19, 1851

An elder named Wicaŋḣpiitetoŋwaŋ (wee-CHAHNK-pee-ee-tay-toon-wah), or Star Face, is the first Dakota to speak to the council. He tells the U.S. delegation that he would rather not make a treaty until all the young men of his band arrive at Traverse des Sioux. Another elder, Iśtaĥba (eesh-TAH-huh-bah), or Sleepy Eyes, also seems reluctant.

Your coming and asking me for my country makes me sad. And your saying I am not able to do anything with my country, makes me still more sad. Those who are coming behind are my near relatives, and I expected to see them here. That is all I have to say.

As Iśtaĥba and the other Dakota elders leave the council, Ramsey threatens to stop all **negotiations** (nih-goh-she-AY-shuhnz). Later, after tempers have cooled, both sides agree to meet again after a one-day recess.

July 21, 1851

Another Dakota elder, Upiyahideya (oo-PEE-yah-hee-day-yah), or Extended Tail Feathers, tells the council that his people want the government to make an offer in writing.

Artist Frank Mayer captured the daily activities of those gathered for the treaty negotiation.

When those sitting around here have seen this paper, had it explained to them, and talked it over among themselves, we will let you know our opinion in regard to it.…we wish to sell, and we will give you our country if we are satisfied with your offers for it.

Ramsey agrees and the council adjourns.

July 22, 1851

The Dakota spend the morning considering the offer that Ramsey wrote the night before. Stephen Riggs and the other missionaries move among the Dakota camps, translating the document. Henry Sibley and his fellow fur traders are also busy trying to convince reluctant Dakota to sign. In the afternoon, a delegation of Dakota hands back the document and promises to sign if certain minor changes are made.

July 23, 1851

The Dakota elders once again seem hesitant to go forward with the treaty. Iṡtaḣba demands that the Dakota be given a copy so they can tell whether the government is keeping its promises. Wicaŋḣpiitetoŋwaŋ says he hopes the government will not try to change the treaty after it is signed. Upiyahideya says he suspects the Dakota will never see much of the money promised them under the treaty.

You think it a great deal you are giving for this country. I don't think so, for both our lands and all we get for them will at last belong to the white men. The money comes to us, but will all go to the white men who trade with us.

Ramsey and another U.S. official sign the treaty. The time to decide has arrived. Despite their many concerns, the Dakota elders come forward to sign one by one. First, they sign two copies of the treaty. Then Stephen Riggs guides them to another table, where they sign another document. Most of the Dakota seem to think they are signing a third copy of the treaty. In fact, they are signing a document that says they will pay back the traders with treaty money.

SKETCHES DRAWN DURING TRAVERSE DES SIOUX TREATY NEGOTIATIONS

The Aftermath

Two weeks after the Sisseton and Wahpeton bands signed the treaty at Traverse des Sioux, the Mdewankanton and Wahpekute bands signed a similar treaty at Mendota. During the talks at Mendota, the government

THE TREATY MAKERS

Early in the treaty negotiations at Traverse des Sioux, negotiators on both sides confronted an important question: who would speak for the Dakota? Several Dakota elders participated in the negotiations, but they all insisted on consulting with their people before making any final decisions. On the second day of negotiations, the Dakota elder Wicaŋḣpiitetoŋwaŋ (Star Face) told Alexander Ramsey that he wanted to wait for a group of young men from his band to arrive:

> *My thoughts are turned toward my young men who are behind and I should be glad if you thought the same way. On looking around yesterday you said you were glad to meet and shake hands with us; but I am sorry you are not willing to wait and shake hands with those who are behind.*

In response, Ramsey insisted that the Dakota elders who were participating in the negotiations were perfectly capable of making decisions on their own:

> *Young men and old men of other bands are here and have been for some time. We suppose they are anxious as we are to get through and return to their families. You who are here are men and chiefs and you should just take hold of this business like men and arrange it at once.*

Over the next few days, the Dakota elders met regularly with each other and with the members of their own bands. Only when they were satisfied that most of their people agreed with the treaty provisions did they sign treaty papers.

threatened to use force against the Dakota when they seemed reluctant to sign the treaty. Together, the two treaties required the Dakota to give up almost all their remaining lands in Minnesota and Iowa—about 35 million acres. In exchange, the government promised to pay more than $3 million and provide a permanent reservation along the Minnesota River where the Dakota could live.

But the Dakota fears that they would be cheated were realized. The U.S. Senate changed the terms of the treaty so that the "permanent" reservation became "temporary." And as the Dakota had suspected, some of the cash that they thought they were going to receive actually went to the fur traders. Some also went to the missionaries, who claimed that the Indians had damaged some of their property.

By 1865, the Ojibwe had also signed treaties giving up much of their land in Minnesota.

Almost immediately after the treaties were signed, streams of white settlers began rushing into Minnesota. During the next three decades, the Dakota and the Ojibwe would sign several other treaties that left them with only a small fraction of their homeland. To Alexander Ramsey, this was how it was meant to be. The treaties, he said, had removed the only remaining obstacles that were keeping Minnesota from "the lofty destination evidently reserved for her." Lost in all the excitement was the fact that the obstacles Ramsey spoke of were people—the Dakota and the Ojibwe.

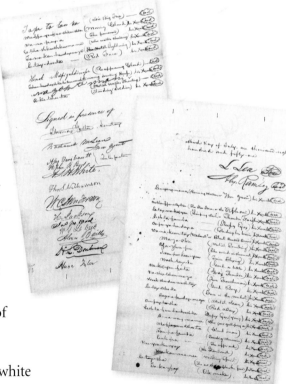

Treaties were handwritten and signed by U.S. government officials and Indian leaders. These are the final two pages of the Treaty of Traverse des Sioux.

IN THEIR OWN WORDS

You have learned what happened at the meetings where the Treaty of Traverse des Sioux was negotiated and signed. Two weeks later at Mendota, a similar treaty was signed with a different group of Dakota. In these treaties the Dakota agreed to give up most of their remaining lands in Minnesota and Iowa—about 35 million acres—to the United States government in exchange for more than $3 million and a permanent reservation. But there is more to history than knowing the facts. Historians also struggle to understand why people made the choices they did.

USE PRIMARY SOURCES TO UNDERSTAND

Historians studying this episode in Minnesota's history investigate primary sources such as speeches, government papers, drawings, paintings, and photographs. They also use their imaginations. When historians use their imaginations, they don't just make up the facts. Instead, they try to think *creatively* about why things happened as they did and why people made the choices that they made.

Look carefully at this painting from the 1850s. **How might a Dakota have seen this landscape? A government official? A farmer?**

USE PRIMARY SOURCES TO UNCOVER POINTS OF VIEW

Historians also try to see points of view that are missing or not obvious. They know, for example, that everything the Dakota representatives said at the 1851 treaty meetings was translated into English, then remembered and written down afterward. Historians also know that many of the speeches by government officials were also recalled and written down later. Did the translators and recorders accurately report what the Dakota and the government officials said? Historians cannot know for sure, but they consider such problems as they work to determine what happened during the treaty meetings.

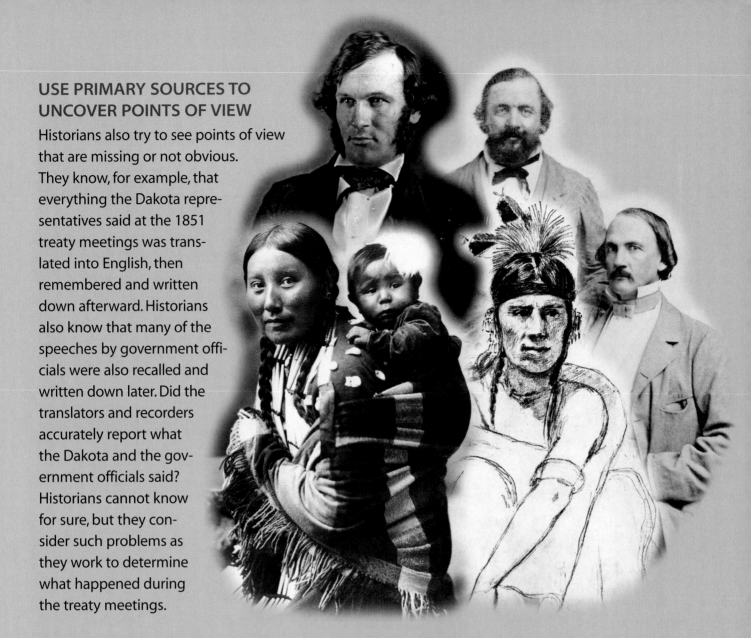

TRAVEL BACK TO 1851

In this investigation, you will examine different perspectives on the treaties of Traverse des Sioux and Mendota. You will read what the Dakota representatives said about the treaties through their translators. You will also examine what the newcomers—U.S. government officials, businessmen, and farmers—said about the treaties. Try putting yourself inside the mind of each Dakota and newcomer as you read. Study their words carefully, and look closely at the pictures that surround those words.

○ **While you study these sources and visuals, take a few notes. You can use your notes to travel back in time to 1851. Follow the directions in the Investigation Guide to write two poems, one from the Dakota perspective and one from the perspective of a newcomer. If you can understand what a Dakota and a newcomer felt in 1851, you will begin to understand why people made the choices that they did.**

DAKOTA

Chief Wapaha**ś**a (WAH-pah-hah-shah), or Red Banner, explained to Luke Lea, Commissioner of Indian Affairs, why he did not want to sign the Treaty of Mendota.

> *You have requested us to sign this [treaty] paper; and you have told these people standing around, that it is for their benefit; but I am of a different opinion. You see these chiefs sitting around. They and others who are dead went to Washington and made a treaty, in which the same things were said; but we have not benefited by them.*

WAPAHA**Ś**A
IN 1858

Taoyateduta (tah-OH-yah-tay-doo-tah), or Little Crow, a respected leader, described to his people what he had seen happening to tribes in the eastern United States.

> *Warriors… We are only little herds of buffaloes left scattered; the great herds that once covered the prairies are no more. See! The white men are like locusts when they fly so thick that the whole sky is a snow storm…. Count your fingers all day long and white men will come faster than you can count.*

Iŋyaŋgmani (EE-yahng-mah-nee), or Running Walker, described the starvation of his people. Both Indian and white people overhunted game in Dakota lands.

> *We kill no game; nothing…. We are poor, very poor. Our ribs may be counted like the poles of a lodge frame, through the skin. Our horses are thin, our dogs are lean, very lean. They are too poor to bark.*

1830s Dakota bison hunt. **How is the hunting life different from the farming life pictured at the top of page 89?**

Sketches and paintings were the most common way of depicting Indian life during this time.

Upiyahideya (oo-PEE-yah-hee-day-yah), or Extended Tail Feathers, a Dakota leader, explained his mistrust of the treaty.

You think it a great deal you are giving for this country. I don't think so; for both our lands and all we get for them will at last belong to the white men....You will take this treaty paper home and show it to the Great Father [the president of the United States], but we want to keep a copy here so that we may look at it and see whether you have changed it.

After many days of difficult negotiations, Taoyateduta agreed to be the first chief to sign the treaty.

I believe this treaty will be best for the Dakota, and I will sign it....We wish to live and die where our Great Father has given us the land forever. The money is small but we are always glad to have it, and so will our children and grandchildren to the end of the fifty years.

TAOYATEDUTA
IN 1858

NEWCOMERS

James M. Goodhue attended the negotiations for the Treaty of Traverse des Sioux and reported the signing in the *Minnesota Pioneer*. Goodhue founded the *Minnesota Pioneer*, now called the *St. Paul Pioneer Press*.

> *The news of the treaty exhilarates our town—It is the greatest event by far in the history of the Territory.*

After Wapaháśa refused to sign the treaty, Luke Lea responded with these words.

> *Suppose your Great Father wanted your lands and did not want a treaty for your good, he could come with 100,000 men and drive you off to the Rocky Mountains…. But your Great Father loves his red children, as he does his white children; and he wishes us to make a treaty which he knows will save you from the trouble which is now coming upon you.*

Mary Henderson Eastman, who lived at Fort Snelling in the 1840s, wrote numerous poems, articles, and books about Dakota culture.

> *White men, Christian men are driving them back [the Dakota]; rooting out their very names from the face of the earth. Ah! these men can seek the country of the Sioux [Dakota] when money is to be gained; but how few care for the sufferings of the Dahcotahs! how few would give a piece of money, a prayer, or even a thought towards their present and eternal good!*

JAMES GOODHUE IN ABOUT 1850

THE CITY OF ST. PAUL IN 1857

William G. Le Duc, a politician and business-man, explained why he thought the treaties should be signed.

FARMER CLEARING LAND

> *The treaties with the Dahcotas had become absolutely necessary both to the Indian and to the whites. The buffaloes which once fed in myriads upon every stream of the Territory now confine their range to the western borders of Minnesota, and have left thousands of red men, who depended almost entirely upon the buffalo for their food and raiment, to destitution and starvation. It is therefore necessary for the Indians ... to change entirely their habits, and become at once an agricultural people.*

In Europe, land belonged primarily to the wealthy. In this letter to relatives in Germany, Minnesota farmer Sebastian May shares his delight in the opportunies available to him.

> *I have been on my land two years. I own 160 acres, 10 of that are woodland. I have two oxen, two cows, and 10 hogs. If I remain in good health I hope to double that. Such progress can be made here in a few years. The beginning is only hard. It took me quite a time to find a suitable place to establish a home. I feel so at home here as if I were in Germany. With little money one can do so much.*

At the Treaty of Traverse des Sioux, Luke Lea shakes hands with a Dakota leader as Alexander Ramsey looks on. **Can you find them in the painting on page 74?**

Luke Lea and Alexander Ramsey reported to Washington, D.C., about the Minnesota territory.

> *Thousands are already eagerly waiting to enter upon this new purchase [Dakota lands] as soon as it is open for settlement. With extreme difficulty can the agents of the Government now restrain them from rushing forward in advance, and occupying the lands without respect to the rights of the Indians or the authority of law.*

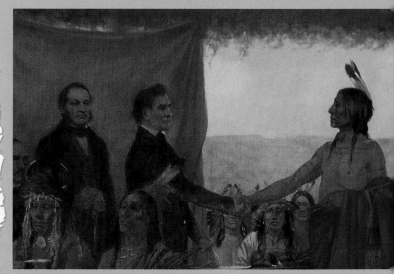

7 Minnesota's Newcomers

Immigrants traveled to Minnesota Territory on steamboats, hoping to find a land of wealth and opportunity.

1787

Northwest Ordinance establishes procedure for lands in Northwest Territory, including part of Minnesota, to become territories and states.

1820

U.S. government offers land to settlers for $1.25 an acre with minimum purchase of 80 acres.

1823

The *Virginia* is the first steamboat to make the trip up the Mississippi River to Minnesota.

1837

John Deere invents the steel plow, making it easier for farmers to break the tough prairie sod.

Samuel Morse invents the telegraph.

1846

The Mexican War is fought between the United States and Mexico.

Elias Howe invents the sewing machine.

1847

Harriet Bishop arrives in St. Paul to become the first public school teacher in Minnesota.

1848

Convention of 61 men meets in Stillwater to begin process of forming Minnesota Territory.

Armed conflicts and crop failures in Europe cause many to emigrate.

Until about 1850, most of the people living in Minnesota were Indians—Dakota and Ojibwe. But by the 1860s, white settlers were in the majority. The speed with which the white settlers took over the land of the Dakota and the Ojibwe was incredible. At the time of the signing of the treaties of Traverse des Sioux and Mendota in 1851, about 6,000 white people were living in Minnesota. By 1854 their number had increased to 30,000. By 1857 it topped 150,000. Between 1849 and 1858, Minnesota was the fastest-growing place in the United States. It had become one of the most popular destinations in a great migration of people from east to west.

As more and more people arrived, Minnesota itself changed in countless ways. The newcomers made a new Minnesota. Their experiences combined to form an amazing tale of a land transformed.

LOOK FOR

♦ What was life like for Minnesota's first public-school teacher?

♦ Why did people move to Minnesota Territory?

♦ What happened to the Indians when settlers began to move into Minnesota Territory?

♦ What sorts of problems did early settlers like Hans Mattson face?

♦ How did the early settlers affect Minnesota?

KEY TERMS

temperance
reservation
immigrant
recruiter

1849

Minnesota becomes a territory. President Zachary Taylor appoints Alexander Ramsey as territorial governor.

Minnesota Historical Society is organized.

1851

Treaties between the Dakota and the U.S. government are signed at Traverse des Sioux and Mendota, opening up southwestern Minnesota for white settlement.

1853

Swedish immigrant Hans Mattson arrives in Minnesota.

1855

Minneapolis is established.

First bridge over Mississippi River opens in St. Anthony.

1858

Minnesota becomes the thirty-second state in the Union.

Henry Sibley becomes the first governor of the state of Minnesota.

1860

Abraham Lincoln is elected president of the United States.

TRANSPORTATION

For as long as anyone could remember, there had been two main ways to travel through Minnesota — by foot or by canoe. But by the 1850s, people had a few more choices.

In 1847, steamboats started making regular stops at the village of St. Paul. The boats carried people and supplies. Great numbers of immigrants took trains from the East Coast to Mississippi River towns such as Galena, Illinois, and then boarded steamboats bound for Minnesota. The boats could run only from April to November, when the river was clear of ice.

Those who wanted to travel to Minnesota during the winter could take a stagecoach from Galena, but it wasn't an easy trip. The journey could take up to six days — compared to two days for the steamboat. Snowstorms often made travel impossible and forced passengers and their drivers to find lodging in the cabins of friendly strangers.

The oxcart was another common form of transportation beginning in the 1850s. It was used by the Métis people of the Red River valley in northern Minnesota and Canada. The Métis used the oxcarts to transport furs, buffalo skins, and other goods from the Red River to St. Paul. A train of oxcarts could make the trip in 30 to 40 days.

The New England Schoolteacher

In July 1847, a young woman named Harriet Bishop stepped off the Mississippi riverboat *Argo* and onto the landing at a small settlement called St. Paul. Several children were there to greet her when she arrived. She had come to be their new teacher—their *first* teacher.

Bishop had grown up in Vermont and had trained to become a teacher, one of the few careers open to women at that time. But teaching jobs were hard for women to find on the East Coast. When Bishop heard that an organization called the National Board of Popular Education was recruiting women to establish schools in newly settled lands to the west, she jumped at the chance. Her assignment was to teach the unschooled children of St. Paul.

The main mode of travel for immigrants was steamboats, which carried cargo as well as people. The four steamboats shown here are docked in St. Paul in 1859.

St. Paul was hardly even a town in 1847. The buildings were mostly just log huts. The streets were rutted and muddy. A few hundred people lived there, and most of them were men. A dozen or so families with school-aged children lived in the surrounding area. About half of the parents had never learned to read.

Harriet Bishop knew that teaching children under these circumstances would not be easy, but she seemed to relish the challenge. "Here was a field to be cultivated," she later recalled, "a garden of untrained flowers to be tended, and the heart raised a thank-offering to heaven and cheerfully entered upon its work."

Her new school was an abandoned blacksmith's shop. Mud plaster held the log walls together. Small, grimy windows let in hardly any sunlight. Rats and snakes lurked in the corners. Bishop got to work. She cleaned up her schoolroom as best she could and decorated the walls with evergreen branches. She seemed to enjoy her new surroundings. "Why should I pine for halls of science and literature, when such glorious privileges are mine," she wrote. "There was not a spot in earth's broad domain that could have tempted me to an exchange."

Three days after arriving in St. Paul, Bishop opened her little schoolhouse for the first day of class.

Energetic, businesslike, intelligent, and confident, Harriet Bishop was an effective teacher and community leader.

Strong Feelings

temperance: a reform movement whose followers worked to make alcohol illegal

Harriet Bishop did more than just teach children. She established St. Paul's first Sunday school. She helped organize a **temperance** group, whose members believed that drinking alcohol was harmful and should be illegal. And she led several women's organizations that raised money for community projects. Bishop believed that all these things would help "civilize" the frontier country of Minnesota. Ten years after arriving in St. Paul, she wrote that Minnesota was a land for people with high ideals.

> *I have known Minnesota from its infancy, and have loved it as a parent does a child, till my very being is entwined with her interests; and to me it is fit for paradise. Come to Minnesota, but bring with you principles firm and unyielding.*

Bishop was just one of a growing number of New Englanders who were making new homes in

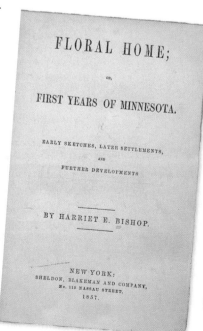

FLORAL HOME;

or,

FIRST YEARS OF MINNESOTA.

EARLY SKETCHES, LATER SETTLEMENTS,

AND

FURTHER DEVELOPMENTS

BY HARRIET E. BISHOP.

NEW YORK:
SHELDON, BLAKEMAN AND COMPANY,
No. 115 NASSAU STREET.
1857.

Harriet Bishop's book *Floral Home*, published in 1857, describes her early experiences in St. Paul.

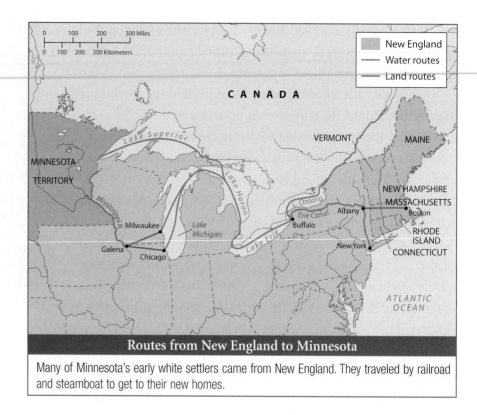

Routes from New England to Minnesota

Many of Minnesota's early white settlers came from New England. They traveled by railroad and steamboat to get to their new homes.

Minnesota. Many of these newcomers had worked in the lumber industry in the East, and they were now looking to make their fortunes off the vast timberlands of Wisconsin and Minnesota. Like Harriet Bishop, these New Englanders often had strong feelings about democracy, laws, schools, and churches. They had plans for Minnesota's future. Many of these New Englanders became leaders in the towns that were developing along Minnesota's rivers. Because of them, Minnesota was often called the New England of the West.

Minnesota Territory

In 1848, 61 men met in the growing lumber town of Stillwater, along the St. Croix River, and agreed to send a delegate to Washington. He would ask Congress to make Minnesota a legal territory, with a

Becoming a Territory	
In 1787, the Northwest Ordinance set the process for new public lands north of the Ohio River and east of the Mississippi River to become territories and states.	
Must have 5,000 adults living in it.	Minnesota had 4,535 adults in 1849.
A convention has to elect a legislature and a non-voting representative to the U.S. Congress.	Sixty-one men met in Stillwater in 1848 to elect Henry Sibley to represent them in Congress.
U.S. Congress passes a law creating the territory and authorizing its legislature to make laws.	Congress created Minnesota Territory on March 3, 1849. Alexander Ramsey became first governor of the territory.

governor, a legislature, and courts of its own. This was the first step to becoming a state. They chose the successful fur trader Henry Sibley of Mendota.

In 1849, after much political arguing about where to draw the boundaries, Minnesota became a U.S. territory. Now the citizens could send an elected delegate to Congress, and Minnesotans again chose Henry Sibley. The territory's other important officer was a governor, appointed by the president of the United States. President Zachary Taylor chose Alexander Ramsey, a Pennsylvanian.

Both Ramsey and Sibley played important roles in Minnesota's development over the following years. One of their first goals was to get the Dakota to give up their lands in southern Minnesota. They achieved that goal in 1851 with the signing of the treaties of Traverse des Sioux and Mendota.

Alexander Ramsey had been the territorial governor of Minnesota for almost a year when this photograph was taken in 1850.

Turning Point

The 1851 treaties marked the beginning of a radical change in Minnesota's population. By 1852, white settlers were starting to pour onto the land, even though the treaties said they were supposed to stay away until 1854. They began claiming land that they hoped to buy from the government when it became legal to do so. The white trespassers rarely showed much concern for the Indians who were living there.

Many of these new arrivals came to Minnesota with hopes of owning their own land and being their own boss. The vast majority of them were from Europe and New England, where land ownership was considered a source of wealth and status. Minnesota appealed

reservation: land set aside, or reserved, by the U.S. government specifically for Indians

THE RESERVATION SYSTEM

Where were Indians supposed to go when white settlement pushed them off their land? The answer, according to the U.S. government, was **reservations.**

Reservations were pieces of land that the government set aside specifically for Indians. To the Indians, reservations were often the only homes they had left. To the government, reservations were places where Indians could be kept separate from white settlers and be encouraged to give up their traditional customs. The government pieced together its reservation policy over several decades in the mid-1800s.

The U.S. government created more than a dozen reservations in Minnesota during the 1850s. Ojibwe reservations were set aside in places such as Fond du Lac, Grand Portage, and Mille Lacs. The Dakota reservation ran for 10 miles along the Minnesota River. Many Ojibwe and Dakota resisted moving to the reservations because they needed more land for hunting than the reservations allowed. The government wanted them to learn how to farm like white settlers, but they preferred to hunt, fish, and plant their traditional foods as they always had — on lands that went beyond the reservation.

New immigrants arrived in busy port cities like New York before making their way to Minnesota. As people set off for the West, they traveled by wagon, train, steamboat, or foot toward their new life.

to many of these newcomers because its landscape was similar to the places they left behind. It felt familiar to them.

The Swedish Immigrant

Hans Mattson arrived in Minnesota in the fall of 1853. His journey to the young territory had been a long one. Mattson had grown up on a small farm in southern Sweden. Mattson's life was good there, but he yearned for adventure. He had heard stories about the United States—how huge stretches of fertile land were opening to settlers, many of whom came from Europe. He decided to become one of those settlers.

In 1850, at age 17, Mattson boarded a ship and made the long journey across the Atlantic. During the next two years, he lived on the East Coast, working at various jobs and saving up enough money to buy his own land out west. He wrote letters to his family and even to newspapers in Sweden, urging others to join him. At age 20, Mattson led a group of fellow Swedish **immigrants**—including his parents, his sister, and his brother-in-law—to find a new home, in Minnesota.

The land they claimed was about 12 miles west of Red Wing. It was difficult to reach. "The first four miles we followed the territorial road," Mattson wrote. "After that, we had nothing but Indian trails to guide us."

immigrant: a person who comes into a country to live there

Almost nothing about living in Minnesota was easy. Mattson spent most of the winter in Red Wing, chopping firewood to fuel the stoves and engines of Mississippi River steamboats. In January 1854, he and his brother-in-law, S. I. Willard, decided to make a trip to the land they had claimed. They wanted to chop down some trees there so they would have enough logs to build a house in the spring. They set out with two other men and a team of horses pulling a sleigh. The weather was mild when they started, but overnight the temperature dropped. Mattson and the others learned how dangerous a Minnesota winter could be:

Hans Mattson quickly adapted to his new home. When the Civil War started in 1861, Mattson volunteered for the military, serving as an officer in the Third Minnesota Regiment until the end of the war.

> We soon found that going over the wild, trackless prairie against the wind, with the thermometer 40 degrees below zero was a struggle for life, and in order to keep warm we took turns to walk or run behind the sleigh. In taking his turn Mr. Willard suddenly sat down in the snow and would not stir. We returned to him, and it required all our power of persuasion to make him take his seat in the sleigh again. He felt very comfortable, he said, and would soon catch up with us again if we only would have left him alone. If we had followed his advice, he never would have left his cold seat again.

Mattson and the others survived their ordeal and chopped down enough trees for a log house. In March, the small group of Swedish immigrants bought as many supplies as they could afford from the stores in Red Wing and set out to build their new homes:

> Hundreds of thousands of immigrants have had the same experience, and can realize how we felt on that fine March morning, starting from Red Wing with a wagon loaded with some boards on the bottom of a cook stove and utensils, doors, windows, a keg of nails, a few trunks, and a little box containing our spotted pig... all of us full of hope, strength and determination to overcome all obstacles and conquer the wildness.

Mattson and his family built a small log cabin. But their first few weeks were difficult. The weather was bad, and their supplies were running out. They could have gone back to Red Wing, but things weren't much better there. The town's store shelves were nearly empty after the long winter. But in April the ice broke up on the Mississippi River, and steamboats began arriving with fresh supplies. Mattson went to town, stocked up on smoked ham, flour, molasses, coffee, salt, and sugar, and carried the merchandise back to the little cabin. He and his fellow Swedes had survived their first winter in Minnesota.

Red Wing
Vasa

A Community Grows

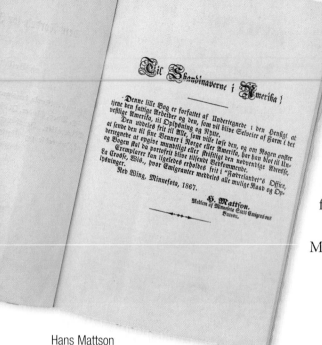

Hans Mattson
wrote many articles, letters,
and speeches to encourage settlers
to come to Minnesota.

Mattson began writing a series of letters that were published in *Hemlandet* ("The Homeland"), a Swedish-language newspaper published in Chicago. The letters described life in Minnesota and urged other Swedes to come. Many did just that. In the summer of 1855, the growing group of Swedes who lived in Mattson's settlement officially formed a township. They called it Vasa, after a Swedish king.

But the Swedes weren't the only immigrants arriving in Minnesota at this time. Hans Mattson recalled what it was like:

While the Swedes were pouring into our place... our friends, the Norwegians, had started a prosperous settlement a few miles to the south, many of them coming overland from Wisconsin, bringing cattle, implements and other valuables of which the Swedes, being mostly poor newcomers, were destitute. Many immigrants of both nationalities came as deck passengers on the Mississippi steamers to Red Wing.

Thousands of new settlers arrived in Minnesota each year, seeking a better life. Many of the Norwegians had left Norway because land and jobs were scarce there. Families from southern Ireland had come to escape the terrible famines in their homeland. Germans, many of whom were fleeing wars back home, arrived in larger numbers than any other immigrant group in the 1850s. Newcomers from New England and other parts of the East continued to arrive, too.

Boatload after boatload of immigrants landed in the towns along the rivers and spread out into the country beyond. Soon there were

recruiter: somebody who encourages others to join a group

ATTRACTING NEWCOMERS

The immigrants who came to Minnesota could have settled in any number of places. So why did they choose this place?

For one thing, they had heard good things about it.

Many of the first newcomers to settle in Minnesota wrote letters to their friends and relatives back home. The letters often described Minnesota in glowing terms. A German immigrant named Wenzel Petran

sent a series of such letters to his aunt and uncle. Minnesota "has a very healthy climate," he wrote, "beautiful country and natural scenery, and with its clean, fresh air it reminds me strongly of the northern part of Germany."

Politicians, newspaper editors, land speculators, and other **recruiters** also spread the word about Minnesota. Often they exaggerated the territory's good

points. Sometimes they outright lied. Among their far-fetched claims was that disease was almost unheard of in Minnesota—thanks, they said, to the chilly climate. Anyone who had battled colds and flu symptoms—or worse—during Minnesota's long, tough winters knew that such claims were questionable at best.

whole communities where hardly anyone spoke English. The names of some of these places told where people had come from. Besides Vasa, there were New Ulm, New Prague, St. Patrick, Scandia, Heidelberg, and many other names that called to mind homelands far away. Before long, Minnesota was not only the New England of the West. It also was the New Sweden, the New Norway, and the New Germany.

Minnesota Statehood

With its population exploding, Minnesota's leaders launched a drive for statehood. There were many advantages to being a state rather than a territory. As a state, Minnesota would control its own finances and be in a better position to attract the railroad companies that were laying tracks to the west. It also would have a real voice in national affairs.

On May 11, 1858, Minnesota became the thirty-second state of the Union. In a speech to the legislature, the state's first governor—Henry Sibley—described Minnesota as the newest member of the American family.

> She extends a friendly hand to all her sisters, north and south, and gives them assurance that she joins their ranks—not to provoke sectional discord or to engender strife…but to promote harmony and good will, and to lend her aid, on all occasions, in maintaining the integrity of the Union.

Sibley, and most other Minnesotans, realized that the family they had just joined was about to break apart. The Civil War that erupted in 1861 would last four long years.

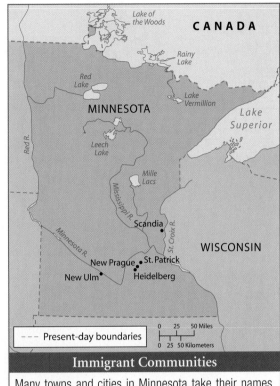

Immigrant Communities

Many towns and cities in Minnesota take their names from the homelands of the first settlers. **Which ethnic groups do the towns on this map represent?**

Statehood for Minnesota

In 1856, a group of Minnesotans decided they were ready for statehood and petitioned Congress for admission to the United States as a state.

Congress must pass a law allowing the territory to proceed toward becoming a state.	In 1857, Congress passed the law allowing Minnesota to begin the process toward statehood.
A group of residents must convene to write the state constitution.	Minnesota's constitution was written at a convention in Stillwater in 1857.
Voters must approve the constitution and elect officials and legislators.	Minnesotans approved the constitution by a vote of 30,055 to 571 and elected Henry Sibley as governor.
Congress must pass a law admitting the state into the Union.	Congress admitted Minnesota into the Union as the thirty-second state on May 11, 1858.

Writing Home, Writing Minnesota

Many immigrants brought large trunks like these with them as they traveled to Minnesota. **If a trunk were your only baggage, which of your possessions would you take?**

Settlers who came to Minnesota Territory between 1849 and 1858 knew the area was rich in natural resources. Early immigrants hoped to turn southern prairies into farmlands, northern forests into lumber, and rivers into power sources for mills. Whether businessman or farmer, these settlers were struck by a sense of great opportunity. All Minnesota needed was just one more resource: people to do the work.

The territorial government took this need so seriously that it hired an emigration commissioner, whose job was to recruit people to Minnesota. Private citizens took up the cause as well, and land developers, newspaper editors, and guidebook authors busied themselves promoting Minnesota to immigrants.

In contrast to the intentional efforts of these people, another method of recruitment also occurred. Many new immigrants wrote letters home to their families and friends that described their new surroundings and opportunities. These letters inspired many people to join their countrymen in Minnesota. By studying these immigrant letters and the guidebooks, posters, and brochures written by recruiters, historians can compare what the immigrants and recruiters thought were Minnesota's good qualities.

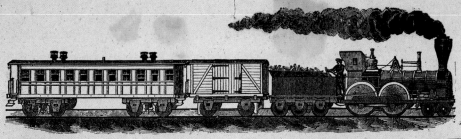

EMIGRATION

UP THE MISSISSIPPI RIVER.

The attention of Emigrants and the Public generally, is called to the now rapidly improving

TERRITORY OF MINNESOTA,

Containing a population of 150,000, and goes into the Union as a State during the present year. According to an act of Congress passed last February, the State is munificently endowed with Lands for Public Schools and State Universities, also granting five per cent. on all sales of U. S. Lands for Internal Improvements. On the 3d March, 1857, grants of Land from Congress was made to the leading Trunk Railroads in Minnesota, so that in a short time the trip from New Orleans to any part of the State will be made in from two and a half to three days. The

CITY OF NININGER,

Situated on the Mississippi River, 35 miles below St. Paul, is now a prominent point for a large Commercial Town, being backed by an extensive Agricultural, Grazing and Farming Country; has fine streams in the interior, well adapted for Milling in all its branches; and Manufacturing **WATER POWER** to any extent.

Mr. JOHN NININGER, (a Gentleman of large means, ideas and liberality, speaking the various languages,) is the principal Proprietor of **Nininger**. He laid it out on such principles as to encourage all **MECHANICS,** Merchants, or Professions of all kinds, on the same equality and footing; the consequence is, the place has gone ahead with such rapidity that it is now an established City, and will annually double in population for years to come.

Persons arriving by Ship or otherwise, can be transferred without expense to Steamers going to Saint Louis; or stop at Cairo, and take Railroad to Dunleith (on the Mississippi). Steamboats leave Saint Louis and Dunleith daily for **NININGER,** and make the trip from Dunleith in 36 to 48 hours.

NOTICES.

1. All Railroads and Steamboats giving this card a conspicuous place, or *gratuitous insertion* in their cards, **AIDS THE EMIGRANT** and forwards their own interest.

2. For authentic documents, reliable information, and all particulars in regard to Occupations, Wages, Preëmpting Lands (in neighborhood), Lumber, Price of Lots, Expenses, &c., apply to

THOMAS B. WINSTON, 27 Camp street, New Orleans.
ROBERT CAMPBELL, St. Louis.
JOSEPH B. FORBES, Dunleith.

This advertisement was made in 1857. **Who made the advertisement? What reasons does it present for coming to Minnesota?**

Now, imagine that you are a recruiter living in Minnesota Territory. Study what the recruiters and letter writers are saying. Think about which aspects of Minnesota Territory you would advertise. Use the Investigation Guide to record your research; then, create a poster, brochure, or guidebook that will convince an immigrant of the 1850s to choose Minnesota.

MINNESOTA!

CURE FOR THE PANIC

Emigrate to Minnesota !

Where no Banks exist ; a supension is unknown. Land and Water of best kind. No Ague and Fever there. CLAIMS can be made by rich and poor.

THE MAN OF SMALL MEANS

CAN SOON REACH COMPETENCY.

Climate dry and healthy. The rich respect and assist the poor—all labor together. The finest Lands are open to pre-emption.

Saint Paul is the great stopping place,

From there you can go to any point, as emigrant settlers start daily to the various Land Offices and Districts.

T. B. W.

Thos. E. Sutton, Printer, 142 Fulton Street, New York.

This advertisement refers to the Panic of 1857, a financial crisis in the East that caused bank failures, unemployment, and bankruptcy. **Who might have written this advertisement?**

RECRUITMENT EFFORTS

J. W. Bond, in his guidebook *Minnesota and Its Resources,* originally published in 1853, wrote:

> The Sioux [Dakota] treaties having been ratified by the senate of the United States, more than twenty million acres of land are open for settlement, before it can be surveyed — *BEFORE IT CAN BE MONOPOLISED BY SPECULATORS.* The sun never shone on a more beautiful or fertile land. A [healthier] country, old or new, exists not in the broad domain of the east or west.
>
> Go to work, men, in the states — men of industry, enterprise, and intelligence. Organize your emigration companies, shake the dust from your feet, and hasten on to the wild lands of Minnesota, which bid you take them, without money and without price.

Edward H. Hall, in a guidebook titled *Ho! For the West!!* wrote of Minnesota in 1858:

> Its northern latitude and healthy climate, are calculated to foster habits of industry and enterprise. ... Perhaps the most striking feature in the natural aspect of the country, is the great abundance of water contained within its limits, and the peculiar facilities which its rivers and lakes afford for inland navigation and for purposes of manufacture. Every portion of the territory may be reached by inland navigation. ... It is a country of great fertility, of picturesque scenery, and is probably rich in mineral treasures; it also possesses a healthy climate and abundant water-power; thus offering an inviting field for manufacturing and agricultural pursuits.

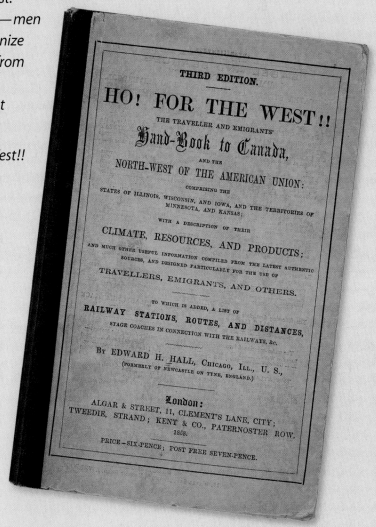

On board the Steamer
"Golden Era" down the Mississippi
June 2, 1855.

Dear Friends,
To day at twelve oclock we loosed our cables &
commenced floating down the "Father of waters" turning our
backs upon the Saints & setting our faces homewards. (this it may be
a long time before they are seen there.) We have been to the head of
navigation on this mighty river, thousands of miles from its mouth & there

IMMIGRANT LETTERS

David W. Humphrey traveled up the Mississippi to Minnesota in the summer of 1855. In June, he wrote to his friends back in Massachusetts:

> This [area], although to you seeming away out of the world, is a beautiful place, in prospect at least.... The country is fast filling up, beyond what one at the east can conceive of.... But there is still room for more. ...St. Anthony is already a town of some thousand inhabitants + looks like a N. England village, with its neat white houses + general appearance of thrift, + indeed I learned that very many of the inhabitants were from the good old N. England States.

Stillwater was a growing town in 1856, when this image was printed. **What about the town might have appealed to Friedrich Schmitz and other immigrants?**

Friedrich Schmitz (SHMIHTS), a German immigrant in Stillwater, wrote to his parents in Germany in April 1858:

> If a man there has a handful of land more than you, you have to bow and scrape, and take off your hat to him. That is certainly not true here. In this country a man who is healthy, even if he has nothing, can get along better than a man in our village in Germany who has property worth $1000.... A girl, if she behaves herself, can make a good marriage here, even if she has no money, for no one considers wealth. Women in general have a good life. Even maids do not have to work in the fields.

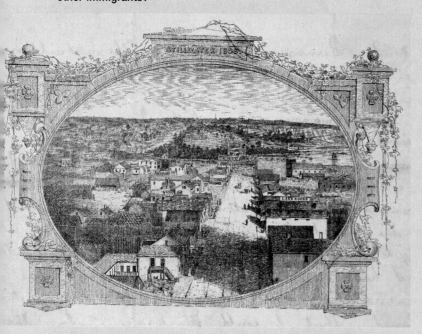

Theodore Bost emigrated from Switzerland to the United States in 1851. After a few years of working and traveling on the East Coast and in Canada, he made plans to move to Minnesota. In February 1855, he wrote to his parents:

The Territory of Minnesota, the place I want to go, [is very large]. … I have bought a book, Minnesota and Its Resources; it is very interesting, very impartial, giving the bad side as well as the good, and seeking only to attract those who have strength, courage, and goodwill, but giving assurances that such people will succeed. … You can see that I am eager to get back to working the land, but at the same time I want, if I do go back to farming, to take some of my friends from Canada out to Minnesota with me to form a sort of colony of Protestant Christians and build ourselves a church.

THEODORE BOST AND HIS FAMILY IN 1874

Guri Sanders-Datter and her husband Svend Svenssen were Norwegian immigrants who settled near St. Peter in Nicollet County in the late 1850s. In February 1860, she wrote to their friends back in Norway:

Now, to give you our honest opinion about emigration, which I know many of you want to hear about. I can say truthfully that I do not regret our coming here, especially when I think of the heavy burdens we escaped from. I feel very glad about it all, for example, when I remember the plight of the cattle in winter, the difficulty of getting hay, and the problem of subsistence. From all this, with God's help, I regard myself as freed, not in that I want anybody to think that we have escaped all worry by having come here. Still, there is a big difference, especially for women.

Women who immigrated to Minnesota in the 1850s brought clothes that were both practical and beautiful. This stylish bonnet helped protect its owner from sun and insects. The dress was probably worn as a wedding dress.

On July 2, 1863, First Minnesota Infantry Regiment soldiers
charged Confederate lines during the Battle of Gettysburg.

1819	**1820**	**1835–1860**	**1849**	**1850**	**1854**	**1857**
Construction of the future Fort Snelling begins.	U.S. Congress passes the Missouri Compromise, excluding slavery in territories north of latitude 36° 30′ and allowing it south of this line.	Fashionable Tours of the Upper Mississippi River are popular.	Minnesota becomes a territory. Alexander Ramsey is appointed governor.	Compromise of 1850 is passed, repealing the Missouri Compromise and setting up a stronger fugitive-slave law.	U.S. Congress passes the Kansas-Nebraska Act allowing these two territories to decide whether to allow slavery.	U.S. Supreme Court hands down the Dred Scott decision.

On July 4, 1858, a new star was officially added to the blue field of the United States flag. It represented the nation's newest state—Minnesota. There were 32 stars on the flag now, each representing a different state. But all was not well in the land of the Stars and Stripes. In fewer than three years, the nation would be at war, and thousands of Minnesotans would head off to join the fight.

By 1858, many Americans had come to think of their nation as having two parts—North and South. The two regions had many similarities, but they also had many differences. The North was a place of big cities, big factories, and small farms producing enough food for a growing population. The South had only a few large cities and factories. On its farms grew a variety of crops, but its agricultural economy depended largely on three —sugar, tobacco, and especially cotton. Its population was growing more slowly than the North's.

These were all major differences. But one, more than any other, was driving a wedge between North and South. That difference was slavery.

LOOK FOR

◆ What were the differences between the North and South that led to war?

◆ How did people in Minnesota react to slavery and the visiting slave Eliza Winston?

◆ What happened to Charley Goddard during the Civil War?

◆ What problems did the former slave Robert Hickman face when he tried to resettle in Minnesota?

◆ What were the consequences of the Civil War for Minnesota?

KEY TERMS

abolitionist

secede

Union

Confederacy

Emancipation Proclamation

1858	1860	1861	1862	1863	1864	1865
Minnesota becomes a state.	Abraham Lincoln is elected president.	Civil War begins.	Dakota War begins in south central Minnesota.	President Lincoln issues Emancipation Proclamation.	President Lincoln is re-elected.	Thirteenth Amendment abolishes slavery.
	South Carolina secedes from the Union, followed by 10 other Southern states the following year.	Governor Ramsey is the first to offer volunteers for the Union army.	Battle of Antietam is fought in Maryland.	Battle of Gettysburg is fought in Pennsylvania.	General Sherman leads Union troops on march to the sea.	Civil War ends with Confederate surrender.
		Battle of Bull Run is fought in Manassas, Virginia.				President Lincoln is assassinated.

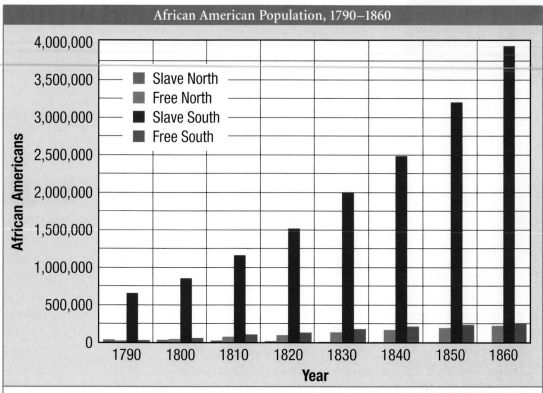

African American Population, 1790–1860

- ■ Slave North
- ■ Free North
- ■ Slave South
- ■ Free South

Y-axis: African Americans (0 to 4,000,000)

X-axis: Year (1790, 1800, 1810, 1820, 1830, 1840, 1850, 1860)

The African American population grew from about 750,000 in 1790 to almost 4.5 million in 1860, one year before the Civil War began.

Land of the Free?

The division over slavery had begun about 60 years earlier. Before then, both Northerners and Southerners had owned slaves. But by 1800 that was changing. In the North, more and more people were beginning to believe that slavery was both unprofitable and morally wrong. By 1804 all the northern states had officially abolished slavery, although in some places it was still practiced.

The South was a different story. White southern farmers needed cheap labor. A new type of cotton plant and the invention of the cotton gin—a machine that separated the fiber of the cotton plant from its seeds—had turned cotton into a very lucrative crop. Southern plantation owners depended more than ever on their slaves to pick cotton.

Southerners were not the only people who supported slavery. Many Northerners believed that the South should be allowed to keep slavery and that runaway slaves should be returned to their owners. But most people in the North did agree on one thing: they didn't want slavery to spread into the West as new states were formed. White Southerners did. Of all the questions involving slavery, this one seemed hardest to resolve.

Like most Northerners, Minnesotans had mixed feelings about slavery and what to do about it. In 1860 those feelings were put to the test.

Freedom for Eliza Winston

The Mississippi River had become a highway between Minnesota and the cotton plantations of the South. Hundreds of steamboats traveled on the river, carrying passengers in comfort and style. Many of these passengers were wealthy Southerners taking what was called the Fashionable Tour. Hotels in St. Anthony and Minneapolis welcomed the Southern visitors because they were good for business. But the Southerners also created a problem: they sometimes brought their household slaves with them.

In the summer of 1860, a well-to-do Mississippi plantation owner named Richard Christmas arrived in St. Anthony with his wife, their baby, and a slave named Eliza Winston. Winston's duties were to care for the baby and to wait on a sickly Mrs. Mary Christmas.

When Winston reached Minnesota, she knew she was in a free state and could walk away from her master. But where would she go? How would she live? Would anyone help her? These questions were answered when she met Emily and Ralph Grey, a free African American couple who lived in St. Anthony. The Greys were friends of the African American **abolitionist** Frederick Douglass. Abolitionists made up a nationwide movement of blacks and whites who sought freedom for all slaves.

The Greys wanted to help Eliza Winston become free. So, with the help of some white friends, the Greys convinced Judge Charles Vandenburgh to consider Winston's case. Vandenburgh sent a sheriff to the house where the Christmases were staying with an order to take Winston into custody.

The next day, the judge held a hearing. The whole town was excited. Abolitionists were joyful because they believed the law was being enforced. Others claimed that Winston had been illegally kidnapped and worried that publicity about the case would drive away rich Southern visitors. Minnesota merchants depended on the money these visitors spent. Vandenburgh heard arguments from both sides and then quickly gave his ruling: Eliza Winston was no longer a slave. She was free to go where she pleased.

But finding a place to go would not be easy.

That night a mob of people surrounded the Greys' house where they thought Winston was staying and demanded that she be returned to the Christmases. They threw stones through the windows, and some men tried to climb through them. Meanwhile, others broke into the home and searched for Winston, but she was not there. The Greys and their friends had sent Winston even farther north—to Canada. She

abolitionist: someone who opposes slavery

The August 23, 1860 *St. Anthony Evening News* featured the story of Eliza Winston's fight for freedom.

> SLAVE EXCITEMENT IN MINNEAPOLIS—HEARING BEFORE COURT—SLAVE DISCHARGED—CONFLICTING STORIES.—Tuesday witnessed a high excitement in Minneapolis; W. D. Babbitt, a Mrs. Gates (white) and a Mrs. Gray (colored) made complaint that Eliza Winston (a slave) was restrained of her liberty by Col. Christmas of Mississippi. A writ was issued and placed in the hands of Sheriff Strout who proceeded to the house of Mrs. Thornton, on Lake Harriet where the parties were residing, and brought Eliza for a hearing before Judge Vanderburgh. F. R. E. Cornell, Esq., appeared as Counsel for the Complainants, and —— Freemen Esq., of Mississippi, for the defence. Col. Christmas made no attempt at a technical defence, admitting that the woman was free and at liberty to choose whether to remain with him or to go at large. The Court consequently ordered her to be discharged from the custody of the sheriff. Then came the

DRED AND HARRIET SCOTT

Dred Scott and his future wife, Harriet, were slaves brought to Fort Snelling by their owners. In 1836 they were married, and Harriet's owner, the Indian agent Lawrence Taliaferro, sold her to Dred's owner, John Emerson, a military surgeon stationed at the fort. Fort Snelling was in free territory. Slavery was illegal, but there were no courts and no one tried to enforce the law. When Emerson returned to Missouri—a state where slavery *was* legal—he took the Scotts with him.

In 1846, the Scotts sued in the Missouri courts. They claimed that because they had been taken to live in a free territory, they were free. For the next 11 years, the case filtered through the court system until it reached the U.S. Supreme Court. In a landmark 1857 decision, the U.S. Supreme Court ruled against the Scotts and refused to give them their freedom, arguing that African Americans were not citizens and had no rights under the Constitution. The ruling also stated that slaves were considered property and that citizens could not be deprived of property.

That same year, though, the Scotts' owners freed them. In 1858, Dred Scott died of tuberculosis.

While many white Southerners supported the decision, abolitionists in the free states were outraged and did not agree that black people could be property. Abolitionists in Minnesota believed Eliza Winston could become free while she was in Minnesota. But under the court's ruling in the Dred Scott case, she would still be a slave if she went back to Mississippi with the Christmas family.

apparently returned to Minnesota a few months later to speak to an abolitionist group, but it's not clear what happened to her after that.

Home of the Brave

By the fall of 1860, many Minnesotans were turning their attention to politics. In November they joined with voters—only white men at that time—in other Northern states and helped to elect Abraham Lincoln president of the United States. It was a turning point in the nation's history. Southerners were convinced that Lincoln's election marked the beginning of the end of what they considered the Southern way of life, a way of life that depended on slavery. Southern states responded by **seceding,** leaving the United States to form the Confederate States of America. In response, President Lincoln said he would not allow the United States to split in two. By the spring of 1861, the North and the South—the **Union** and the **Confederacy**—were at war.

Both sides immediately began building up armies, with each state expected to provide its share of soldiers. Minnesota's first contribution to the war effort was a volunteer regiment of 1,009 men. It was made up of soldiers from St. Anthony, St. Paul, and nearby towns. It trained at Fort Snelling and was known as the First Minnesota Volunteer Infantry Regiment.

secede: to withdraw from the Union of states

Union: the Northern states during the Civil War

Confederacy: the 11 Southern states that seceded from the Union during the Civil War

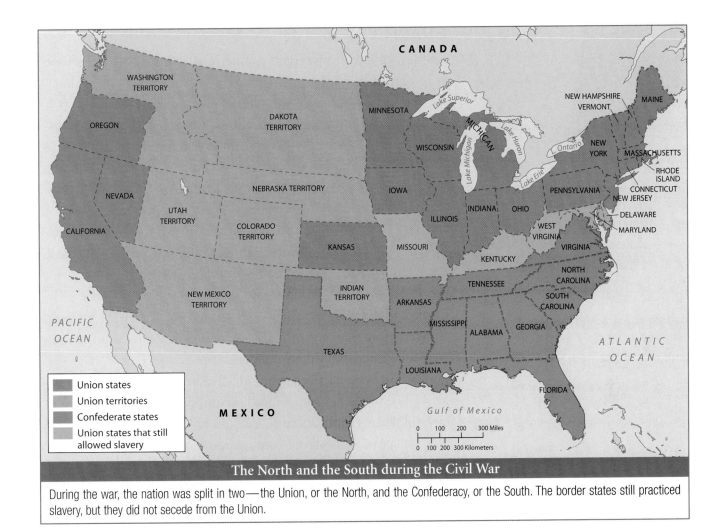

The North and the South during the Civil War

During the war, the nation was split in two—the Union, or the North, and the Confederacy, or the South. The border states still practiced slavery, but they did not secede from the Union.

Legend:
- Union states
- Union territories
- Confederate states
- Union states that still allowed slavery

Charley Goddard Goes to War

Charley Goddard was 15 years old when the call for volunteers went out. Charley lived in the Mississippi River town of Winona. He was an adventuresome boy. When he was 12, he had scared his mother—and many other people in town—by swimming all the way across the river through its dangerous currents. Now he was determined to join in what he figured would be the adventure of a lifetime—war.

There was just one problem: he wasn't old enough. Men had to be 18 to enlist.

That didn't stop Charley. When Winona men started enlisting, he lied about his age and signed up, too. A few days later, he and 75 other Winona volunteers boarded a steamboat and traveled upriver to Fort Snelling. For nearly two months, Charley trained to become a soldier. He learned how to march in formation, fire a musket, and follow orders. On June 22, 1861, Charley and the rest of the First Minnesota Regiment left Fort Snelling and headed for Washington, D.C. He had just turned 16.

Winona•

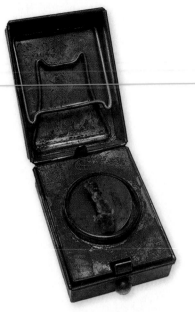

Northern soldiers cooked their own meals on cookstoves like this one.

CHARLEY AT 16

Charley started writing to his mother, Catharine Goddard, as soon as he reached Washington. In an early letter he admitted that he was looking forward to his first taste of battle. "The truth of it is," he wrote, "I would like to be in a little more danger where I could have a chance at some Secession soldiers and finish up the job and go home to old Winona." Charley didn't know better. He didn't yet realize how terrifying and bloody war could be.

About a month after arriving in Washington, Charley and the rest of the First Minnesota Regiment set out for the first major fight of the Civil War, the first Battle of Bull Run, on July 21, 1861. On the way there, Charley got sick and had to stay behind. It was just as well for Charley. After hours of fierce combat, the Confederates forced the Union army to retreat. The First Minnesota suffered more than any other Union regiment at Bull Run: 42 men were killed, and 108 were wounded.

Back in Winona, Catharine Goddard heard about the regiment's losses. She wrote her son, reminding him that he was too young to be a soldier. He replied that she should not worry. "I hope that you will not speak to me about coming home yet unless it is your direct order," he wrote. "I want to do some good before I go back home."

Charley did not see much fighting as a 16-year-old. He wouldn't see the terrible realities of war until the next year.

Charley Goddard wore his uniform for this photograph.

CHARLEY AT 17

That fall, the Confederate army invaded the North. The Union forces rushed to turn back the Confederates. The two sides met near Antietam Creek in Maryland. September 17, 1862, turned out to be the bloodiest day in the nation's history: 26,000 men were killed or wounded. "If the horrors of war cannot be seen on this battlefield," wrote Charley, "they can't be seen anywhere."

Charley survived the Battle of Antietam, but some of his friends did not. Among the dead was William Smith, a 26-year-old corporal from Winona. Charley broke the news in a letter to his mother:

I enclose a lock of Corporal William Smith's hair which I wish you would please give to his mother. Tell her that he fought bravely for the stars and stripes. His remains will be seen to by the boys of our company.

CHARLEY AT 18

Charley again witnessed the ravages of war during July 1863. It happened at a little town in Pennsylvania called Gettysburg.

The Battle of Gettysburg lasted for three hot, bloody days—July 1 through 3. On the second day, the First Minnesota Regiment played a crucial role in what turned out to be an important Union victory. After repeated attacks on the Union lines, Confederate soldiers were on the verge of breaking through. About the only thing standing in their way was the First Minnesota. The Minnesotans charged forward, knowing they probably would not survive. For about 10 minutes, they fought the Southerners almost face to face—both sides shooting and bayoneting each other. The Minnesotans stopped the Confederates just long enough for reinforcements to arrive.

When the fighting was over, the ground was covered with dead and wounded men. Charley Goddard had been seriously wounded —shot in the leg and shoulder. But he lived. From his hospital bed, he wrote to his mother about the Winona soldiers who had been killed or wounded at Gettysburg.

Nurses and women volunteers at hospital camps helped wounded soldiers keep in touch with their families by writing letters for them.

> *We have engaged the enemy again but this time in a free country and our company as well as the regiment has suffered much. . . . Don't let anybody see this letter but if they want to know if any of their friends are wounded you can tell them.*

The true story was that at least 160 Minnesotans were killed or wounded during the second day of fighting at Gettysburg. More than 50 others were killed or wounded the next day.

Unlike many wounded soldiers, Charley recovered from his wounds. He returned to his company and fought in several more battles. In February 1864, he and the surviving members of the First Minnesota Regiment headed home because their term of enlistment had ended, though the war would continue for another year. Charley returned to Winona. He died just four years later after a brief illness at age 23.

The First Minnesota was one of 22 Minnesota units that served during the four years of the Civil War.

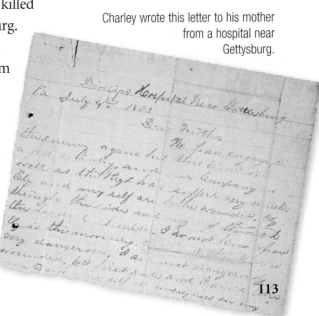

Charley wrote this letter to his mother from a hospital near Gettysburg.

113

In all, the state sent about 25,000 men—whites, blacks, mixed-bloods, and Ojibwe—to fight the South. More than 600 were killed in battle. Three times that number died in crowded army camps and in prison camps, where disease spread quickly.

Land of the Free

To most Minnesotans, the Civil War had begun as a fight to preserve the Union. But as time went on, many Minnesotans began to see that there was another reason for the conflict. On January 1, 1863, President Lincoln issued the **Emancipation Proclamation,** which made it clear that if the North won the war, all slaves would be free. Suddenly, the soldiers of the North were fighting not just to hold the Union together but also to free the slaves.

Charley Goddard, for one, was happy to fight for this cause. "I am for dislodging any officer who does not give the President's proclamation his entire support," he wrote.

But what about the people back home? Two years earlier, many white Minnesotans had responded angrily to the freeing of the slave Eliza Winston. How would they react when other former slaves began arriving in the state?

Emancipation Proclamation: the presidential decree that stated that as of January 1, 1863, the slaves in the Confederate states were free

Journey to Freedom

Robert Hickman became an influential member of the African American community in St. Paul when he arrived in 1863.

Robert Hickman was one of the first slaves to make the journey to freedom in Minnesota. He had been born into slavery in Missouri in 1831. As an adult slave, he had worked as a rail-splitter. But Hickman had other skills. He had learned to read and write, which most slaves weren't allowed to do. He preached the Bible to his fellow slaves. He was a leader in his community.

Then, in 1863, Hickman heard about the Emancipation Proclamation and was inspired to escape. He gathered together a large group of slaves who escaped and headed north. They called themselves "the pilgrims." There are many conflicting stories about how they made the trip. One tells of how they received help from Union soldiers. Another recounts how they built a crude raft out of logs that was towed upriver by a steamboat. But what is known is that, in May 1863, two steamboats docked in St. Paul, carrying about 300 African Americans.

HOME FRONT

The people of St. Paul reacted in different ways to the arrival of this large group of former slaves. Workers on the riverfront were afraid that the newcomers might take their jobs, and they tried to stop the boats from landing. But many Minnesotans welcomed these Missourians. One newspaper reported that it much preferred what it called the "quiet, civil, and inoffensive manner" of the African Americans to the behavior of the riverfront laborers.

Some of the new arrivals went on to Minneapolis and Stillwater, but most of them stayed in St. Paul. Soon Hickman and his followers established Pilgrim Baptist Church. They had no building to worship in, so they held services in members' homes. Pilgrim Baptist was St. Paul's first African American congregation, and it still exists today.

The North finally defeated the South in 1865. The war was over, but the nation had paid a terrible price. More than 600,000 soldiers and countless civilians had lost their lives. Many parts of the South were in ruins. In contrast, Minnesota had escaped most of the ravages of the Civil War. The state's economy had flourished. Prices for farm products had risen. Wheat production had doubled. Immigrants had continued to move in, encouraged by a new federal law that gave away government land to settlers. Perhaps more importantly, Minnesotans had learned—partly through their exposure to the horrors of war and the evils of slavery—that their lives were firmly connected to those of other Americans.

But all was not well in Minnesota. Families were broken and bodies were crippled for life. Even worse, three years earlier—around the time Charley Goddard and his regiment had been fighting at Antietam— another conflict had been raging in the southern part of the state. This one also inflicted deep wounds that would cause great pain for years to come.

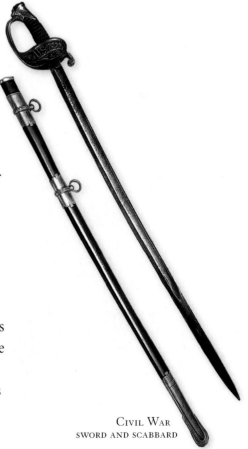

CIVIL WAR
SWORD AND SCABBARD

Missionary Ridge, the "Soldier's Battle"

Jeremiah C. Donahower, from St. Peter, Minnesota, was an officer in the Second Minnesota. **Can you find him in Volk's painting?**

PROBLEM AT THE CAPITOL

The people of Minnesota were upset! It was 1905, and the new capitol building in St. Paul had just opened to the public. The walls and ceilings inside the capitol were decorated with beautiful murals—but the paintings depicted mostly ancient history and mythology. Minnesotans wanted to see *Minnesota* history in the capitol. A group of citizens and war veterans decided to take action. They raised money to hire famous American artists to paint pictures about Minnesota history and Minnesotans in the Civil War.

The artist Douglas Volk was chosen to paint the Civil War's Battle of Missionary Ridge in Tennessee. The painting was going to be big: six feet high and eight feet long. When Volk met with the capitol commissioning board in 1905, they had just one request: make your painting as accurate as possible.

This coat was worn by Captain Donahower. Look carefully at the coats in the Volk painting. **Do they look like this one?**

WHERE COULD VOLK GET HIS INFORMATION?

Although the battle happened in 1863—42 years earlier—Douglas Volk knew that Civil War veterans were still alive. He knew there were letters, diaries, and reports from the actual battles that he could study. Objects such as uniforms, medical equipment, guns, and ammunition could easily be found. There were even photographs of soldiers from the Second Minnesota Infantry Regiment and photographs of Missionary Ridge in the 1860s. But one thing was missing: there were no action shots of the battle. "Fast action" film had not been developed in the 1860s. So Volk had to do research and imagine what had happened.

To paint the Battle of Missionary Ridge *in action* was Volk's job. He knew he needed to make his painting as historically accurate as possible, but he also wanted viewers to feel the excitement and drama of the battle. He wanted everyone who looked at the painting to see how brave and daring the soldiers of the Second Minnesota had been.

THE SECOND MINNESOTA AT THE BATTLE OF MISSION RIDGE, BY DOUGLAS VOLK, *1906*

Compare the primary-source photos, objects, and diary in this investigation to those same people and objects in Douglas Volk's painting. Now decide for yourself: Is Douglas Volk's painting an accurate portrayal of a Civil War battle? From his painting do you feel the excitement and daring of the Second Minnesota at the Battle of Missionary Ridge?

The Berdan Sharps rifle was popular with soldiers because it was accurate, fast to load, and easy to clean. **How many rifles and other weapons can you spot in Volk's painting?**

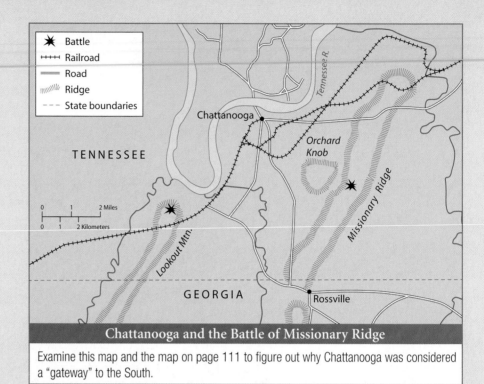

Chattanooga and the Battle of Missionary Ridge

* Battle
+ Railroad
Road
Ridge
State boundaries

Examine this map and the map on page 111 to figure out why Chattanooga was considered a "gateway" to the South.

WHERE IS MISSIONARY RIDGE LOCATED?

Missionary Ridge is part of a chain of steep, craggy mountains in southern Tennessee, next to the city of Chattanooga. Chattanooga was one of the war's most important strategic locations. To get to the city by road or by rail, you had to cross over Missionary Ridge. Both the Union and the Confederacy wanted to control the city of Chattanooga.

WHAT HAPPENED AT MISSIONARY RIDGE?

In November 1863, Confederate soldiers were in control of Missionary Ridge, cutting off the rail line to the north that brought Union supplies of food and ammunition. The Second Minnesota, along with 20,000 other Union troops, was stationed in the valley to the west of Missionary Ridge. On November 25, they were ordered to capture the Confederate rifle pits—deep ditches that hid men and guns—at the base of Missionary Ridge. After overrunning the first rifle pits, the Second Minnesota and others continued charging up the ridge even though they had been ordered to stop. Their charge was so fierce and unexpected that the Confederates fell back in retreat.

Take a close look at this photograph of Lookout Mountain, a mountain close to Missionary Ridge. **Does the landscape in Volk's painting look like the landscape in this 1863 photograph?**

118

The victory at Missionary Ridge enabled the North to control the vital rail center at Chattanooga. Now the Union could move troops, guns, and supplies easily to the South. Equally important, the South lost the use of this essential transportation link. Because the men charged on their own initiative, with no orders, this battle was nicknamed the "Soldier's Battle."

MOVING IN CLOSER

Color Bearers

At the heart of Volk's painting are the flags, or "colors." Each regiment carried a national flag and a regimental flag. Some regiments painted the names of the battles they fought on the stripes of their flags.

Compare the flags in Volk's painting to the actual flags of the Second Minnesota below. Do you think Volk ever looked at the real flags?

Each regiment had several soldiers whose job was to carry and protect the colors. Carrying the colors was a dangerous job but also an honor. Soldiers carried the flags at the front of the regiment while marching and in battle. Men in battle would look for their colors to see where to move and to keep from being separated from their regiment. Generals would watch enemy colors from afar to track regiments. The enemy shot at the color bearers to confuse the troops, because if a flag went down, soldiers could lose track of the movement of their regiment.

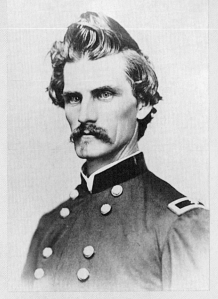

Judson Wade Bishop of Chatfield, Minnesota, was the commanding officer of the Second Minnesota at Missionary Ridge. Officers could be recognized by the shoulder straps on their uniforms. **Can you identify Colonel Judson Wade Bishop—and other officers—in Volk's painting?**

SECOND MINNESOTA REGIMENTAL BANNER

SECOND MINNESOTA NATIONAL BANNER

When a regiment won a battle, the colors were planted in the ground to signify victory. Fighting took a toll on the flags. Flags often had holes from bullets and even cannonballs that had been shot through them.

Musicians

Drummers and buglers were essential parts of the army. In fact, there were more than 50 distinct bugle calls that told men when to charge, shoot, and retreat. Like color bearers, buglers had a dangerous job during battle. They needed to be close to commanding officers, who were often at the front of the regiment. Because they were making noise and had shiny instruments, they were easy targets for the enemy.

Has Volk placed the color bearers and musicians realistically?

CIVIL WAR BUGLE

Hand-to-Hand Combat

In the Battle of Missionary Ridge, the Second Minnesota's ultimate goal was to drive the Confederate soldiers off the ridge. Drummer William Bircher wrote the following account of the battle on November 25, shortly after he witnessed it:

> At 4:30 p.m., from a signal gun at Orchard Knob, the entire army moved as one man ... towards the first line of works [Confederate rifle pits], which we soon reached, and drove the rebels [Confederate soldiers] out. Before we reached the first line of works, we crossed an open piece of ground, and, as we left our cover of trees and entered this piece of ground, the top of the ridge was one sheet of flame and smoke from the enemy's [cannons] ... After taking the first line of works, the troops followed the fleeing rebels up the ridge and charged over the second line of works.

This Civil War bayonet is 18 inches long and attaches to the end of a rifle. **How close would you need to be to the enemy to use a bayonet?**

How does this firsthand account of the Battle of Missionary Ridge compare to Volk's painting?

Infantry soldiers in the Civil War fought with single-shot rifles, bayonets (long, knifelike daggers attached to the end of the rifles), swords, and revolvers. They had artillery to back them up. Typically, soldiers in a regiment began a battle standing in an orderly formation. They then marched closer and closer to the enemy, stopping frequently to reload and fire. The formations would begin to waver as men scrambled over steep hills and brambles, were wounded, or came face-to-face with the enemy.

Look carefully in the middle of Volk's painting. Can you see the blue lines of soldiers fighting across the length of Missionary Ridge? Can you spot their regimental colors?

DID VOLK SUCCEED?

You have examined photos, objects, and a firsthand account from the Battle of Missionary Ridge. Did Volk paint an accurate picture of the battle? We know he did extensive research, including visiting the site of the battle twice before he painted the piece. We also know he used live models dressed in real Civil War uniforms and full-size reproductions of the flags as references while he painted. Go back over the evidence. How is *The Second Minnesota at the Battle of Mission Ridge* historically accurate? How does this painting bring the drama of war to life?

The type of musket balls that were fired at Missionary Ridge are shown here at their actual size.

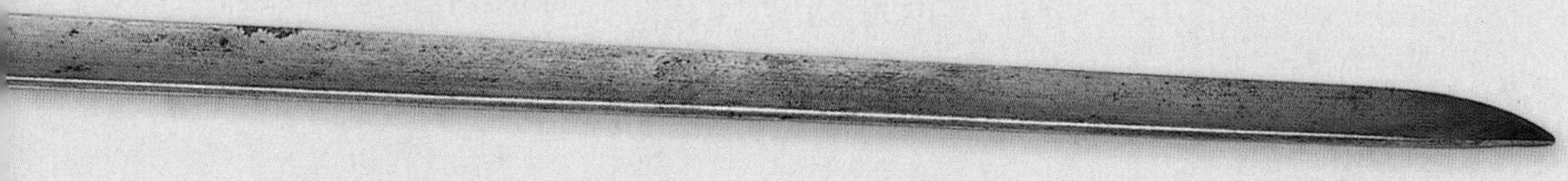

This painting depicts the Dakota attack on New Ulm on August 23, 1862.

1850

Minnesota's non-Indian population is 6,076.

1851

Land treaties at Traverse des Sioux and Mendota are signed between the Dakota and the United States.

1853

Lower Sioux Agency and Fort Ridgely are established to manage U.S.–Dakota relations.

1858

Treaty between Dakota and United States turns over the northern part of the Dakota reservation on the Minnesota River to the United States.

1860

Telegraph services reach St. Paul, St. Anthony, and Minneapolis.

Minnesota's non-Indian population is 169,654.

1861

U.S. Civil War erupts in April.

Telegraph wires cross the United States from New York City to San Francisco.

1862

Homestead Act makes free land available to settlers.

First train in Minnesota runs from St. Paul to St. Anthony.

Even as the Civil War was splitting the nation in two, another struggle was threatening the lives and futures of many Minnesotans. This one pitted Minnesota's oldest residents—the Dakota—against its newest residents—the white settlers.

By the early 1860s, the Dakota's traditional homelands were rapidly filling up with farms and small towns. The 1851 treaties of Traverse des Sioux and Mendota—and another treaty in 1858—had left the Dakota just a 10-mile-wide strip of land along the southern side of the Minnesota River and a promise of an annual payment, called an **annuity**. But even there, the Dakota could not feel secure. White settlers were taking over land where the Dakota still hunted game and gathered food. Other white people lived and worked among the Dakota, trying to convince them to give up their traditional ways. Food supplies were short, and many Dakota were starving. The annuities due from the government were late. Tensions were rising. All that was needed was a spark for disaster to strike. In the summer of 1862, the spark came. It ignited one of the bloodiest episodes in Minnesota's history.

LOOK FOR

- ◆ What were the tensions between the traditional and farm Dakota?
- ◆ How did the agent and traders at the Lower Sioux Agency treat the Dakota?
- ◆ Why did Taoyateduta (Little Crow) agree to lead the Dakota?
- ◆ What happened to the people at the Lower Sioux Agency during the Dakota War?
- ◆ What happened to the Dakota after the war?

KEY TERMS

annuity
agency
traditional Dakota
farm Dakota

annuity: annual payment of food and money that the government promised the Indians in return for their land

Aug. 1862	**Dec. 1862**	**1863**	**1865**	**1866**	**1869**	**1871**
Dakota War breaks out with attack on Lower Sioux Agency.	Thirty-eight Dakota are hanged for their role in the Dakota War.	Dakota are moved to the Crow Creek Reservation in South Dakota. Taoyateduta is killed by a white farmer while picking berries in a field near Hutchinson.	U.S. Civil War ends in April.	Dakota at Crow Creek are moved to Santee Reservation in Nebraska.	Transcontinental railroad completed.	Congress passes law forbidding any more treaties with Indian nations.

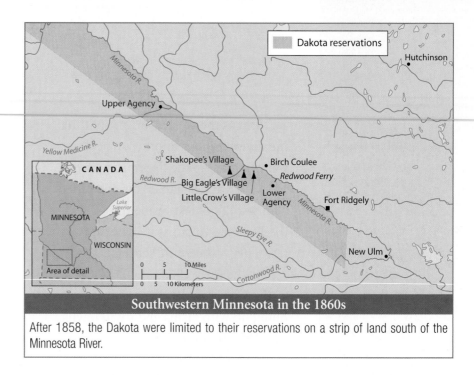

Southwestern Minnesota in the 1860s

After 1858, the Dakota were limited to their reservations on a strip of land south of the Minnesota River.

Setting the Stage at the Lower Sioux Agency

agency: a U.S. government field office

The Dakota's narrow strip of land along the Minnesota River was split into two reservations—each with its own government field office, or **agency**. The Upper Sioux Agency was close to the junction of the Minnesota and Yellow Medicine Rivers. The Lower Sioux Agency was near the junction of the Minnesota and Redwood Rivers. By 1862, both agencies had grown into small towns. The town at the Lower Sioux Agency was an especially busy place with homes, mills, warehouses, stores, a stable, a steamboat landing, and a schoolhouse.

The people who lived at the Lower Sioux Agency and on the reservation surrounding it represented cultures and viewpoints whose differences eventually led to a tragic confrontation.

IN THEIR OWN WORDS
THOMAS GALBRAITH

Thomas Galbraith, the Indian agent at the Lower Sioux Agency, expressed his views about the Dakota:

"The [beliefs] and habits of the Indian must be eradicated; habits of industry and economy must be introduced in the place of idleness ...; the peaceful pursuit of home life must be substituted for the war-path, the chase, and the dance; and more than all, the hostility of the Indian opposed to this policy must be met on the threshold."

GOVERNMENT PERSONNEL

In 1862, the top government official at the Upper and Lower Sioux Agencies was the Indian agent, Thomas Galbraith. He was the person responsible for carrying out the U.S. government policy regarding the reservations, which was designed to make the Dakota reject their culture and accept white culture. Among other things, the agent distributed the annuities of food and money that the U.S. government had promised the

Dakota under the treaties of 1851 and 1858. The agent also oversaw a host of government workers, including blacksmiths, carpenters, and a doctor. Many of these people lived and worked in a cluster of buildings surrounding the agency headquarters.

TRADERS

The government allowed a small group of traders—including the unpopular Andrew Myrick—to run stores where the Dakota could get additional food and supplies. The stores were located on the agency's west side. The traders usually worked on a credit system. They provided goods to the Dakota with the understanding that the Dakota would pay their debts when they received their annuities. The traders kept written records of every business deal they made. The Dakota did not. As a result, dishonest traders were able to cheat the Dakota by claiming debts that the Dakota did not actually owe.

IN THEIR OWN WORDS
ANDREW MYRICK

Andrew Myrick was a trader who kept two stores—one at the Upper and one at the Lower Sioux Agency. Several historical accounts suggest that Myrick enraged the Dakota when he dismissed their appeals for food in August 1862. According to one version of the story, Myrick said:

"So far as I am concerned, if they are hungry, let them eat grass."

MISSIONARIES

By 1862, two missionaries, Samuel Hinman and John Williamson, had each founded churches just east of the Lower Sioux Agency. Their main goal was to convince the Dakota to give up their own spiritual traditions and accept Christianity. The U.S. government's policies toward the Dakota supported this goal because government officials

IN THEIR OWN WORDS
STEPHEN RIGGS

Stephen Riggs was one of the missionaries who participated in the treaty negotiations of 1851. He and a small group of Dakota had founded a farming community on the Upper Reservation in 1856. The community disbanded in 1860 because of constant harassment from the traditional Dakota.

"It is true that the change of dress does not change their hearts, but in their estimation it does change their relations to the Dakota religion and customs. It is quite a step for an Indian to take. . . . It is related of the wife of one of these men at the Lower Sioux Agency, that, whenever she looked at the [short hair] of her husband, she cried."

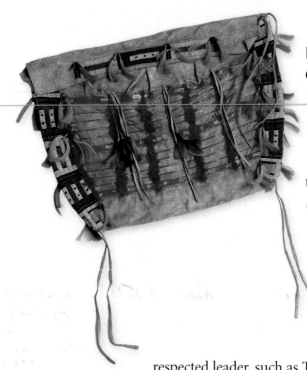

Traditional Dakota preferred a hunting lifestyle. Hunters used game bags to carry muskrats, duck, and other small game.

believed that Dakota who accepted white, Christian spiritual beliefs were more likely to accept other parts of white culture, as well. The missionaries lived among the Dakota, got to know many of them well, and often spoke up for the Dakota when they had disagreements with the traders and the agent.

TRADITIONAL DAKOTA

In the summer of 1862, many Dakota on the Lower Reservation lived in tipis and bark lodge villages along the south side of the Minnesota River. Each village was led by a respected leader, such as Taoyeduta (tah-OH-yah-tay-doo-tah), or Little Crow, Makato (mah-KAH-toh), or Blue Earth, and Wapaháśa (WAH-pah-hah-shah), or Red Banner. Families in these villages wanted to continue their traditional ways of life. They kept their sacred rituals and beliefs despite the missionaries' efforts to convert them to Christianity. These **traditional Dakota** often moved off the reservations to hunt game and gather food despite the government's attempts to turn them into full-time farmers.

traditional Dakota: Dakota who wanted to maintain their culture and resist efforts to make them live like whites

FARM DAKOTA

By 1862, several hundred Dakota on the Lower Reservation were living on farms. They grew crops, raised livestock, and lived in wood or brick houses along the main road that cut through the reservation. Most of them—including the Dakota leader Taopi (tah-OH-pee), or Wounded Man—abandoned traditional Dakota customs and adapted to the white people's way of life. These **farm Dakota** were expected to wear white people's clothing and attend the missionaries' churches. The men were pressured to cut their hair short like the white men on the reservation.

farm Dakota: Dakota who adopted some white ways, including farming like white farmers

Tensions Rise

A main source of tension on the reservation was the combined effort of the government and the missionaries to remake Dakota culture. "The whites were always trying to make the Indians give up their life and live like white men," recalled the traditional Dakota leader Waŋmbditaŋka (wahn-buh-DEE-tahn-kah), or Big Eagle. "The Indians wanted to live as they did before. . . . If the Indians had tried to make the whites live like them, the whites would have resisted, and it was the same way with many Indians."

As more and more Dakota accepted the whites' ways, tensions rose among the Dakota themselves. Traditional Dakota looked down on farm Dakota for abandoning their heritage. Many of the traditional Dakota were also angry because the government gave extra food, as well as tools and livestock, to the farm Dakota. For their part, the farm Dakota believed that they were doing what was best for their futures. They resented the way the traditional Dakota treated them.

A group of Dakota in the summer of 1862. **What evidence of Dakota culture do you see? What evidence of the Dakota adopting some white ways?**

Another source of tension was the relationship between the Dakota and the government. Under the treaties of 1851 and 1858, government personnel were supposed to make regular distributions of money, food, and supplies to the Dakota. In a short time the Dakota became dependent on the distributions. But often those annuities were late and smaller than the Dakota expected.

The Dakota's relationship with the traders was equally strained. The credit system—with its many opportunities for trader cheating— had always been a big part of the problem. But in the summer of 1862, traders shut down the entire credit system. They refused to extend any more credit because annuity payments were late. They were worried that, without the annuities, the Dakota would be unable to pay off their debts. When a group of Dakota leaders from the Lower Reservation asked the traders to reopen their stores, the traders refused. "From that time the Indians and the traders were unfriendly," recalled a Dakota woman named Wicaŋhpiwaśtewiŋ (wee-CHAHNK-pee-wahsh-tay-wee), or Good Star Woman.

By the middle of August 1862, the Dakota on the Lower Reservation —especially the traditional Dakota—were hungry, frustrated, and angry. The annuity payments were late—again—and Agent Galbraith refused to give them their food from the agency storehouse until the money arrived. The government personnel and the traders did not seem to care. The missionaries were either unable or unwilling to get involved. When a crisis erupted, many Dakota decided to take what they thought would be their last chance to get back their land.

Taoyateduta was a tough negotiator and a brave soldier. His sharp memory, intelligence, and confidence made him a natural leader.

Conflict

On August 17, 1862, the tensions turned to bloodshed. Though the details of the confrontation are still debated, the basic facts are these: four young Dakota men killed five white settlers near the town of Acton in an argument over eggs. That night, traditional Dakota on the Lower Reservation discussed the situation among themselves. Some believed that the young men who killed the settlers should be handed over to the government for punishment. But many others believed that surrendering the young men would do no good—that the white people would use the killings as an excuse to punish all the Dakota. They said that the Dakota should strike out at their enemies before their enemies struck out at them. The time was right, they said. The U.S. military would not fight back, they thought, because its attention was focused elsewhere, on the Civil War.

Finally, the traditional Dakota turned to one of their leaders—Taoyateduta. At first, Taoyateduta spoke for peace even as many of the young men argued for war. "If you strike at the white people," he said, "they will turn on you and devour you and your women and little children just as the locusts in their time fall on the trees and devour all the leaves in one day." Despite his misgivings, Taoyateduta agreed that night to lead his people into war. "Taoyateduta is not a coward," he told them. "He will die with you."

On the following morning, August 18, 1862, Dakota soldiers attacked the Lower Sioux Agency. They struck first at the traders' houses, killing —among others—the trader Andrew Myrick, and stuffed grass into his mouth. Then they moved east to the agency headquarters. At the ferry crossing on the Minnesota River, they ambushed a group of U.S. soldiers. Soon they were fanning out beyond the reservation, overrunning small farms, and killing settlers before they could escape.

All across both reservations, the farm Dakota were beginning to fear for their lives. Taopi, a farmer who lived near the Lower Sioux Agency, began preparing

IN THEIR OWN WORDS
WAᗺMBDITAᗺKA

Waŋmbditaŋka was the leader of one of the traditional Dakota villages on the Lower Reservation. He was a reluctant participant in the fighting. Years later he told his story (through an interpreter) to a newspaper reporter.

"I was still of the belief that it was not best [to go to war], but I thought I must go with my band and my nation, and I said to my men that I would lead them into the war, and we would all act like brave Dakotas and do the best we could."

Wicaŋhpiwaštewiŋ was eight years old when the war broke out. She told her story more than 70 years later to Frances Densmore, who studied the Dakota and other Indian groups.

"An Indian came riding into the camp, so frightened that he could not tell them what was the trouble.... At last he said, 'The Dakota are killing the whites.' This was taking place four or five miles away but they could hear the guns. The children wakened and began to cry."

for trouble as soon as he heard the gunshots. "I went up to the top of my house, and from there I could hear the shouts of the Indians, and see them plundering the stores," he recalled. "The men of my band now began to assemble at my house. We counseled, but could do nothing to resist the hostile Indians because we were so few and they were between us and the settlements." Later, some of them helped arrange the release of many white prisoners who were being held by traditional Dakota.

Taopi and many of the other farm Dakota tried their best to stay away from the fighting.

Meanwhile, on the prairie beyond the reservation, hundreds of white settlers were fleeing their homes and warning each other of the danger. The refugees included a young German immigrant, Mary Schwandt (SHVAHNT). Mary was working in the home of another family when

These refugees fled the fighting at the Upper Sioux Agency on August 19. This image, taken on August 21, is the only known photo taken during the Dakota War.

Mary Schwandt was 14 years old when the war began. Her parents, her sister, and two of her brothers were killed in the fighting. Her recollections of the war were published in 1894.

"While in Little Crow's village I saw some of my father's cattle and many of our household goods in the hands of the Indians. I now knew that my family had been plundered, and I believed murdered. I was very, very wretched, and cared not how soon I too was killed."

news of the Dakota attacks arrived. She fled in a wagon with two other girls, Mattie Williams and Mary Anderson, and two men—one named Mr. Patoile (pah-TWAHL) and one named Mr. Davis. About eight miles from the town of New Ulm, they encountered a large group of Dakota. "Two of them dashed forward to us, one on each side of the wagon, and ordered us to halt," Mary recalled. "Mr. Patoile turned the wagon to one side of the road, and all of us jumped out except him. As we leaped out Mr. Davis cried, 'We are lost!'" Mary watched as the Dakota killed Patoile and Davis. She and the other two girls were captured and taken to the village of Taoyeduta.

In the days that followed, the Dakota launched a series of attacks on New Ulm and on the nearby Fort Ridgely. But the people of New Ulm beat back the Dakota each time the Dakota attacked. Nine days after the fighting began, Colonel Henry Sibley, the former Minnesota governor, led 1,600 well-armed soldiers into the prairie to battle the Dakota. Soon it became clear to many Dakota that they could not win. By the end of September, the Dakota War was over. The Dakota were defeated. More than 500 whites and at least 21 Dakota were killed.

The battle at Fort Ridgely was considered a key event in the Dakota War. After three days of fighting, the Dakota retreated and did not advance any farther east. The burning buildings are the stable and a store.

Henry Sibley held the trials of the accused Dakota in this trader's cabin at the Lower Sioux Agency. Soldiers guarded these prisoners as they awaited their trial.

The Aftermath

That fall, in the kitchen of one of the Lower Sioux Agency's trading houses, Colonel Sibley set up what he called a "court" to judge the hundreds of Dakota that his men had taken prisoner. But it was a court in name only. The judges were a panel of army officers who just days before had fought in the Dakota War. The panel rushed through dozens of cases each day. The Dakota defendants often appeared before the panel chained together in groups. They had no lawyers to represent them. The missionary Stephen Riggs, who had worked for years among the Dakota, was troubled by what he considered a rush to judgment. "I dislike the way the trials were conducted," he wrote. "If the Indians have done wickedness they should have something like a fair trial, even for our own sake."

Unlike Riggs, most white Minnesotans were outraged by the Dakota War and supported Sibley's court. The Dakota soldiers had killed hundreds of people. The white survivors had been forced to witness the deaths of their friends and families. White Minnesotans demanded revenge. Newspapers such as the Faribault *Central Republican* expressed this yearning for vengeance in stark terms: "Extermination, swift, sure, and terrible is the only thing that can give the people of Minnesota satisfaction, or a sense of security."

Sibley's court took 39 days to sentence 303 Dakota men to death. But under the law, none of those men could be executed without the approval of President Abraham Lincoln. At the urging of Minnesota missionary Henry Whipple, Lincoln reviewed the cases. The more he learned, the more troubled he felt. In November, he met with Whipple, who described the conditions on the reservation and asked the president to show mercy. In the end, Lincoln approved the execution of 39 Dakota who had been convicted of crimes against civilians. He ordered that the remaining prisoners be sent to a military prison camp in Iowa.

Bishop Henry Whipple was called "Straight Tongue" by the Dakota because of his directness and honesty.

IN THEIR OWN WORDS
ḢDAIŊYAŊKA

Ḣdaiŋyaŋka(huh-dah-EE-yahnk-kah), or Ran with the Sound of a Rattle, was the son-in-law of Wapaháśa, a respected Dakota leader. Sentenced to death, he wrote of his frustration at being wrongly accused.

> "I have not killed, wounded, or injured a white man, or any white persons. I have not participated in the plunder of their property; and yet to-day I am set apart for execution, and must die in a few days.... My wife and my children are dear to me. Let them not grieve for me. Let them remember that the brave should be prepared to meet death; and I will do as becomes a Dakota."

On the morning of December 26, 1862, the 39 Dakota singled out by Lincoln, minus one who was spared at the last minute, were hanged in front of a large crowd in Mankato's public square. It was the largest mass execution in U.S. history, before or since.

The government ordered the rest of the Dakota—including those who did not participate in the attacks—to an outdoor prison camp at Fort Snelling. About 1,600 men, women, and children spent a miserable winter there. More than 130 people died from extreme crowding, cold weather, and disease.

In the spring of 1863, the surviving Dakota prisoners at Fort Snelling were banished from Minnesota. Steamboats and barges carried them down the Mississippi River and then up the Missouri River to a reservation at Crow Creek in what is now South Dakota. It was a desolate place and food was scarce. The government sent food, but it was never enough and almost always came late. Hundreds of Dakota died from hunger and disease. The missionary John P. Williamson, who had worked with the Dakota in Minnesota, went to visit. He was appalled by the conditions there. He called Crow Creek "a desert"—a place that was "totally unfit for the habitation of any human being." In 1866 the government finally let the banished Dakota move to a new reservation in Nebraska. The land was better there than it had been in South Dakota, but it was nothing like home. It was not Minnesota.

About 1,600 Dakota spent the winter of 1862–1863 at this prison camp below Fort Snelling.

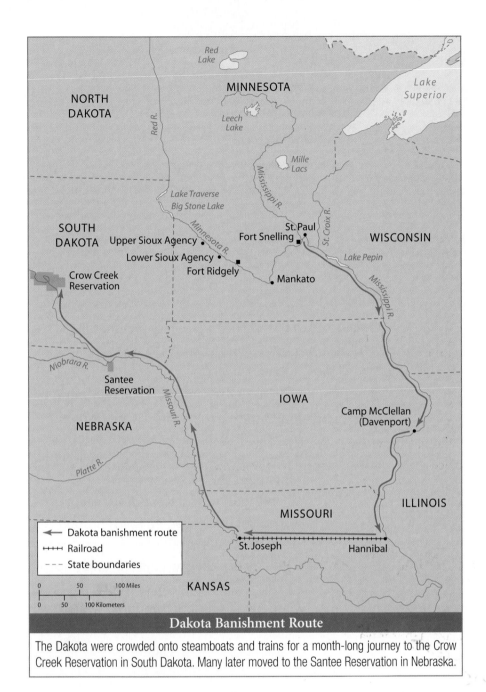

Dakota Banishment Route

The Dakota were crowded onto steamboats and trains for a month-long journey to the Crow Creek Reservation in South Dakota. Many later moved to the Santee Reservation in Nebraska.

By the summer of 1863, southwestern Minnesota was almost empty of people. Nearly all the white settlers in the region had abandoned their homes during the war. Most of the Dakota had either been banished from the state or had fled to the west. Only about 200 Dakota who had helped the whites during the war were allowed to stay.

But as the years went by, people came back. Many of the Dakota who had been forced to leave their homeland returned and established new communities—at the old Upper and Lower Sioux Agencies, at Wabasha, at Prairie Island, at Grey Cloud Island, and at Prior Lake. But the land the Dakota came back to had already changed beyond recognition. Thousands of new settlers had moved to Minnesota, and they were fencing in the landscape as quickly as they could.

Untold Stories of the Dakota War

The handwritten letter reads:

> Santee Agency Neb
> Sept 28 th 1900
>
> my Dear adopted daughter
> I Received your letter ... was glad to here from
> you; I want to tell you
> what I think about
> comeing to mendota
> I think it is to cold
> to come now. I will
> weat till spring that is
> if I live that long.
> after I write to you
> I was sick fore two
> weeks I was geting
> better now I will be ...
> ... was writing to you
> your mother
> Maggie Brass

You have heard the expression "Every picture tells a story." You may not realize, though, that every picture can tell more than one story.

Study the picture of the two women on the right. Why are these two women, who don't seem to be related, together? What clues does the letter on the left give you about their relationship?

Although this letter doesn't mention it, both of these women lived through the Dakota War. Both of them saw fighting and experienced the fear and uncertainty of that time. Fate brought them together—as much younger women—and they both lived to tell their own stories many years later.

Their experiences during the Dakota War, along with the stories of two other eyewitnesses, appear on the following pages. None of these eyewitnesses fought in battles, and none of these accounts was reported in the newspapers of 1862. In fact, most of these "untold" stories were first recorded many years later.

The two women in the photo exchanged this letter in 1900.

As you read the following four stories, imagine that you are a newspaper reporter who can go back in time. Which story would you most want to report to the people of Minnesota in 1862?

Use your Investigation Guide to set up your news story.

Snana's Story

Snana (SNAH-nah), or Ringing Sound, or Maggie Brass, was a 23-year-old Mdewakanton Dakota, and the mother of two when the Dakota War began. She favored peace over war, and when captured settlers were brought to her village, Snana decided to protect an immigrant girl named Mary Schwandt. She later explained that she adopted the girl as a way of grieving for her own daughter who had died several weeks before. Here, she describes how she protected Mary…

During the outbreak, when some of the Indians got killed, they began to kill some of the captives. At such times I always hid my dear captive white girl.… I thought to myself that if they would kill my girl they must kill me first. Though I had two of my own children at that time with me, I thought of this girl just as much as of the others.…Once, [when Mary was in danger] I dug a hole inside my tent and put some poles across, and then spread my blankets over and sat on top of them, as if nothing unusual had happened. But who do you suppose were inside the hole? My dear captive girl, Mary Schwandt, and my own two little children.

SNANA IN ABOUT 1860

Snana kept Mary hidden in a tipi like this one.

Mary's Story

Mary Schwandt was 14 years old during the Dakota War. She and her brother August were the only surviving members of her family of seven. She was captured on August 18 and spent nearly six weeks as a captive. In this part of her account, she had already been a captive for several weeks and had just met Snana. Mary explains…

MARY SCHWANDT AS A YOUNG WOMAN

An old Indian woman called Wamnuȟawiŋ [wahm-NOO-hah-wee]… took compassion on me and bought me of the Indian who claimed me, giving a pony for me. She gave me to her daughter, whose Indian name was Snana, but the whites called her Maggie…. Maggie and her mother were both very kind to me, and Maggie could not have treated me more tenderly if I had been her daughter. Often and often she preserved me from danger, and sometimes, I think, she saved my life. Many a time… she and her mother hid me, piling blankets and buffalo robes upon me until I would be nearly smothered, and then they would tell everybody that I had left them…. But Maggie never relaxed her watchful care over me, and forbade my going about the camp alone or hardly anywhere out of her sight. She gave me a clean white blanket… and embroidered for me a most beautiful pair of white moccasins, and I put them on in place of the clothing I wore when I was captured.

DAKOTA MOCCASINS

A watercolor from 1846 shows farm land on the Minnesota prairie.

Alomina's Story

By 1862, Alomina Hamm Hurd and her husband had farmed for three years on land 60 miles from New Ulm. They knew many of the Dakota who came to the area, and Alomina had learned to speak a little of the Dakota language. Her husband was gone on the afternoon of August 20, when 20 Dakota came to her homestead. While her hired man was killed and her home destroyed, Alomina, her infant son, and her three-year-old son William were spared. In her search for safety, she wandered across open prairie for six days and almost 70 miles before she joined other settlers. She later described the difficulty of her journey…

ALOMINA
HAMM HURD

I could not bear to lie down with my little ones on the unknown, trackless waste, over which we had been wandering. But this weakness was for a moment only. I took courage and started on the road to New Ulm. When it became quite dark, I halted for the night. That night I passed as before, without sleep. In the early morning I started on. It was foggy and the grass was wet. William was so sick that he could not walk much of the time, so I was obliged to carry both little boys. I was now sensibly reduced in strength and felt great hunger. My boy no longer asked for food, but was thirsty and drank frequently from pools by the wayside. No longer able to carry both of my boys at the same time, I took one a distance of a quarter or half a mile, laid him on the grass, and returned for the other. In this way I traveled twelve miles to a place called Dutch Charley's, sixteen miles from Lake Shetek, arriving about sunset, sustained on my weary journey by the sweet hope of relief.

Lorenzo's Story

In August of 1862, Lorenzo Lawrence, or Tonwaŋiteton (too-WAH-ee-tay-too), was a Dakota farmer living with his family near Lac qui Parle in southern Minnesota. One year earlier, he had become the first Dakota to receive Minnesota state citizenship. He did not participate in any battles during the Dakota War, but in a daring and difficult rescue, traveling mostly by boat at night, he took ten settlers and his own family to Fort Ridgely for safety. This part of his account begins early on the fourth day of the trip…

We waited expectantly till daylight. Then we looked around and saw a house some distance off. So I went to see who was there. When I got close I saw that the door stood open. Then I saw where some one had been at work hewing a log with a broadax, and he had been shot while he was at work.…

Seeing these dead bodies moved my heart very much. I looked around and found a spade at the stable, and I took the bodies and buried them as well as I could. Then I went to the door of the house and I wrote on a piece of paper:
"I am Lorenzo Lawrence. I am fleeing from the Indians with some White women and children, and my own wife and children. We are going down in boats, and when we come here we found the dead bodies of a man and boy, and I buried them near the house under the mound of dirt. I have ten captive women and children that I am fleeing with, and I write this so any one who comes can tell who was here."

Then I tacked the paper on the door. Afterward I went in the house and took a kettle and dish and knife, and went back to where the women and children were. And we made a fire and stewed some of the meat we had, and the women and children were very glad to get some cooked meat soup. And the women asked me, "What did you see at the house where you went?" But I did not want to tell them I had found the dead bodies and buried them, because I thought it would frighten them, so I did not tell them that.…

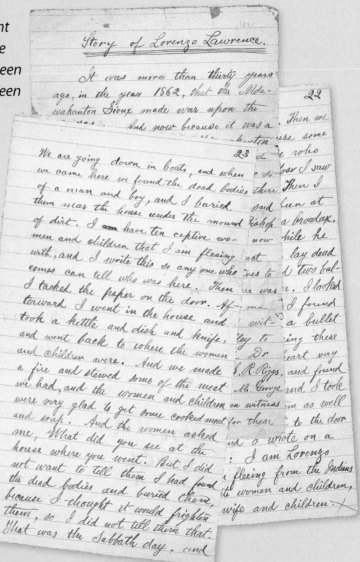

Although no known pictures of Lorenzo Lawrence exist, we do have his original handwritten account, shown here.

At harvest time, Minnesota farmers collected crops to help feed the growing state and nation.

1857

Kerosene lamps are developed and soon replace oil lamps.

1858

Minnesota becomes a state.

1862

Dakota War is fought in Minnesota.

Homestead Act is passed.

1865

Civil War ends.

1867

Oliver Kelley helps organize the Grange.

Minnesota Board of Immigration is established to encourage immigration to the state.

1869

Louisa May Alcott writes *Little Women*.

1870

Construction begins on the Northern Pacific railroad that will reach from Minnesota to the Pacific Ocean.

Minnesota's population reaches 439,706.

innesota was emerging from turbulent times. The Dakota had tried and failed to win back their lands. The Civil War had ended. The state was heading into what most people assumed would be a time of peace and prosperity, a prosperity based largely on agriculture. Southern Minnesota appeared to be superb farming country. The land was relatively flat. Its rich soil would nourish many kinds of crops. It had just about everything going for it—except that it hadn't been "broken" yet.

The unbroken prairie land of Minnesota was covered with tall grasses that had a heavy tangle of roots called sod. For thousands of years the sod had fed plants that gave food and shelter to insects, birds, and animals. Those, in turn, had made life possible for people. The thick sod also protected the soil beneath it and stored water during dry seasons. It was the soil underneath that held such promise for farming.

By the late 1860s, settlers were pouring into Minnesota, hoping to make a living off this rich land. They were a great mix of people—Yankees from the New England states and New York as well as Canadians,

LOOK FOR

◆ What challenges did the Tainter family face in their first year on the prairie?

◆ How did the U.S. government encourage people to settle in farming areas?

◆ How was the arrival of the railroads both good and bad?

◆ How did the railroads change western Minnesota?

◆ Who were the Grangers, and what did they do?

KEY TERMS

Homestead Act
subsistence farmers
diversified farming
cooperative
land speculator

1871	1874	1876	1877	1878	1879	1880
Lincoln County is opened for settlement.	Joseph Glidden of Illinois invents barbed wire.	Alexander Graham Bell invents the telephone. Mark Twain writes *The Adventures of Tom Sawyer*.	Governor John Pillsbury declares an official day of prayer for relief from the grasshopper invasions. Thomas Edison invents the phonograph.	Tainter family arrives in Lincoln County.	Railroad reaches Lake Benton in Lincoln County. Thomas Edison invents the electric lightbulb.	Minnesota has more than 3,000 miles of railroad track.

Swedes, Norwegians, Germans, Irish, and English. They knew that farming in Minnesota would be hard work. Before they could plant any crops, they would have to cut through the sod to get to the rich soil underneath. But they were confident that it would be worth the effort.

Starting Small in Lincoln County

LINCOLN COUNTY

In September 1878, a covered wagon led by a man and pulled by a team of oxen, came to a stop on a wide expanse of prairie. The man, John Tainter, could tell this was the right place. He and his wife, Sarah, had staked a claim on 80 acres of this land the previous spring. John looked to his wife and smiled. "Well, we've got home," he said. Sarah gazed over the landscape. All she saw was tall grass, rippling in the breeze. There were no houses to be seen, no trees. This was her new home? She burst into tears. After some reassuring words from her husband, Sarah found the courage to face the work in front of her. She wiped her eyes, climbed down from the wagon, and set foot for the first time on Lincoln County soil.

The Tainters had come to this place, with their three children, to start a new life. Their first job was to put a roof over their heads. The next morning, John set off for Canby, the nearest town, 18 miles away. He came back with some lumber and got to work. A few days later, the Tainters moved into a small shanty that would be their home for years to come.

Most farmers built houses out of milled lumber, just as the Tainters did. But if they couldn't afford to buy lumber they had to use materials that were easy to find. If there were woods nearby, they could cut logs for a cabin. On the treeless prairies of southern and western Minnesota, settlers often built their first house from blocks of sod.

The Tainters were not the first settlers to move to Lincoln County, nor were they the last. The government had surveyed the county and opened it up for settlement in 1871. People had been

The Tainters' first house, built in 1878, was constructed for utility, not beauty. The black tar paper minimized drafts, and the boards sloping to the barrel collected rainwater.

staking claims under the federal government's **Homestead Act** ever since. By 1878, when the Tainters arrived, several hundred families were living there, getting by as best they could.

The Tainters and other early settlers in Lincoln County were **subsistence farmers** at first, producing just enough food to feed themselves and trade with neighbors. Typically, during their first year, Lincoln County farmers broke a few acres and planted crops such as potatoes, turnips, and corn. Sometimes they planted wheat, but usually it was just enough to make flour for their own use. The nearest gristmill was 35 miles away. Even if they did produce extra grain, they had no easy, reliable way to bring it to market.

Years later, the Tainters and other early settlers told stories about the challenges they faced on the prairie during those early years. They recalled their struggles to keep their families decently fed, and the four summers in a row during the 1870s when enormous swarms of grasshoppers "obscured the sun" and destroyed crops. They remembered the incredibly long and harsh winter of 1880–1881, when settlers tied a clothesline to their house and themselves before venturing outside so they could find their way back home in the deep snow.

But they also told stories about good times: about the fun the children had during the winters, sliding down snow-covered rooftops, and about simple holiday celebrations when family members gave each other pincushions and dolls made in secret from scraps of cloth.

Leaky, dirty, and full of bugs, sod houses were a temporary solution for shelter. Most settlers built wooden houses as soon as they could.

Homestead Act: 1862 law that provided up to 160 acres of land to settlers who would live on it and farm it for five years

subsistence farmers: families who produced enough food to feed themselves, but not enough to sell at market

To fight the grasshopper plagues, farmers tried everything they could: squashing the pests, capturing them with nets like the ones shown here, trapping them in tar, burning the fields, and praying.

Every farm family had plenty of work to do. If someone needed help, the other family members would pitch in. But even though they shared the work, men, women, and children had different jobs on the farm.

For a man, farming meant heavy work in the fields. When a farmer was not busy plowing, planting, or harvesting, he had to repair buildings and care for the animals. With few neighbors, a farmer had to rely on his own skills as a logger, veterinarian, lawyer, well digger, and accountant.

A farm woman's jobs ended only when her strength ran out. She tended to the children and cooked three meals a day over a wood-burning stove. She rubbed her hands raw doing the laundry over a rough metal washboard. Dirt was everywhere. She made soap, sewed and mended clothes, and preserved fruits and vegetables for winter. She also cared for the chickens and cows and made butter and cheese from the cows' milk. The vegetable garden was usually her job, too.

As soon as children were big enough, they carried firewood and brought water from the well. Weeding the garden, gathering eggs, and bringing in the cows for milking were other chores for boys and girls. When they were older they helped in the fields or cared for younger brothers and sisters.

Changes on the Farm

The experiences of the Tainters were very similar to those of other early settlers in Minnesota. The first years were always the hardest. It wasn't enough to have a piece of land. Farm families also needed a house, a barn, fences, tools, animals, seed, and many more things. All of these cost money. Even with inexpensive land, farmers often had to borrow money to get started. They needed plows, axes, spades, pitchforks, scythes, pots and pans, stoves, needles, thread, and all sorts of other tools and household goods. Without these things, farm families could not start work. Most farmers also owned a team of oxen. Oxen were slower than horses, but they could pull heavy loads and plows. Many families also had a cow or two and a few chickens or pigs.

Many of Minnesota's early settlers were subsistence farmers first, but, like the Tainters, they did not want to continue to grow crops for their families alone. As soon as they were established, they worked hard to better themselves by growing crops to sell. They needed a cash crop with a reliable market.

During the 1860s and 1870s, this often meant planting wheat. Wheat was a relatively easy crop to cultivate, and prices were good because demand for wheat flour was growing. For a while, many Minnesota farmers depended almost entirely on wheat. But that turned out to be a mistake. One-crop farming

Cutting through the dense sod was grueling, backbreaking work. Oxen were needed to pull the plow through the thick tangle of grass and roots.

demanded too much of the soil and depleted its nutrients. Also, farmers who depended on just one crop had a more difficult time earning money when prices fell. This happened when harvests were so good that farmers produced more of their crop than they could sell.

Farm families realized that they would be better off if they could produce a variety of crops and livestock. This was called **diversified farming**. But how would they learn to do this?

They could learn by sharing information with each other.

In 1867, seven settlers, including Oliver H. Kelley of Elk River, Minnesota, founded the first nationwide farmers' association. It was called the Grange, or the Patrons of Husbandry. The Grange was an organization in which farming men and women could share their concerns, learn about new ways to succeed on the farm, and enjoy each other's company. Grangers gathered for socials and lectures on farming topics. They also joined together to form **cooperatives** to sell their produce and buy the things they needed on the farm. Unlike most organizations of the time, the Grange also welcomed women as equal members. By 1869, Minnesota had 40 local Granges, more than any other state. Five years later, it had 538.

At first, the Grangers stayed away from politics. They thought it might threaten the unity of their organization. But it didn't take long for the Grangers to become politically active. Many of them banded together against what they believed was their common enemy—the railroad. This was quite a switch. During the early days of settlement, most people in rural Minnesota had looked forward to the railroad's arrival.

Oliver Kelley

diversified farming: the practice of producing a variety of crops and livestock

cooperative: an organization formed to buy or sell products as a large group in order to get better prices

Grange buttons identified the wearer's role in the organization.

Grange meetings like this one in Northfield in 1875 offered a welcome break from the toil and routine of working on the farm.

Thinking Big in Lincoln County

Railroad companies issued tickets for trips, but they also gave out passes like these, which could be used over and over during a one-year period.

It was September 16, 1879, and the people who had assembled at the village of Lake Benton in southern Lincoln County were talking excitedly among themselves. Many of them craned their necks to see what was happening less than a quarter mile to the east. The railroad was coming! About 200 men—tracklayers, bridge builders, surfacers, tie-men, and pile-driver operators—were working quickly. They had gotten past the curved section of the road and were now working on the straightaway toward the village.

By noon, the track reached Lake Benton and the first train arrived. The crowd cheered. The people of Lincoln County had been waiting years for this day. Now, boasted the editor of the Lake Benton *Times*, everything was going to change:

A few weeks will make a marked change in the appearance of our village. Business men have all been awaiting the completion of the road so they might obtain lumber at cheaper rates, and get their goods transported at a less cost. As material can soon be obtained, building will doubtless commence at once, and Lake Benton will contain at least seventy-five buildings before the snow flies.

The railroad connected Lincoln County to much of the rest of Minnesota, and to much of the rest of the United States. Everything seemed closer now. Before the train, a trip to Marshall—the nearest big town, 16 miles away—had taken a full day. Now it took just a couple hours. People could even travel to the Twin Cities of Minneapolis and St. Paul in less than a day. Mail traveled between post offices faster than ever before. Until this time, county residents were mainly limited to trading with their neighbors. Now, with the arrival of the train, they could buy from and sell goods to people far from home. The people of Lake Benton had become part of a larger market.

This was especially good news for farmers like the Tainters. Now, instead of producing just enough to feed themselves and trade with neighbors, they had a good reason to produce more. The more they

Building a railroad took a large work crew to complete many different steps. **How many construction jobs do you see being done on this railroad?**

146

Settlers who needed land to farm had several ways of getting it. The Homestead Act of 1862 provided one way. A homestead was a section of public land—up to 160 acres. If settlers claimed a section, lived on it for five years, built a house, and cultivated the soil, the government let them have the property for a registration fee of $14. But settlers also used several other methods to get the land they wanted. Some bought it directly from the railroads. Some settled on public land without permission and then bought it from the government at bargain prices. Still others took advantage of government programs that granted free land to soldiers.

But not everyone who obtained land in these ways actually intended to live on it or farm it. Many people wanted the land only so they could sell it to somebody else at a profit. These people were called **land speculators,** and they often made a great deal of money by guessing which land settlers would want to buy. Consider the case of Louis Fertile, a speculator in Lincoln County. Records show that Fertile once paid the government $8 for 160 acres. Ten days later, he sold those same 160 acres for $1,200. Not all speculators were as lucky as Louis Fertile, though. Many lost their life's savings by guessing wrong about the land's value.

grew, the more they could sell on the open market. The more they sold, they believed, the better off they would be. So John and Sarah decided to buy more land for growing crops.

The Tainters had claimed 80 acres under the Homestead Act. They knew the government would give them the land for $14 if they stayed there for five years and "improved" it by plowing, planting, and building a house. But now they wanted to add another 40 acres that belonged, not to the government, but to the Winona and St. Peter Railroad. The railroad had been given the land by the federal government and was eager to sell. That was how it raised the cash it needed to build the line. In 1883, after several years of scrimping, John and Sarah bought an additional 40 acres for $160. The crops they grew on that new land would eventually earn enough money to pay for a larger farmhouse elsewhere on their homestead. The Tainters were grateful to the railroad for selling them the land at what they felt was a good price. But would they remain grateful?

land speculator: someone who buys and sells land, hoping to make a profit, often at great financial risk

The Railroad: Friend or Foe?

Lincoln County was not the only place in Minnesota that changed once the trains came. Railroads transformed the entire state, especially the western part. In 1860 Minnesota had no railroads. Twenty years later, more than 3,000 miles of track crisscrossed the state.

The arrival of a train in a small town was an important event, bringing new settlers, visitors, mail, news, and goods faster and more often than in the days before the railroads.

CANADA

Lake Superior

MINNESOTA

NORTH DAKOTA

SOUTH DAKOTA

MICHIGAN

WISCONSIN

IOWA

0   25   50 Miles
0   25   50 Kilometers

Railroads in Minnesota, 1870 to 1880

In the years following the Civil War, railroad companies built thousands of miles of track in Minnesota. Tracks soon stretched across southern Minnesota and into the northern parts of the state.

During that same period, the state's population grew from 172,000 to 780,000. This was not a coincidence. The railroads played an active role in attracting immigrants and encouraging settlement.

If not for the railroads, it might have been hard to convince people to settle in places like Lincoln County. The land of western Minnesota was good for farming, but it wasn't very easy to reach. There were few rivers that could handle boat traffic and even fewer roads. Western Minnesota needed railroads to attract settlers. The question was how to attract the railroads.

The federal government's answer was to give the railroad companies millions of acres of land in western Minnesota for free. The companies then sold the land and used that money to pay for the construction of their lines. Railroad land was popular among settlers. The closer they were to the railroad lines, the easier it was to send their crops east and to visit friends and relatives in nearby towns. This system worked well

JAMES J. HILL

Of all the people who ran railroads in Minnesota, none was more successful or powerful than James J. Hill. Hill was a short, broad-shouldered man with a disability that he kept hidden from others—he was partially blind in one eye due to a boyhood bow-and-arrow accident. But more than anything else, Hill was a businessman with an immense drive to get things done. He was a fierce and, some said, unfair competitor. People called him the Empire Builder. The nickname fit.

Hill had entered the railroad business in 1878, when he and some business partners completed a rail line between the Twin Cities and Winnipeg, Manitoba. During the 1880s, he improved the existing railroad, built more tracks, and named his new company the Great Northern Railway. Hill continued to expand his holdings and eventually became one of the country's most powerful business leaders. He owned coal mines, iron mines, waterpower facilities, and Great Lakes steamships. He collected fine art. Additionally, he spent much time, effort, and money promoting and developing agriculture in Minnesota and other regions served by his rail lines. Hill knew that most farmers depended on railroads to send their produce to market. The more they produced, the more money he made.

for the railroads, too. Not only did they make money on the land sales, but they also made sure there would be new customers along the line.

At first, almost everybody seemed happy with this arrangement. But then, feelings began to change. The railroads started charging more for shipping and storing crops—pocketing up to one-third of the price that wheat farmers received for their grain. To make matters worse, some of the companies' inspectors often cheated the farmers by telling them that their grain wasn't worth as much as it really was. The farmers didn't like what was happening, but what could they do about it?

Once again, the Grange played an important role. Although the Grange had started out as a social and educational organization, the dispute over railroad freight rates helped change it into a political organization as well. Grange members began pressuring the state legislature to regulate railroads. In the 1870s the legislature passed a series of laws setting maximum fares and rates and creating the Office of Railroad Commissioner. These "Granger laws" signaled the beginning of railroad regulation in Minnesota.

The vast, sod-covered prairies of southwestern Minnesota were turning into fields of wheat, corn, oats, potatoes, and hay. Thousands of settlers were changing the land to fit their needs and their dreams. Towns and counties that hadn't even existed a few years earlier were bursting with new buildings and businesses. Trains cut through the landscape, carrying freight and passengers to and from the growing cities to the east. Life was getting faster—even in rural Minnesota. And this was just the beginning.

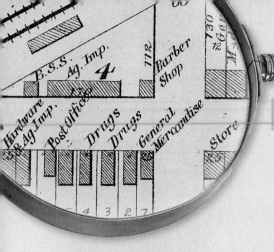

Small Town Life

Forest Mills

Hidden in the southeastern hills of Minnesota are the ruins of a town that flourished more than 100 years ago. Weeds grow among the heavy rock foundations. The Zumbro River has swept away most signs of the dam and mill. Some houses still stand in the fields, but few people remember the history of Forest Mills.

In the 1870s, the sounds of hammers and saws filled Forest Mills as settlers built their homes and their dreams. Like other settlers in Minnesota, the people of Forest Mills hoped their town would grow into a regional center for trade and business. But this was not to be. Forest Mills never managed to grow as fast as its rival, the nearby town of Zumbrota. In the 1880s, businesses began to move to Zumbrota, and by 1900, it was clear that Forest Mills was withering away.

Why did Forest Mills die and other towns survive? Success depended on both natural resources and human factors: Was the town in a good location? Would a rail line pass through? How well was the town planned and promoted? As you read about the factors that affected small town growth, you will create your own town and see how you would fare as a town developer.

STAKING A CLAIM

As is often said in real estate, the secret to success is "location, location, location." When land speculators came to western Minnesota, they looked for town sites that had access to natural resources: a navigable river, good soil for crops, a waterfall that could power a mill, or timber to build houses. There were other considerations, too. A good town site would be located near a crossroads or well-traveled road. It should be the right distance from other towns—not too close, or the new town citizens would go to buy goods in the old town, and not too far, or people might think the location was too remote. Finding such a site was tricky. Few places had everything.

Shotley, in Beltrami County, was one of the dozens of towns in Minnesota that became a ghost town. **Why might a town succeed or fail?**

150

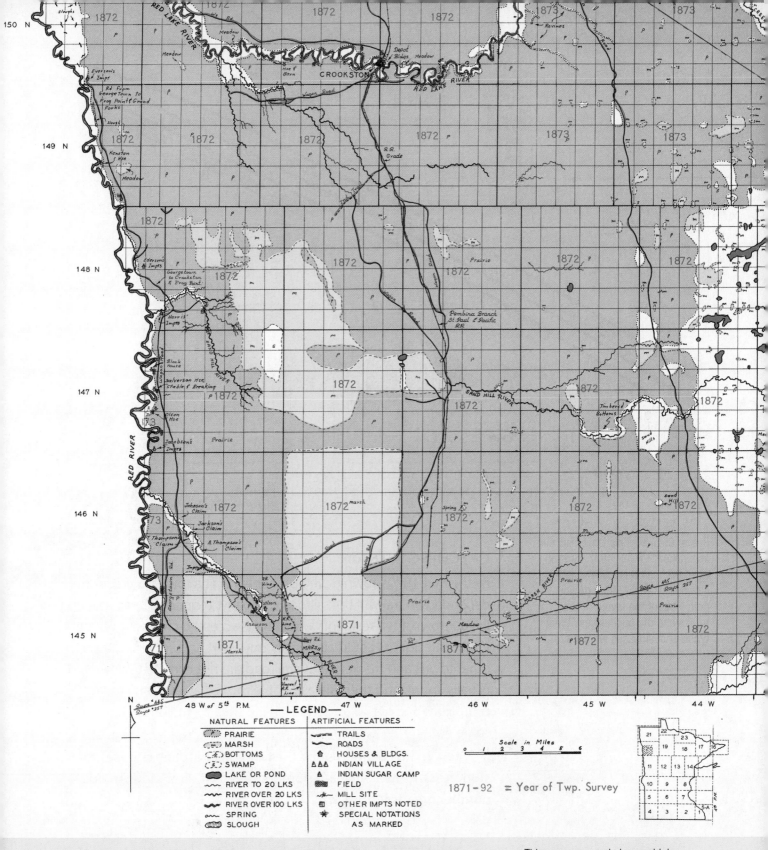

—LEGEND—

NATURAL FEATURES	ARTIFICIAL FEATURES
PRAIRIE	TRAILS
MARSH	ROADS
BOTTOMS	HOUSES & BLDGS.
SWAMP	INDIAN VILLAGE
LAKE OR POND	INDIAN SUGAR CAMP
RIVER TO 20 LKS	FIELD
RIVER OVER 20 LKS	MILL SITE
RIVER OVER 100 LKS	OTHER IMPTS NOTED
SPRING	SPECIAL NOTATIONS
SLOUGH	AS MARKED

Scale in Miles

0 1 2 3 4 5 6

1871–92 = Year of Twp. Survey

Step 1: This map shows an area on the east side of the Red River before it was densely settled. Where would you choose to build a town? On a large piece of paper, sketch an enlarged copy of your chosen site and show its natural resources. This is your "county map."

This map was made by combining several original survey maps from the 1870s. Identify natural features such as prairies, marshes, and rivers. **Which location will make the best town site?**

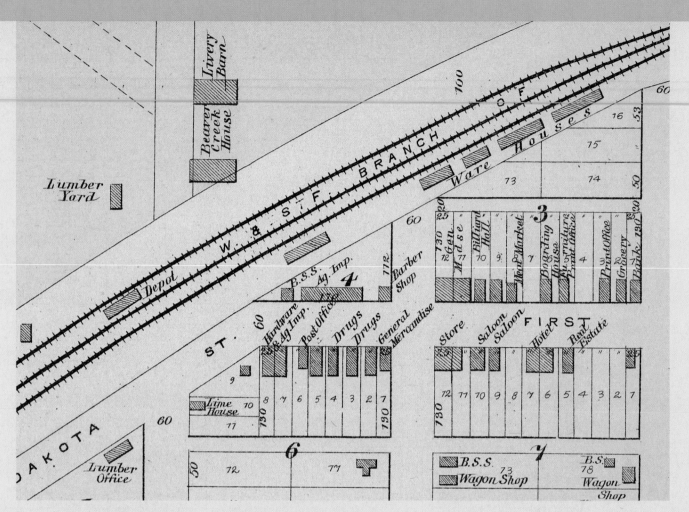

Beaver Creek was platted, or laid out, as a railroad town in 1877. By 1886, when this map was made, it had grown significantly. **What do you notice about the layout of the tracks and the businesses? What types of businesses were there?**

CATCHING A TRAIN

By the mid-1870s, town developers knew that a town's success often depended on trains. If the railroad company decided to build a station in your town, then residents would have access to cheaper goods and lumber. Residents could also easily transport and sell products to other towns and markets. If the railroad did not come, a town would usually shrink and then die as people moved away. Many towns campaigned to get railroads to come to their town, some successfully, some not.

○ **Step 2: Roll a die to see if the railroad company chooses to stop in your town. An even number means it does stop. An odd number means it does not.**

PLATTING OUT THE FUTURE

Railroad or no railroad, a town developer had to work hard to plat, or plan, all the details of a town. They laid out the streets and decided where the churches, mills, businesses, and homes would go. Sometimes speculators didn't plat parks or cemeteries, since that took up land that could be sold as business or home sites. If a train track was going to be built, the town developer would have to choose where to place the track.

Step 3: Name your town and create its town plat. For ideas, study how towns such as Beaver Creek, Wilno, and Hallock were laid out. Ask yourself these questions: What businesses should be located near each other? Pay attention to the scale of your drawing. How long is each block? Include these features:

A. Main streets and side streets

B. Business district

C. Residential district, where homes will be located

D. Roads to farms and river

E. School, church, town hall, park, cemetery

F. Train tracks and depot

WILNO

Scale 200 feet to one Inch.

Towns like Wilno were platted without a railroad and had to find other ways to attract settlers. **What types of immigrants do you think the speculators of Wilno were trying to attract?**

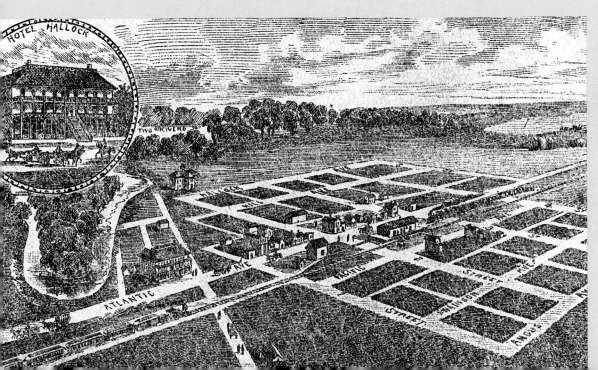

Study this image to see how the town of Hallock was platted. **Do you think the people of Hallock were more connected to the river or to the railroad? Why?**

After platting the town, the developer had to choose which types of people to recruit. Would the town need a doctor? What about a blacksmith? Or an innkeeper? What businesses help a town grow?

The gazetteer was a business directory that gave short descriptions of towns and listed some of the businesses located there. Gazetteers are good sources for learning about small town businesses and occupations.

○ **Step 4:** Look at the town listings on this gazetteer page. What kinds of businesses and jobs do you see? What other types of small town jobs were there? Make a list that shows the top 15 jobs that your town needs to fill.

NATHAN FORD CLOUGH & WARREN AND ESTEY ORGANS, 92 and 94 E. Third Street, ST. PAUL, MINNESOTA.

LAC AND BUSINESS DIRECTORY. LAK 363

Chalmars H J, artist.
Erickson Ama, milliner.
Farnham & Himle, publrs Lac Qui Parle Press.
Jacobson & Oadson, machinery agents.
Jerdu C O, lawyer.
Lac Qui Parle Press, Farnham & Himle publrs.
Paige C W, justice of peace.

LA CRESCENT. In Houston county, at the junction of C., St. P. & M. line of the C., M. & St. P. Ry, with the S. M. div. of the same road. It is 1 mile from the Mississippi river, where a strong water power runs a grist mill and a woolen factory. Catholic, Presbyterian and Methodist churches and a district school are here. Bank at La Crosse, Wis. Ships wheat, flour, stone and live stock. Exp., Am. Tel., W. U. Population, 350. Thomas Minshall, postmaster.

Anderson Wm R, carpenter.
Bock Edward, railroad and express agent.
Boynton Charles E, blacksmith.
Boynton George W, blacksmith.
Brant P, live stock.
Brown James M, gardener.
Caple Rev George (Methodist).
Donald George, constable.
Donald Thomas, meats.
Ferguson Peter, general store.
Groff Bros (Benjamin and Theodore), flour mill, 7 miles w.
Gurley H D, blacksmith.
Harris & Sons (John S, Frank and G Eugene), nurserymen.
Keith Albert, wagon mnfr.
Keith Solomon, wagon mnfr.
Knapp Jerome, carpenter.
Kramer John C, nurseryman.
McCollum Gustavus, boots and shoes.
Minshall Thomas, Druggist and Postmaster.
Pernin Rev Peter (Catholic).
Potter George F, lawyer.
Potter Wm E, Farmer.
Richardson David, justice of peace.
Sawyer House, W S Wolcott Propr.
Sawyer J O, Hotel Propr and Justice.
Stiles Frank I, Stone Mnfr. (See adv, opp Stone in classified.)
Webster Edward B, justice of peace.
Webster Mathew M, woolen mill.
Wheeler E A, wheat buyer.
Wilford Rev T (Methodist).
Williams J M, wagonmaker.
Wilsey John R, hotel propr.
Wolcott Walter S, Propr Sawyer House.

LAFOND. On the N. P. R. R., in Morrison county, 7 miles west of Little Falls, the county seat and bank location. Population, 30. M. Lafond, postmaster.

LAFONTAINE. A discontinued postoffice in Polk county, 18 miles from Crookston, the county seat and shipping point. Send mail to Red Lake Falls.

LAKE AMELIA. In Pope county, 5 miles from Glenwood, the county seat, nearest railroad and banking point. Postoffice discontinued. Send mail to Otto.

LAKE ANDREW. In Kandiyohi county, 12 miles north of Willmar, the judicial seat, nearest shipping point and bank location, on the St. P., M. & M. Ry. Stages semi-weekly to Willmar. Population, 80. L. Hedin, postmaster.

Applequist C J, blacksmith.
Chinelin Hans, general store.
Goodhamer H H, general store.
Quist P M, railroad agent.
Selvig O, express agent.

LAKE BELT. In Martin county, 3 miles from the State line, 15 from Fairmont, the judicial seat and bank location, and 8 from Sherburne, the nearest railroad point, on the C., M. & St. P. Ry. Stage semi-weekly, to Sherburne, and Estherville, Iowa. W. Headley, postmaster and general store.

LAKE BENTON. On the C. & N. W. Ry, at the foot of Lake Benton, in Lincoln county, of which it is the county seat. Settled in 1872, it contains a steam flour mill, a bank, 2 churches and a weekly paper, the Lake Benton *News.* Stages semi-weekly to Pipe Stone and Wilno. Exp., Am. Tel., W. U. Population, 600. John L. Cass, postmaster.

Aldsworth Wm, harnessmaker.
Allen H A, clerk J W Bush.
Anderson K, farm impts.
Anderson R L, boots and shoes.
Andrews C W, lawyer and collections.
Andrews & Ware, lawyers.
Bradley George H, hardware and furniture.
Bradley W H, grocer.
Brightman J M, loans and insurance.
Bryan Wilbur, agent Winona mill co.
Burt Wm H, pres Lincoln County bank.
Bush J W, grocer.
Calkins Melville, printer.
Carlisle C H, clerk W H Roberts.

G. F. Farrington, Exclusive Merchant Tailor, 239 Nicollet Ave, Minneapolis, Minn. SEE PAGE 3.

FINANCIAL AGENTS
The Farnsworth Loan and Realty Co., Correspondence Solicited. Minneapolis, Minn.

25

This gazetteer was published in 1886–1887. Compare the town descriptions and the jobs listed. **Which towns do you think will succeed and which will fail?**

THE LUCK OF THE DRAW

After identifying what types of workers to recruit, a developer began promoting the town. Developers created posters and newspaper advertisements, gave speeches, handed out cards, and did whatever they could to encourage people to move to their town.

Step 5: Roll a die twice and add up the two numbers. Then choose that many jobs from your list of 15. Congratulations! You have attracted people to fill these positions. Be sure to choose the jobs you fill carefully, since this will be important in attracting other settlers.

PROMOTING THE LAND

Once the first wave of settlers arrived in a town, speculators faced a decision. What should they charge for land? Some developers might lower land prices to encourage more people to come. Others might keep prices high, hoping to make as much profit as possible.

Step 6: Make a poster or brochure for your town. What natural resources does your town have? Who do you want to move there? What will you charge for land? Are there special things about your town that you want to boast about? Your answers to these questions are the kinds of details to include in your poster or brochure.

Despite the efforts of town developers and townspeople, many early towns died. Compare the land you chose for your town to a modern map. Are there any towns or railroads located near where you put your town? Did you choose your site wisely?

Railroad companies sold land, too, and they held land fairs to advertise the affordability and fertility of the land they sold. **What methods are they using to advertise land in this photo?**

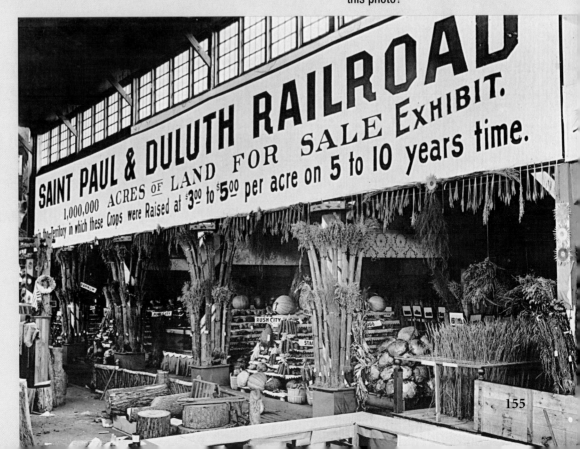

155

11 Flour, Lumber, and Iron

This 1885 advertisement for Pillsbury flour shows the busy company's location at the Falls of St. Anthony.

DAILY CAPACITY 10,500 BARRELS.

CHAS. A. PILLSBURY & Co

MERCHANT MILLERS, Pillsbury's BEST XXXX Minneapolis, Minn. MINNEAPOLIS

1839
First commercial sawmill in Minnesota is built along the St. Croix River near Stillwater.

1854
Minnesota's first commerical flour mills are built at the Falls of St. Anthony.

1869
Charles Pillsbury comes to Minneapolis to work in the flour milling industry.

Tunnel collapse at St. Anthony Falls almost destroys the falls.

1878
Washburn A Mill in Minneapolis explodes, killing 18 workers and destroying seven other flour mills.

1881
Minneapolis becomes the flour milling capital of the world, producing more flour per year than any other city.

1883
Northern Pacific Railway completes a transcontinental route from Minnesota to the Pacific Ocean.

1887
Minneapolis flour mill owners build the Soo Line railroad to cut their shipping costs.

The trains that chugged across the landscape during the late 1800s signaled the arrival of a new era in Minnesota—an era of **industrialization.** It was a time of big machines and big businesses. Companies that had been owned by one person or by several partners grew into corporations—companies with many owners, called stockholders. By forming a corporation and selling stock, businesses could bring together the money of many people. This allowed them to hire more workers, buy expensive machinery, and expand their operations. Entire **industries** developed that specialized in certain products or services. The railroad industry was one example of this trend, but there were many others.

In Minnesota's early **economy**, three industries became particularly important: flour milling, lumbering, and iron mining. Each of these industries succeeded by finding the right mix of at least three key ingredients:

- *Natural resources* that could be used to make products
- *Machines* that made it easier to use those natural resources
- *People* who were willing to invest money, ideas, and physical labor to make use of both natural resources and machines to make products

LOOK FOR

- Why were Minnesota's rivers important for industries?
- How did Charles Pillsbury become a leading flour miller in Minneapolis?
- What did Frederick Weyerhaeuser do to change the lumber industry?
- How did new machines contribute to Minnesota's industries?
- What were work conditions like in the iron mines?

KEY TERMS

industrialization

industry

economy

industrialist

iron ore

labor union

industrialization: the process of developing large-scale, mechanical factories

industry: a specific branch of business that provides a certain product or service

economy: the system for producing, distributing, and consuming or using goods and services

1889	1890	1891	1902	1907	1909	1910
William Mayo and his two sons establish the Mayo Clinic in Rochester with the opening of St. Mary's Hospital.	Frederick Weyerhaeuser's lumber company buys timberland in northern Minnesota. The Merritt brothers discover iron ore north of Duluth.	Minnesota's first state park, Itasca State Park, is established.	Minnesota Mining and Manufacturing Company (3M) is founded at Two Harbors on the north shore of Lake Superior.	Iron miners in Minnesota strike for better pay and working conditions.	President Theodore Roosevelt establishes Superior National Forest in northern Minnesota.	Split Rock Lighthouse on Lake Superior begins operations that continue for 59 years.

Minnesota's flour milling, lumber, and iron mining industries took advantage of these and other factors to grow bigger and more profitable during the late 1800s and early 1900s. Their owners became rich. Their workers earned a living. And in the process, employers and employees often found themselves at odds with each other.

An Industrialist's Story: Charles Pillsbury and the Flour Milling Industry

Minneapolis was a town of small businesses when 27-year-old Charles Pillsbury arrived in 1869. Pillsbury had grown up in New Hampshire and had learned the ins and outs of the business world while working for a company that distributed farm produce to markets in Montreal. He had come to Minneapolis to go into business for himself, and he was thinking big, not small. The business he chose was flour milling.

Flour mills had been grinding wheat into flour at the Falls of St. Anthony for 15 years by the time Pillsbury arrived. But the amount of flour produced at those mills was small compared to the production of major milling centers such as St. Louis, Missouri. Pillsbury and a few other **industrialists** set out to change that. A few years after arriving in Minneapolis, Pillsbury became part owner of a failing flour mill. He knew he was taking a gamble. "The other fellows in the business rather pitied me," he recalled, "and said that another poor devil had got caught in the milling business."

But Pillsbury didn't need pity. He knew he was getting into a tough business and worked hard to succeed. Within five years, his business was flourishing. Soon after, he could afford to make improvements to his mill and buy additional ones. By the late 1870s, production at his mills had increased from 300 barrels of flour a day to 3,000 barrels a day. Other mill owners also expanded their operations in Minneapolis with similar increases in production. Such rapid expansion resulted from a combination of natural resources, new machines, and the efforts of people.

industrialist: an owner or manager of a large business

Charles Pillsbury, pictured in his office in Minneapolis, built a flour milling company that helped make Minneapolis the flour milling capital of the nation.

THE FLOUR MILLING EQUATION

In many ways, the flour milling industry's success began with water-power. The cascading waters of the Falls of St. Anthony turned the turbines that spun the shafts that powered the grindstones inside the mills. But the industry would not have thrived without new machines, the investment and effort of industrialists and workers, and the growing demand for flour by families across the United States and in Europe.

Natural Resources

The rich farmland of southern and western Minnesota had a soil that was ideal for growing wheat, which was the preferred grain of the flour millers. As more farmers moved into the state, the supply of wheat increased dramatically—from 1,400 bushels in 1850 to nearly 19 million bushels in 1870 to more than 52 million in 1890. Minnesota had become the leading wheat-producing state in the nation. Of course, this growth in wheat production did not just happen. The state's expanding railroad system was making it easier to move wheat from the farms to the mills, opening new markets for the farmers' grain.

Machines

Until the 1870s, flour made from Minnesota wheat was speckled with brown flecks of bran—a flaw that made bread less appealing, slower to rise, and faster to decay than pure white flour did. In Pillsbury's words, it "was way down at the bottom of the heap." But then the

Compare this 1898 photograph of the milling district to the advertisement on pages 156–157. **In your opinion, how realistic is the ad?**

Steel rollers made large-scale production of flour possible, but required constant attention.

159

Minneapolis millers started using new machines that greatly improved the quality of their flour. One machine called the middlings purifier removed the brown flecks and turned Minnesota wheat into the pure, white flour that consumers preferred. Steel rollers ground the flour finer and faster than the old millstones, improving the quality and increasing the production of wheat flour. By the early 1880s, Minnesota flour was considered among the best in the world.

People

Charles Pillsbury and the other Minneapolis flour mill owners employed thousands of people. The highest-paid workers were the ones who tended the huge machines at the mills. Their jobs were also the most dangerous—many lost an arm or a hand in the big machines. The packers who caught the flour in barrels and bags as it poured off the assembly lines were among the lowest-paid workers in the mills. Those workers who nailed the flour barrels shut and who swept the floor also received low wages. The unskilled jobs were boring and repetitive, and they offered little chance of moving up to better-paying jobs.

By 1880, Charles Pillsbury and his fellow mill owners had—with considerable help from their workers—turned Minneapolis into the nation's leading flour producer. As production rose, large milling companies began buying up small milling companies. By 1890, four corporations accounted for 87 percent of the city's flour production. Of those four corporations, C. A. Pillsbury and Company was the largest.

A company's name and logo were important sales tools for flour companies trying to compete in a tough market.

A Worker's Story: Horace Glenn and the Lumber Industry

Minnesota's lumber industry was operating at its peak in the winter of 1900 to 1901, when 21-year-old Horace Glenn arrived in Minnesota's northeastern Arrowhead region to work as a lumberjack. Glenn had come for money and adventure. He considered himself well educated and well mannered—the superior of the other lumberjacks he worked with. But in letters to his parents in Aberdeen, South Dakota, he said he was glad to be there:

I enjoy the work better than any I ever did before. For me, sawing is the best job in the woods. The time passes quickly, and although it is very cold, from zero to 30 below so far, you don't notice it as so

Loggers started their day at about 4:00 A.M. in the bunkhouse they shared with up to 20 other men. Huge meals fueled the men for a long, hard day of work.

much in the timber, and what I eat at home would be scarcely a light lunch for me here.

Horace Glenn worked as a swamper, cutting branches off felled trees. For Glenn and his fellow lumberjacks, the day started at four in the morning. They woke up, ate a big breakfast of pancakes, pork, and beans, and headed out into the woods for the rest of the day—snow, rain, or shine. The camp cooks brought lunch at midday. In the winter most lumberjacks learned to eat quickly before the food froze. After returning to camp, they ate dinner and then headed to the bunkhouse. Most were asleep by nine o'clock.

Lumberjacks had one day off—Sunday. Men occasionally attended church services conducted by traveling ministers, but mostly they spent the day playing cards, writing letters, and paying at least a little attention to personal hygiene. If nothing else, it was a day to boil your clothes and kill the lice that infested them. Horace Glenn tried his best to stay clean, but it was difficult with no running water, little soap, and shared bathwater. "I have the barber's itch now," he wrote his parents, describing a rash caused by a skin fungus. "My face is a fright, but it's healing up."

By March, Glenn was itching to join up with a work crew on a springtime log drive. All winter, workers stacked logs by the side of the river. When the ice melted on the river, crews drove the logs downstream to the sawmills. Log driving was dangerous work, but the wages were good—as much as $2.50 a day. Glenn hoped to make enough money on the river to pay for a trip back to South Dakota.

Saws, cant hooks, and steel-tipped pike poles were some of the tools loggers used.

This logjam blocked the St. Croix River at Taylors Falls in 1886. It took 200 men six weeks using dynamite and hard work to break the logs loose. **How many men can you find in this photo?**

THE LUMBER EQUATION

Rivers and waterfalls were just as important to the lumber industry as they were to the flour milling industry. Rivers served as transportation highways for millions of logs. Lumber companies built sawmills and booms—where logs were sorted and stored—at several of the state's waterfalls. Towns grew up near the sawmills and booms, as people came to work in the industry.

Natural Resources

For hundreds of years, vast forests of white pine—a tree highly prized for its high-quality lumber—covered much of northern Minnesota. The white pine could grow more than 125 feet tall, and the straight trunks had no branches for many feet above the ground. These straight and strong trees made superior boards for construction. Though logging in Minnesota began in the late 1830s, it wasn't until the 1880s that lumber companies started making major investments of money, machines, and people to harvest the trees.

Machines

Crosscut saws, axes, hammers, and hooks were always important tools of the lumber trade, but as the years went on, companies invented new machines to make the business more efficient. Hot-water pumps kept the water near sawmills from freezing so that mills could run all winter. Faster steam-powered saws helped increase lumber production. But few innovations were as important as the railways. At first, most logs were hauled to rivers by horses and floated downstream to the mills. But in the 1890s, lumber companies started using freight trains to move logs out of the forests that weren't near rivers.

Lumberjacks loaded logs onto large sleds and took them to rivers, where they were easily moved downstream.

People

Lumberjacks like Horace Glenn provided the muscle to fell the trees and to send logs downriver, but they were just part of the story. Minnesota's lumber industry would never have developed as quickly as it did without business owners like Frederick Weyerhaeuser (WEHR-how-ser). In 1890, Weyerhaeuser and his partners made their first big investment in Minnesota, purchasing hard-to-reach timberland in the central part of the state. He eventually expanded his control to sawmills, booms, and small railroad lines. Because he controlled every step of the lumbering process, he could tightly control costs and profits. By 1900, more than 400 lumber companies (including several belonging to Weyerhaeuser) were operating in the state, and Minnesota ranked third in the nation in lumber production. Towns and cities throughout the Midwest were built using Minnesota lumber.

It was probably a good thing that Horace Glenn didn't want to make a career out of lumberjacking. By 1905, Minnesota's white pines had been cut down and lumber production was beginning to decline. Minnesotans started talking seriously about conserving trees and planting new ones, but by then it was too late. Many lumber mills in Minnesota closed and lumber operations moved west to uncut white pine forests. Lumberjacks who wanted to keep working in the lucrative white pine forests had to follow the companies west. Others turned to harvesting different kinds of trees, and the rest had to find new work. Horace Glenn never returned to the lumber camps. He became a lawyer instead.

Minnesota's Pine Forest around 1830

In the 1830s, lumbermen estimated Minnesota's pine forests would provide lumber for more than 100 years. Actually, almost all of the white pine trees were gone by 1905.

Frederick Weyerhaeuser's lumber companies cut millions of acres of white pine forest in Minnesota and then moved on to the Pacific Northwest.

To see in the underground mines, miners wore helmets with kerosene-powered headlamps.

iron ore: the rock source that contains iron

labor union: a group of workers organized to bargain collectively for better wages and working conditions

A Labor Activist's Story: Anton Antilla and the Iron Mining Industry

Seventeen-year-old Anton Antilla arrived in the tiny mining community of Biwabik (bih-WAH-bihk) in 1906. He had come all the way from Finland to live and work on Minnesota's Mesabi Range. Thousands of other Finns had done the same during the previous decade or so. It took Antilla less than a day to find work in an underground mine nearby.

Antilla learned immediately how hard the work was. For more than 10 hours a day, he worked deep underground, shoveling **iron ore** into wheelbarrows and tramcars so that machines could lift it up the mine shaft. It was dangerous work—the mine shafts were dark and dusty and could collapse, especially when miners used dynamite to break up the rock. A few months after Antilla arrived on the range, five tramcars loaded with ore raced out of control and killed six men at a mine near Eveleth.

The longer Antilla worked in the mines, the more he became convinced that the mining companies were treating him and his fellow miners unfairly. Hours were long—up to 14 hours a day. And since the miners were paid by the amount of iron ore they produced—instead of by the hour or by the day—they had to bribe foremen to let them work in places where the ore was plentiful and easy to remove. An unlucky miner earned wages as low as $1.80 a day. By the summer of 1907, Antilla and thousands of his coworkers had had enough. They joined a **labor union** and walked off the job, demanding better pay and working conditions. It was the first widespread, organized strike the Iron Range had ever seen.

The mining companies were determined to keep the mines open and force the labor union to give up its strike. They brought in replacements—immigrant workers from southern and eastern European countries, such as Greece, Italy, Slovenia, Croatia, and Montenegro. They hired hundreds of guards to protect the new workers and intimidate the strikers.

Antilla and other striking miners tried

Wages in 1900		Prices in 1900	
Blacksmith	$2.43/day	Root beer float from soda fountain	5¢
Dressmaker	$2.00/day	Sewing machine	$12.00
Iron miner	$2.00/day	Eggs from grocer	12¢/doz.
Lumberjack	$0.56/day+room and board	Roast beef dinner	15¢
Miller	$3.80/day (1882)	Ice cream and cake dessert	15¢
Schoolteacher	$450.00/year ($2.50/day)	House	$3,000.00
Cabinetmaker	$2.25/day	Trolley-car fare	5¢

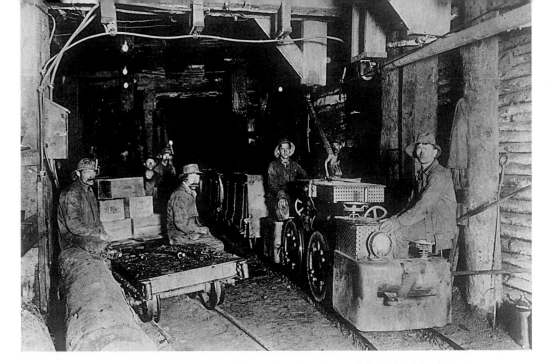

Miners were paid low wages for dangerous work in underground mines—like this one shown in 1910 near Virginia.

to convince the replacement workers, who they called scabs, to honor the strike, but most of the newcomers needed the jobs they had been offered. The mines reopened. Soon, the men who had gone on strike began returning to work. The strike was over. The strikers had gained nothing. Minnesota's iron mining companies turned their attention back to other business, but they would be faced with labor concerns again and again in the years to come.

UNIONS: WORKING FOR WORKERS

Labor unions in Minnesota and across the nation began fighting for better pay and working conditions during the late 1800s, but success came slowly. Strikes—like those on Minnesota's Iron Range—often failed to produce immediate improvements in the workplace. But eventually, workers and their unions began to make progress. During the first four decades of the 1900s, successful strikes took place in other states and in industries such as textiles, steel, and railroads. The U.S. government also passed a variety of federal laws that benefited working people. By the middle of the twentieth century, the combined efforts of labor unions and government reform had achieved all of the aims listed in the chart below.

Issues	Common Working Conditions in 1880s	Aims of Labor Movement
Workday and workweek	10 to 14 hours a day, 6 to 7 days a week	8 hours a day, 5 days a week
Child labor	Long hours and unsafe conditions	Hours and conditions restricted
Minimum wage	Employers set wages as low as they could	Minimum wage set by law
Workplace safety laws	Workers responsible for own safety	Safe and clean workplaces required by law
Paid vacations	No vacation time or paid time off	Paid time off for vacation and sickness each year
Workers compensation	No requirements to compensate workers injured on the job	Employers required to pay wages and medical costs of workers injured on the job

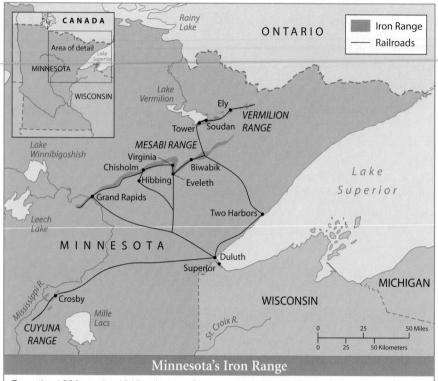

Minnesota's Iron Range

From the 1880s to the 1910s, dozens of towns were built near the huge iron ore deposits in northeastern Minnesota.

THE IRON MINING EQUATION

Most of Minnesota's iron ore country was less than 100 miles away from Lake Superior, and that was an important part of the industry's success. Trains hauled ore from the mines to the lake. From there, large ships carried the ore to mills in Pennsylvania and Ohio, where it was turned into steel used in skyscrapers, bridges, railroad cars, trucks, and automobiles. But proximity to Lake Superior was just part of Minnesota's success in iron mining.

Natural Resources

Minnesota's state geologist first reported finding iron ore in the northeastern part of the state in 1865, but it wasn't until the 1890s that the true magnitude of Minnesota's iron wealth became clear. In 1890, brothers Leonidas and Alfred Merritt discovered that parts of the Mesabi Hills, north of Duluth, were covered with soft, granular iron ore that could be shoveled up like dirt. They had found the iron deposits of what would soon be called the Mesabi Range. As it turned out, the Mesabi—along with the smaller Vermilion and Cuyuna Ranges—formed one of the largest masses of high-grade iron ore in the world.

Machines

To be profitable, iron mining requires an enormous investment in heavy machinery and transportation. Before the mining companies could make any money, they had to build railroads to haul the iron ore to Lake Superior; they had to construct ore-loading docks on the lakeshores in Duluth, Two Harbors, and Superior, Wisconsin; and they had to build a fleet of ships to carry the ore across the Great Lakes. At first, they used massive, steam-powered shovels to dig the ore out of open-pit mines and steam-powered trains to haul the ore to Lake Superior. As technology progressed, electric shovels replaced the steam shovels and diesel engines replaced steam trains.

People

Minnesota's iron mining industry depended heavily on the men who worked in the mines, but it needed more than labor. It needed the money of people who were willing to take tremendous financial risks. The seven Merritt brothers of Duluth were among the first of those risk takers (they made—and lost—their family's fortune between 1890 and 1895). But as the promise of the industry grew, eastern investors with deeper pockets stepped in with even more money. During the 1890s, several of the country's most powerful industrialists invested in mining operations on the Mesabi Range. A few of them, such as John D. Rockefeller, J. P. Morgan, and Andrew Carnegie, were well known. Others, such as Henry Oliver, were less famous but just as influential. All but Duluth's Merritt brothers lived in the East—and took the money they made from Minnesota iron ore out of the state.

After striking in 1907, Anton Antilla returned to the mines, but he didn't stay there long. He had earned a reputation as a union trouble-maker—the kind of worker the company didn't want around. After a few days back on the job, he was fired. He looked for another mining job, but no one would hire him. "I had been speaking my mind," he later recalled. "I got blacklisted."

Antilla turned to farming and never returned to mining, but his labor-union efforts marked the start of a long struggle to improve the lives of Iron Range workers. In the years that followed, miners on the Iron Range continued their attempts to bargain with the companies. In 1935, the U.S. Congress passed a law that made it easier for miners and other working people to form labor unions to bargain collectively with their employers. Finally, in 1943, 36 years after their first strike, miners on the Iron Range signed their first contract with the mining companies.

The flour milling, lumber, and iron mining industries continued to drive Minnesota's economy well into the twentieth century. Abundant natural resources, technological innovations, and hard-working, enterprising people all played vital roles in creating a thriving business economy in Minnesota.

After he quit mining, Anton Antilla bought a farm near Palo in northeastern Minnesota. Here, he poses with his family in front of their farmhouse.

167

Picturing Working Life

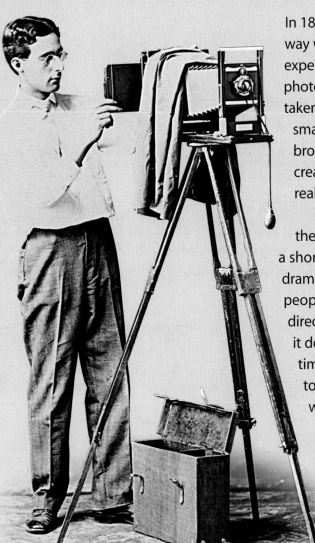

In 1839, a new invention—the camera—changed the way we record and view history. At first, cameras were expensive and difficult to use, and people traveled to a photographer's studio to have formal, posed portraits taken. Soon, technological advances made the camera smaller, cheaper, and easier to use, and cameras were brought to homes, battlefields, ballparks, and factories, creating an opportunity to see what people's lives were really like outside of a studio.

If it's true that a picture is worth a thousand words, then studying photographs can be a lot like studying a short story. What you first see may be the central, dramatic events, but small details can reveal more about people's thoughts and feelings. Photography doesn't directly capture the sounds or smells of a moment, but it does capture the appearance, action, people, location, time, and sometimes meaning of a moment. By learning to study what is obvious and subtle in a photograph, we can learn to uncover stories from our past.

In the 1880s, photographers began taking their cameras into the factories and workplaces of Minnesota, capturing images of how and where people worked. As you study these photos, think about the stories they are telling.

What was working life like between 1880 and 1920?

Cooperage shop, Hamm Brewing Company, 1905

Study these images as a detective would. **How do these scenes differ?**

People posing in a photographer's studio, 1890

Women attaching labels to boxes, International Stock Food Company, 1900

🔍 **Step 1: Observe**
When looking at a historical photograph, your first job as a historian is to take a few minutes to study it. Let your eyes wander over the image, and observe its drama and detail. Do not take notes or try to record your impressions; simply let yourself become familiar with the image.

M. A. Gedney Bottling and Pickling Company, 1912

🔍 **Step 2: What is going on here?**
After you have become familiar with a photo, start to record what you see. What appears to be going on here? What event is happening? Note the action that the photo has captured. Can you infer what just happened? Or what is about to happen?

Step 3: Who is involved?

Study the people in the image. Describe each one's age, sex, occupation, and ethnic background if you can. Try to figure out the relationships between the people in the photo. Are they family? Friends? Co-workers? Are they strangers? Based on what you see, can you make an inference about who might be just outside the photo's frame? We know that the photographer was there, although we cannot see him or her, but is there evidence of other people, too?

UNIDENTIFIED ST. PAUL BUSINESS, 1900

EMPLOYEES POSING OUTSIDE THEIR FACTORY, 1890

○ Step 4: Where was the photograph taken?

Describe where the photograph was taken. Was it taken outside or inside? What kinds of buildings are visible? What kinds of natural environment? Are there landmarks or signs that show you exactly where this photograph was taken?

○ Step 5: When was the photograph taken?

Study the photograph for clues about the time of day, season, and year. Is daylight visible? Are people dressed for daytime or nighttime activities? Can you see evidence of the season? Do the fashions, transportation, or environment give you clues about the time period of the photo?

PACKINGHOUSE WORKERS LEAVING WORK, SOUTH ST. PAUL

Step 6: Why was the photograph taken?

Photographers take pictures for many different reasons. While a journalist might take a picture to show newspaper readers who won a race, parents take pictures at their children's graduations to help remember that proud moment. Sometimes the reason that a photo is taken can be obvious; other times it is more difficult—or even impossible—to know why a picture was taken.

To understand why a photograph was taken, consider what the subject of the photograph is. Did the photographer focus on the place, the people, the event, or the things? What is the relationship between the people and the photographer? Are the people in the photograph aware of the camera? Does the subject of the photograph seem natural or staged?

Modern fire escape and pleasant grounds surrounding Guiterman Bros. Garment Factory, St. Paul, ca. 1910

Step 7: What are the stories of these photographs?

Now that you have learned to analyze photographs like a historian, choose one of these images to focus on. Observe your photograph carefully, then try to understand the what, who, where, when, and why of the image. Can you uncover the hidden story from the past?

Downtown St. Paul was bustling in 1908, when this Wabasha street scene was painted.

1869	**1870**	**1871**	**1872**	**1885**	**1889**	**1890**
Duluth is established and grows rapidly.	About 15 percent of Minnesota's population lives in urban areas.	Railroads reach Duluth and Moorhead from St. Paul.	St. Anthony and Minneapolis merge into one city.	The safety bicycle, with chain-driven gears, is invented in England.	Electric streetcars begin operation in Minneapolis.	The Guaranty Loan building opens in Minneapolis.

In the early days of statehood, people usually thought of Minnesota as a land of farms and farmers. But at the end of the 1800s, Minnesota was changing. Its cities were growing—and growing fast. In a few cities, factories and mills grew. There, workers turned raw materials such as timber and grain into finished goods such as furniture and flour. Each Minnesota city played an important and unique role in the state's development. But the most dominant city was the rapidly expanding area known as Minneapolis–St. Paul, or the Twin Cities.

The *Twin Cities*—this was a new term that reflected a new way of thinking. For years, people had thought of St. Paul and Minneapolis as distinct cities. St. Paul was older and dignified, a center of business and politics. Minneapolis was younger, a vibrant manufacturing center. Minneapolis had grown to become the state's biggest city shortly after absorbing the town of St. Anthony in 1872. St. Paul and Minneapolis had always been rivals, but by the turn of

LOOK FOR

- ◆ Why did Knud Wefald dislike the cities so much?
- ◆ How did the people, buildings, and pace of city life change at this time?
- ◆ What differences were there between Minnesota's rural and urban areas?
- ◆ What types of problems developed in cities?
- ◆ How did people try to solve city problems?

KEY TERMS

metropolitan

urban

rural

working class

boom

lifestyle

settlement house

1895
Automobiles first appear in the Twin Cities.

1902
Minneapolis has an estimated 125 automobiles.

1903
In North Carolina, Orville and Wilbur Wright make the first airplane flight, which lasts 12 seconds.

1905
Aerial bridge in Duluth begins operating.

1910
Split Rock Lighthouse, located on Lake Superior's north shore, opens.

1912
Knud Wefald is elected to state legislature.

1914
World War I begins in Europe.

metropolitan: of or relating to a large city

urban: of or relating to the city

rural: of or relating to the country

the century people in and out of the state often thought of the two cities as a single **metropolitan** area.

The Twin Cities and the other **urban** areas in Minnesota were very different from **rural** areas—the farms and small towns of Minnesota. The cities were a jumble of contrasts. They were places of staggering wealth and extreme poverty. They promised an exciting future, but they also presented problems that sometimes seemed beyond anyone's ability to solve.

Noise, Hum, and Clatter

In January of 1913, a 44-year-old lumberyard owner named Knud Wefald (NOOD WAY-fahld) arrived in the big city of St. Paul. Wefald had come all the way from Hawley, a small town of about 800 near Moorhead in western Minnesota. His neighbors there had recently elected him to the Minnesota House of Representatives. Since the legislature did its work at the state capitol in St. Paul, St. Paul is where he went.

When Knud Wefald came to St. Paul after being elected to the state legislature in 1913, he was awed by the crowded atmosphere.

It didn't take long for Knud Wefald to decide that he would much rather be in Hawley than in St. Paul. To him, the city was an overwhelming place that beat down the human spirit. He described his first impressions in a long letter to his hometown newspaper, the *Clay County Herald*:

> The noise, hum and clatter almost drives a person crazy to begin with. The hotel and rooming house air chokes me; the baker's bread poisons me, and this looking only against high and dirty stone walls makes a fellow stupid. It is a dreary contrast to the far-reaching view of snow-covered, white and beautiful Clay County rolling prairie, with its invigorating air. I cannot see how people can tie themselves down to live in a city, even with all the modern conveniences they have that we in the villages and on the farm do not have.

Wefald was not alone in his dislike of the city. For several decades, rural Minnesotans had watched from a distance as the cities grew in size and importance. Many especially resented the Twin Cities area. They suspected that the agricultural businesses headquartered there were swindling them. Like Wefald, they considered the city a confining, suffocating place.

But not everyone felt this way. To many Minnesotans, the city was an exciting place full of possibilities. Sure, city life had its problems, but these were problems that could be fixed if people put their minds to them. Things were bigger, taller, and faster in the city, and many Minnesotans liked it that way.

A Mass of People

One of the first things Knud Wefald noticed when he arrived in the Twin Cities was what he called "the whole mass" of people on the streets and sidewalks. Back in his hometown of Hawley, people did not gather and move in crowds—there weren't enough of them. But the city was different. As Wefald described it in his letter to the *Herald*, the people trudged through the city with "no joy and pleasure to see in any face."

In downtown St. Paul in 1914, the intersection of Seventh Street and Wabasha was full of action.

> *A steady stream of human beings goes surging and seething up and down the narrow streets, in and out of doors of the dirty black and brown buildings. It reminds me of ants and ant heaps.*

177

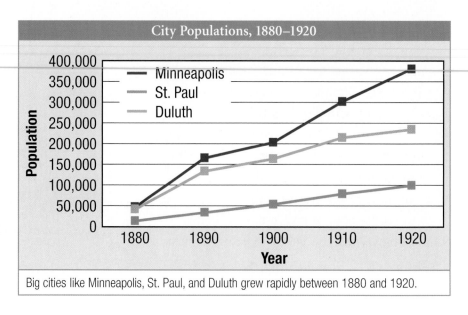

City Populations, 1880–1920

Big cities like Minneapolis, St. Paul, and Duluth grew rapidly between 1880 and 1920.

Trains brought thousands of immigrants—including this group in 1910—to their new homes in Minnesota.

Agree or disagree with him, Wefald was right about at least one thing: the cities were bursting with people. Minneapolis especially had grown beyond most people's expectations. In 1880, Minneapolis's population was about 46,000. By 1890, it had jumped to about 165,000. The population reached 203,000 in 1900 and 301,000 in 1910. And Minneapolis was not alone. Other cities in the state experienced similar, although less dramatic, growth. By 1920, more than 40 percent of the people in Minnesota lived in urban areas—up from about 15 percent in 1870.

Many of these new urban dwellers came from farms and small towns in Minnesota. They were often young people who liked the excitement

of the city and considered it a place of opportunity. Rural newspapers tried to stop the young people from leaving the country by painting an ugly picture of city life. They described the cities as places where swindlers and thieves infested grimy streets and dark alleys. Still, Minnesotans continued to move to the cities.

Immigrants also came to Minnesota's cities. Many of these new arrivals came from countries that were unfamiliar to native-born Minnesotans. Until the 1890s, most immigrants to the state were from northern and western Europe. By the early 1900s, newcomers came from countries like Italy, Greece, and Poland, in southern and eastern Europe. The state's good farmland was already claimed, so most of these immigrants went to the cities or the iron mines in northern Minnesota.

In the cities, immigrants took hard, low-paying jobs in mills and factories. Few understood English, and many of them could not read or write. They often lived with other people from the **working class** in areas like Northeast Minneapolis, the West Side of St. Paul, and West Duluth. They spoke their own languages, and to their Minnesota-born neighbors, they often seemed slow in adopting American ways. African Americans migrated from other parts of the United States to the Twin Cities. They, too, faced prejudice and discrimination, so they formed their own neighborhoods and community institutions.

Bohemian Flats, shown here in 1910, was a neighborhood in Minneapolis named after the eastern European immigrants who lived there.

working class: people who work for hourly wages, usually in jobs that require physical labor

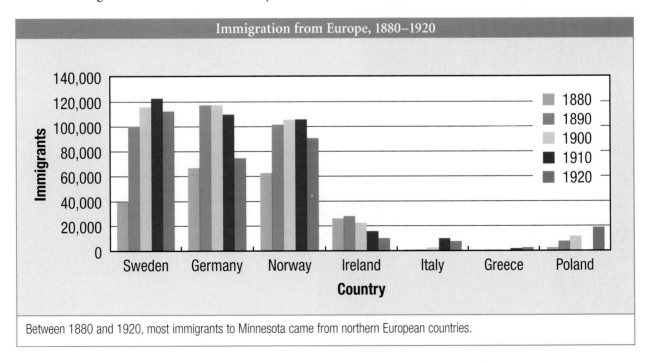

Between 1880 and 1920, most immigrants to Minnesota came from northern European countries.

As more and more people crammed into the cities, the problems of urban life increased. Swelling populations of workers competed for a limited number of low-paying jobs. Those who couldn't find steady work often watched their families slip into poverty. As poverty increased, crime increased. Diseases such as diphtheria and tuberculosis spread in the cities' tightly packed homes, apartments, and boarding houses. All these problems were worse in cities than they were in the country.

Still, many city dwellers enjoyed being part of such a large mass. They liked having so many different ways to spend their time. They liked being able to live their lives without being noticed by the thousands of people around them. They could blend into the crowd. For those who had come from small towns, this was something new. As Knud Wefald put it, small town people "know what everybody else is doing." Wefald thought that was a good thing. Many city people disagreed. They preferred the anonymity that the big city provided.

Building Boom

The problems that came with crowding troubled Knud Wefald, but they weren't the only things that bothered him. He also disliked what he considered St Paul's obsession with newer, bigger, and taller buildings. Wefald gawked at the hotels and office buildings that towered above him. Some of them were more than 10 stories high. He was amazed that city people could walk by such buildings without giving them a second glance.

We [country people] stop and half break our necks to see the top of the high buildings. They just bow their head a little, gather their clothes about them, put one shoulder to the wind and press on. We run around the corner to find out where the fire is when we hear a fire whistle. They never mind it, I suppose, until the fire has developed into something worth seeing.

Completed in Minneapolis in 1890, the Northwestern Guaranty Loan Building rose up as an example of urban growth.

180

It may have seemed to Wefald that city dwellers were unimpressed with all the construction going on around them. But city people actually took pride in their buildings. Urban residents often boasted about their tallest buildings, pointing to them as examples of how up-to-date their cities really were.

By 1890, new materials such as steel allowed businesses to build skyscrapers that rose taller than 100 feet. That same year, the Northwestern Guaranty Loan Association opened a new office building in downtown Minneapolis. The Guaranty Loan, as the people of Minneapolis called it, was the tallest structure west of Chicago.

On the day the Guaranty Loan opened to the public, hundreds of people pressed through the main entrances to marvel at the breathtaking sight. They stood in the towering courtyard and gazed at the clouds through the windows of the twelfth-floor skylight. They packed into elevators for up-and-down trips that, in the words of one visitor, were "twice as thrilling as a roller coaster ride." They climbed stairs to the fashionable rooftop garden. They inched toward the building's edge for a glimpse at the antlike pedestrians who scurried over the streets and sidewalks 200 feet below.

To the people of Minneapolis, the Guaranty Loan was proof that their city had joined the ranks of the nation's major metropolitan areas. "It is of immense importance," wrote the *Minneapolis Journal*, "because it demonstrates that the spirit of Northwestern enterprise is

Traffic jams, such as this one in 1905 at the corner of Sixth and Nicollet Avenues in Minneapolis, were common. **Can you find five different modes of transportation?**

Electric streetcar service began in St. Paul on Grand Avenue in 1890.

boom: a period of rapid economic growth

leading this favored region into national, indeed, international prominence." During the next decade, the city experienced a building **boom.** By 1900, Minneapolis had about 40,000 buildings and nearly half of them were newer than the Guaranty Loan. Soon, taller buildings rose over Minneapolis and rearranged the city's skyline. But, until it was torn down in 1961, the Guaranty Loan (by then renamed the Metropolitan Life Building) stood as a reminder of a time when a 12-story building was a source of pride and amazement.

A Faster Pace of Life

Knud Wefald may have frowned upon the city's throngs of people and towering buildings, but more than anything he disliked the pace of city life. The sidewalks were full of men and women rushing from one place to another. Streetcars and automobiles raced through the streets. Wefald was convinced that "the big treadmills of civilization" were taking the joy out of life. He believed that the people of the Twin Cities would be happier if they took life more slowly—as country people did.

> *How I wish the farmers would come in and tie their teams in front of the stores and hotels here. How pleasing it would be to see a bunch of cattle come straying loose up the street to eat hay out of the farmer's wagons, with now and then a stray pig, the same as in Hawley. How I long to see Mr. Sill's chickens as they come over the yard to visit me.*

The pace of city life had been speeding up for years by the time Wefald arrived in the Twin Cities. New and faster methods of transportation were leading the way. One of the first big changes in Minnesota transportation began on December 23, 1889. Crowds of people lined the streets to watch as eight new electric streetcars set out on their first run through Minneapolis. Until this time, horses had pulled the streetcars of Minneapolis. The new cars ran on electricity provided by thin wires strung above the street. The drivers and conductors stared straight ahead, looking dignified in their long coats with brass buttons. The passengers smiled and waved at the crowds. The electric cars of the busy Fourth Avenue line made their round-trip in 48 minutes—16 minutes faster than the horsecars had managed.

In 1885, bicycles gained chain-driven gears, which made pedaling easier. These new safety bicycles also had a chain guard to prevent clothing from getting caught.

In 1895, Minnesota saw its first automobile. Some early cars, like this one, used electricity instead of gasoline. They were recharged at night in special garages.

A few years after electric streetcars arrived, the people of the Twin Cities welcomed another new form of transportation: the bicycle. Bicycles began appearing on city streets during the 1890s and soon became popular among men and women alike. Not everyone was happy about the changes this brought to their **lifestyle**. Previously, people had stayed close to their families and neighborhoods. Now bicyclists could ride far away from the watchful eyes of their families. Some people were disturbed by the sight of women pedaling their "wheels" through the city. A group known as the Women's Rescue League called the bicycle a threat to health and morals. Most city dwellers, however, including the editors at the *St. Paul Pioneer Press*, said the league was doing "more harm than good."

But nothing made the pace of city life move faster than the automobile. The first "horseless carriages" had begun chugging and bouncing through Twin Cities streets in 1895. By 1902, Minneapolis alone had an estimated 125 automobiles. Motorists dressed up in proper driving clothes—dusters (overcoats that protected them from dust and dirt), gloves, goggles (for men), and veils (for women). Drivers challenged each other to hill-climbing competitions and other contests. And they loved to go fast—sometimes as fast as 20 miles per hour—which caused many Twin Cities residents

lifestyle: the typical way of life of a person, group, or culture

Motorists wore clothes like these gloves, goggles, and coat to keep dust and dirt off themselves as they drove.

183

to worry about their safety. The *Minneapolis Journal* warned "automobilists" to show better manners:

> *A little more thought for others, a little more willingness to divide the "right of the road" with slower vehicles and pedestrians, and a little less of the mad desire to violate all the laws regulating speed, will solve the problem.*

The automobile continued to grow in popularity. By 1920, the growing number of cars was beginning to push horses, wagons, and buggies off city streets for good. Fewer people rode streetcars. Ridership began to drop off and would continue to decline until 1954 when the Twin Cities' streetcar system finally went out of business.

City Problems, City Answers

Knud Wefald surveyed the city landscape—its masses of people, its towering buildings, its hectic pace—and concluded that the growing dominance of the cities was bad for Minnesota. "If we are to make men happy and virtuous, we should legislate against letting people build big cities," he wrote. "Cities about the size of Hawley are big enough— those bigger than Moorhead should not be allowed."

Wefald never did try to pass laws against big cities. He realized it was too late for that. But he and others did call attention to problems in growing cities. Slowly but surely, government and private groups started taking action to solve some of those problems. Charities offered help to poor families. Local boards of health passed rules aimed at controlling the spread of disease. **Settlement houses**, like the Pillsbury Settlement House in

settlement house: a place that helped new immigrants with employment, housing, health care, education, and citizenship

By 1910, settlement houses like the Pillsbury House in Minneapolis were helping new immigrants adjust to life in Minnesota.

BIRTH OF A CITY: DULUTH

Duluth's transformation from a tiny settlement into a major city did not happen in the same way as it did in St. Paul and Minneapolis. Its growth came in spurts financed largely by wealthy investors from outside the state.

Duluth was a frontier village of about 100 people in 1868, when Jay Cooke and some other businessmen and bankers from Philadelphia came to visit. They were trying to decide if they should invest money in the area. The men liked what they saw. There was a natural harbor—a perfect place for a major port. On the hills above the town was the edge of a vast pine forest—a seemingly endless source of timber. It was easy to imagine Duluth becoming a great rail and shipping center where lumber, wheat, cattle, and other products could be moved from train to ship. Cooke and

his fellow investors were so impressed that they began putting money into railroads and land around Duluth.

By 1869, Duluth was a boomtown. Houses could not be built fast enough for all the railroad workers, land buyers, and other newcomers. By 1871, railroads ran south to St. Paul and west to Moorhead. To make access easier for ships, workers cut a canal through Minnesota Point, a peninsula that blocked much of the entrance to the harbor. Now, ships would come to Duluth instead of Superior, Wisconsin, on the other side of the

harbor. But in 1873, hard times swept the country. Investors like Jay Cooke ran out of money. Duluth's first boom was over.

The next boom came in the 1880s, with the discovery of iron ore on Minnesota's Iron Range. During the next 20 years, Duluth kept growing. The waterfront, pictured below in 1898, was crowded with grain elevators and lumberyards. Hundreds of ships steamed through the canal each year. In 1916, a giant steel mill was added. Minnesotans began to realize that their state had a third big city.

Minneapolis and the Neighborhood House in St. Paul, helped newly arrived immigrants feel more at home. St. Paul, Minneapolis, and other Minnesota cities began setting aside land for parks, museums, libraries, and other public spaces that made cities more inviting.

These and other efforts improved the cities, but they weren't enough to change Knud Wefald's mind about the advantages of country life over city life. "When we learn to understand it, there is poetry in the unchangeable laws of nature," he wrote. "When we look for it we find there is nothing new under the sun."

Minnesota might once have been known mostly as a land of farms and farmers, but by 1920 its image had changed for good. The homesteading of Minnesota farmland had stopped in 1918. The cities' share of the state's population was increasing steadily. A few decades later, half of all Minnesotans would live in cities. But no matter where people lived in Minnesota, more and more of them were encountering common problems that needed solving.

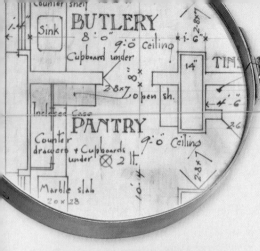

BLUEPRINTS OF OUR PAST

Prairie School designs often use simple or geometric patterns. Victorian designs are often flowery and intricate. **Which style describes each of these two designs?**

In the late 1800s and early 1900s, Minnesota's cities were not only growing bigger, taller, and faster, but also more modern. Many citizens wanted their homes to be just as modern and sophisticated as their cities. To do this, they built the biggest and grandest houses they could. In turn-of-the-century St. Paul, the grandest place to build those homes was Summit Avenue.

In the late 1800s, known as the Victorian age, Summit Avenue home owners hired St. Paul's finest architects to design homes that looked like old English countryside manors or medieval castles. Towers, dormers, steep gables, and verandas helped these Victorian homes look like royal palaces. Inside, expensively decorated formal rooms were meant to impress guests.

But around 1900, people started to think differently about architecture. In the Midwest, a new style of architecture called the Prairie School was born. This style featured simple, no-frills houses without any old-fashioned or fancy details. Prairie School homes had low rooflines that mimicked the land. Wide bands of windows welcomed in natural light and a view of the outside world. These homes featured fewer, more open rooms and eliminated formal rooms that had been seldom used, such as a library or a music room. Prairie School architects designed homes for people who wanted to look toward the future, not back to the past.

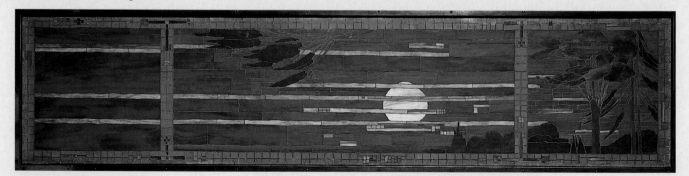

Between 1890 and 1920, a quiet revolution took place along Summit Avenue. When William Elsinger built his home in 1898, he asked for the popular Victorian style. In 1912, when Ward and Bessa Beebe faced a similar decision, they chose a Prairie School home. This shift between Victorian homes and Prairie School homes was about more than just appearance. Different house styles mirrored different family lifestyles—the way a family lives, works, eats, relaxes, and plays. Family lifestyles were changing, so houses were changing, too.

Study the Elsinger and Beebe homes to uncover how architecture and family lifestyles changed in the early 1900s. Then, design your own floor plan of a Victorian or Prairie School home.

THE EXTERIOR OF THE ELSINGERS' VICTORIAN HOME

THE EXTERIOR

To most people, the first and most obvious difference between Victorian and Prairie School homes is the design of the outside, or exterior. The design of the doors, windows, and roofline give the home a certain look and feel. Building materials such as wood, concrete, brick, plaster, and stone also can affect how a house looks and feels. Colors like pink or tan might seem friendly, while all-white homes can seem cold.

Look at the images of the Elsinger house and the Beebe house. How are the exteriors of these houses different? What impressions do these houses make?

THE INTERIOR

While the outside of a house affects what other people think about the house, the interior, or inside, affects how people *live* in the house. Most homes have three main types of interior spaces.

THE EXTERIOR OF THE BEEBES' PRAIRIE SCHOOL HOME

Public spaces are where the family entertains guests. These include parlors, dining rooms, and living rooms. *Private spaces,* such as bedrooms, are generally used just by the family. *Service spaces* are places to accomplish the work of running a home, such as the kitchen, laundry room, and workshop.

By studying these three types of interior spaces, historians can get a sense of how families in the past lived and how lifestyles changed.

187

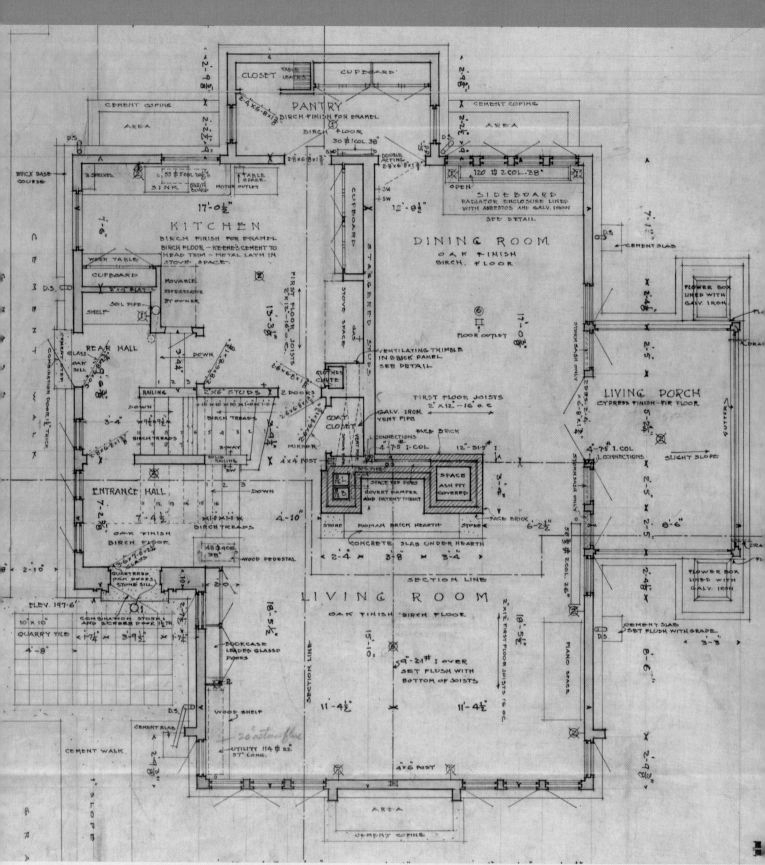

The first floor of the Beebes' Prairie School home

Public Spaces

Look at the floor plans for the Elsinger and Beebe homes and study the public spaces that the architects designed. Notice the types of spaces and how they are arranged.

○ **What do these public spaces say about how the home owners lived and how they entertained guests?**

Service Spaces

Keeping a home and its family in good shape takes a lot of work. Houses have plumbing, heating systems, and electrical systems that need maintenance. People need maintenance, too, such as feeding and cleaning. When architects design homes, they consider how all of this work is to be done.

○ **Study each home to see how the service spaces are designed. Where are the bathrooms? Which house would be easier to clean? Can you tell if the family or servants did most of the work?**

The first floor of the Elsingers' Victorian home

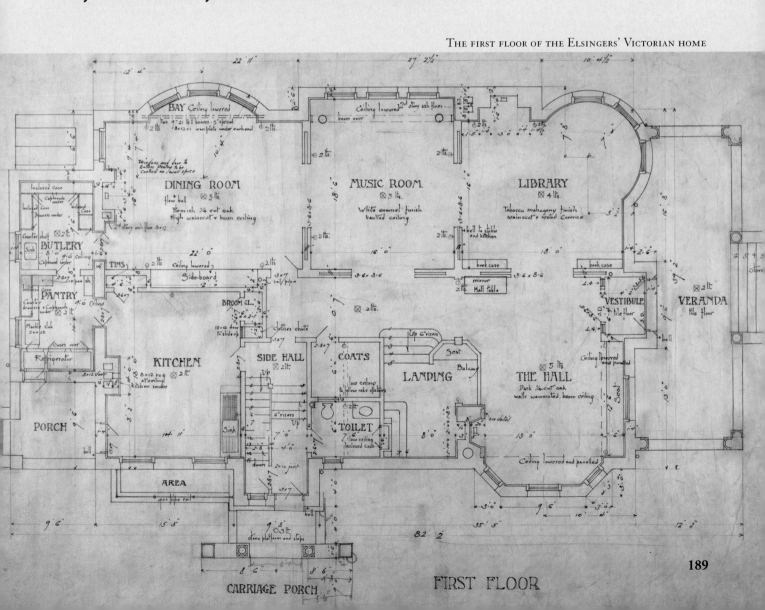

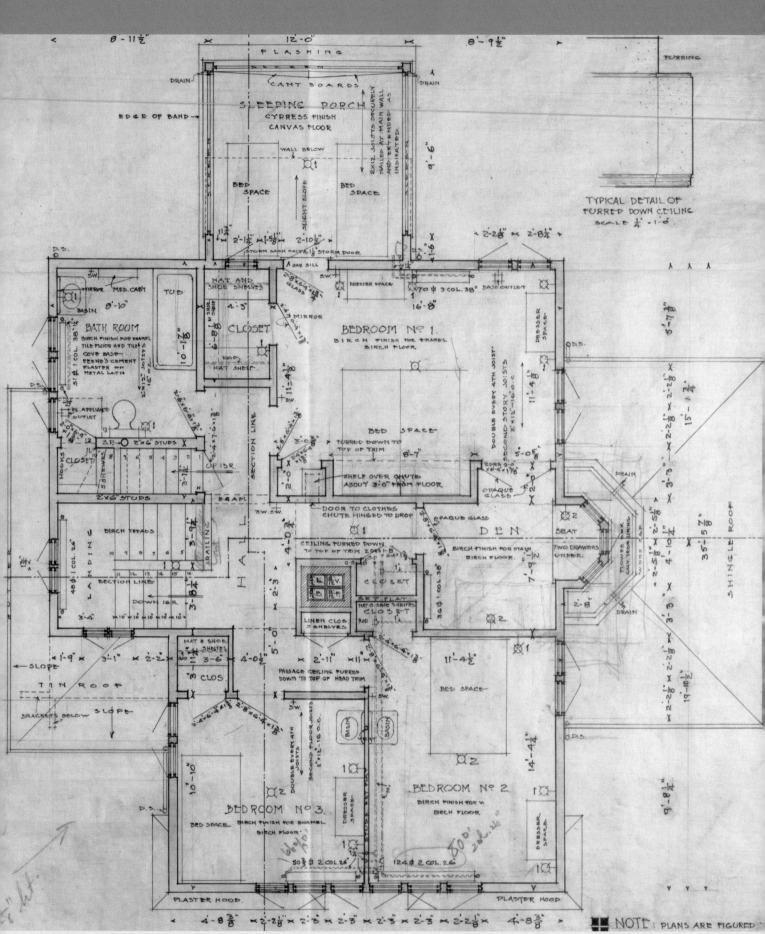

The second floor of the Beebes' Prairie School home

Private Spaces

In many homes, the private spaces where the family can relax are on the second floor. These spaces are mainly bedrooms (called chambers in the Victorian era), but sometimes there are offices or dens.

🔍 **Look at the private spaces in each of these second-floor plans. Are there differences between them? What do these differences tell us about how the people lived?**

LIFESTYLE CHANGES

Historians study the past using all types of evidence, not just books and papers. By studying homes built at the turn of the twentieth century, historians can see how people's lives were changing.

🔍 **Think about all the differences between Victorian and Prairie School homes. What do these differences tell us about how family life changed around 1900? Now it is your turn to be an architect as well as a historian. Use what you have learned to design a floor plan for either a Victorian home or a Prairie School home.**

THE SECOND FLOOR OF THE ELSINGERS' VICTORIAN HOME

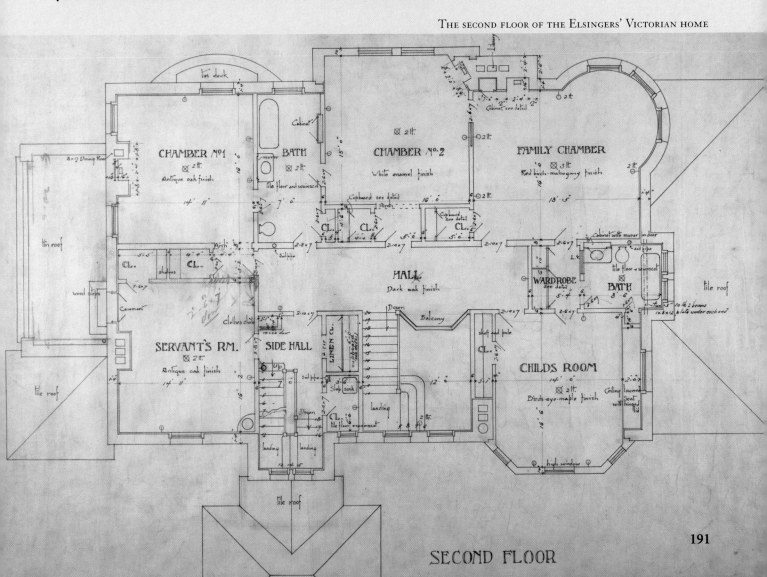

SECOND FLOOR

191

MINNEAPOLIS TURNS OUT IN FORCE TO WITNESS ITS FIRST SUFFRAGE PARADE AND OUTDOOR DEMONSTR

Nearly 2,000 March In Suffrage Parade

Caught by Camera When "Votes for Women" Par

Continued from First Page.

Second avenue side of the Church of the Redeemer had the American flag draped about the windows. Women had taken possession of the band stand diagonally across the street, which was covered with yellow bunting.

Cheers From Bank Building.

Cheers and handclapping came from the McKnight building, and more cheers from the Security Bank building, which was decorated with small American flags.

"Yankee Doodle" broke from the band and "Columbia the Gem of the Ocean" followed.

The parade made the turn into Nicollet to face a crowd of people such as has been seen along that thoroughfare only on days of big turnouts. Curbs and sidewalks were lined; it was difficult to pass at all, and there were lines of people four and five deep, on the asphalt paving.

Suffrage States Shown.

Mrs. A. H. Bright led the Woman Suffrage Association of Minnesota, and the crowd cheered the organization and cheered the several young women each of whom carried a banner representing a state where women now have the right to vote. Dr. Ethel Hurd led the Political Equality Club in the second division of which Mrs. Jessie Haw was marshal. The crowds applauded when the big American flag, borne blanket-like, its sides and corners held by marching women moved past. Miss Anna Bloomquist of the Scandinavian Suffrage Association led that organization and Mrs. Andreas Ueland, who marched in that section, caried a small pennant. The Socialist Suffrage club was headed by Mrs. Guy Williams and Mrs. Thomas Van Lear.

Temperance Cause Represented.

Miss Blanche McDonald, marshall of the third section, wore a red colonial hat and led the home makers under Mrs. Carl Wallace, the Woman's Christian Temperance Union, under Mrs. Mary Girard Andrews and the Prohibitionists under Mrs. George F. Wells.

Miss Ruth Byers, headed the fourth section, the Scandinavian Women in National costume forming the lead. This was one of the most effective divisions of the entire line. The native costumes of Sweden, Norway, Denmark and Finland were worn. The flags of these nations flapped in the breeze and the band played the national airs.

Banner Attracts Notice.

Professions were represented in the fourth section. Physicians were headed by Miss Grace Harrison, nurses by Miss Ethel Plympton, attorneys by Miss Virginia Blythe, social workers by Miss Kate Finkle, librarians by Miss Ruth Rosholt, and teachers by Miss Laurie Stahley. The 1915 club came next, led by [...]ler, and the [...] women and [...] Miss Lillian [...] Fox. Some [...] headquarters [...] to the advisab[...] ner that her[...] prominent in [...] dealers and gamblers are unanimous in opposing woman suffrage."

neers and afterward participated in the demonstration in the auditorium.

In the forefront of the St. Paul division was Will J. Massingham, author and poet.

More than 1,500 women attended the suffrage meeting in the St. Paul auditorium yesterday. The principal addresses were by Ole Sageng and Mrs. Minona Jones of Chicago. Following the parade the women marched to Rice park and then boarded cars for Minneapolis. The number in the parade was estimated at 900, only seventy of whom were men.

A resolution was passed calling on congress to pass the Bristow-Mondell resolution, now before that body, which would provide for equal suffrage.

BELIEVE IN EQUAL SUFFRAGE

to right, F. Corser, F. W. [...] Civic and Commerce as-

participation therein with[...] ng ourselves of the most [...]sistance we can possibly [...]rking out the problems of [...] society.

"But to say that man needs woman's assistance at the ballot box is only half

HITS AT OPPOSITION

By 1914, the suffrage movement had gained wide support both locally and nationally. The May 2 parade in Minneapolis was big news.

Insert [...] phine Sch[...] she was astride her parade.

NAMES [...] IN T[...]

When [...] suffrage [...] Raymond [...] those in [...] R. M. [...] der, W. [...] Sprague, [...] man Men[...] Roberts, [...] Dr. E. F. C[...] Sneller, [...] Edwards, [...] D. T. Jon[...] Thorp, Ke[...]ler, S. O[...] F. Corser [...] Livingsto[...] Purdy, W[...] rand, H. [...] Stavenhe[...] Schwartz [...] neth Tay[...] Walter, [...] Youngdah[...] S. Rodge[...] John Low[...] Ernest L [...] tel of Ho[...] mer Mor[...]

1887
U.S. Congress passes the Dawes Act to allow allotment on Indian reservations.

1893–1894
Massive forest fires destroy the towns of Virginia, Merritt, Hinckley, and Mountain Iron, killing more than 400 people.

1896
U.S. Congress reduces the size of the Red Lake Reservation in order to sell timber and farmland to lumber companies and land speculators.

1904
Newspaper reporter Lincoln Steffens publishes *The Shame of the Cities*.

1905
Minnesota legislature passes timberland conservation law to slow the rate of logging in forests.

1906
U.S. Congress passes the Pure Food and Drug Act to help ensure that processed foods and drugs are safe.

1908
A major forest fire wipes out Chisholm and the surrounding area.

By the late 1800s and early 1900s, Minnesota was a home for people of many different racial and ethnic backgrounds. But even though Minnesota's population was becoming more diverse, its people were becoming more dependent on each other. Citizens were making goods to sell and buying more manufactured goods, rather than supplying everything they needed themselves. Farmers, for example—with the help of new and better machinery—were producing more crops for market and less for themselves. At the same time, many Minnesotans were moving away from farmlands to live in the state's bustling towns and cities. They were joining large communities where the actions of one person could directly affect the lives of many others—in good ways and bad ways.

As the towns and cities grew, old ideas about self-sufficiency began giving way to a new concern for what some people—including President Theodore Roosevelt—called the **"common good."** The idea was that individuals should work to improve life not just for themselves, but also for society as a whole. Many Minnesotans worked hard during the late 1800s

LOOK FOR

- What was the "common good"?
- Why couldn't women vote?
- What was public health like at the turn of the twentieth century?
- Why did Minnesotans begin to protect the forests?
- What obstacles did African Americans face?
- How did allotment and boarding schools affect the Ojibwe?
- Why did the legislature create the Commission of Public Safety, and what did it do?

KEY TERMS

common good
Progressivism
reformer
suffrage
conserve
assimilate
allotment

common good: a popular attitude that people should work for social and political changes that benefit everyone

1909	1913	1914	1917	1918	1919	1920
National Association for the Advancement of Colored People (NAACP) is founded in New York City.	Minnesota legislature passes a workers compensation law.	Woman suffrage parade is held in Minneapolis. World War I begins in Europe.	United States enters World War I. Minnesota Commission of Public Safety is created by the state legislature.	World War I ends.	Minnesota becomes the fifteenth state to approve the Nineteenth Amendment, which grants women the right to vote in federal elections.	Prohibition goes into effect to limit the sale of alcohol. The Nineteenth Amendment becomes law.

and early 1900s to act in ways that they believed contributed to the common good. Sometimes they succeeded. Sometimes they did not.

Common Problems

As communities grew, people began to identify common problems that needed to be solved for the good of everyone. This new awareness of the problems plaguing society led to a movement called **Progressivism.** Progressive **reformers** sought to improve people's lives by organizing groups and campaigning for government changes. The targets of their reforms included the government, corporations, and social problems.

In Minnesota, Progressives came from all parts of the state and from all political parties. Almost every governor between 1900 and 1920—Republican and Democrat—pushed for reforms that many people considered progressive.

PROGRESSIVE TARGET: GOVERNMENT

By the early 1900s, many Minnesotans came to believe that government itself was broken and needed fixing. So reformers set out to reform government. Sometimes the reformers went after government officials. Sometimes they set out to change the way officials were elected in the first place.

Government Corruption

Reformers were especially concerned with corruption in city governments. In 1904, Lincoln Steffens, a New York reporter, wrote a book called *The Shame of the Cities.* One chapter described how the mayor of Minneapolis had taken bribes from illegal gambling operations. Many Minnesotans were outraged by this and other similar incidents, and they began to demand changes at all levels of the government. State and local politicians responded to these demands by passing new laws designed to clean up government actions and make the government more responsive to the people.

Votes for Women

Some Minnesota women had been asking for the right to vote, or **suffrage,** since the founding of the state, but they'd had little success. By 1900, they could vote only for the members of school and library boards. Opponents argued that women were homemakers, supported and protected by

Progressivism: a movement to solve various social and political problems through government action

reformer: a person who supports changes that are intended to improve society

suffrage: the right to vote

The popular book *The Shame of the Cities* exposed corruption in Minneapolis's city government.

THE SHAME OF THE CITIES

LINCOLN STEFFENS

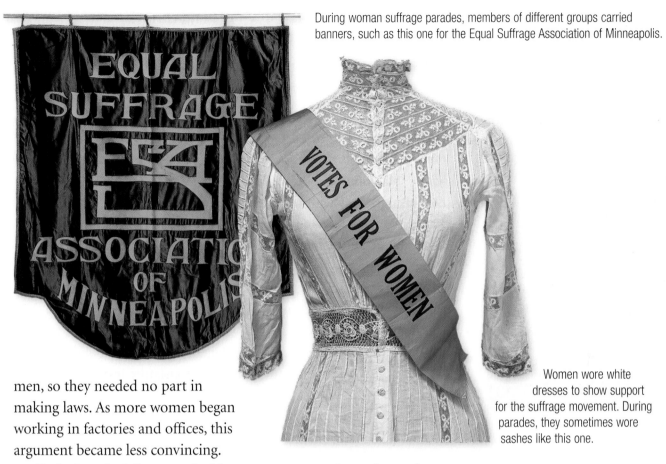

During woman suffrage parades, members of different groups carried banners, such as this one for the Equal Suffrage Association of Minneapolis.

EQUAL SUFFRAGE ASSOCIATION OF MINNEAPOLIS

VOTES FOR WOMEN

Women wore white dresses to show support for the suffrage movement. During parades, they sometimes wore sashes like this one.

men, so they needed no part in making laws. As more women began working in factories and offices, this argument became less convincing.

Each time the Minnesota legislature met, women brought up the issue. They pointed to other states, like Wyoming, that already had woman suffrage. But still, the lawmakers refused. At last, in 1919, the state legislature allowed women to vote for president. A year later, the Nineteenth Amendment to the U.S. Constitution gave American women the same voting rights as men.

CLARA UELAND

Woman Suffrage Leader

Clara Ueland was a former schoolteacher, the wife of a prominent lawyer, and mother of six children. She was a leader in the movement to open free kindergartens in Minneapolis. She also campaigned for clean streets, clean water, and clean air. In 1910, Ueland decided to take up another cause: woman suffrage.

Ueland started hosting suffrage fundraising parties at her Minneapolis home. In May of 1914, Ueland organized a huge woman suffrage parade in Minneapolis. Later that year, the Minnesota Woman Suffrage Association rewarded her efforts by electing her president.

Ueland embraced her new role. In January of 1915, she went to the state capitol to support women's right to vote. Some lawmakers argued that women actually were better off without the vote. Ueland disagreed. "It is utter nonsense," she said. "It is foolish. What greater influence can any body of persons have than the possession of the right to vote?"

When the Nineteenth Amendment became law in 1920, Clara Ueland was ecstatic. "It is my happiest day," she said.

PROGRESSIVE TARGET: CORPORATIONS

Government was not the only institution that the Progressives wanted to reform. Big business was another major target. The reformers believed that corporations had become too powerful. They demanded that government step in to protect workers and consumers.

Railroad Monopolies

One of the first big fights over corporate power began in 1901, when Minnesota's railroad tycoon, James J. Hill, tried to merge his Great Northern Railway with two other major railroads. He planned to create a single company to control most of the railroad traffic in the northwestern part of the country. Many Minnesotans objected to Hill's plan. They thought one company should not control, or monopolize, such a large part of the nation's transportation system. Minnesota Governor Samuel Van Sant agreed, and he organized those who were against the merger. In 1904, he and other merger opponents cheered when the U.S. Supreme Court decided against Hill's railroad monopoly.

In the years after 1904, the Minnesota legislature imposed a series of rules and regulations to curb corporate power. They included regulations on rail rates, insurance rates, and factory conditions. Later laws established a system for workers compensation and minimum wages, also limiting the number of hours women and children could work.

Logging Practices

By the late 1800s, the vast pine forests of northern Minnesota were beginning to disappear. Lumber companies were cutting down white pines as fast as they could, leaving behind cutover brush—scarred landscapes littered with leftover branches, limbs, and stumps. Reformers in Minnesota argued that lumber companies needed to be restrained in order to protect the few forests that remained, but they had a hard time getting anyone to listen.

Governor Samuel Van Sant's progressive reform efforts made him popular with the public, but not with the leaders of corporations.

An uncut pine forest still remained in northern Minnesota in 1903.

After the October 1918 forest fire raced through the town, Cloquet was left in ruins.

Then disaster struck. Not just once, but repeatedly.

In 1894, a huge fire fueled by cutover brush destroyed the town of Hinckley and burned 160,000 acres of surrounding forests and farmland. Four hundred thirteen people died. Over the next 25 years, a series of similar fires devastated several other north woods communities. In 1908, the mining town of Chisholm was destroyed. In 1910, Baudette and Spooner, near the Canadian border, went up in flames. The worst of the big forest fires struck in 1918, when a firestorm consumed Moose Lake, Cloquet (kloh-KAY), and 25 other towns, killing 483 people.

Each of these fires helped convince Minnesotans that the state's forests needed to be protected and **conserved,** with some made off-limits to lumber companies. Lawmakers responded by enacting a series of laws designed to prevent forest fires. They created the Office of Fire Commissioner and, later, the Minnesota State Forest Service, and the University of Minnesota opened a school of forestry.

conserve: to preserve or carefully use something, particularly natural resources

In the 1920s, farmers used explosives to remove tree stumps and transform cutover areas to farmland.

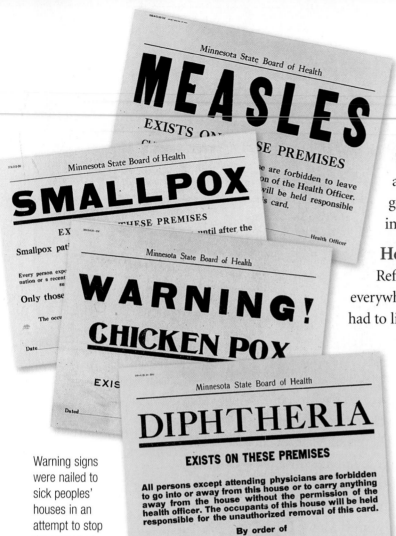

Warning signs were nailed to sick peoples' houses in an attempt to stop the spread of contagious diseases.

PROGRESSIVE TARGET: SOCIAL PROBLEMS

Minnesotans of the late 1800s faced a wide variety of social problems that often seemed beyond their control. Progressive reformers attacked these problems by demanding government action and by banding together to increase their social and political power.

Health Dangers

Reformers saw threats to public health nearly everywhere they looked. In cities and towns, women had to lift up their long skirts to avoid dragging them over filthy streets and sidewalks covered with horse manure and tobacco spit. The carcasses of horses, cattle, hogs, and other animals were regularly seen floating in the Mississippi River near an intake pipe that supplied the city's drinking water. In St. Paul, a police officer and his wife lost three of their children in one day to typhoid, a contagious disease spread through water. The spread of disease was an increasing concern as people packed into the densely populated cities. A flu epidemic in 1918 and 1919 killed 10,100 Minnesotans. Reformers demanded that the government do something.

By the turn of the twentieth century, reformers were beginning to make progress. Minnesota's State Board of Health was working actively to prevent and control disease. It promoted good sanitation and sponsored laws requiring quarantines against diseases such as smallpox and diphtheria. It also set up vaccination programs.

The state and federal governments also began making rules to improve the quality and safety of food. Minnesotans, like other Americans, were buying more and more food that had been processed in factories. They wanted to know that the food they were eating was safe. The State Board of Health had been an early supporter of food safety regulations. In 1906, the federal government enacted the Pure Food and Drug Act and a new meat inspection law to help make sure that Americans' food would be safe.

Racial Discrimination

In the years following the Civil War, Minnesota had enacted a series of civil rights laws designed to protect the rights of all Minnesotans,

AMANDA AND THOMAS LYLES

Community Activists

Very few African Americans lived in Minnesota when Amanda and Thomas Lyles arrived in St. Paul in 1876. Those who did live in the state experienced racism regularly. They often were unwelcome in hotels and restaurants. They were unable to rent or purchase homes in many neighborhoods. Almost from the moment they arrived, Amanda and Thomas Lyles set out to help their fellow African Americans cope with inequalities.

Thomas opened a barbershop when he and Amanda arrived. He entered the real estate business, buying homes that he would rent or sell to other African Americans. He and Amanda helped found a church in St. Paul, and she became the choir director and organist. She also started a hair-styling business, and Thomas became the first African American mortician in Minnesota when he opened a funeral home in 1906.

Thomas was an active member of the Republican Party, and he is credited with convincing the mayor of St. Paul to hire the city's first black policeman in 1881. He also helped launch an African American newspaper and a publishing company.

Amanda Lyles devoted much of her time to important causes. She called for laws to protect black people from mobs of angry whites, who would lynch, or execute, blacks without a trial. She supported the woman suffrage movement. She spoke out against the selling of alcohol. She called for an end to job and housing discrimination. She also raised money to establish an orphanage and school for African American children in Chicago.

When Thomas Lyles died in 1920, Amanda Lyles took over the funeral home business. She successfully ran Lyles Funeral Home until her death in 1937.

including African Americans. But the state's growing black population still faced many obstacles. White Minnesotans often broke the law and discriminated against African Americans.

African Americans responded to this discrimination by organizing into groups that would take action. In 1887, black leaders in the Twin Cities rallied support for William Hazel, an African American architect who had been refused lodging at a local hotel. With their help, Hazel sued the hotel and won, but he was awarded just $25 in damages. Many African Americans were insulted by the award. They believed the hotel should have received a harsher punishment for discriminating against black people. Many of the same African American leaders who had supported Hazel then formed the Minnesota chapter of the Protective and Industrial League—a national organization designed to promote and protect the civil rights of blacks. It was just the first of several civil rights organizations formed in Minnesota during the late 1800s and early 1900s. Several local black leaders went on to lead national civil rights organizations.

Good for Whom?

Minnesotans who claimed they were acting in the public interest fought for many changes they thought would make the state a better place to live. But sometimes their efforts backfired. Changes that were intended

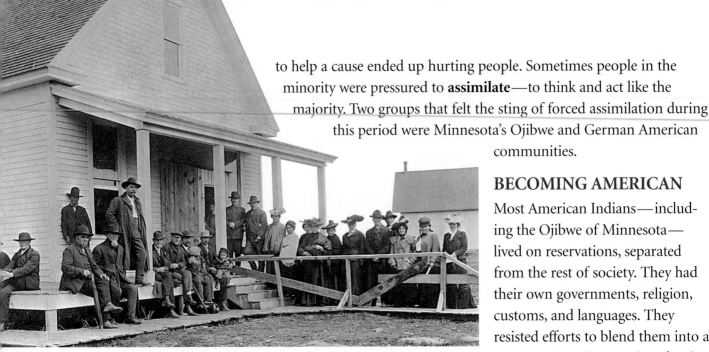

to help a cause ended up hurting people. Sometimes people in the minority were pressured to **assimilate**—to think and act like the majority. Two groups that felt the sting of forced assimilation during this period were Minnesota's Ojibwe and German American communities.

In 1905, Ojibwe gathered at the White Earth Agency to register for their allotment land.

assimilate: to adopt the values and habits of a larger group

allotment: a share, or portion, determined by a plan for dividing a larger quantity

BECOMING AMERICAN

Most American Indians—including the Ojibwe of Minnesota—lived on reservations, separated from the rest of society. They had their own governments, religion, customs, and languages. They resisted efforts to blend them into a common American society dominated by white people. Once again, lawmakers tried to overcome the Indians' resistance to white culture by starting two new programs. One tried to change Indians' traditional relationship with the land. The other encouraged Indian children to become more like white children.

Allotment

By the late 1800s, the federal government's policies toward Indians focused mostly on one goal: ending the practice of Indians owning land in common. In 1887, the federal government passed a law named the Dawes Act that used a policy called **allotment.** Under allotment, reservation lands—including those belonging to Minnesota's Ojibwe—were divided among members of the tribe. Each family was supposed to receive 160 acres, which could then be farmed. This policy was meant to encourage the Indians to give up their ways of life and blend into the larger society. But it did not work out that way.

In Minnesota, many Ojibwe were cheated out of their land. The Dawes Act said that the land left over after allotment could be sold to outsiders for settlement or lumbering. Only a few of those who kept their land became self-sufficient farmers. As the years went by, so many Indians sold their land—through fraud or by force—that non-Indians eventually owned most reservation land. The poverty that was the unintended result of allotment still haunts Ojibwe communities today. Only the Ojibwe at the Red Lake Reservation kept their reservation intact. They refused to accept allotment and continued to hold their land in common.

Boarding Schools

In 1893, the federal government began requiring Indian children—including many from Minnesota's Ojibwe reservations—to go to

WEKWAA-GIIZHIG

Ojibwe Boarding School Student

Wekwaa-giizhig (WAY-KWAH-GEE-zhihg) was six years old in 1896, when he and his two sisters were taken against their parents' wishes to attend a boarding school in South Dakota. He had grown up on Minnesota's White Earth Reservation and had not spent much time away from his family.

Over the next six years, the teachers tried to make Wekwaa-giizhig stop thinking and acting like an Ojibwe. They gave him a new name—John Rogers. They told him to stop speaking the Ojibwe language. They discouraged visits and letters from his family. Eventually, Wekwaa-giizhig convinced his sisters to cut his long hair so he would look like the rest of the boys.

But Wekwaa-giizhig never forgot that he was an Ojibwe. In 1902, he returned to the reservation with his sisters. Years later he remembered what it was like to see his mother again:

> She looked up from her work, and we children made a mad scramble toward her. . . . What a reunion that was! She endeavored to gather us all into her arms at once. She started talking joyously, but we couldn't understand very well what she said, for we had forgotten much of the Indian language during our six years away from home. But all that mattered was we were welcome here in mother's wigwam—the home of our birth.

After spending a year with their mother, Wekwaa-giizhig and his sisters left again for boarding school. This one was closer—in the town of White Earth on their own reservation.

boarding schools. Usually, these schools were built off the reservations. Children who attended them lived away from their families and were taught to reject Indian ways of life.

Life at the boarding schools was unlike life on the reservation. One of the first things that the Indian students had to do was learn English. They had no choice. "They told us they'd wash our mouths out with soap if we talked our own language," recalled one former student. The Indian children took courses in reading, writing, math, history, and geography. But they also had to learn other skills that white educators considered valuable. Boys learned how to be farmers, shoemakers, blacksmiths, and carpenters. Girls were taught how to be seamstresses, maids, and farm wives. The courses were designed to prepare Indian children for lives off the reservation, but many who attended boarding schools returned to the reservation. Their ties to the Ojibwe homelands were strong—too strong to be broken by the boarding school.

The government eventually realized its policy of sending Indian children to boarding schools had not worked as they had hoped. Instead, it moved toward opening day schools on reservations. These were much more popular among Indians because children returned to their homes each day after classes. By 1910, Minnesota had more day schools for Indians than boarding schools.

At boarding schools, girls and boys often attended separate classes. **How is this boarding school classroom similar to or different from your own?**

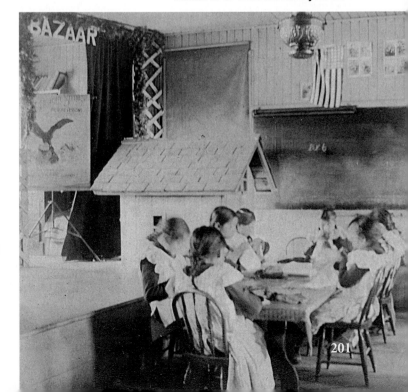

The Central Powers—so named because they were located in central Europe—were surrounded by Allied Nations in World War I.

World War I

PROVING PATRIOTISM

In April of 1917, the United States entered what people at the time called "The Great War"—World War I. The war had started in Europe in 1914. On one side were the Allies—led by Great Britain, France, Russia, and Italy. On the other side were the Central Powers—led by Germany, Austria-Hungary, and Turkey. At first, most Americans and most Minnesotans wanted the United States to stay out of the war because it involved issues of European power that did not seem relevant to the United States. But those who believed that the United States should join the war on the Allies' side worked hard to change people's minds. They argued that a German victory would shift the balance of power in Europe in ways that would hurt the United States. They started to spread stories that German soldiers had tortured and killed Belgian women and children. As the war raged on and German submarines attacked American ships, the United States could no longer stay neutral. In April of 1917, President Woodrow Wilson asked Congress to declare war on Germany and its partners. After that, most Americans supported the war effort. Those who did not were often accused of being disloyal.

Fear of disloyalty spread through Minnesota like a disease. Shortly after war was declared, the Minnesota legislature—with almost no opposition—created the Commission of Public Safety (CPS). The CPS had power to do almost anything to support the war effort. It spied on organizations suspected of disloyalty. And it ordered all Minnesotans who were not American citizens to register with the state. German Americans and German immigrants were among the CPS's prime targets.

Americans were swept by super-patriotism. In blind support of the U. S. war effort, many thought everything German was bad. Schools stopped teaching German. Families with names like Schmidt tried to prove their loyalty by changing their names to Smith. People no longer referred to sauerkraut by its German name—they called it "liberty cabbage."

Minnesotans from Hutchinson showed their support for the war effort at a parade in November 1917. They carried signs with anti-German slogans. "Hun" was an insult that compared Germans to a barbarian people called Huns who invaded Europe at the end of the Roman era.

LOUIS A. FRITSCHE

Mayor of New Ulm

Louis A. Fritsche was more than just New Ulm's mayor. He was one of Minnesota's most distinguished surgeons—among the first in the state to perform a successful appendectomy. But in 1917, in his role as mayor of New Ulm, Fritsche briefly became one of the most despised men in the state.

Fritsche had presided over the public meeting in which the people of New Ulm asked the government to stop sending German Americans to fight in World War I. His involvement with that meeting made him an easy target for Minnesotans who believed the people of New Ulm were disloyal. A month after the meeting, Fritsche received a letter from an old friend. The letter put into words the kind of hatred that Fritsche faced:

> It gives me great distress to hear of the treason, which you are manifesting toward your country in which you have prospered and enjoyed life exceptionally for many years. I hold a pleasant memory of you—now it is replaced with detestation. I despise a traitor… I hope that I am not truly informed concerning your position, but if I am I hope that I will be selected to individually carry out a sentence of death upon you by a loyal court of martial law.

The uproar over the meeting eventually forced Fritsche from office, but Fritsche did not stay down for long. When the war was over, the people of New Ulm reelected him in a landslide victory.

In the summer of 1917, anti-German feelings reached a new level. German Americans in New Ulm held a peaceful meeting to discuss the war. The speakers talked of loyalty to the U. S. and the importance of obeying laws. But they also agreed to ask the government not to send their young men overseas to fight against their own kinfolk. This did not sit well with many Minnesotans. Newspapers around the state called the people of New Ulm traitors. Governor Joseph Burnquist even removed the German American mayor of New Ulm from office because he feared the mayor was disloyal.

By the time World War I ended in November of 1918, it had left a number of permanent scars on Minnesota: 3,480 Minnesotans had died in the war, and nearly 5,000 had been wounded. But Minnesota suffered other casualties as well. Many German Americans in the state felt bitter about the way they had been treated during the war. Many other Minnesotans were embarrassed that their state had stooped to persecution, treating some of its own people cruelly.

These events of the late 1800s and early 1900s demonstrated how positive *and* negative things could happen when Minnesotans worked for what they believed was the common good. Thanks largely to the efforts of the Progressives, government and businesses became more accountable to the people. Water was made safer to drink and forests were protected. Women gained the right to vote. But the events of this period also raised some troubling questions. Who is to decide what the common good is? Should people be forced to think or act a certain way if a majority thinks it's in the public interest?

New Ulm

Why Is Miss R. Sick?

Medical reports from 1907 show the case of 14-year-old Miss R. For a week she complained of feeling sick, but she kept going to school—she didn't want to miss the neighborhood sleigh ride, and she couldn't attend an evening event without going to school. But the night of the sleigh ride, things took a turn for the worse. Miss R. began to have chills, to shake, and to run a fever. Rapidly she grew worse. Over the next few days, her fever climbed to 105°F.

Her doctor didn't know what was wrong with her. At first he thought she was having an attack of the flu. When the fever did not subside, he thought she might have pneumonia. She could hardly eat, and at night she was delirious. Finally, when red spots appeared on her stomach, her doctor knew: Miss R. had typhoid fever.

In 1907 there was no cure for typhoid fever. Doctors weren't exactly sure where it came from. For weeks, Miss R.'s parents bathed her and fed her broth. Slowly her fever died down. She grew stronger. Miss R. was lucky, but many others in the early 1900s were not.

TOWN OF COUNTY OF STATE OF MINNESOTA.

Married, Single, or Widowed.	Age Years	Months	Days	Place of Birth (Township or City.)	Date of Arrival in Minnesota Month	Day	Year	Disease, or Cause of Death.	Place of Death (Township or City)	Occupation	Names of Parents	Birth-Place of Parents	When Registered
Single	1	10	2	Fillmore	Aug	2	1879	Spinal Fever	Fillmore	—	Wm E Ploof / Margret	Canida / Minn	Dec 28th
Married	58		1	Ireland	Apr	26	1855	Typhoid Fever	Fillmore	Farmer	Not Known		
Single		10	6	Minn	Apr	19	1880	Lung fever	Wykoff		Milford N Beardsley / Myra	NY / NY	Dec 31st
Single	1	7		Minn	May	23	1880	Typhoid fever	Wykoff		Lawran G Kilborn / Fanny	Ohio / Illinois	Dec 31st
Single	1	10		Minn	Aug	11	1879	Spinal Fever	Wykoff		Thomas Kelley / M Ellen	Illinois / Wisconsin	Dec 31st
Married	31	8	21	Germany	Mar	22	1869	Child Birth	Fillmore		Not Known	Germany	Dec 31st
Single			12	Fillmore	June	17	18[illegible]		Fillmore		Chas Tyse / Mary	Germany	Dec 31st
Married	31	—		Wisconsin	Nov		72	Child-Birth	Wykoff		Fredrick Erdman / Mary	Germany	Dec 31st
Single	84			Ireland			1868	Old Age	Fillmore		Edward Cummings / Cathrine	Ireland	Dec 31st
Married	61	3	27	Canida	June	22	1856	Typhoid fever	Wykoff		Joseph Kilborn / Huldah	NY	Dec 31st
Single	1	5	19	Minn	Apr	27	1880	Typhoid Fever	Wykoff		Peter Jorris / Della	Wisconsin / Ind	Lumber Merch[illegible]
Mar	63			Newyork	May		1855	Lung fever	Fillmore	Farmer	Not Known		Dec 31st
Single	12	7	7	Minn	Oct	28	1868	Typhoid Fever	Fillmore		Wm Rundell / Dora	Illinois / Ind	
Single			19	Minn	Sept	5	1881		Fillmore		Wm Smith / Mary	New York	Dec 31st
			1	Minn	Nov	18	1881		Fillmore		Herman Affeldt / Albertina	Germany / Wisconsin	Dec 31st
Married	82			New York	Mar	18	1868	Typhoid fever	Fillmore	Farmer	Austin Clark / Pheba	New York	Dec 31st
Single		8	24	Fillmore	June	19	1881	Typhoid fever	Fillmore		Ira G Clark / Caroline	New York / Ohio	Dec 31st
			1	Minn	Mar	0	1881		Fillmore		John Stender / Johanna	Germany	Dec 31st
Married	59	7		Germany	Apr	14	1874	Typhoid fever	Fillmore	Farmer	Michael Wollman / Katie	Germany	

Study the Fillmore death registry. **From what causes did people die in 1881?**

Today children in Minnesota do not die from, or even get, typhoid fever. The past 100 years have seen a revolution in the field of medicine. During this time, public health reformers in Minnesota have fought to control disease and to get people to care about something called "public health." They have understood that what we do as a community affects everyone's health. Dirty water, polluted streets, and crowded conditions can make all of us sick.

Study this photo of city life from the early 1900s. Consider what you know about disease today. **What health risks did these children face?**

On the next few pages you will find several primary sources from the late 1800s and early 1900s. These sources tell you about typhoid fever, a major health crisis facing Minnesota citizens during the turn of the twentieth century. The sources will also tell you how public health reformers tried to solve the typhoid fever problem.

🔵 **Use your Investigation Guide to keep track of what you learn about typhoid fever. As you go, track what public health reformers did to solve the crisis. Afterward, it will be your turn to investigate and fight a disease.**

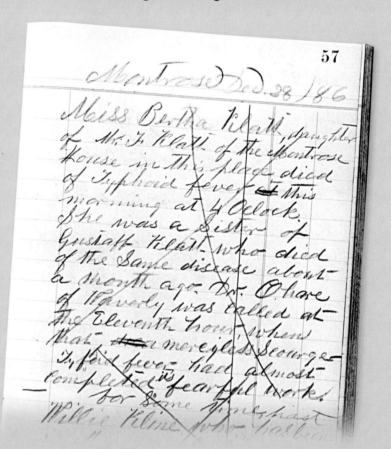

Examine the 1886 diary from the Thomas Gunn family on the right. **How did typhoid fever affect the Gunn family?**

WHAT IS TYPHOID FEVER?

Typhoid fever begins with a high fever and terrible chills. Victims soon find themselves too weak to stand. Headaches, vomiting, and diarrhea often set in after the first few days. Typhoid fever lasts several weeks, after which time the disease will either go away or progress into pneumonia, intestinal bleeding, and even death.

Today we know that typhoid fever is caused by a specific bacterium—a germ—that grows in water, milk, or solid food that has been contaminated by human or animal feces. We know that typhoid fever is not transmitted through the air. But it took doctors and public health reformers a long time to learn about the disease.

LEARNING ABOUT TYPHOID FEVER

It wasn't until 1864 that a French scientist named Louis Pasteur published his "germ theory." It stated that disease was spread by microscopic organisms that survived in garbage, body fluids, and human and animal waste. At the time, this was a radical idea. It seemed foolish to most people in the 1800s. The fact that these invisible germs traveled through the air, in the water, and on the feet of insects seemed even more ridiculous. Most people in Minnesota did not believe in the germ theory, at first. But progressive doctors caught on quickly.

STATE BOARD OF HEALTH
OF MINNESOTA.
TRACT NO. 3, 1881.

TYPHOID FEVER,

HOW TO PREVENT IT, OR IF IT OCCURS HOW TO STOP ITS SPREAD.

TYPHOID FEVER.

Typhoid fever is at the date of this report, threatening to again become epidemic in the State, and the probabilities are that the fall of 1881 will be accompanied by its unusual prevalence. The State Board of Health therefore repeat the statements already made in various ways:

1st. That typhoid fever is peculiarly associated with filth in air and water, so much so that it is called the "filth fever." Therefore when it occurs, in a family, all premises should be thoroughly examined, especially cess pools, privies, manure heaps, cellars, and every other place where decaying vegetable or animal matter is ever permitted to collect. The chief danger is that the water supply has been infected by leachings from such collections, through the soil.

2d. The disease is infectious by means of the discharges from its victims which gain entrance to the bodies of other people, chiefly through water, but also probably by soiled clothing or bedding, and possibly by means of the poison floating in the air.

3d. The peculiar poison of the disease probably escapes from the bodies of the sick in the discharges from the bowels alone.

4th. That if these discharges are thoroughly disinfected immediately on their escape from the body, the probabilities are that the spread of the disease beyond the sufferer will be reduced to the

Examine this brochure circulated by the State Board of Health. **What facts about typhoid fever did the doctors have correct in 1881? Can you find any mistaken conclusions?**

Typhoid Fever: This disease killed 4,532 persons in Minnesota during the past ten years. Minneapolis and St. Paul are but a few miles apart. Minneapolis uses a polluted river supply and is never free from typhoid fever. St. Paul has a safe drinking supply of water and has an extremely low typhoid rate, even with its imported cases. It is time that this state was waking up to its responsibilities in protecting the municipal and rural water supply.

Study the State Board of Health report from a meeting in 1899. **What did the board want the state to do to end typhoid fever?**

Public Health Fair, mid 1900s

What are this cartoon and the public health fair display trying to tell people?

St. Paul Pioneer Press, 1909

Doctors published and distributed thousands of informational brochures to help the people of Minnesota learn about dangerous diseases like typhoid fever.

While the germ theory was catching on in universities, ordinary people were slow to make changes that stopped the spread of germs. Health care reformers worked hard to spread the word—and to pass laws that enforced sanitation.

Public health reformers distributed educational pamphlets, hung posters, and published articles and cartoons in local newspapers. They even hosted health fairs, with informational booths, speakers, and games to educate people about disease. But still, in 1910, almost 700 Minnesotans died of typhoid fever, a preventable disease.

PROGRESSIVE SOLUTIONS FOR TYPHOID FEVER

Typhoid fever had one main solution: clean water. But providing clean water for people was not an easy task. By 1900, most public water sources were contaminated. Outhouses were built too close to water sources. Garbage and sewage were dumped directly into lakes and rivers.

Where did people get their drinking water in the 1800s? The 1854 photo above shows one source.

Developing a safe water supply would take organization and lots of money. Who could be trusted with such a big job? At first, private companies charged people for clean water. But stopping the spread of typhoid fever meant clean water for everyone, not just for people who could afford it. Public health reformers believed the only way to protect the common good—and to provide clean water for all people—was to have the government take charge of the water supply.

Income and sales taxes paid for Progressive improvements like the one shown in this 1934 photograph. **Can you tell what the men were building?**

Reformers convinced city officials to take action: armed guards began patrolling designated water sources. Thousands of miles of sewer pipes were installed, along with a separate system for clean water. By 1912, drinking water was treated with chlorine to kill germs. By the 1920s, water filtration plants were under construction to further safeguard the public water supply.

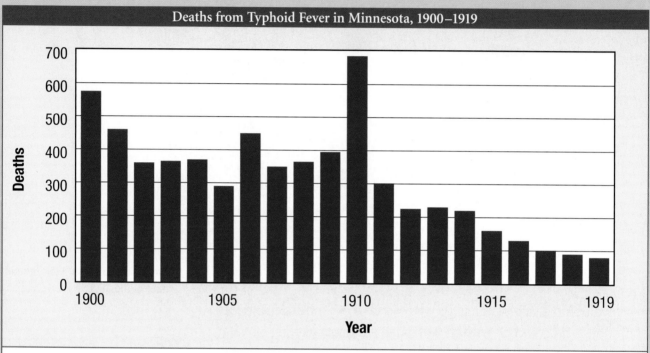

Deaths from Typhoid Fever in Minnesota, 1900–1919

This graph was published in the Minnesota Public Health Association Journal in 1920. **What does it show about the fight against typhoid fever?**

PROGRESSIVE CHANGE: DID THEIR EFFORTS PAY OFF?

It wasn't easy to change things. Public health reformers spent years promoting changes that controlled the spread of typhoid fever and other diseases.

Look back at the sources you just studied. How many years did Minnesota reformers spend battling typhoid fever?

YOUR CHANCE TO BE A PROGRESSIVE

Typhoid fever and the need for clean water were only one public health problem faced by the Progressives. The photo on the right shows an unfortunate girl with another disease that reformers fought—smallpox.

Using the information you have learned about typhoid fever, create a plan for your own public health campaign. First, select a disease, like smallpox, or another public health problem. Then,

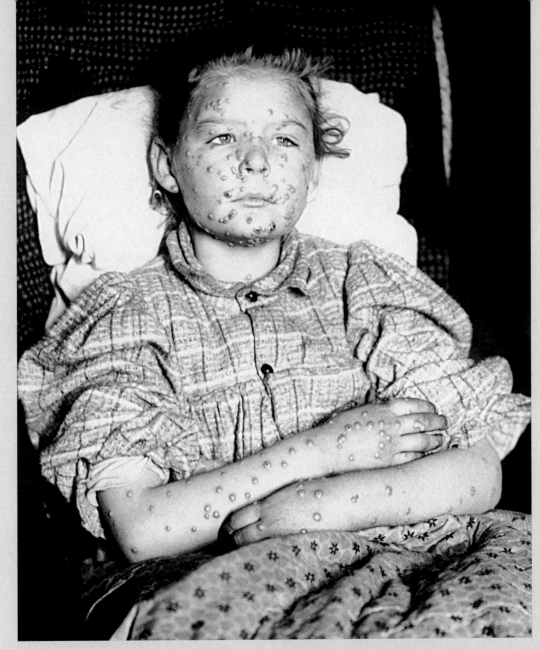

Doctor C.P. Gibson had this 1900 photo taken of Dottie Lake, his first smallpox patient. A smallpox vaccine was introduced in 1796. Still, even in 1900, many people were afraid and refused the vaccine.

brainstorm ways to attack the problem. Remember that a successful campaign requires many different strategies. Review Chapter 13 to learn how Progressive reformers were able to bring change and solve problems.

Use your Investigation Guide to take notes about the methods reformers used to bring about changes. Can you use some of these same methods in your public health campaign? Can you think of other methods that will be effective?

In the late 1800s, leaders in cities and towns in Minnesota began building public parks—like this one in Rochester—where people could enjoy their free time.

1870s	**1872**	**1876**	**1879**	**1881**	**1888**	**1895**
Minneapolis and St. Paul begin building public parks and sewer systems.	The brand name Pillsbury's Best first appears on flour packaging. Montgomery Ward starts the nation's first mail-order catalog business in Chicago.	Alexander Graham Bell invents the telephone in Massachusetts.	Minneapolis and St. Paul get their first telephones. Thomas Edison invents the electric lightbulb in New Jersey.	Duluth gets its first telephones.	After starting Sears Roebuck in Redwood Falls, Minnesota, Richard Sears publishes his first mail-order catalog in Chicago.	Guglielmo Marconi invents the radio in Italy.

The late 1800s and the early 1900s were an exciting time for many Minnesotans, especially for those in the **middle class.** They were people who worked in offices and stores instead of factories and mines. These men and women were clerks, accountants, teachers, doctors, and lawyers. As the century turned, these middle-class Minnesotans were earning higher wages and salaries, so they had more money in their pockets. Many of them also were spending less time on the job, giving them more **leisure,** or free time, than they'd ever had before. Some got Saturdays off. Others were lucky enough to take an occasional vacation.

With more money in their pockets, middle-class Minnesotans began looking for new things to buy. Companies began producing and marketing a mind-boggling variety of affordable **consumer goods**— everything from telephones to toilets.

With more time on their hands, middle-class Minnesotans began looking for new things to do. This led to a growing interest in leisure activities—everything from picnics in the park to baseball at the stadium.

LOOK FOR

- How did leisure time and buying patterns change between the 1880s and early 1900s?
- What new products and inventions were developed during this period?
- How did companies create a greater demand for their products?
- Where did new products first arrive? Why?
- What did children do for fun in the early 1900s?

KEY TERMS

middle class

leisure

consumer goods

spectator sport

brand name

middle class: the section of society made up largely of people who work in business and professional jobs

leisure: time that is free from work or duties

consumer goods: mass-produced items—such as food, clothing, or toys—that people buy

1900
Minnesota's population reaches 1,751,394.

1902
In Minneapolis, George Dayton starts Dayton's department store, later known as Marshall Field's.

1910
Over 20,000 movie theaters are operating in the United States.

About 10 million Americans are shopping by mail.

1913
Minnesotans own more than 40,000 automobiles.

1915
Baseball overtakes boxing as the leading spectator sport in Minnesota.

1921
General Mills creates Betty Crocker as advertising spokesperson for the company's consumer products.

1922
The University of Minnesota starts WLB (now known as KUOM), the first licensed radio station in Minnesota.

DEPARTMENT STORES

By 1900, a new kind of city store was turning shopping into entertainment. It was called the department store. The department store was often housed in a large, almost palace-like building with grand staircases and fancy lighting. It sold almost every product imaginable—clothes, furniture, carpets, toys, cooking utensils. It encouraged customers to go on buying sprees by holding regular sales and by showing off merchandise in colorful displays, often behind plate glass windows. Even people who did not have enough money to buy things at the department store liked to go there. It was an exciting place where people could dream of the good life.

Minnesota's early department stores included Dayton's, Donaldson's, Powers, Glass Block, and Golden Rule. Many continued to do business for decades, but by the late 1900s all but Dayton's had either gone out of business or had been acquired by other companies. In 2001, Dayton's, too, became a name of the past when it changed its name to Marshall Field's, a company Dayton's had purchased in 1990.

4331. Dayton Dry Goods Co., and Raddison Hotel, Minneapolis, Minn.

This focus on consumer goods and on leisure time became typical of middle-class people in cities and small towns, but this lifestyle affected people throughout the state. Working-class people, such as factory workers and miners, wanted to buy new things and enjoy more time off, too. So did people who lived on farms in the countryside. Nearly all Minnesotans wanted a part of this new culture of the good life. Just how good they had it, though, depended largely on how much money they had and where they lived.

Melvin Frank: Growing Up in the City

Melvin Frank and his brother Clifford posed for this photo in 1913. Melvin is on the right.

Melvin Frank was born in 1907 and grew up in a working-class neighborhood near the Mississippi River sawmills of North Minneapolis. His father operated a power substation that fed electricity to the city's streetcars. His mother stayed at home to take care of Melvin and his brother and sister. Years later, Melvin looked back with fondness on his childhood. "North Minneapolis was a great place to be a boy during the first couple of decades of this century," he remembered. "A kid was always aware of the adventures possible along the river, and there was always the aroma of freshly cut pine lumber and the smell of wood smoke from the steam plant of the Northland Pine Company sawmill."

Still, life was not always easy for the Frank family. Melvin's father worked long hours for a modest wage. The Franks often had only enough money to pay for food, clothing, and the rent on their house. But like other Minnesotans, they could see that times were changing. Companies were producing new products designed to make life easier and more enjoyable. People were finding new ways to spend leisure time. The Franks may have been a working-class family, but they wanted to enjoy modern life just as much as any middle-class family did.

GOOD THINGS: INDOOR PLUMBING AND ELECTRICITY

Melvin Frank did not like outhouses. "Making that early morning or late-at-night walk out to the outdoor toilet was adventure indeed during the cold winter months," he recalled. "Having a flush toilet was devoutly to be wished for in Minneapolis!"

Even in the cities, outhouses were still common sights until 1920. Minneapolis and St. Paul had begun building sewer systems during the 1870s, but it was a slow process. Year after year, people complained about smelly streets and rivers fouled with stagnant pools of human waste. At first, only those home owners who were wealthy enough to pay for hookups to the city sewer lines were able to install the new flush toilets in their houses. But gradually, the city installed lines to all homes. By 1911, six out of every ten homes in St. Paul had sewer service. In 1918, Melvin Frank was thrilled when his family moved into what he called "a modern apartment" with indoor plumbing.

This electric toaster was state-of-the-art technology at the beginning of the twentieth century.

Until sewer systems were built, many homes had an outhouse like this.

But the modern home of the early 1900s had more than just indoor plumbing. Above all else, it had electricity. For many people, the biggest benefit of electricity was electric lighting. Electric lights were brighter and cleaner than gas lamps. Gas lamps gave off smoke as they burned, creating dirty soot that clung to the walls and ceiling. People whose homes were wired for electricity could also use a host of new appliances that were designed to make life easier. These new products included the washing machine, the refrigerator, the electric iron, the electric fan, the vacuum cleaner, and the toaster.

GOOD TIMES: GOING TO THE PARK

Consumers bought the most popular toys of the time, including the spinning top, the jack-in-the-box, and the flipping acrobat.

Melvin Frank and his friends played many games at Farview Park in Minneapolis, shown here in 1905.

One of Melvin Frank's favorite things about living in North Minneapolis was Farview Park. Farview had baseball diamonds, a playground, picnic areas, and tennis courts. During the winter, Melvin and his friends spent countless hours on the park's hills riding sleds called Flexible Flyers. In the summer, thoughts turned to baseball. "From somewhere a catcher's pad and mask turned up," Melvin recalled, "and I was frequently found behind the plate in the receiver's spot. I did not like the bruised shins or stung fingers from foul tips, but I caught when no one else would, and usually no one else would."

Minneapolis and St. Paul began creating a network of public parks in the 1870s. At first, some critics complained that these parks were just playgrounds for the rich. But soon people from all walks of life were enjoying them. Family and group picnics were especially popular.

City people also began to gather in large numbers for another type of leisure activity: **spectator sports.** At first, boxing was the most popular, but by 1915, baseball had become the nation's—and Minnesota's—leading spectator sport. The Minneapolis Millers and the St. Paul Saints forged a fierce rivalry that lasted for many years. Melvin Frank remembered how "Rube" Schauer, a pitcher for the Millers, would sometimes give pointers to the boys who played at Farview Park. "We were proud to have the big pro from the Millers show us how it was done," he recalled.

Melvin Frank used bats, balls, catcher's masks, and shoes like these when he played baseball.

Gerhard Ellestad: Life in a Small Town

Gerhard Ellestad was born in 1898 in the southeastern Minnesota town of Lanesboro. Gerhard's family was solidly middle class. His father was a skilled watchmaker who owned a thriving jewelry store in town. His mother was a former salesclerk. Their home was carefully decorated with fancy rugs and wallpaper. An upright piano stood in the parlor. Painted still lifes and photographic portraits hung from the walls. The Ellestads lived a comfortable life.

But because they lived in a small town, Gerhard and his family sometimes had to wait to experience all the good things of modern middle-class life. As Gerhard later recalled, Lanesboro was "a pleasant and stimulating place," but it lacked many of the "comforts and conveniences" that had already arrived in big cities like Minneapolis and St. Paul. Small-town people often had to make their own comforts and conveniences during the early 1900s.

spectator sport: a sports event that is watched by an audience

Lanesboro

The Ellestad family sat for this picture in 1903. Gerhard is the boy facing the camera. His father, Gilbert, took the photograph by pulling a string attached to the camera.

MERCHANDISING

Manufacturers in the early 1900s used all sorts of new techniques to make people want to buy their products — to create consumer demand. These techniques included advertising, **brand names,** and convenient packaging.

By 1900, American companies were spending nearly $100 million a year to advertise their products — about 10 times more than they spent in 1865. They placed most of their ads in newspapers and magazines and on billboards. The ads introduced people to new products and gave them new reasons to buy existing ones.

Companies also created demand by giving their products easy-to-remember brand names. Two Minnesota flour companies — Pillsbury and Washburn-Crosby — were among the first big companies to use this strategy successfully. Pillsbury labeled its flour Pillsbury's Best. Washburn-Crosby used the brand name Gold Medal. Advertising campaigns helped turn both flours into national brands that people all over the country recognized and trusted.

At the same time, companies began changing the way they packaged their products. Before, many goods were sold in bulk out of barrels, jars, bins, and sacks. By the early 1900s, many manufacturers were packaging their products in individual wrappers, cartons, and bottles. Quaker Oats, for example, became available in 16-ounce cardboard cylinders instead of the usual 8-pound sacks it had been in. Consumers found these smaller packages appealing and easier to carry and store.

brand name: name given to a product to encourage consumers to recognize and buy it

Circus-themed toys — and circuses themselves — were popular in cities and small towns during the early 1900s.

GOOD THINGS: TALKING MACHINES

Gerhard and his two brothers spent much of their childhood trying to duplicate new inventions they read about in books and magazines. They built a wireless telegraph that sent and received signals 30 miles away. As a prank, they hooked up a homemade battery to an outhouse seat just to see what would happen when someone sat down. (The unlucky user received a mild shock.) They liked experimenting with machine parts. Like their father, they were top-notch tinkerers. Tinkerers were often the first people to introduce new technologies to small towns. Such was the case with the Ellestads and the telephone.

In the early 1900s, the telephone became increasingly common in Minnesota's urban areas. Minneapolis and St. Paul got their first telephones in 1879, and Duluth followed suit two years later. But telephone companies were often slow to expand their services to rural areas and small towns. That often meant that do-it-yourselfers had to step in. Gerhard's father built a home telephone from scratch, using a few old magnets, some lengths of wire, a sheet of brass, and a hodgepodge of scrap lumber. It connected to another homemade phone that was mounted high on a wall in the family jewelry store. Gerhard had to stand on a chair to reach it.

Children and adults alike gathered at soda fountains to swap stories and meet friends. This Minneapolis soda fountain was photographed in 1894.

GOOD TIMES: ICE CREAM AND A MOVIE

In Lanesboro, ice-cream season started in late spring and ran to early fall. People there preferred hot coffee during the winter, Gerhard said. Lanesboro had two stores with soda fountains where people could buy ice cream. The fountains included equipment for making ice-cream treats and long marble counters—decorated with fancy wood trimmings—for serving the treats. The clerks who worked behind the counters were called soda jerks. They made ice-cream sodas, sundaes, and cones for 10¢ apiece. Gerhard was very fond of ice cream, but the prices in Lanesboro outraged him. "What made the matter more galling," he said, "was the fact that in some neighboring villages you could buy an ice-cream soda for a nickel."

Another favorite gathering place was the movie theater. Gerhard vividly remembered that in 1905, he watched one of the first silent movies in a makeshift theater above a corner drugstore in Lanesboro. Called *The Great Train Robbery*, the film seemed so real that it gave him nightmares. A few years later, a real movie theater opened in Lanesboro, and Gerhard got a job operating the hand-cranked film projector. He was part of a fast-growing industry. By 1910, 20,000 movie theaters were operating across the nation. Movies were distributed nationally, which meant that audiences in Lanesboro got to see the same movies as audiences in big cities like New York.

Soda fountains often had fancy cash registers like this one. **How does this compare with a modern cash register?**

Lakeville

Nellie Stone Johnson: Working the Farm

Nellie Stone Johnson was born in 1905 on a farm near Lakeville, about 25 miles south of the Twin Cities. Her mother had taught school in Kentucky and Chicago. Her father came from a family of successful farmers in Missouri. Like many African Americans who moved to Minnesota, Nellie's parents had come to the state looking for jobs. They met, fell in love, and got married. Shortly after their wedding, they decided to start a dairy farm. They made their living selling milk to a company in Minneapolis.

Years later, Nellie remembered her childhood as a happy time. "I thought my family life was pretty good," she said. "We always had plenty of milk to drink and plenty of chickens to eat and everything else. We butchered our own beef and all of our pork." But Nellie's family had to make do without many modern conveniences that people in towns and cities were already beginning to take for granted. For example, they had no electricity. Electric companies in the early 1900s often refused to extend their lines out to farms because they thought it wouldn't be profitable. Too few people lived in rural areas to pay for the costs of providing electricity to rural communities. The good things and the good times of modern life would come to Minnesota's farms—but they would come slowly.

Nellie Stone Johnson, pictured on the upper right, was about 10 years old when this photograph was taken. With her are her siblings, Richard (back) and Herbert and Mayme (front).

GOOD THINGS: WHEELS

Nellie liked growing up on a farm, even though life could be hard. She learned many skills that she never would have learned elsewhere. She remembered one day when she and her father were putting a new roof on a shed. "Gosh," she said to her father, "I can hire myself out now as a carpenter." Nellie's father was proud of his daughter's skill with a hammer, but he didn't want her to think too highly of herself. "You're not quite there yet," he said.

By the age of 10, Nellie had learned another skill that was becoming more common in the early 1900s: she learned to drive. Her parents had bought a Model T Ford automobile, nicknamed the Tin Lizzie, in 1914. It cost $400, but it was a good investment. The automobile cut the amount of time it took to travel into town or up to the Twin Cities, if the roads weren't too muddy. Nellie also learned to drive another modern machine: the tractor. "I did a little plowing," she later recalled. "I tried to do a little cultivating. Most every girl on the farm knew how to run a tractor if their people had a tractor."

The automobile and the tractor were among the few modern inventions that seemed like necessities to farmers during the early 1900s. By 1913, Minnesotans owned more than 40,000 automobiles. About half of them were registered in rural areas. With new cars and trucks, farmers demanded newer and better roads. In 1920, Minnesota began a new road-building program that would become part of a statewide highway system.

Fire pumps were once pulled by horses. This toy is the ancestor of the modern toy fire truck.

The Model T automobile, built by the Ford Motor Company, was the first mass-produced car. Its low price made it the most popular car of the early twentieth century.

GOOD TIMES: MAKING THE MOST OF FARM LIFE

Nellie's days were packed with work and school. Nellie started the day at 6:30 in the morning milking the cows—something she had learned how to do at the age of six. By the time she was in high school, she was milking 30 of them each day. After breakfast, Nellie walked two miles to the tiny schoolhouse where one teacher taught students from kindergarten to eighth grade. Some of Nellie's schoolmates skipped classes —especially during the fall—to help their families with harvesting and other chores.

But life on the farm was not all work and study. During the winter, Nellie and her friends spent many hours skating on a nearby pond. When the weather turned warm, they played baseball. While city dwellers and townsfolk had their public parks, spectator sports, ice-cream fountains, and movie theaters, farming families often enjoyed simpler pleasures. They got together for church picnics and school graduations. Even adults who disliked each other managed to behave during these community get-togethers. "We all got along," Nellie recalled. "The parents didn't fight and fuss with each other."

Nellie Stone Johnson learned to drive a tractor that looked much like this one from 1910.

MAIL-ORDER CATALOGS

During most of the 1800s, people who lived on farms and in small towns bought many of the things they needed at the local country store. The stores sold all the essentials, including groceries, medicines, and fabric for clothing. But a country store's selection of goods was not nearly as big as the selection found in large city stores. That's why rural people were so excited about the arrival of the mail-order catalog in the 1870s.

Sears Roebuck and Montgomery Ward were the two biggest mail-order companies. Each year they sent out millions of catalogs—thick books loaded with drawings and descriptions of all kinds of merchandise—to people throughout the United States. By 1910, about 10 million Americans were shopping by mail.

In rural communities, the mail-order catalog touched almost everyone's life—from birth (baby carriages) to death (coffins). At the turn of the nineteenth century, a woman from Minnesota ordered embalming fluid from Montgomery Ward so that she could properly bury her husband when he died. She included a note with the order: "When you send the stuff please send instructions with it. Must I pour it down his throat just before he dies, or must I rub it on after he is dead? Please rush."

Though Melvin Frank, Gerhard Ellestad, and Nellie Stone Johnson came from different backgrounds and lived in different places, they shared many of the same dreams and experiences. They and their families were absorbing some of the values and aspirations of the growing middle class. They were spending money on widely available goods and spending time on new forms of recreation and entertainment. The good life of the early 1900s produced a feeling of contentment among Minnesotans that would continue to grow well into the 1920s. At the time, no one could have guessed how quickly things would change.

Capturing Leisure in Scrapbooks and Diaries

What do you and your friends like to do with your free time? What did your parents like to do for fun when they were your age? What about your grandparents? Or even your great-grandparents?

By 1900, Minnesotans had many new ways to spend their money and free time. New games, toys, and activities encouraged people to relax and have fun together. So, what did people actually do for fun?

One popular leisure activity was creating scrapbooks. People, especially school-aged children and teenagers, spent hours pasting photos, ticket stubs, letters, and other items into these "memory books." In the early 1900s, two young Minnesotans, Dorothy Walton and Foster Kienholz, created their own memory books. Today, these books are records of what Dorothy and Foster did for fun nearly 100 years ago.

Small, portable, and easy to use, the Brownie camera was popular with children and amateur photographers. Many people used Brownie cameras to capture scenes of everyday life.

Scrapbooks, photo albums, diaries, and memory books can tell us a lot about how people used to live their lives. **What can you learn from studying these sources?**

As you study these artifacts, keep track of the details of the leisure activities in your Investigation Guide. What kinds of leisure activities are shown? Who was involved? What did they wear? When you are finished, create your own memory book of what you like to do with your leisure time. Then, compare your activities with the ones in Dorothy's and Foster's books.

Foster's Photo Album

Foster Kienholz grew up in St. Paul and went on to study graphic and fine arts at the University of Minnesota. In his photo album, which he called "Proofs of a Few Good Times," Foster collected images of the leisure time he spent with family and friends. As an artist, he often added sketches and clever captions to the photos.

They don't have to tell fish stories.

What types of activities did Foster and his friends like? Are they similar to the activities you enjoy today?

The smile that wont come off

One end of the canoe

What kinds of clothes did Foster and his friends wear in their free time?

Marshmallows.

Where did Foster and his friends spend their leisure time? Indoors? Outdoors? In private or public spaces?

Dorothy's Memory Book

Dorothy Walton (called "Tom" by her friends) lived in a neighborhood south of downtown Minneapolis with her parents and two sisters. In 1908, she was an active 14-year-old who enjoyed playing with her friends and attending lots of parties and gatherings. For years, Dorothy wrote in her memory book nearly every day, leaving a record of what her leisure time was like.

With whom did Dorothy spend her free time? With neighborhood friends, family, or school friends?

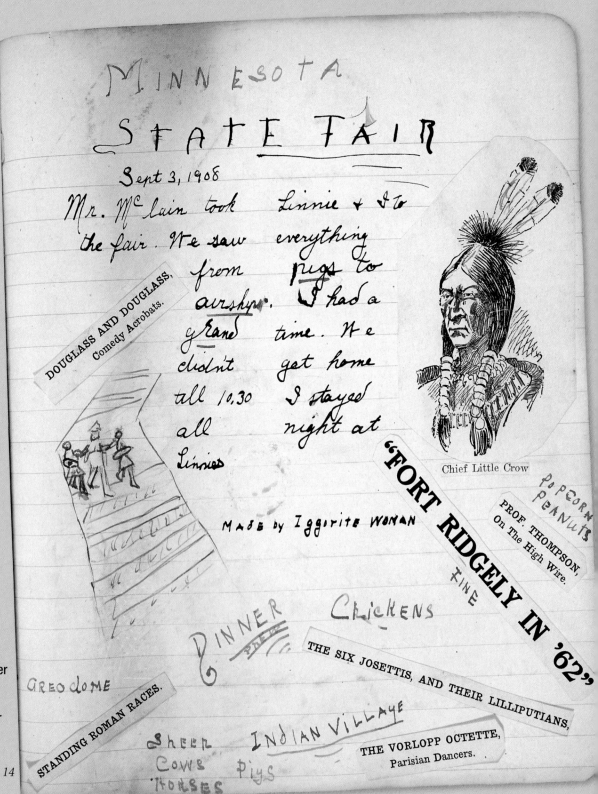

MINNESOTA
STATE FAIR
Sept 3, 1908

Mr. M^c lain took Linnie & I to the fair. We saw everything from pigs to airships. I had a grand time. We didn't get home till 10.30 I stayed all night at Linnies

DOUGLASS AND DOUGLASS, Comedy Acrobats.

MADE by Iggorite WOMAN

Chief Little Crow

"FORT RIDGELY IN '62"

POPCORN PEANUTS

PROF. THOMPSON, On The High Wire.

DINNER CHICKENS FINE

GREO DOME

STANDING ROMAN RACES.

THE SIX JOSETTIS, AND THEIR LILLIPUTIANS,

SHEEP COWS HORSES PIGS

INDIAN VILLAGE

THE VORLOPP OCTETTE, Parisian Dancers.

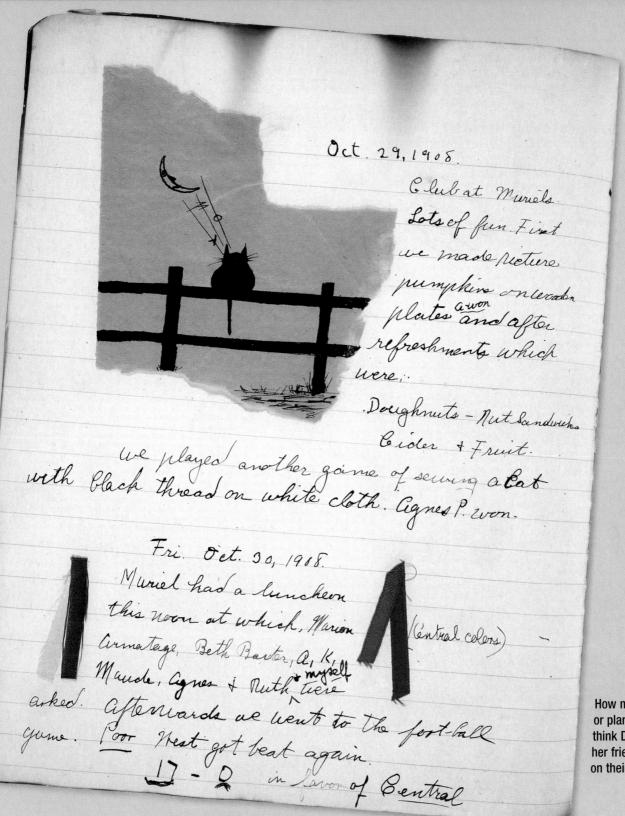

Oct. 29, 1908.

Club at Muriels. Lots of fun. First we made picture pumpkins on wooden plates a won and after refreshments which were:

Doughnuts - Nut Sandwiches
Cider + Fruit.

we played another game of sewing a Cat with black thread on white cloth. Agnes P. won.

Fri. Oct. 30, 1908.

Muriel had a luncheon this noon at which, Marion Armatage, Beth Baxter, A, K, Maude, Agnes & Ruth myself were (Central colors) — arked. Afterwards we went to the foot-ball game. Poor West got beat again.

17 - 0   in favor of Central

How much money or planning do you think Dorothy and her friends spent on their free time?

🔍 Over the years, many things have changed, including how people spend their leisure time. Now it's your turn to create a memory book like Foster's or Dorothy's. What activities will you include?

In 1933, during the Great Depression, people gathered outside the employment offices in Minneapolis in hopes of finding a job in the city.

1920

In January, Prohibition goes into effect. The previous year, Minnesota's Andrew Volstead had sponsored the law.

1921

The first radio station in the United States begins broadcasting from Pittsburgh, Pennsylvania.

1925

Minnesotan F. Scott Fitzgerald writes *The Great Gatsby*.

1927

Minnesotan Charles A. Lindbergh, Jr., becomes the first pilot to fly alone and nonstop between New York and Paris.

1929

Stock market crashes, signaling the beginning of the Great Depression.

1930

Richard Drew, a lab technician at 3M in St. Paul, develops Scotch tape.

1932

Franklin D. Roosevelt wins the first of four presidential elections.

A Minnesotan named Wilbur Foshay had always admired the Washington Monument in Washington, D.C. For years he had dreamed of building an office tower modeled after the famous obelisk. All he needed was a few million dollars.

But where was he going to find that kind of money?

In 1916, Foshay borrowed $6,000 and started buying up small public utilities—gas, electric, and water companies. He combined these utilities into one large company and then sold shares, or stocks, in that company on the stock market. Investors liked Foshay's ideas. They put thousands and thousands of dollars into his company. By 1927, Foshay had built a fortune of about $22 million—more than enough money to build that skyscraper he had been dreaming about. He decided to construct his office obelisk in downtown Minneapolis.

The people of Minneapolis watched with wonder as Foshay's tower rose higher and higher above the city's skyline. The magnificent structure, the tallest building west of the Mississippi River, symbolized their hopes for the future. It seemed to prove that anything was possible.

LOOK FOR

- ◆ What events combined to cause the Great Depression?
- ◆ What was the Jazz Age?
- ◆ What problems did farmers face in the 1920s and 1930s?
- ◆ How did Elizabeth and Conrad Toso feed their nine children during the Great Depression?
- ◆ How did local and private organizations work to relieve the problems of the Great Depression?
- ◆ How did the New Deal change the role of the government?

KEY TERMS

Great Depression
Prohibition
bootlegger
foreclosure
welfare
New Deal

1933	**1934**	**1935**	**1936**	**1937**	**1939**	**1940**
Prohibition ends.	GangsterJohn Dillinger escapes from a gun battle with the FBI in St. Paul.	Farmers protest low crop prices by marching to the state capitol in St. Paul.	Moorhead reports a record high temperature of 114°F.	U.S. Congress establishes Pipestone National Monument in southwestern Minnesota.	World War II begins in Europe.	The first Minneapolis Aquatennial summer festival is held in July.

A blizzard on Armistice Day (November 11) drops 27 inches of snow and kills 49 people. |

THE CRASH AND THE GREAT DEPRESSION

Some Americans of the late 1920s saw the stock market as a way to get rich quickly. They could hardly be blamed for thinking that way. Stock prices were doubling and tripling as more and more investors scrambled to buy shares in all sorts of companies. Many people spent all their savings on stocks. Others borrowed money to join the action.

But all that ended with the crash. When people talk about the crash of 1929, they are referring to the sudden fall of stock prices and the panic that fed that collapse. All of a sudden, investors were scrambling to *sell* their stocks—not *buy* them. But they couldn't sell if no one wanted to buy. Prices sank lower and lower.

The crash brought on a nationwide economic crisis that we now call the Great Depression. The year before the crash, a slight economic downturn had caused many businesses to lay off workers and cancel orders for new equipment.

Without the crash, the downturn probably would have corrected itself. But the crash caused people to panic. As more people lost their jobs and were unable to purchase goods, more businesses went bankrupt. That caused even *more* people to lose their jobs. Worried Americans began holding onto their money instead of spending it. The economy kept getting worse. The Great Depression lasted for more than a decade and it touched all Americans—rich, poor, and in between.

Great Depression: the 1930s economic crisis that was triggered by the stock market crash of 1929

Wilbur Foshay's obelisk towered over the Minneapolis skyline when it was built in 1929.

In August 1929, Foshay held a three-day celebration to mark the completion of his 32-story Foshay Tower. He was, as they say, on top of the world.

But he did not stay there for long. Two months later, on October 29, 1929, the stock market crashed. Foshay's fortune, which was based on the value of his company's stock, disappeared. By November, he was broke. So were many of the people who had invested in his company.

The stock market crash of 1929 was a turning point from boom to bust in the history of the United States and Minnesota. Before the crash, the economy was booming and many city dwellers believed that life was good and would only get better. Even farmers, who struggled during the 1920s, had hoped that better times were ahead. After the crash, everything was different. The bust started an economic crisis that we now call the **Great Depression,** which swept across the nation and touched lives throughout Minnesota—from cities to small towns to farms.

Before the Crash: The Jazz Age

Carl Warmington was 10 years old and living in Minneapolis when he first heard the new music that everyone seemed to be listening to after World War I. It was fast, happy, and fun. It came out of the African American neighborhoods of New Orleans, Louisiana, and St. Louis, Missouri, and spread across the nation over the radio and on phonographs. People called the music jazz, and they called the 1920s the Jazz Age. As Carl grew older, he spent hours and hours playing jazz records on his family's Victrola. But Carl wasn't satisfied just listening to jazz—he wanted to *play* jazz. He started taking trumpet lessons.

Soon he was playing in amateur bands around the Twin Cities. In 1923, at the age of 15, Carl joined a nine-piece youth orchestra that performed in theaters all over Minnesota. A few years later, he picked up the trombone. By the time he was attending the University of Minnesota, Carl was earning good money as a trombonist in several dance bands.

Dancers gathered in 1925 at a Minneapolis dance hall to learn the latest jazz moves. Women were called "flappers" when they cut their hair short and wore clothes like these.

As he toured the theaters, resorts, and roadhouses of Minnesota, Carl soaked up the giddy excitement of the Jazz Age. The country was at peace. Investors were getting rich in the stock market. Carl noticed that attitudes were changing in this new era of jazz. Women shortened their skirts and their hair. Even though **Prohibition** was in force and liquor was illegal, people drank and danced at illegal bars called speakeasies. "New intimate dancing styles such as the 'Bunny Hug' were introduced," Carl later recalled. "Speakeasies and **bootleggers** became popular, and parties stimulated by illegal liquor took on more gaiety. Jazz music fit nicely into this new mood."

In the summer of 1929, Carl played with a dance orchestra at the Breezy Point Lodge on Big Pelican Lake in central Minnesota. The lodge had an illegal gambling casino and served illegal liquor. Breezy Point was a popular destination among gangsters and Hollywood movie stars. Guests arrived in fancy cars and wore fancy clothes. Carl did not make much money at the lodge, but he enjoyed hobnobbing with people who seemed to have more money than they could spend. The summer went quickly. In August, Carl returned to the Twin Cities to continue college. Two months later, the stock market crashed.

Carl, like many Minnesotans, did not worry very much at first about the effects of the crash. During the months that followed, he finished his college education and made plans for the coming summer. "President Herbert Hoover gave me encouragement when he said that business was sound and the economy would improve," he recalled. "So I signed on for another season at Breezy Point Lodge."

The summer of 1930 was Carl's last carefree summer for a very long time. Like many Minnesotans, he was about to discover that the exciting days of the Jazz Age were over.

Prohibition: the period from 1920 to 1933, when the manufacture and sale of alcohol was illegal

bootlegger: person who makes or sells illegal alcohol

Breezy Point Lodge

Carl Warmington played in the jazz band at Breezy Point Lodge in the summers of 1929 and 1930.

PROHIBITION

In 1919, the U.S. Constitution was amended to ban the sale of liquor. This ban was called Prohibition. The law that officially made liquor sales illegal was called the Volstead Act—named after Andrew Volstead, a Minnesota congressman who headed the committee that wrote the law.

Supporters of Prohibition, such as the Women's Christian Temperance Union, believed that it would reduce the problem of drunkenness. They hoped Prohibition would make the nation a better and safer place. It did not. If anything, Prohibition made drinking alcohol more fashionable. Illegal saloons called speakeasies opened up in nearly every city and gangsters moved in to control the supply of bootleg.

Minnesota was a perfect location for bootleggers. They smuggled liquor across Minnesota's border with Canada and sent it by train to St. Paul. Police raids like the one pictured here did little to control illegal liquor. Profits from this illegal activity turned several small-time bootleggers in St. Paul into powerful criminal bosses. They bribed city officials and police officers to protect their illegal bootleg business. Well-known gangsters like George "Machine Gun Kelly" Barnes and John Dillinger hid out in St. Paul because they knew they would be safe. Gangster Alvin "Creepy" Karpis put it this way:

> *Of all the Midwest cities, the one that I knew best was St. Paul, and it was a crook's haven. Every criminal of any importance in the 1930s made his home at one time or another in St. Paul. If you were looking for a guy you hadn't seen for a few months, you usually thought of two places—prison or St. Paul. If he wasn't locked up in one, he was probably hanging out in the other.*

By the 1930s, most Americans believed that Prohibition was a mistake. Drinking was still common, and crime had increased because of illegal liquor sales. In 1933, the nation changed its Constitution again—this time to get rid of Prohibition. The bootleggers were out of business. St. Paul's gangster era soon came to an end.

Before the Crash: The Farm Crisis

The 1920s had been good years for many city dwellers, but they were hard years for the people of Minnesota's small towns and farming communities. Rural Minnesota's problems had started shortly after World War I. During the war, the government had encouraged farmers to produce more food to keep up with the rising worldwide demand. But after the war, farmers continued to increase production even though the demand for their goods decreased. As a result, prices for farm products plummeted. By 1922, farmers were getting less than half the money they had received three years earlier for their wheat and corn. The prices they got for their hogs and beef cattle were not much better. Farmers who owed money on their farms found it increasingly difficult to repay their debts. More and more of them went broke.

The people of Otter Tail County, in the west-central part of the state, were among thousands of Minnesotans who felt the sting of the 1920s farm crisis. Otter Tail County's economy depended heavily on farms, meat processing plants, and businesses that served farmers' needs.

Maplewood

OTTER TAIL COUNTY

When farmers could no longer afford to buy what they'd bought before, local businesses began to fail. People from all walks of life went further and further into debt.

In one way, Otter Tail County was better off than most rural areas in the state. Over the years as the soil wore out, the county's farmers turned from growing wheat to running dairy farms. By the late 1920s, Otter Tail County was a top producer of dairy products in Minnesota. And since prices for dairy products did not drop as much as those for wheat, corn, hogs, and cattle, Otter Tail County farmers did not suffer as much as other farmers in the state.

Conrad and Elizabeth Toso were among the many Otter Tail County farmers who made the switch to dairy farming. They lived with their nine children in Maplewood, a heavily wooded township that was difficult to farm. Their farm was small—40 acres. They never had more than 10 milk cows on it at one time. The Tosos' small dairy operation did not produce much income, but it was enough to help the family get by. Like many Otter Tail County farmers, the Tosos were largely self-sufficient. They kept hogs and chickens and had a vegetable garden. "We never went hungry," Conrad recalled, "but the table was always clean. The children ate what was on the table."

The Tosos and most other Otter Tail County farmers managed to hold onto their farms through the tough years of the 1920s. But then the stock market crashed. Hard times on Minnesota farms were far from over.

Conrad and Elizabeth Toso posed with their nine children and Elizabeth's mother around 1936.

foreclosure: the sale of a house or farm to cover unpaid debts

FARMERS HOLIDAY ASSOCIATION

In 1932, the Great Depression tightened its grip on the nation's farm economy. Prices for farm products continued to drop. In the Upper Midwest, many farmers decided to take action. They banded together to form the Farmers Holiday Association.

One of the association's main goals was to keep food from getting to market until farm prices rose. Association members refused to sell their own produce, and they set up roadblocks to keep other farmers from selling theirs. By keeping the supply of food low, association members helped force prices up.

Association members also tried to stop **foreclosures**—the selling of farms to cover unpaid debts. When banks auctioned off a farmer's possessions, association members sometimes bid pennies for each item placed on the auction block. When the auction was over, banks gained only a few dollars. Association members returned the goods they bought to the original owner.

All farmers wanted a law to stop foreclosures until times were better. In February 1933, Governor Floyd Olson declared a farm emergency. Governor Olson, shown here at his desk, stopped all foreclosures in Minnesota.

After the Crash: The Soup Line

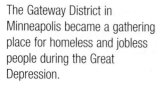

1930S RADIO

welfare: aid in the form of money or necessities for people who are poor, elderly, disabled, or unemployed

Back in the city, Carl Warmington was getting a rude surprise. It was the fall of 1930—a year after the crash. He had just finished his orchestra gig at the Breezy Point Lodge and was looking for a new job. But he could not find one. Not in Minneapolis, not anywhere. The economic crisis triggered by the stock market crash—the Great Depression—was spreading quickly through Minnesota and the rest of the nation. By the fall of 1930, private organizations like the Salvation Army were struggling to give **welfare** to a growing population of unemployed and homeless people. Carl thought his college degree would help him find a job, even in tough times like this. He was wrong. "I looked in vain for any kind of full-time position," he recalled. "I watched the want ads and filled out employment applications without a call back."

Even though he had no job, Carl still felt luckier than many people since he had a place to live with his parents. One day in December of 1930, he visited a friend's father who worked for a private agency that gave vouchers for meals and lodging to homeless men in the Gateway District of Minneapolis. Years later, he described his impressions of what was called the "soup line":

> *What a dark and dreary sight. It had begun to snow and the wind was howling down this deserted lane. Stretched along the side of an empty building was a long line of shivering men, many with only light jackets. The line reached down the alley to a fire escape that crawled up the side of this dark warehouse to the second floor. The only action from this long queue of men was from their stomping feet in the snow.*

In many cases, these were men who had mined Minnesota's Iron Range, plowed Minnesota's fields, logged Minnesota's forests, or built Minnesota's industries. Now these same men were jobless and waiting in line for a chance to eat a hot meal and sleep in a warm bed. The

The Gateway District in Minneapolis became a gathering place for homeless and jobless people during the Great Depression.

times were even harder for African Americans and Native Americans, who had been struggling even before the depression hit. They were often the first to lose their jobs.

A few months later, in early 1931, Carl finally landed an office job with the city. Before long, he was transferred to the city's department of public relief, the agency that helped people who needed housing, food, counseling, health care, and clothing. By this time, about 35,000 people in a workforce of 212,000—one in six—were out of work in Minneapolis.

Over the next few years, Carl and his fellow relief workers tried hard to make life better for the thousands of Minneapolis residents who needed help. But there was only so much Carl's organization could do. The Great Depression was a national, or federal, crisis—not a city crisis. "City funds were limited," Carl recalled. "It was not until federal funds were made available that improved care for homeless people was possible."

In 1932, the American people elected a new president with a new vision. Franklin D. Roosevelt had won by promising "a new deal for the American people." His first challenge was to fight the people's panic and restore confidence in the country's economic system. Within his first 100 days in office, President Roosevelt sent—and Congress passed—15 bills to deal with the crisis. The president took his ideas and his programs straight to the American people in a series of radio broadcasts called "fireside chats." Many Americans liked Roosevelt's plans, and Congress approved most **New Deal** proposals. People felt hope for the future now that the government was trying to relieve their misery.

New Deal: the federal programs developed during Franklin D. Roosevelt's presidency to improve the economy and provide public relief

THE NEW DEAL

The New Deal was an experiment. No one really knew how to end the Depression. President Roosevelt and his advisors based their ideas on the progressive view that government could and should improve economic conditions for all Americans, provide relief for the poor, and curb abuses by the powerful. While the New Deal failed to end the Great Depression, it did provide work and welfare for the unemployed. The New Dealers also greatly enlarged the federal government, adding new responsibilities to regulate banks and the stock market, to assist farmers and unemployed workers, and to increase the general welfare of the people.

Many Americans loved Roosevelt. Many others hated him. Generally, public opinion divided along class lines. Those hit hard by the depression—especially farmers and laborers—helped elect him to a record four terms. The wealthy—including bankers and industrialists—often accused him of making government larger and more expensive. They believed the New Deal would undermine the American economic system. But no matter how people felt about Roosevelt and his policies, the ideals behind the New Deal have inspired reformers since the 1930s.

After the Crash: The New Deal

The New Deal sounded like good news to rural people like the Tosos of Otter Tail County. By 1932, the Great Depression had driven prices for farm products lower than they had been even during the darkest days of the 1920s. It looked like the state's farm economy was on the verge of collapse. Families throughout rural Minnesota were frightened. They hoped help would come soon.

In 1933, a new federal agency called the Agricultural Adjustment Administration (AAA) started a program to raise prices for farm goods and provide relief for farmers. President Roosevelt went on the radio to explain how the AAA and other New Deal programs would work. Many farmers, including Conrad and Elizabeth Toso, were skeptical at first. "He promised us that he was going to give everybody work," Conrad recalled. "And of course that puzzled us. We wondered how he could do that."

The Tosos' questions were answered the following year, when drought struck a large part of Minnesota, including Otter Tail County. Fields dried up from lack of rain. Farmers who were already struggling wondered what else could go wrong. In Otter Tail County, farmers could not find enough feed to keep their dairy cattle alive. Conrad Toso, for example, had to feed his milk cows Russian thistle, a plant that was hard for the animals to digest. But then the federal government stepped in. The AAA offered to buy any cattle that farmers in Otter Tail County could not afford to keep. The Tosos sold all but four of their cows for $20 apiece. The money they received from this New Deal program helped them get through the summer.

During the 1930s, many Americans listened to the "fireside chats" that President Roosevelt broadcast over the radio.

Farmers in western Minnesota faced severe droughts in the 1930s. In the summer of 1936, this farmer's soil was dry enough to sift through his fingers.

In 1936, drought struck again, and another government agency came to the rescue. The Works Progress Administration (WPA) provided money for public projects such as renovating schools, improving roads, and building new ball fields. In Otter Tail County, drought-stricken farmers worked on WPA road projects and received feed and seed as payment. It was hard work, hacking through brush to clear the way for new roads, but Conrad Toso was happy to do it. "There were no jobs to get whatsoever," he recalled. "It was the only thing you could do."

Throughout the United States, REA work crews strung electrical wires across rural areas. This crew worked in northern Minnesota in the 1930s.

Of all the New Deal agencies, none was as popular in rural Minnesota as the Rural Electrification Administration (REA). Most Minnesota farms still had no electricity by the 1930s. The REA set out to change that by encouraging farmers to form electric cooperatives. The cooperatives bought electricity from existing power plants and then built power lines to carry that electricity to the farms. By 1939, about 800 farmers in Otter Tail County were enjoying the benefits of the REA, but Conrad and Elizabeth Toso were not among them. "We didn't have the cash to do it," recalled Conrad. "I wanted it in the worst way." Rural electrification went slowly. Most Minnesota farms did not get electricity for another 10 or 15 years. But without the REA, getting electricity would have taken much longer.

The New Deal pumped more than $1 billion into Minnesota between 1933 and 1939. It put people to work, gave people hope, and propped up the economy. It also convinced many Minnesotans that government could—and should—play an active role in people's lives. But for all the things the New Deal accomplished during the 1930s, it did not end the Great Depression. Farm prices remained low and millions of people were still out of work. It would take another world war to shake the United States and Minnesota out of their long economic nightmare.

The Hamline Playground building in St. Paul, designed by architect Cap Wigington, was one of many built by the WPA.

St. Paul's Gangster Era

Throughout the 1920s and early 1930s, though St. Paul was the home of some of the country's worst gangsters, it was actually a remarkably safe place to live. A system of bribery made this possible. The criminals and police had an agreement: as long as the criminals paid the police money and did not commit crimes *in* St. Paul, the police would not arrest them for crimes committed *outside* St. Paul. Since St. Paul itself was a safer place to live, many of its citizens were happy to ignore the corruption.

But when Prohibition ended in 1933, a crime wave swept through St. Paul. Since gangsters could no longer make money by selling illegal alcohol, they began to look for other ways to make money. When crimes like murder, bank robbery, and kidnapping increased both outside *and* inside the city limits, St. Paul's citizens decided to act.

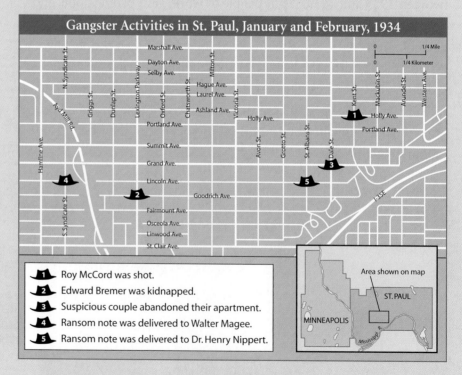

Gangster Activities in St. Paul, January and February, 1934

1. Roy McCord was shot.
2. Edward Bremer was kidnapped.
3. Suspicious couple abandoned their apartment.
4. Ransom note was delivered to Walter Magee.
5. Ransom note was delivered to Dr. Henry Nippert.

Area shown on map

ST. PAUL

MINNEAPOLIS

St. Paul Dispatch

Minnesota Weather
Partly cloudy tonight and Friday; somewhat colder in extreme west tonight and in extreme east Friday.

The unruly boy they have ideas; don't suppress him, Angelo Patri warns on Page 10 to-day.

TWO CENTS IN ST. PAUL.

VOL. 66. NO. 112. 18 PAGES *Exclusive Service of the Associated Press.*

ST. PAUL, MINN., THURSDAY, JANUARY 18, 1934. cx☆

EDW. G. BREMER KIDNAPED; $200,000 RANSOM ASKED

WASHINGTON

TWO MONTHS have passed since America took Russia back to her bosom. Ambassadors have been exchanged and preliminary work looking to the opening of new trade channels is well under way.

As condition No. 2 Washington's recognition of the Soviet government President Roosevelt made Moscow promise it would not lift a finger—by outlay of money or otherwise—to foment communistic tendencies in the United States. Nothing was said about the Amtorg in the agreement Commissar Litvinoff signed but our secret agents have good reason to believe this Russian-controlled New York City trading corporation has been financing many of the principal "red" agitators in recent years.

Have communistic demonstrations and activities diminished since November 16? An hour's talk with federal operatives and police officials who check reports from all over the country proves illuminating.

THE ANSWER is that agitation is proceeding on about the same scale as before. Organizers and speakers continue to tour from city to city attempting to stir up unrest among the poorest classes. In the larger centers demonstrations of more or less consequence are still staged periodically.

Our undercover men are a little reluctant to openly charge a newly recognized nation with breaking faith so soon but they are convinced the old order still prevails. At least their investigations have not developed any change for the better.

COMMUNIST spokesmen undoubtedly will seize on this statement as proof of the contention Moscow never did underwrite the American malcontents. They can argue that the movement in this country is 100 per cent domestic and carried on only by Americans.

But where does the jack come from? ask the police. Men and women can't be paid regularly and sent all over the country on speaking tours unless a war chest exists somewhere.

Again Red leaders would answer that the coin comes from small contributions collected from a large number of sympathizers. They would say further that the "brothers" and "sisters" working for the cause draw mere pittances, being in the movement because of deep-rooted conviction.

BUT, REPLY the officers, there is no central treasury organization. And as for collections, a recent meeting in Washington is typical. About 80 persons were present. Rent of the hall was $4. It was announced the Unemployed council would contribute $2 if the audience would chip in the rest. After the hat was passed a careful count totaled $1.84. A final stirring appeal brought out another quarter to save the night. This left up to others the speaker's traveling expenses here and on to the next city.

ABOUT two weeks before President...

ABDUCTION VICTIM, KIN AND KIDNAP SQUAD

COURT RESTRAINS BANCO STOCK SIFT

Molyneaux Signs Order Halting Action of State Commerce Commission.

4 OTHER KIDNAPINGS IN 30 MONTHS HERE

Obtained $128,400 of $310,000 Demanded; Eight of 20 Suspects in Prison.

Secrecy Veils Second Major Seizure Here

Victim Member of One of St. Paul's Wealthiest Families, Son of Adolph and Nephew of Otto Bremer, Minnesota Manager of Home Owners Loan Corporation; Phone Call Gave "Tip."

VANISHED AFTER TAKING HIS DAUGHTER TO SUMMIT SCHOOL ON GOODRICH AVENUE

Edward G. Bremer, president of the Commercial State bank and a member of one of St. Paul's wealthiest families, was kidnaped for $200,000 ransom Wednesday morning.

Police say they have received no official notification of the crime and the family refused to discuss it. Thomas Dahill, chief of police, said he was investigating reports of the crime.

Mr. Bremer is 37 years old and resides at 92 North Mississippi River boulevard. It is known he returned Tuesday from a business trip to Chicago. Efforts to effect his release are reported to have failed thus far.

SECOND MAJOR CASE IN 7 MONTHS.

It was the second big abduction in seven months of a member of a St. Paul brewing family. William Hamm Jr., president of the Hamm Brewing Co., paid $100,000 for his release last June.

Mr. Bremer is the son of Adolph Bremer, 855 West Seventh street, part owner of the Jacob Schmidt Brewing Co., and is a nephew of Otto Bremer, 1344 Summit avenue, a Democratic power, chairman of the American National bank and Minnesota manager of the Home

U. S. Agent on Way Here by Plane

Dallas, Jan. 18.—(AP)—Frank J. Blake, Department of Justice agent who directed most of the search for the kidnapers of Charles F. Urschel, Oklahoma City oil millionaire, left by plane today for St. Paul.

Owners Loan corporation. He also is a nephew of Paul Bremer, 145 Amherst avenue.

Kidnapers are reported to have seized him between 8:15 A. M. and 10 A. M. Wednesday, possibly on Summit avenue or in downtown St. Paul.

As was his custom, he drove his 8-year-old daughter, Betty, to Summit school, 1150 Goodrich avenue, where she is a pupil in the third grade, and apparently continued on his way to the bank at...

The kidnapping of Edward Bremer was just one of the many gangster-related crimes in St. Paul during this era.

Detectives from the Federal Bureau of Investigation (FBI) arrived, and the ordinary citizens of St. Paul resolved to clean up their city.

In the spring of 1934—after months of investigating—the FBI detectives finally got a break. While investigating the kidnapping of the banker Edward Bremer, the detectives uncovered enough evidence to arrest the worst criminals and bring St. Paul's gangster era to an end.

○ **Using the historical evidence and your Investigation Guide, imagine that you are a detective on the Bremer case. You will need to gather and analyze the evidence, make connections, consider various possible conclusions, and—ultimately—decide for yourself who the criminals were. Can you put the criminals behind bars?**

CLUE #1: A DRIVE-BY SHOOTING

January 13, 1934. Late at night, Northwest Airlines radio operator Roy McCord noticed three suspicious-looking men in a Chevrolet coupe driving through his St. Paul neighborhood. McCord was concerned and thought the men might be prowlers. Still dressed in his work uniform (a peaked hat and dark jacket with brass buttons), McCord decided to follow them in his car. When he pulled up next to them, a man jumped out of the coupe with a machine gun and fired nearly 50 bullets at McCord! McCord survived and was even able to recall the license plate, which was registered to an E. V. Davis. But the shooting was a mystery.

Why might a man shoot at Roy McCord for simply stopping his car?

CLUE #2: A BANKER IS KIDNAPPED!

January 17, 1934. The day started out like any normal one for Edward Bremer, the president of the Commercial State Bank in downtown St. Paul. Following his usual routine, Bremer ate breakfast, then drove his daughter to school. Two blocks beyond the school, he halted at a stop sign. Bremer later reported to the FBI what happened next:

> As I sat there, the [right] door opened and next to me an arm came in with a gun and a voice said: "Don't move or I'll kill you." I attempted to put the car in low gear and as I glanced up again there was a car crosswise in front of me. My next move was to grab the handle on the left door to get out of the door. By the time I grabbed the handle the fellow on the right side must have been in the car and hit me across the

Detectives re-created the scene of the Bremer kidnapping. **Does this scene match what Bremer describes?**

```
head with a gun. The
[left] door opened. I
don't know whether I
opened it or not. On
the other side, a
fellow came in and
I was crashed on that
side. After the man
grabbed me, he pulled
me down. I tried to
hold my foot out of
the door as long as I
could to see whether I
could stall them along
enough for someone to
drive up.... They grabbed me and beat me in
the head and I felt I was going to pass out
of the picture. I could not see because the
blood was coming over my eyes.... The car
started and we went away.
```

Bremer was blindfolded. After many hours, the car finally stopped and he was led into the house where he would be held for the next 21 days.

Back in St. Paul, Bremer's friends and family were frantic. Around 10:40 on the night that Bremer was kidnapped, his friend Walter Magee received a phone call. A voice said, "Hello, we've snatched your friend Ed Bremer. We want 200 grand." The caller then directed Magee to a ransom note that had been left outside his house. Magee quickly informed the Bremers and the police. The FBI began to investigate, too.

If you were an FBI agent, what clues would you use to help solve the crime?

CLUE #3: A SUSPICIOUS COUPLE

In the days after Bremer's kidnapping, several kinds of clues began to surface. More ransom notes were delivered. Witnesses came forward with reports of suspicious activities.

A newspaper article published in the *St. Paul Dispatch* on February 10, 1934, described a suspicious couple. That article, which appears to the right, provides a clue to help solve the Bremer case.

How was the couple linked to the kidnapping?

COUPLE SOUGHT IN BREMER CASE SIFT

U. S. Agents Try to Trace Man and Woman Who Had Apartment.

Federal authorities, the Dispatch learned today, have been attempting for the past several days to identify a man and woman who abandoned their apartment at 628 Grand avenue, a few hours after the kidnaping, January 17 of Edward G. Bremer, 37-year-old St. Paul banker.

The hurried, unannounced abandonment of the apartment was discovered by federal agents checking apartment buildings in the vicinity of Dale street and Grand avenue.

It was from an apartment in that vicinity that the telephone call was made to the home of Dr. H. T. Nippert, 706 Lincoln avenue. Dr. Nippert, Bremer family physician, received the call at 7 A. M., January 20. He was instructed by a man to look for an envelope under his front door. The envelope contained the first contact instructions to the victim's family.

The manager of the apartment building at 628 Grand avenue said that a woman who identified herself as a "Mrs. B—" rented a first floor apartment December 7 and paid a month's rent in bills of small denomination.

"The woman was dark, the building manager said. "She had a decided Irish brogue. I never saw her husband once during the time they lived here."

The woman told the apartment manager that her husband worked for a newsgathering agency. This was checked later and was found to be erroneous.

"The people did a lot of drinking and always had friends in their apartment, although they never were noisy or troublesome," the manager said.

The couple had an automobile, a small black, wire-wheeled coupe, the make of which the building manager never knew. The machine, the license numbers of which were unknown to the manager, always was kept at the rear.

Gone Day After Abduction.

"On January 7," the building manager continued, "the woman arranged to rent the apartment for another month. She paid the rent that time with a $50 bill."

Federal agents were especially interested in that angle, the manager observed.

"About 6:30 A. M. January 18, the day after Bremer was kidnaped," the manager said, "I discovered that the apartment occupied by these people was abandoned. The front door was found to be wide open and all the lights were burning. No one saw them leave."

Federal agents, it was learned, made a minute examination of the apartment and found two or three bottles which might bear fingerprints.

Were Seen in Drug Store.

A clerk at the Grandendale pharmacy, Dale street and Grand avenue, said that he had been queried by government investigators about purchases by the couple at the drug store.

"I remember both the man and woman," the clerk recalled, "but never knew their name."

His description of the woman tallied with that given by the apartment manager.

"The man was rather short and sandy complexioned," he said, "and not flashily dressed."

Division of Investigation
U. S. Department of Justice
Post Office Box 515
Saint Paul, Minnesota.

January 25, 1934.

7-576-73

RECORDED
&
INDEXED

JAN 27 1934

JAN 30 1934

FILE

Director,
Division of Investigation,
U. S. Department of Justice,
Washington, D. C.

Re: UNKNOWN SUBJECTS.
EDWARD C. BREMER, Victim.
KIDNAPING.
St. Paul File 7-30.

Dear Sir:

Enclosed please find fingerprint cards of Doctor H. T. Nippert, whose impressions possibly may appear on the various ransom notes forwarded to the Division.

There is some indication that the Barker-Karpis Gang again has been in the vicinity of St. Paul during this kidnaping and it might perhaps be advisable to examine their prints in connection with any prints found on any of the documents that have been forwarded in connection with the above matter. It is suggested that the prints of the following be kept in mind:

Volney Davis, McAlester, Okla. Pen. #12808;
Harry Campbell alias Dave Campbell, Sheriff's Office, Tulsa, Okla #9420;
Arthur R. Barker alias Doc Barker, McAlester, Okla. Pen. #11906;
Fred Barker, Lansing, Kans. Pen. #9856;
Alvin Karpis, Lansing, Kans. Pen. #1539.

Very truly yours,

Werner Hanni

WERNER HANNI,
Special Agent in Charge.

WH:IM
Encls.(2)
AIR MAIL
COPIES DESTROYED
20 MAR 17 1965

JAN 26 1934

CLUE #4: FBI MEMO ON SUSPECTS

January 25, 1934. After uncovering some information about possible suspects, FBI detective Werner Hanni wrote a letter to FBI director J. Edgar Hoover.

○ **Whom did Hanni suspect, and why?**

CLUE #5: A STRANGE PURCHASE

January 27, 1934. A man wearing a dark wool jacket, high-topped leather boots, and a wool cap pulled down to his eyes, entered the Grand Silver department store in St. Paul. The clerk, Mrs. Florence Humphrey, remembered his strange request.

He came into the store and bought the flashlights on a Saturday....In his hand he held a red lens, and he asked if we carried lenses of that kind. I told him we did not, and I directed him to a place where I thought he could obtain them. He then bought three flashlights, with necessary bulbs and batteries, and left.

She later described him as being of medium height and somewhat thin.

○ **How do you think Mrs. Humphrey's information helped solve the crime?**

STATE OF MINNESOTA, BUREAU OF CRIMINAL APPREHENSION
STATE CAPITOL BUILDING · ST. PAUL, MINNESOTA

Record from _Police Dpt_

On the above line please state whether Police Department, Sheriff's Office, or County Jail

(Address) _Tulsa - Okla_

Received from _____ County

Date received _Mar 23 · 1934_

Charge _Robbery_

Sentence _____

Place of birth _____

Nationality _____

Age _32_   Height _5'-3 1/2_

Weight _112_   Hair _Chest_

Build _Med_   Eyes _Blue_

Complexion _Med_

Marks and Scars _____

Brother of Fred Barker.

Paroled _____

ARTHUR "DOC" BARKER'S MUG CARD

CLUE #6: THE BARKER-KARPIS GANG

The Barker-Karpis gang was a group of criminals led by Alvin Karpis and the Barker brothers. Women were in the gang, too, but they committed minor crimes like shoplifting.

🔍 **What did these three mug cards reveal about these men from the Barker-Karpis Gang?**

STATE OF MINNESOTA, BUREAU OF CRIMINAL APPREHENSION
STATE CAPITOL BUILDING · ST. PAUL, MINNESOTA

Record from _Sheriff Office_

On the above line please state whether Police Department, Sheriff's Office, or County Jail

(Address) _West Plains Mo_

Received from _____ County

Date received _____

Charge _Murder_

Sentence _____

Place of birth _Kansas_

Nationality _____

Age _22 - 1921_   Height _5-9_

Weight _120_   Hair _Med Dark_

Build _Slim_   Eyes _Blue_

Complexion _Fair_

Marks and Scars _Scar at base_
left index finger.

Paroled _____

ALVIN KARPIS' MUG CARD

STATE OF MINNESOTA, BUREAU OF CRIMINAL APPREHENSION
STATE CAPITOL BUILDING · ST. PAUL, MINNESOTA

Record from _Sheriff Office_

On the above line please state whether Police Department, Sheriff's Office, or County Jail

(Address) _West Plains Mo_

Received from _____ County

Date received _____

Charge _Murder_

Sentence _____

Place of birth _Mo_

Nationality _____

Age _29 (1931)_   Height _5-4_

Weight _120_   Hair _sandy_

Build _slim_   Eyes _blue_

Complexion _fair_

Marks and Scars _Teeth: 2 upper and_
2 lower frt. crowned. Has
shot sc. outer left knee.

Paroled _____

FRED BARKER'S MUG CARD

Kate "Ma" Barker, the mother of Fred and Arthur Barker, was blonde and 5 feet, 4 inches tall.

CLUE #7: THE RANSOM IS PAID

February 6, 1934. The kidnappers sent instructions for the payment of the ransom. After packing up the $200,000 ransom, Magee drove to the location where the kidnappers told him he would find a black Chevrolet coupe. After transferring the money, Magee drove the coupe toward Zumbrota in southeastern Minnesota. As instructed, when he saw three red lights along the side of the road, Magee stopped the car and left the ransom money on the road. Later, when FBI agents examined the car, they found a blue cap.

What new clues could the FBI get from this payment of the ransom?

CLUE #8: BREMER IS RETURNED!

February 7, 1934. After 21 days of captivity, Bremer could barely believe the kidnappers when they said his ransom had been paid and he would be freed. After dressing him in new clothes and blindfolding him, they drove him away in a car. He described what happened next:

> Then the car stopped and they took me out and they put me in this other car. There were gasoline cans because I could smell them in this car. I had to bend down with my head in my hands. There were rattling noises in the car. Does a machine gun have clips on it that would rattle? Anyhow, we drove. We stopped once and they took this gasoline can out and filled the car. Anyhow, then I had room to stretch out my legs and I laid down in the [back].

After his release, Edward Bremer returned to the home of his father, Adolph Bremer, where they were photographed together.

The FBI uncovered four gas cans, as well as many other pieces of evidence connected to the Bremer kidnapping. **What other evidence do you see?**

Hours later, Bremer was dropped off in Rochester and instructed to catch a bus back to St. Paul. When he walked onto the back porch of his father's home and was greeted by his sister, Bremer was shaken and exhausted.

Did Bremer know any facts that could help solve the crime?

CLUE #9: GAS CANS DISCOVERED

February 10, 1934. Near Portage, Wisconsin, four gas cans and a funnel were discovered by a farmer. The FBI tested the cans and found that one of them had Arthur Barker's fingerprints on it.

How did this evidence connect to the crime?

In the months after Bremer's return, the search for his kidnappers continued. The FBI followed leads across the country, tracking down where the ransom money went, and even uncovering the kidnapping hideout. As the FBI increased the heat on all gangsters, St. Paul's era of crime ended. Within two years, the FBI had solved the crime, and Bremer's kidnappers were all dead or behind bars.

So who were the criminals? Can you solve the crime?

During World War II, the U.S. government created thousands of colorful posters to promote the war effort.

1932	1933	1934	1935	1936	1937	1939
Worldwide unemployment reaches 30 million people.	In January, Adolf Hitler of the National Socialist Party (Nazi) is elected chancellor of Germany. He is given absolute power in March.	Girl Scouts begin selling cookies as a fund-raiser.	First successful color motion picture is released.	President Franklin D. Roosevelt is elected to the second of his four terms.	Hormel develops SPAM luncheon meat.	World War II begins in Europe when Germany invades Poland.

Buy
WAR
BONDS

©1943—BY THE SEVEN-UP CO.
ST. LOUIS, MO. LITHO IN U.S.A.

While Minnesota, the United States, and most of the world struggled to cope with the hardships of the Great Depression, a second world war was brewing. The depression made life miserable for people all over the world—not just in the United States. People were unemployed and businesses were failing. In much of Europe, countries still struggled to rebuild economies that had been destroyed during World War I. Starvation threatened millions of Europeans. Fear and frustration led them to question their leaders, creating opportunities for new leaders. In Germany and Italy, harsh and repressive dictators rose to power. In 1936, these two nations signed a partnership agreement, forming what became known as the **Axis** powers.

Germany's dictator, Adolf Hitler, promised to restore the strength and pride his nation had enjoyed before World War I. Part of his plan was to seize land from neighboring countries. In 1939, his troops invaded Poland. Great Britain, France, and several other countries responded by declaring war on Germany. World War II had begun.

At first, most Americans—and most Minnesotans—wanted to stay

LOOK FOR

- ◆ Why did the United States enter the war?
- ◆ How did Hildred Long and other Minnesotans deal with life on the home front?
- ◆ Why were German prisoners of war put to work in Minnesota?
- ◆ What did William Cummings do to help the Allies win the war?
- ◆ What sacrifices did Minnesotans make during the war?

KEY TERMS

Axis
Allies
home front
war effort
rationing
victory gardens

Axis: the nations led by Germany, Italy, and Japan during World War II

1940	1941	1942	1943	1944	1945	1947
United States begins sending war supplies to Great Britain.	United States begins a secret program to develop an atomic bomb. Japan attacks Pearl Harbor, Hawaii, and the United States enters World War II.	After years of oppressing Europe's Jews and others, Nazi Germany begins killing them methodically. At Battle of Midway, Allies keep the Pacific from Japan's control.	Minnesota farmers begin using prisoners of war to work in their fields.	Plans for the United Nations are made at the Dumbarton Oaks Conference. Allies invade German-occupied France on D-Day (June 6).	President Roosevelt dies in April, shortly before Germany surrenders. United States drops atomic bombs on two Japanese cities in August, forcing Japan to surrender.	The Cold War— a long period of distrust and tension between the United States and the Soviet Union— begins.

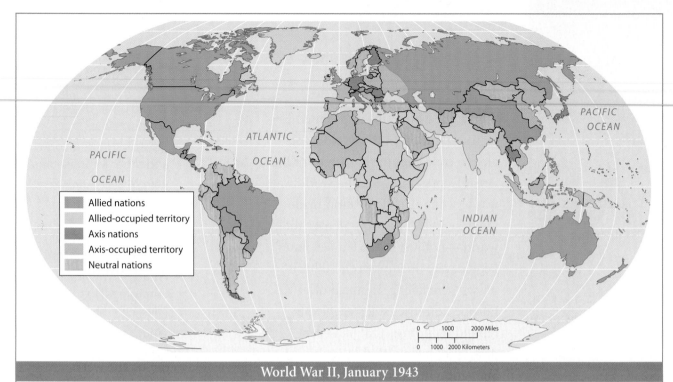

World War II, January 1943

Nations from every continent except Antarctica participated in World War II. While armies fought in Europe, Asia, and Africa, the combatants' air forces, navies, and marines expanded the war to the seas and skies.

Legend:
- Allied nations
- Allied-occupied territory
- Axis nations
- Axis-occupied territory
- Neutral nations

out of what people considered a European war. But the United States could not ignore what was happening in Europe. In 1940, after defeating Poland and occupying much of Eastern Europe, Germany's army swept through and occupied Denmark, Norway, the Netherlands, Belgium, Luxembourg, and France. Then, in 1941, Germany invaded the Soviet Union. Great Britain suffered nightly bombing raids and feared a German invasion. The United States became alarmed and started sending weapons and supplies to Great Britain to help it hold off the Germans.

Meanwhile, the island empire of Japan had invaded northern China, Korea, and Southeast Asia. By 1940, Japan had joined the Axis powers of Germany and Italy. During the next year, Japan and the United States tried to negotiate their differences. But military leaders in Japan believed that Japan should go to war against the United States. Then, on December 7, 1941, Japan attacked the U.S. naval base at Pearl Harbor, Hawaii. The United States was at war. Joining the fight against the Axis, the United States became a part of the **Allied** nations that included Great Britain and the Soviet Union.

Allies: the nations led by Great Britain, the Soviet Union, and the United States during World War II.

World War II touched the lives of Minnesotans and other Americans in all sorts of ways. It brought new jobs and pumped money into the economy. But it also forced almost everyone to make sacrifices. And, like every war, it destroyed lives and shattered dreams. Life in Minnesota changed drastically during the war. People worried about very basic concerns, like getting enough food and keeping their loved ones safe.

The Home Front

Most Minnesotans spent the war at home, in Minnesota. They lived their lives as best they could—working, making sacrifices, and worrying about loved ones who were off fighting the war. William Cummings and Hildred Long were among the hundreds of thousands of people who spent the war on the Minnesota **home front.**

William Cummings was a restless young man who worked for four employers in the Twin Cities over the course of the war. Cummings and his wife Betty followed the war news and wondered constantly whether he would be called to fight.

William Cummings was in his twenties when World War II broke out. He wrote in his diary daily about the events of the war and his life on the home front.

December 7, 1941

Something happened today that I thought would never happen at all. Japan declared war on the United States!...It is hard to realize that we are now actually engaged in war. My friend Eugene Larson is a gunner's mate in the U.S. Navy on the Pacific Ocean.

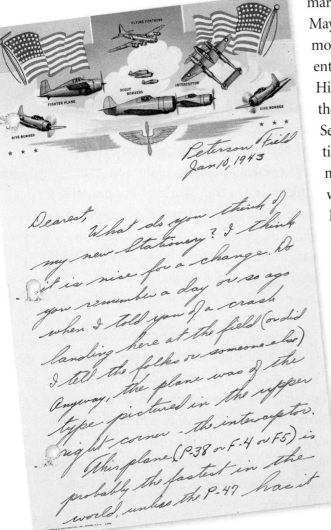

LETTER FROM FRANK LONG TO HIS WIFE, HILDRED

Hildred Shelland married Frank Long in May 1942—just one month before Frank entered the army. Hildred Long worked for the New Deal's Farm Security Administration, teaching homemaking skills to women around Detroit Lakes. Later she took another government job in Ada. Hildred and Frank Long wrote to each other almost every day they were apart. Their letters provide personal glimpses of life during World War II.

home front: the area of civilian (nonmilitary) activity during a war

War Work

As I came to work, a long freight train went by. It was all flatcars. Each flatcar had two new army trucks on it. This is the first time I had seen anything like that.

In November 1941, William Cummings heard that a new plant in New Brighton that made ammunition was hiring workers. "The pay is really good there," he wrote in his diary. But competition for the jobs at Twin Cities Ordnance was fierce. Cummings finally landed a job there, inspecting bullet casings. "It was really interesting to see the bullets form from chunks of metal," he wrote after his first day on the job. "And the noise from these machines! One has to shout to be heard."

Ever since the war had begun in 1939—a year and a half before the attack on Pearl Harbor—the United States had been preparing for war, mostly to help supply the Allies in Europe. Military planners also knew that if the United States entered the war, the nation would need all sorts of supplies—especially weapons and ammunition—for its own soldiers. These planners pushed for a huge increase in the production of war-related supplies. Twin Cities Ordnance was one of more than 200 government-owned weapons factories that opened in the United States between 1940 and 1945.

MANUFACTURERS

war effort: the combined efforts of civilians and the military to help win a war

Many Minnesota companies also contributed to the **war effort.** Some companies started making new products that the military needed. Others increased production of things that were suddenly in high demand. For example, Munsingwear, a Minnesota underwear manufacturer, made military clothing. Crown Iron Works of Minneapolis produced portable bridges and pontoons. Andersen Corporation, a window manufacturer in Bayport, made easy-to-assemble huts for military use. Meat processor Hormel made millions of cans of SPAM luncheon meat to feed soldiers and civilians around the world.

AGRICULTURE

Minnesota's farmers also increased production during the war, but a shortage of farm workers made it difficult. Many farm men had gone off to war, and thousands of rural men and women had taken high-paying defense jobs in the cities. The government tried to ease the shortage by exempting farm workers from serving in the military. The state urged women, children, and the elderly to help out with farm work. In 1944, several thousand German prisoners of war and foreign workers from countries such as Mexico, Jamaica, and Barbados were put to work on Minnesota's farms.

As more and more men went off to war, many women filled defense jobs. This worker is sorting bullets at the Twin Cities Ordnance plant.

IRON ORE AND TIMBER

World War II also pumped new life into Minnesota's iron ore and timber industries. Many mines on the iron ranges had shut down during the Great Depression of the 1930s. But when the United States began preparing for war in 1939, everything changed. Mines on the Mesabi, Vermilion, and Cuyuna Ranges resumed full-time production. These mines sent off millions of tons of iron ore to be turned into guns, tanks, bombs, and ships. Minnesota's timber industry had a hard time keeping up with increased demand for lumber and paper products. In November 1943, officials estimated that the state had a shortage of about 4,000 loggers. The following year, lumber companies—like farms—began employing German prisoners of war.

rationing: limiting the amount of certain foods or materials that one is allowed to purchase

Making Sacrifices

In the first few months after the attack on Pearl Harbor, life seemed to go on as usual for many Minnesotans. But by the spring of 1942, things were changing. The U.S. government started a system of **rationing,** limiting the amount of certain items that people could buy. Sugar was one of the first foods to be rationed. Some people, like William Cummings, stocked up on sugar before the rationing took effect. Others, like Hildred Long, found they could make do with less. "I bought

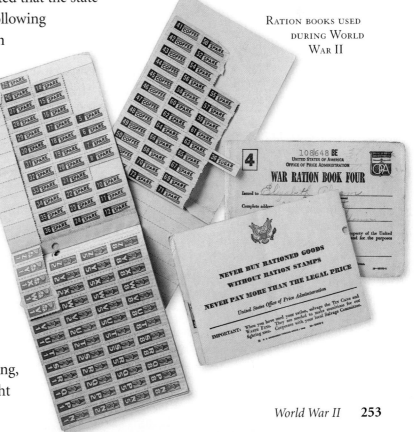

RATION BOOKS USED DURING WORLD WAR II

VICTORY GARDEN POSTER

victory gardens: private or community gardens that people planted to help relieve food shortages during wartime

At Franklin School in St. Paul, Boy Scouts helped gather scrap metal for the war effort in 1941.

some more sugar tonight," she wrote in a letter to Frank. "If I don't begin using it I will have all my containers full and people will begin accusing me of hoarding."

In early 1943, the government announced that the armed forces of the United States and its allies needed 25 percent of all the food the nation produced. The government began rationing a wide variety of foods, including meat, milk, eggs, soups, juices, and almost every kind of canned, dried, or frozen fruit and vegetable. People had to have special government-issued ration stamps to buy these foods. Each person got a certain number of points. Many Minnesotans, including Hildred Long, struggled at first with the rationing system. "We're to have only 48 points for our canned food rationing," she wrote, "with Number 2 can peas counting 16 or 18 points—other foods accordingly—fruits more and soups and baby foods less. It will amount to about a can a week per person." In order to make up for the smaller amounts of food they could buy, many Americans began to grow their own food in what were called **victory gardens.**

Other new consumer goods, like safety pins, refrigerators, cars, and tires, became hard or impossible to find. Raw materials such as copper, brass, and rubber were being used to make military hardware instead of everyday items. People learned to conserve, reuse, or repair the things they needed. Because the military needed gasoline and rubber for tanks, trucks, and planes, both were rationed throughout the war. Minnesotans walked or relied on public buses, trains, and trolleys.

By late 1943, it seemed like everything was in short supply—even nylon stockings. Hildred Long wrote that it was "a tragedy" when she discovered "a wide run in a perfectly good pair of nylon hose."

Across the country, Americans contributed to the war effort by buying war bonds—loans that the government promised to pay back with interest after the war was over. Buying war bonds left people with less money to spend, but many—including William Cummings—considered it their patriotic duty. "I'm glad to do that little bit toward helping out in this war," he wrote.

Posters encouraged people to carpool, since conserving tires and fuel could help win the war.

Joining the Fight

More than 300,000 Minnesotans served in the army, the army air forces, the navy, the marines, or the Coast Guard during World War II. They came from every part of the state and from every racial and ethnic background, although blacks served in segregated units and were mostly limited to a few types of jobs. Hundreds of Dakota and Ojibwe also served in the war. Many people throughout the state volunteered. Many others were drafted, or called by the government to serve in the military. They served in Europe, Africa, the Pacific, and throughout the United States. All of them understood that the war was a serious matter with deadly consequences.

Minnesotans on the home front understood this, too.

William Cummings, for one, struggled with mixed feelings about the war. He wanted to help his country win, but he worried about what

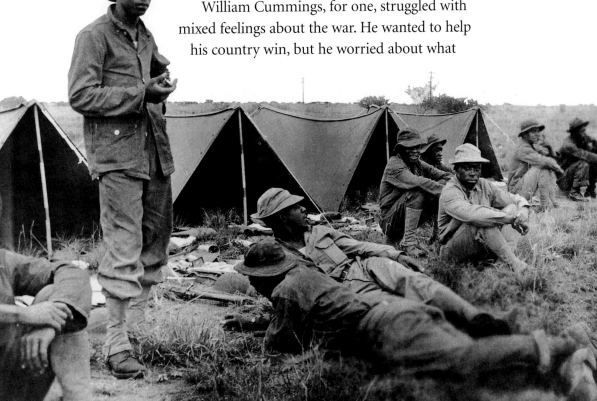

In World War II, African American soldiers served in separate units. In 1948, President Harry S. Truman integrated the armed forces.

255

would happen if he went off to fight. "If I only knew I would come back for sure I wouldn't mind going so much," he wrote, "but oh, I would hate to die so young!" Cummings tried to enlist in December 1943, but when he took a physical, doctors determined that because of stomach trouble he was not healthy enough to join the military. He returned home from his physical and told his wife the news. "Betty was so happy when I got home that she laughed and cried," he wrote.

Hildred Long's husband, on the other hand, did go away to fight in the war. "I miss you so much," she wrote shortly after he joined the army. "You have been gone for only a week and it seems like a year." Frank Long spent nearly three years serving on various assignments in the United States, but his wife worried that he might be sent into harm's way. Finally, in 1945, he shipped off to the Pacific. But he never got close to the fighting. Germany surrendered in May. In August, the United States dropped a new kind of weapon—the atomic bomb— on the Japanese cities of Hiroshima and Nagasaki. Japan surrendered a few weeks later on September 2. The war was over. The Allies had won. Frank Long went home to Minnesota and Hildred.

WILLIAM CUMMINGS' DIARY

June 6, 1944

At last the day we have all been waiting for has arrived—"D-Day"— the invasion of Europe.... It seems the invasion has been underway in fine shape. It must be literal hell for many of the men there.

May 8, 1945

All the sirens, whistles and bells blew and rang.... Much emphasis was made that we have a lot to do yet with the war with Japan.... V-E Day has been different than I thought it would [be]. It was a gradual affair.

HILDRED LONG'S LETTER

August 7, 1945

I suppose you have heard a great deal about this new atomic bomb. It offers, at least its principle offers, just such an enormous possibility for good and bad that we little realize just how tremendously it will change our future civilization.

Not all Minnesotans came home. Nearly 6,000 Minnesotans died in World War II. Countless others were wounded. Some were missing and never found. But most of the state's servicemen and servicewomen returned safe and sound. They came back to hugs and kisses and parades. They were considered heroes. As friends and families settled down and got reacquainted with each other, many Minnesotans looked forward to a bright future. But the future was cloudy. Americans soon realized that the postwar world was full of new dangers that forced them to rethink what it meant to be secure.

A SOLDIER'S STORY

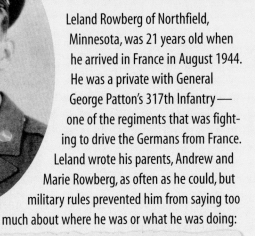

Leland Rowberg of Northfield, Minnesota, was 21 years old when he arrived in France in August 1944. He was a private with General George Patton's 317th Infantry— one of the regiments that was fighting to drive the Germans from France. Leland wrote his parents, Andrew and Marie Rowberg, as often as he could, but military rules prevented him from saying too much about where he was or what he was doing:

August 22, 1944

There isn't much I can say about what I am doing. Have run into some Germans. They are everything that you have read about them. Some are fanatical in their devotion to the Nazi cause while others seem quite reticent about sacrificing their lives for the Führer.

September 10, 1944

Well, I am 22 today and it was some birthday. I wanted to go to church today but was too busy.... Have seen quite a few instances of Nazi efficiency that they have favored the French with. It seems impossible to believe that people can be so vicious in this day and age. The war news is certainly excellent. It seems like the war should end within another month or so.

September 27, 1944

War news continues to be good and I am quite optimistic about its end. However, the Germans we have been meeting are quite fanatical and are fighting hard.

September 30, 1944

I had an opportunity to take a shower today and you can't imagine how good it felt. I don't believe I ever was as dirty as I was until that shower.

October 2, 1944

I am sorry I can't write you oftener but circumstances prevent me from doing so. We have been so busy that we seldom have time even to think about writing.... There isn't much more to say except that I am feeling fine and am anxiously awaiting the packages you have been sending.

Andrew and Marie Rowberg looked forward to their son's letters and wrote him almost every day. They tried not to let him know how worried they were about him, but sometimes their fears came through:

October 8, 1944

We are following the war developments in France anxiously and of course still wondering where you are and in what actions you have been.... Hope this letter will find you well and with morale high.... Love, Dad

October 10, 1944

A month ago today since you wrote the letter we received last—and it has seemed a lifetime ... Most important of all, write us a letter. We are getting quite worried. Loads of love, Mom

October 21, 1944

I am sure you are "on the line" again. God help and protect you! As we would have heard from you otherwise.... Love, Mom

October 23, 1944

We are afraid you are back "on the line" again. Hope you can get back to get some rest. I know this must sound terribly absurd to you where you are and what you do, see, and hear. The trouble is we do know something of what is going on and we feel so helpless.... Love, Mom

Leland never read any of these letters from his parents. On October 9, 1944, he was killed as his company tried to reclaim a small French village from the Germans. His parents did not hear anything about him until October 24—the day after they sent their final letter. Even then, the telegram they received informed them only that Leland was missing. It was another week before they learned that he was dead.

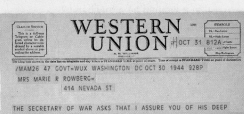

Virginia Mae Hope: World War II Pilot

Can a woman be a mechanic? A pilot? Before World War II, these jobs were considered "men's work." But a shortage of workers during the war began to change that idea, and government posters, like the one above, challenged people to think—and work—differently.

Virginia Mae Hope—Ginny—of Winnebago, Minnesota, had a dream: she wanted to fly airplanes for a living. In 1941, the same year that the Japanese bombed Pearl Harbor, she started flight school and earned her private and commercial pilot licenses. She was only 20 years old.

But after Ginny had earned her pilot licenses, no one would hire her. Although women had been some of the earliest pilots, many people in the 1940s did not think women could—or should—fly airplanes. Instead of working as a pilot, Ginny began training as an air traffic controller at the Minneapolis airport. This, too, was considered a "man's job," and she was hired only because it was wartime and men were not available.

While Ginny was training to become an air traffic controller, the U.S. Army began to run short of pilots to fly their planes at home and overseas. In 1942, the army came up with a solution to the pilot shortage: they would recruit women to fly planes.

The army called this new group of pilots the Women Airforce Service Pilots, or WASPs. The WASPs flew noncombat missions around the United States for the army air forces. This plan freed male pilots to fly planes in battle. From the moment Ginny heard about the WASP program, she knew that this was how she wanted to serve her country.

But the army refused to admit her into the WASPs. Her work as an air traffic controller was too important for her to leave. Ginny was crushed, but she did not give up her dream.

VIRGINIA MAE HOPE AT THE CONTROLS OF AN AIRPLANE

In this Investigation, you will explore primary sources that tell Ginny's story. These sources come from her cousin Lyle, from a flight instructor, from Ginny herself, and from her friend Winifred. As you study these sources, try to put together the story of Virginia Mae Hope.

What part of Ginny's story do each of these four people tell? As you read, use your Investigation Guide to keep track of the information you find.

GINNY AT ABOUT AGE SIX

Virginia Mae Hope (Ginny)
(1921-1944)

In her younger years, Cousin "Ginny" was called a tom-boy. Anything a boy could do - she could go one better. It could be in hunting, driving farm machinery, flying, eating corn on the cob, and even a couple of times would show me how to catch fish. (the biggest + the most) "Ginny was also tops in high school + in college.
She attended both: Gustavus Adolphus in St Peter, Mn + NorthWestern Univ. in Evanston, Ill.
"Ginny" could fix anything: and was a certified aircraft mechanic.

LETTER WRITTEN BY GINNY'S COUSIN LYLE

Ginny wrote these three quotes on the inside of her flight notebook. **What do they tell you about her as a pilot?**

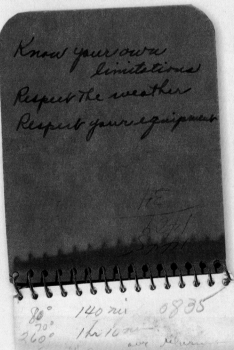

COUSIN LYLE REMEMBERS

Born on August 17, 1921, Ginny loved riding horses and was a great kidder and teaser. She was especially close to her father and, as an only child, spent a lot of time with him on the family farm in Winnebago.

Ginny was good at school, but she was also handy and loved tinkering with engines. Like a lot of farm kids, Ginny drove a car and tractor from an early age. Her cousin Lyle Schmidt remembered her as a "hot rod jockey." Lyle, who often spent summers on the Hopes' farm, described her in a letter.

What does Cousin Lyle's letter tell you about Ginny?

A FLIGHT INSTRUCTOR'S RECORD OF GINNY

Ginny learned to fly through the Civilian Pilot Training Program. This program was set up by the government to meet the growing need for pilots. Just one in ten students in the program could be female. Like any new student, Ginny had strengths and weaknesses.

RATING SHEET
CONTROLLED PRIVATE FLYING COURSE
Stage B
Minimum, 5 Hrs.—2 Hrs. Dual Check
Grade Maneuvers During Instruction

Ident. No. NC 26714
Make and model Cub 3C
Engine Lyc Hp. 50
Time up _____ a. m. _____ p. m.
Time down _____ a. m. _____ p. m.
Date 4-15-41

Note.—Keep time by stages.

Ground Instr. Time	DUAL Hr.	DUAL Min.	SOLO Hr.	SOLO Min.
Time this flight				30
Previous time		45	1	15
Total stage time			1	45
Total course time	8	45	1	45

Solo Practice

Lesson No. 7.

To read the score card:
1—excellent
2—above average
3—average
4—below average
5—poor

Wind direction	Wind velocity	Judgment	Aptitude	Number of landings	Taxiing	Take-offs	Climbs and turns	Glides and turns	Approaches (180°)	Landings	Forced landings	Coordination exercises	S turns	30° 8's
W	1	2	3	3	4	3	3	3	3	3	4		4	

Landing too fast. Student dissatisfied with own ability to land.

Check number in each column indicating student's characteristics

A	ATTITUDE	B	PHYSICAL TRAITS	C	MENTAL TRAITS	D		FLYING HABITS		E	SPECIAL FAULTS
1	Eager to learn.	1	Relaxed.	1	Alert.	1	Good coordination.	7	Good timing.	1	Cocky.
2	Cooperative.	2	Good control touch.	2	Careful.	2	Good speed sense.	8	Climbs too steep.	2	Disobedient.
3	Punctual.	3	Tired.	3	Consistent.	3	Poor coordination.	9	Skids on turns.	3	Overconfident.
4	Tardy.	4	Tense.	4	Erratic.	4	Nose too high.	10	Slips on turns.	4	Overcautious.
5	Indifferent.	5	Forgetful.	5	Forgetful.	5	Nose too low.	11	Lands too fast.	5	Irresponsible.
6	Hard-headed.	6	Airsick.	6	Mechanical.	6	Dives in glide.	12	Reacts slowly.	6	Reckless.

Above instruction given.

(Instructor's signature) 13849 1820 _(Cert. No.)_ _(Rating)_

Above-ground and flight instruction received.

Virginia Mae Hope
(Student's signature (first, middle, and last names) must be signed exactly the same on all forms) 16—17685

What can you learn from this rating sheet about Ginny's performance as a beginning pilot?

GETTING THE NEWS

Despite the fact that she was already a licensed pilot, the government did not allow Ginny to join the WASPs. But Ginny did not give up. For months she wrote letters to military officials in Chicago and Washington, pleading to be released from the air traffic control job—so she could join the WASPs. Over and over they refused. Finally, in May 1943, she received this Western Union telegram.

What news did this telegram bring to Ginny?

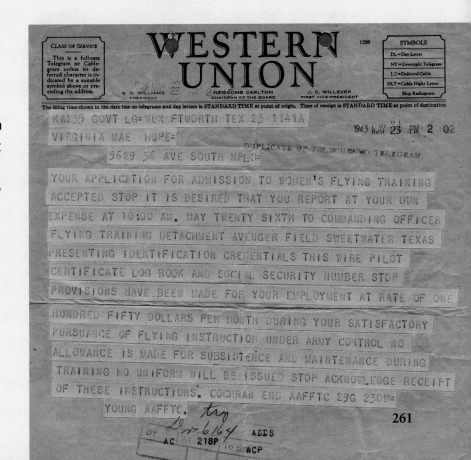

WESTERN UNION

CLASS OF SERVICE
This is a full-rate Telegram or Cablegram unless its deferred character is indicated by a suitable symbol above or preceding the address.

A. N. WILLIAMS
PRESIDENT
NEWCOMB CARLTON
CHAIRMAN OF THE BOARD
J. C. WILLEVER
FIRST VICE-PRESIDENT

SYMBOLS
DL=Day Letter
NT=Overnight Telegram
LC=Deferred Cable
NLT=Cable Night Letter
Ship Radiogram

The filing time shown in the date line on telegrams and day letters is STANDARD TIME at point of origin. Time of receipt is STANDARD TIME at point of destination.

KA255 GOVT LG=WUX FTWORTH TEX 23 1141A

1943 MAY 23 PM 2 02

VIRGINIA MAE HOPE=

5629 36 AVE SOUTH MPLS=

DUPLICATE OF TELEPHONED TELEGRAM

YOUR APPLICATION FOR ADMISSION TO WOMEN'S FLYING TRAINING ACCEPTED STOP IT IS DESIRED THAT YOU REPORT AT YOUR OWN EXPENSE AT 10:00 AM MAY TWENTY SIXTH TO COMMANDING OFFICER FLYING TRAINING DETACHMENT AVENGER FIELD SWEETWATER TEXAS PRESENTING IDENTIFICATION CREDENTIALS THIS WIRE PILOT CERTIFICATE LOG BOOK AND SOCIAL SECURITY NUMBER STOP PROVISIONS HAVE BEEN MADE FOR YOUR EMPLOYMENT AT RATE OF ONE HUNDRED FIFTY DOLLARS PER MONTH DURING YOUR SATISFACTORY PURSUANCE OF FLYING INSTRUCTION UNDER ARMY CONTROL NO ALLOWANCE IS MADE FOR SUBSISTENCE AND MAINTENANCE DURING TRAINING NO UNIFORM WILL BE ISSUED STOP ACKNOWLEDGE RECEIPT OF THESE INSTRUCTIONS COCHRAN END AAFFTC 29G 230V=

YOUNG AAFFTC.

Size 40

THE WISHING WELL — WAS WET!

THINK IT WILL FLY?

AVENGER, WE ARE HERE

GINNY'S SCRAPBOOK

These photos from Ginny's scrapbook show some of her experiences while training at Avenger Field in Texas. The WASPs trained 16 hours a day, six days a week, sometimes in hand-me-down "zoot suits" made for men. But they also had a lot of fun together. After making her first solo flight, each WASP was thrown into the flight school's wishing well to celebrate.

What can you learn about Ginny from this scrapbook page?

WASPS

"Isn't it just wonderful!" Ginny used to say about flying. Ginny served as a WASP for more than a year, ferrying planes and military personnel around the United States. While female pilots never flew in battles, they did fly the planes to ships that then carried the planes to battles. WASPs also completed dangerous assignments like pulling targets behind their planes so men in other aircraft could practice shooting at the targets — using real bullets.

But as World War II neared an end, returning male pilots took over WASP jobs, and the WASPs disbanded in 1944. Few women remained pilots, since most airlines would not hire them to fly planes.

Ginny was lucky. She was able to secure a job with a ferrying company, flying old military planes to destinations to be sold or taken apart. On December 7, 1944 — the same day her parents received a letter from her telling them she would be home for Christmas — she boarded a military transport plane as a passenger. That plane crashed on takeoff. No one survived.

GINNY'S FRIEND WINIFRED REMEMBERS

More than a year after her death, Ginny's parents received this letter from Winifred Wood, a fellow WASP.

What does this letter tell you about Virginia Mae Hope's life?

Ginny's WASP
BOMBER JACKET

Ginny's
WASP MILITARY
SERVICE PIN

W. Wood
901 Castile Ave.
Coral Gables, Fla.

MIAMI, FLA.
JUN 19
10-PM
1946

AIR 8 CENTS MAIL
UNITED STATES OF AMERICA

June 19, 1946

Dear Mr. & Mrs. Hope,

...Yes, I knew Virginia. I knew her as one of our best pilots and for a 'gallant' girl who loved her flying a great deal. She worked hard to make sure that she would live up to the responsibilites that were entrusted to us. In doing so she left a record that was tops...I also remember the first girl in our class to solo. Yes, it was Virginia and we threw her in the Wishing well. That was quite a day for her and she was so happy. The first one of some hundred girls to take the PT up alone—it was an acheivement.

I cannot say how shocked and saddened we all were to hear the tragic news of Virginia...

THE ALL-ELECTRIC KITCHEN..

THE KITCHEN OF TOMORROW!

- ● **ELECTRIC RANGE**
- ● **ELECTRIC DISHWASHER**
- ● **ELECTRIC WATER HEATER**
- ● **SMALL A**

1945	**1946**	**1947**	**1948**	**1949**	**1950**	**1954**
World War II ends. In New Hampshire, Charles Tupper invents Tupperware.	General Mills introduces Multi-Purpose Food (MPF) for use as a food supplement.	Bell Labs invents the cell phone. In Massachusetts, Dr. Percy Spencer invents the microwave oven.	KSTP, Minnesota's first television station, begins broadcasting.	Soviet Union conducts its first test explosion of an atomic bomb. Betty Crocker cake mixes are introduced.	St. Paul native Charles Schulz begins drawing the comic strip *Peanuts*.	Dr. Jonas Salk develops the polio vaccine.

After World War II, many Minnesotans sought a sense of security. Modern kitchens became popular as people focused on life at home.

CTRIC REFRIGERATOR

CTRIC GARBAGE DISPOSAL

CTRIC HOME FREEZER

CES

LOOK FOR

◆ What caused the Cold War to begin?

◆ How did General Mills market its products during the Cold War?

◆ Who was Betty Crocker?

◆ What was Multi-Purpose Food?

◆ Why did Ed Mahowald build a fallout shelter?

KEY TERMS

communism

capitalism

superpower

Cold War

fallout shelter

civil defense

When World War II ended in 1945, many Minnesotans were looking forward to better times—to peace and prosperity. They dreamed of a postwar world in which they could feel safe and secure.

But another kind of war was just beginning.

In many ways, the postwar world was less secure than it ever had been. America's former ally, the Soviet Union, was using military force to spread its brand of **communism** to other countries. Communism is grounded in the belief that the best society is one in which everyone receives an equal share of their nation's goods and wealth, and all property is held in common. Many Americans—including many Minnesotans—were afraid that communism would spread to the United States and threaten the American ideal of **capitalism,** which allows private individuals to own property and increase their wealth.

communism: an economic system in which property and businesses are owned by the government for the benefit of all citizens

capitalism: an economic system in which property and businesses are privately owned

1956	1957	1958	1961	1963	1965	1969
Federal Highway Act authorizes the construction of an interstate highway system.	In October, the Soviet Union launches Sputnik, the first man-made satellite to orbit Earth. In November, they launch Sputnik II, which carries Laika, a dog, into space.	Congress designates Grand Portage as a national monument.	Soviet cosmonaut Yuri Gagarin becomes first human in outer space. Major-league baseball and football come to Minnesota as the Twins and Vikings begin to play.	Guthrie Theater opens in Minneapolis.	First minicomputers are sold.	U.S. astronaut Neil Armstrong is the first human to walk on the moon.

Cold War: the ongoing conflict between the United States and the Soviet Union from 1945 to 1991

In 1949—four years after the United States dropped atomic bombs on Japan—the Soviet Union exploded its own atomic bomb to test the bomb's abilities. Soon the Americans and the Soviets were threatening each other with nuclear weapons even though they knew a nuclear war could destroy the earth. This standoff between the world's two most powerful nations became known as the **Cold War.**

FROZEN IN A DEADLOCK

The Cold War dominated world events for most of the second half of the twentieth century. This simmering and dangerous standoff featured two **superpowers**— the United States and the Soviet Union. Each feared the other as an enemy bent on world domination.

The United States and the Soviet Union had been reluctant allies during World War II, but their alliances did not last. After the war, the Soviets installed communist governments in many Eastern European countries. Soon, Europe was effectively split in two. On one side— the United States and its allies in Western Europe and Canada. On the other side— the Soviet Union and its communist allies in Eastern Europe. Each side sought alliances with other countries and built up armies to protect itself from the other. By the 1950s, both sides were stockpiling nuclear weapons many times more powerful than the ones dropped on Hiroshima and Nagasaki.

Several times over the years, the United States and the Soviet Union came close to going to war. But each time they stepped back. Instead, the two Cold War rivals fought each other indirectly by taking part in wars involving smaller, less powerful nations.

superpower: an extremely powerful country that influences or controls its allies

To prevent panic, children practiced what they would do during an actual attack.

As this sense of global insecurity grew, more and more Minnesotans responded by trying to build cocoons of security around themselves. They got married in record numbers, had children, and moved into comfortable new homes. They tried to shut out the dangers of the postwar world by concentrating on something they felt they could control: their family's home life. But it wasn't that easy. No home, no matter how happy and secure, could make the dangers of the world go away.

The Cold War also created new business opportunities— especially for companies that understood people's concerns about security and insecurity. One of these companies was a well-established Minneapolis flour manufacturer that knew how to respond to changing markets. Its name was General Mills.

Secure in the Kitchen

By the late 1940s, General Mills was one of the best-known companies in Minnesota—and one of the most successful. It had started out in the 1870s as a flour milling company called Washburn-Crosby and Company. Over the years the company had profited handsomely from the good reputation of its trademark product, Gold Medal flour. But by the end of World War II, General Mills—as the company was now known—faced a big challenge. Its baking flour business was in trouble.

After the war, women were encouraged to find satisfaction in baking and other domestic activities.

At first, it looked like General Mills' flour business would thrive in the postwar world. Hundreds of thousands of young women who had worked in factories during the war were giving up their jobs—willing or not—and taking on the more traditional roles of wife, mother, and homemaker. The company hoped that those new brides would now spend more time making delicious baked goods for their husbands and children. But it didn't turn out that way. Many young women had gotten used to working at a fast wartime pace. They had little or no experience in the kitchen. As a result, they often bought their bread at the store instead of making it from scratch at home. This was bad news for companies that, like General Mills, manufactured flour for home baking.

So General Mills decided to change. It started making new products that appealed to the new generation of postwar housewives. The new products were designed to be convenient. They also were meant to appeal to America's Cold War desire for easy living.

BETTY CROCKER

The centerpiece of General Mills' new corporate strategy was a make-believe kitchen expert named Betty Crocker. The company had created Betty Crocker in the 1920s. It hired an artist to paint her "portrait" and added her "signature" to the recipes and cooking advice it gave out to consumers. Over time, Betty Crocker turned into the main corporate symbol of General Mills. By 1945, 91 percent of American women recognized the Crocker name. As Americans settled into the security of their postwar homes, General Mills once again turned to Betty Crocker to lead the way to prosperity.

General Mills researchers determined that many young American women of the early postwar years longed for "the apprenticeship of the

General Mills updates Betty Crocker's appearance regularly so she always looks current. Portraits of Betty Crocker from 1936, 1955, 1968, and 1996 show how her image has kept up with the times.

Published in 1950, *Betty Crocker's Picture Cook Book* became an instant bestseller.

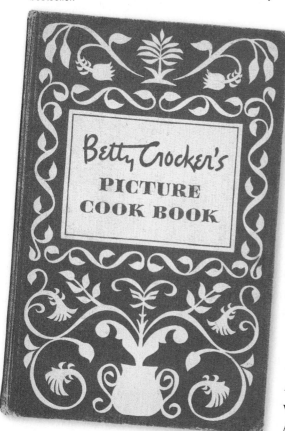

stove"—the opportunity to learn cooking skills from their mothers and grandmothers. As the company saw it, these new homemakers needed someone to show them how to make good meals for their growing families. They needed a patient, knowledgeable, and reassuring guide. Someone like Betty Crocker.

The Cookbook

In 1950, General Mills published a new book that set the foundation for the company's postwar success. *Betty Crocker's Picture Cook Book* was unlike any cookbook ever written before. It was colorful. It was easy to understand. And it included hundreds of photographs that explained, step by step, how to make everything from lemon chiffon cake to chicken à la king. It told young housewives that cooking was "the age old way to express love and concern for their [families'] welfare." And not only that—it was fun and easy.

Betty Crocker's Picture Cook Book was a huge success. In two years, it sold more than two million copies. It convinced many young American women that they—like their mothers and grandmothers—could make wholesome and nutritious family meals. But many of the recipes in the Picture Cook Book were just as elaborate as the ones mother and grandmother used to make. What if the modern homemaker didn't want to spend quite so much time in the kitchen? Could she still "express love" for her family through food without going to too much fuss? The answer, according to General Mills, was a definite yes.

Convenience Foods and Appliances

Betty Crocker's Picture Cook Book may have introduced Americans to fancy recipes like lemon chiffon cake, but it was the modern cake mix that actually changed the way Americans baked. Ready-to-make cakes in eye-catching boxes offered housewives a solution. They could make their families tasty desserts like the ones illustrated in the *Picture Cook Book* without spending so much time in the kitchen and without fear of failure. In the words of one General Mills researcher:

> *For the first time [the housewife] has the possibility of compromise; mixes not only save time, but permit [her] to be creative in new forms…modern ready-mixes permit her to bake at home, but in an easy fashion which assures her success.*

"Big Red," the nickname for *Betty Crocker's Picture Cook Book*, encouraged bakers to make perfect cookies like these.

General Mills introduced its Betty Crocker cake mixes in 1949. Soon the company had a whole line of easy-to-use baking products that appealed to Americans' desire for home-cooked comfort. Among the most successful was an all-purpose baking mix called Bisquick. With a box of Bisquick baking mix and a few additional ingredients, a postwar housewife could whip up a dinner featuring Biscuitburger appetizers, Topsy-Turvy meat pie, and Apple Pan Dowdy for dessert.

America's Cold War devotion to home life also helped convince General Mills to experiment with a new kind of business: home appliances. During World War II, the company had manufactured machinery for the military. After the war, its production lines switched over to making electric irons, toasters, coffeemakers, and pressure cookers. The new appliances were sold under the Betty Crocker name. The company touted them as labor-saving devices that would help the woman of the house create a more comfortable and tidy home.

All of these General Mills products—the cookbooks, the baking mixes, the appliances— fit snugly into the domestic dreams of Cold War America. But some of its other products responded directly to a stark reality: the dangerous Cold War world.

Many of the cookbooks published by General Mills featured recipes that used a specific food product the company made.

Demand for new appliances soared following the war. Factories that had been making war materials switched back to making consumer goods.

Products of Insecurity

Although much of General Mills' success during the last half of the twentieth century came from its focus on the desires of the American family, it couldn't ignore what was happening in the rest of the world. World War II had left millions of people worldwide homeless and hungry. Cold War fears of nuclear destruction and communist expansion were rising. Like other companies, General Mills had to find ways to sell its products even as people worried about growing global dangers. But unlike many other firms, General Mills succeeded in turning this atmosphere of tension to its advantage.

FEEDING THE WORLD

Businesses were encouraged to stock emergency supplies. Local governments gave awards to businesses who stocked emergency supplies.

When World War II ended in 1945, world leaders began worrying about a new problem: hunger and famine. The war had devastated many parts of the world—especially in Europe and Asia. Economies were shattered. Farms were not producing food. People had little or no money. Widespread starvation was a real possibility.

In 1946, General Mills teamed up with a nonprofit group called Meals for Millions to manufacture a high-protein soy food supplement called Multi-Purpose Food, or MPF. MPF looked like cornmeal, but it tasted better (or so the company said). It could be eaten alone, either dry or mixed with water. It could also be added to other foods to make them more nutritious. During the 10 years following its introduction,

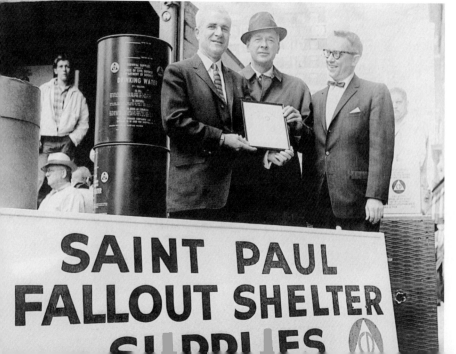

SAINT PAUL FALLOUT SHELTER SUPPLIES

millions of $4\frac{1}{2}$ pound cans of MPF were distributed to relief agencies in more than 100 countries.

After about 10 years of manufacturing MPF for overseas hunger relief, General Mills realized that there might be a large market for the product at home, in the United States. MPF could be what the company called a "survival food product"—the perfect emergency food for the Cold War.

FALLOUT FOOD

Fears of nuclear war had grown throughout the 1950s, as the United States and the Soviet Union built up their stockpiles of nuclear weapons. In 1961, tensions between the two countries were higher than ever. President John F. Kennedy called on all Americans to prepare for a possible nuclear war by building **fallout shelters**—underground rooms designed to protect people from the radioactive fallout created by nuclear blasts. The government put out guidelines for stocking a fallout shelter. Among the most important items on the must-have list was a large supply of nonperishable food.

Here was an opportunity for General Mills. Thousands of Americans were building fallout shelters. Why not try to convince them to stock those shelters with cans of MPF? After all, MPF came in big, stackable cans and had a shelf life of at least five years. In 1961, the company launched a marketing campaign to promote, advertise, and sell MPF. The marketing plan played on Americans' Cold War fears:

> *If a national emergency in the form of nuclear attack was to descend on us at this moment, would you be ready? As a survivor, would you be prepared to exist for 14 days with no outside help? Your answer to this question—probably "No!" General Mills' answer to the survival problem is MPF (Multi-Purpose Food).*

The company's Betty Crocker test kitchens produced a collection of MPF recipes that families could use in the event of a nuclear attack. The recipes included Apricot Nectar with MPF, Jellied Fruit with MPF, and Mashed Potatoes with MPF and Creamed Gravy. Civil defense agencies started stocking public bomb shelters with MPF. Families bought MPF at grocery stores or had it delivered to their homes by door-to-door milkmen. General Mills had found one way to profit from people's sense of insecurity. But it wasn't the only way.

fallout shelter: a place where people could go in the event of a nuclear war to be protected from radiation

Fallout shelter signs designated a public place for people to go in the event of a nuclear attack.

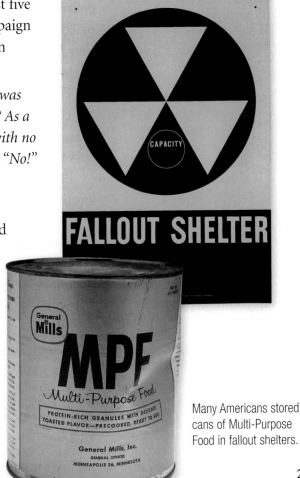

Many Americans stored cans of Multi-Purpose Food in fallout shelters.

Civil defense programs encouraged people to prepare for an attack. **How were these women preparing?**

civil defense: a plan for emergency procedures to protect life and property in the event of a disaster

SEEKING SECURITY UNDERGROUND

Most Minnesotans got through the Cold War without ever setting foot in a fallout shelter. Ed and Thelma Mahowald were among the few who actually built their own.

The Mahowalds lived in the southern Minnesota town of Farmington. Like most Minnesotans, they tried not to think too much about the threat of nuclear war. They had other things to worry about. Money was tight. Their family was growing, and their home was starting to feel cramped. They needed extra room.

In 1961, as the Mahowalds were getting ready to build an addition onto their home, they heard President Kennedy call on all Americans to build fallout shelters. This request got them thinking. They hadn't planned on building a fallout shelter, but now it didn't seem like such a bad idea. They were adding a family room, weren't they? Why not put a shelter beneath it? Ed started making plans. "It was just because the president asked me to do it," he later recalled.

Experts on **civil defense,** who mapped out procedures to help communities handle disasters, said that a well-made fallout shelter should be under 12 inches of concrete. So Ed made a mold and started pouring his own concrete beams. One by one, Ed and his two sons rolled the heavy beams out into the backyard, where they eventually were laid over a concrete block foundation. Before long, Ed and Thelma had their fallout shelter—the first one in Farmington.

The people of Farmington took notice. When the members of the city council started searching for a new civil defense director, they knew where to look. They asked Ed Mahowald—the man who had built his family a fallout shelter—to take the job. He agreed.

Ed didn't have to do much as civil defense director. He went to meetings with civil defense officials from other towns and he tested the city's warning siren once a month, but that was about it. Then, in October of 1962, President Kennedy announced that the Soviet Union was putting nuclear missiles on the island of Cuba, just 90 miles off the U.S. coast. Suddenly, nuclear war was on everyone's mind. "We didn't really feel so close to danger until the Cuba crisis came," Thelma recalled. "I think everybody was running a little scared."

One night during the Cuba crisis, a Farmington police officer came to the Mahowalds' home and interrupted dinner. He told Ed that the city council was holding an emergency meeting and wanted Ed to come. When Ed arrived, the grave-looking council members asked him what the city could do to protect itself from a possible nuclear attack.

By this time, Ed knew that there wasn't much people could do to protect themselves, but he passed along what information he had:

> I told them they should go home and take the doors off their closets, put them down in the basement, lean them against a wall, and then start piling dirt, sand, and gravel against them so that that they got a place to crawl behind. I said that'll keep them busy so they won't be worried so much.

The council members, who had been so serious before that, started laughing. Hide behind a closet door? If their civil defense director thought that was the best defense they had against a nuclear bomb, they weren't going to waste their time worrying about it. They thanked Ed for his advice and told him he was free to go back home and finish his dinner. They would have to hope for the best. After a tense 13-day standoff, the Soviets removed the missiles from Cuba.

The Mahowalds never did have to use their fallout shelter to protect themselves from nuclear war. Ed used it as a photographic dark-room. Thelma stored canned vegetables on its shelves. At Halloween, their children turned it into a haunted house. But the Mahowalds, like other Minnesotans, still knew that the world was a very dangerous place. In the 1960s, fear of communism helped lead the United States into a war in the Southeast Asian country of Vietnam. For several years, Ed and Thelma crossed their fingers, hoping that their two sons would not have to fight in Vietnam. To their great relief, neither son was sent to fight in the war.

Each family member practiced what to do in air raid. **Which task did each person in this photo have?**

During the 1950s and 1960s, schools stocked their basements with water, MPF, medical supplies, sanitation kits, and other supplies. This 1962 photo shows preparations being made at a school in St. Paul.

Playing with History

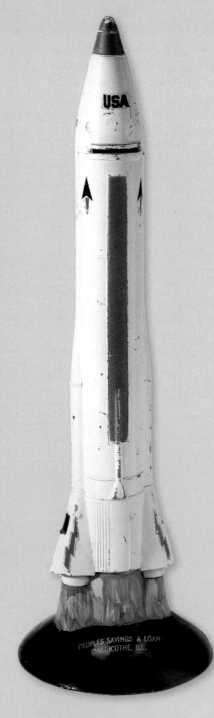

Imagine yourself 50 years from now, sorting through a box of items from your past. Imagine that you rediscover your favorite toy from your childhood. What would that toy be? If you showed the toy to others, would they understand what it meant to you? Could they use that artifact to understand something about the time when you grew up?

As you probably know by now, toys are part of history, too. Toys, like other artifacts, can tell us a lot about the time they were made and the people who used them.

In this Investigation, you will study Cold War toys to see what they can tell us about the values and ideas of the time. As you look at these toys, keep in mind some things that were happening during the fifties, sixties, and seventies: the Cold War, the space race, the growth of TV and movies, and the rapid expansion of the suburbs.

As you study the toys and games on the following pages, use your Investigation Guide to record what they tell us about the people and the culture of the Cold War era.

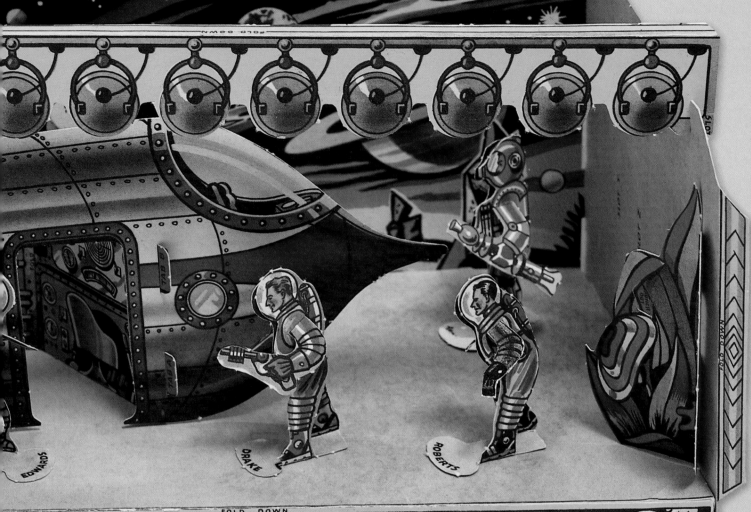

How do toys reflect our culture and our history?

ACTION: (With your magic wand, move Roberts out door of ship and turn him facing Edwards.)

ROBERTS: I'm sure this isn't our proper destination, Edwards. We didn't pass the asteroid belt.

EDWARDS: Where do you think we are, sir?

ACTION: (Move Roberts to the right and toward back of the stage. Turn him part way to the left.)

ROBERTS: Look at that sky, Edwards. Judging from the color of the atmosphere, my guess would be that we are on Mars.

ACTION: (Move Edwards out from ship and toward Roberts.)

EDWARDS: Mars? How can that be, sir? I set the course myself on the control deck.

ACTION: (Move Roberts back to door of ship.)

ROBERTS: I don't know, but you better check Central Radar.

EDWARDS: Aye, aye, sir.

ACTION: (Move Roberts back and move Edwards through door of ship and up to control panel.) Control Bridge X-2 calling Central Radar . . . X-2 calling Central Radar! Come in Central Radar, over!

VOICE: (Make sound like voice in loudspeaker by cupping hands around mouth.) Control Bridge X-2X . . . Central Radar reporting. Go ahead X-2! Over.

EDWARDS: Come in Central Radar. Chief Pilot Edwards. Give me present position of Space Ship Skylark. Believe it off course. Give position of Skylark. Over.

ACTION: (Move Edwards out and to right of door facing Roberts.)

18

⟲ After you have analyzed these toys from the past, think about today's local, national, and global events. Choose an issue and design a toy that is related to it. After you have finished designing your toy, try making it.

NOT SUITABLE FOR CHILDREN UNDER THREE

Toys are designed for certain age groups. The toys you played with when you were two are different from the toys you play with now.

○ **Who would have played with these toys and games? How would they have been used?**

AS SEEN ON TV!

Throughout history, the toys that children played with often reflected events in the news. During the Cold War era, the growing popularity of TV meant that families across the country watched the same shows and saw the same national news. Popular TV shows, inventions, or news events often inspired new games or toys.

What events or inventions may have inspired these toys and games?

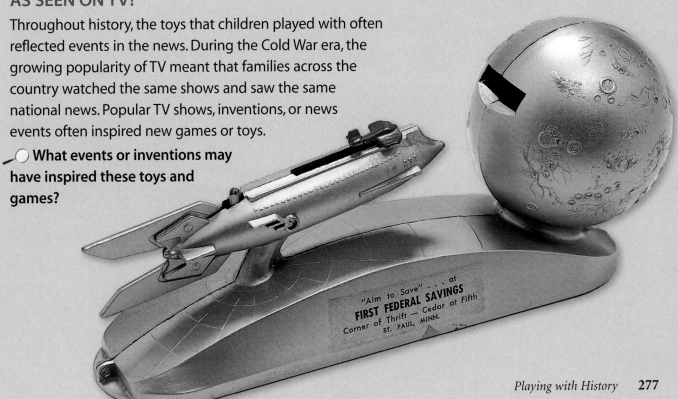

NEW AND IMPROVED!

Most toys become popular because they are fun, new, and interesting. Some classic toys, such as balls and dolls, are always popular. Some toys, such as Pet Rocks, Strawberry Shortcake dolls, Cabbage Patch Kids, Beanie Babies, and Pokémon cards, are fads that soon fade away. Some toys, like roller skates and Slinky, were unusual and unique when they were first produced but are now just as common as balls and dolls.

The toys on this page were classic in some ways, and new in others. Can you tell what was classic and what was new about each of these toys?

LEARN NEW SKILLS!

Just as toys often reflect events in the news, toys also reflect values that are important in a culture. Playing with toys involves thinking and acting, and many toys reinforce popular ideas or skills. Games such as Battleship and Risk reflect an interest in war. Monopoly reflects an interest in business and capitalism. Other games, like Pictionary or charades, encourage creativity and communication skills.

What popular ideas or skills do these toys from the Cold War era reflect?

SPLIT LEVEL DOLL HOUSE

Ⓐ $7.98 57 Pieces

6-Pc. Doll House Family
93c
Ⓒ

Ⓓ

Ⓔ

Ⓐ Split Level Doll House With Pool, the modern home any little girl would love to move into with her playtime friends. It has everything . . . seven rooms fully equipped with bright gay plastic furnishings . . . dining area, living area, bedroom, nursery, bathroom, kitchen, utility room . . . even an outdoor patio with pool and accessories and a shining sports car. There are extra features that make this house extra special, such as a room divider, two-way barbecue, front and inside stairs with railing. Lithographed steel house open at back, abt. 29½x15x14 in. high.
48 T 4590 M—*Mail*. Wt. 9 lbs. 8 oz. 57-Pc. Set **$7.98**

Ⓑ Wishmaker Doll House Has Exclusive Features . . . And A Special Price. It's a lovely six-room suburban design with sun deck . . . the large bay window and smaller windows are trimmed with shutters . . . the Dutch door actually opens. Sturdy steel lithographed to resemble red brick and blue shingles, the back open for furniture arranging; living room, dining room, kitchen, bedroom, bath and nursery all furnished. 18x8x15½ in. high.
48 T 4589 M—*Mail*. Wt. 6 lbs. 10 oz. 30-Pc.Set **$3.98**

Ⓒ Family Fits Either Doll House . . . mother, father, sister and brother are jointed, have attachable platform; little sis, baby are one-piece. Father 3¼ in. tall, others in proportion.
48 T 4588—Ship. wt. 12 oz. . . . . 6-Pc. Set **93c**

Ⓓ Patio Accessory Set has 54 miniature items to make doll house living more delightful . . . paper lawn abt. 16x24 in., with barbecue gear,

Taking a Stand

Police stood guard as University of Minnesota students gathered in 1972 to protest U.S. involvement in the Vietnam War.

1948	1954	1955	1956	1962	1963	1964
By executive order, President Harry S. Truman ends racial segregation in the armed forces.	U.S. Supreme Court rules that segregation in public schools violates the Fourteenth Amendment to the Constitution.	An African American boycott of city buses in Montgomery, Alabama, marks the beginning of the civil rights movement.	Elvis Presley becomes newest teen idol with the song "Heartbreak Hotel."	Folk singer Bob Dylan's "Blowin' in the Wind" is a national hit.	President John F. Kennedy is assassinated in Dallas, Texas, on November 22.	U.S. Congress enacts the Civil Rights Act, which prohibits discrimination in public places based on race, color, religion, or national origin.

Imagine that you couldn't live where you wanted, or that you couldn't get a job you were qualified for, or that you weren't allowed to compete in your favorite sport—just because of who you are. How would you feel? Chances are you would feel angry.

By the mid-1900s, many Americans —including many Minnesotans— were angry about these very things. Although people in Minnesota were proud of their record of fighting **discrimination,** many serious problems remained. African Americans here were often refused housing in white neighborhoods. American Indians living in St. Paul were eight times as likely as other residents to be unemployed. Women and girls did not have the same opportunities as men and boys.

Many of these same people lived in poverty. By the end of the 1960s, one out of every ten Minnesotans was considered poor. Unemployment and poverty hit African Americans, American Indians, and unmarried women especially hard. Discrimination and poverty were making it impossible for many Minnesotans to enjoy the prosperity

LOOK FOR

- ◆ What were the goals of the civil rights movement?
- ◆ How did Rose Mary Freeman take a stand for civil rights?
- ◆ What were the goals of the American Indian Movement?
- ◆ Why did Indian activists take over the Twin Cities Naval Air Station?
- ◆ What were the goals of the women's movement?
- ◆ How did Kathy Striebel take a stand for women's rights?
- ◆ What methods did people use to promote change?

KEY TERMS

discrimination

movement

activist

civil rights

segregation

minority group

women's rights

discrimination: treating people differently because of their race, religion, ethnicity, or sex

1965	1966	1968	1969	1974	1975	1977
Antiwar demonstrations break out in response to U.S. bombing and troop increases in Vietnam. The Beatles come to the Twin Cities and perform at Metropolitan Stadium.	National Organization for Women (NOW) founded.	Martin Luther King, Jr., is assassinated, prompting race riots around the nation. The American Indian Movement (AIM) is founded.	About 70 black students take over a University of Minnesota building.	President Richard M. Nixon resigns after learning that he will likely be impeached.	The United States evacuates its troops, its civilians, and many of its Vietnamese allies from South Vietnam.	Rosalie Wahl becomes the first woman to serve on Minnesota Supreme Court.

On April 27, 1967, Dr. Martin Luther King, Jr., spoke against the Vietnam War to a crowd of students at the University of Minnesota's St. Paul campus.

movement: an organized effort to promote a certain cause or reach a specific goal

activist: a person who works for changes that are intended to improve society

civil rights: rights belonging to a person because he or she is a citizen

that came with the end of World War II. Outrage over these injustices led to action.

Angry Minnesotans began joining with others around the country who felt the same way they did. By the mid-1960s, this anger had erupted into protest **movements** that could not be ignored. Like those involved in the Progressive movement decades earlier, these reformers, or **activists,** wanted to make real changes in American society. They marched, protested, boycotted, and went to court to fight for their rights. They confronted authority wherever they encountered it—in government, in business, and in school. Sometimes these movements represented groups of people who were being denied basic rights. Sometimes they united people around a single cause—like the Vietnam War in Southeast Asia.

But even though they often fought for different things, the people who joined these movements learned from each other. They came to believe that they could make their world—and their state— a better place.

The Civil Rights Movement

When Minnesotans thought about **civil rights,** they often thought of Dr. Martin Luther King, Jr., and his struggle to gain equal rights for African Americans. But King was not the only person fighting for civil rights.

Thousands of Minnesotans—black and white— joined the fight for civil rights. Often Minnesota's civil rights leaders worked for large, well-known groups such as the Urban League or the National Association for the Advancement of Colored People (NAACP). But sometimes they belonged to lesser-known organizations that also managed to make a real and lasting difference.

TAKEOVER AT THE UNIVERSITY

Rose Mary Freeman knew very well what discrimination meant. As a young African American from Mississippi, she remembered not

Rose Mary Freeman and Horace Huntley led the student takeover of Morrill Hall.

MARTIN LUTHER KING, JR.

African Americans had tried repeatedly during the first half of the twentieth century to gain equal rights for themselves, with little success. **Segregation** by race remained legal in many parts of the country as late as the 1960s, but it was especially rigid in the South. Blacks there were separated from whites in public schools, neighborhoods, theaters, restaurants, swimming pools, and churches. They couldn't even use the same drinking fountains or restrooms. By the 1950s, many African Americans were fed up. A new generation of black leaders began demanding the full equality promised by the Fourteenth Amendment.

Dr. Martin Luther King, Jr., was the most prominent and most widely respected of the many civil rights leaders who emerged during the 1950s and 1960s. King played an important part in a series of protests in Alabama that captured national attention: the 1955 bus boycott in Montgomery, the 1963 demonstrations in Birmingham, and the 1965 march from Selma to Montgomery. His eloquent speeches and his commitment to nonviolent protest helped rally millions of Americans to the civil rights cause. The new civil rights movement helped convince leaders in Washington, D.C., to enact new laws, such as the Civil Rights Act of 1964 and the Voting Rights Act of 1965.

On April 4, 1968, an assassin shot and killed Dr. Martin Luther King, Jr., in Memphis, Tennessee. In the months that followed, angry mobs led riots that shook dozens of cities. King's message of nonviolence sometimes seemed forgotten, but it wasn't. Black activists continued to build on King's ideals. They encouraged African Americans to take pride in their history and culture. They continued to work for social and economic justice using nonviolent methods. King's dream for a better a future was still very much alive.

being allowed to go to school with white children, and being forbidden to use the same restrooms that white people used. During high school, she had joined the growing civil rights movement—registering black voters who had long been prevented from voting. Now she lived in Minneapolis. She was in her second year at the University of Minnesota. And she had never felt more like a member of a **minority group.**

It was 1969. Freeman was one of fewer than 250 African American students at the university that year—out of a student body of about 41,000. She and her black classmates constantly felt outnumbered and unappreciated. "It was like you were the fly in the buttermilk," she recalled years later. "If you had class, there was not another black student in that class. Nine times out of ten, your instructor was white."

The year before, in 1968, Freeman had helped organize demonstrations, or protests, on campus following the assassination of Dr. Martin Luther King, Jr. Those demonstrations had helped convince the university to start several new programs for black students. But many African American students, including Freeman, believed that much more needed to be done. Perhaps more than anything, they wanted the university to establish a new department of African American studies.

And now they were ready to do something about it.

segregation: the separation of a group of people from the rest of society

minority group: a group that is considered different from the majority of society

During the takeover, students gathered outside Morrill Hall.

On a cold afternoon in January 1969, Rose Mary Freeman and about 70 other black students walked into an office at the university's Morrill Hall administration building and announced that they were taking over the building. After the staff had cleared out, the students wired doors shut with twisted coat hangers and barricaded the entrances with overturned desks and file cabinets. "We've turned the tables on them," one of the protesters said. "These doors have always been closed to us. Now we're closing the doors on them." The activists said they planned to stay until university officials agreed to meet a list of demands— including the establishment of an African American studies program.

University officials, including university president Malcolm Moos, were alarmed. Several other colleges and universities around the nation had become the targets of student activism in recent months, and many of those confrontations had ended in violence. Moos and the other administrators wanted to make sure the occupation of Morrill Hall ended peacefully.

That evening, university officials met inside Morrill Hall with Rose Mary Freeman and six other members of the black student group that she headed—the Afro-American Action Committee (AAAC). The university made a proposal. The AAAC rejected it. The two sides agreed to call off negotiations for the night and try again in the morning.

Tensions began to mount. By morning, word of the takeover had spread around campus. Several hundred students gathered outside Morrill Hall. Some of them supported the goals of the African American activists inside. Others did not. Some of them yelled encouragement to the black students. Others hurled insults and racial slurs. Many of the protesters inside worried that the crowds outside might grow violent. "It was pretty shaky," Freeman said.

HUBERT H. HUMPHREY

Most politicians of the 1940s and 1950s avoided talking about civil rights. But Hubert H. Humphrey of Minnesota was not like most politicians. He believed that African Americans and other minorities should have the same rights as everyone else. And unlike most politicians, he was willing to do something about it.

In the mid-1940s, when Humphrey was mayor of Minneapolis, he worked hard to improve opportunities for the city's minorities—especially blacks. He pushed through a law that made job discrimination illegal and set up a committee of experts to investigate cases of discrimination. He took African-American guests to segregated restaurants and made sure that newspapers covered the story. He led a successful campaign to end segregation in Twin Cities bowling alleys.

In 1948, Humphrey brought his civil rights message to a national audience. He helped write a new platform for the national Democratic Party. Humphrey wanted the platform to include a strong statement in favor of civil rights, but many Democrats disagreed with him. At the Democratic National Convention, he delivered what some people consider the best speech of his life. Humphrey said the time had come to take a stand against discrimination. Looking back to the 1776 Declaration of Independence he said, "There are those who say to you—we are rushing this issue of civil rights. I say we are 172 years too late."

The Democratic Party adopted the civil rights statement. Humphrey became a leading national voice for civil rights.

During the years that followed, Humphrey remained a strong advocate of equal rights for all Americans. As a U.S. senator from 1949 to 1965, he introduced or supported many civil rights bills. Most of these bills failed to pass, but Humphrey won a big victory with the passage of the 1964 Civil Rights Act, the first national civil rights legislation since 1877. As vice president under President Lyndon B. Johnson, Humphrey continued to fight against poverty and discrimination.

In 1968, the Democrats nominated Humphrey for president at their convention in Chicago. At the convention, disagreements about President Johnson's Vietnam War policies overshadowed other issues. Violent clashes between antiwar protestors and the police set the convention's tone. Damaged by his support of President Johnson's policies, Humphrey lost the election to Richard M. Nixon.

Humphrey returned to the Senate in 1971 and served until his death in 1978. In these later years, he gained the respect and affection of many Americans for his stand on civil rights. His stature as an inspirational political figure was summarized in President Jimmy Carter's eulogy: "From time to time, our nation is blessed by the presence of men and women who bear the mark of greatness, who help us see a better vision of what we can become. Hubert Humphrey was such a man."

Negotiations between the two sides resumed. By early afternoon, they reached an agreement. The AAAC did not get everything it wanted, but it did convince the university to establish an African American studies department. The new department would, in the words of President Moos, "bring a full reflection of the experience of black people in America."

Freeman felt her efforts had been worthwhile. For one thing, the takeover of Morrill Hall had made Minnesotans pay attention to some important African American concerns. A few years later, Freeman was among the first group of students to graduate from the University of Minnesota with a degree in African American studies.

The American Indian Movement

The number of American Indians living in Minnesota's biggest cities was growing quickly in the 1960s, partly because of a government policy to move Indians from the reservations to the cities. In 1950, fewer than 500 Indians lived in Minneapolis. By 1960, the number was more than 2,000. By 1970, it was nearly 6,000. These new urban Indians often had a hard time finding jobs and resisted efforts to blend into white society. They often felt alone and rootless. Before long, several American Indian organizations formed in the Twin Cities to help. One of these groups eventually grew into the best-known American Indian organization in the world. And it earned its fame by confronting the federal government.

STAKING A CLAIM

The Twin Cities Naval Air Station at the Minneapolis–St. Paul International Airport was a pretty quiet place in the spring of 1971. The government was in the process of closing it down. Only a handful of sailors and marines worked there. Hardly anyone paid any attention to it.

But to one group of American Indians, it was the perfect place to take a stand.

On the evening in May 17, 1971, an Ojibwe named Dennis Banks walked up to the air station's security guard and announced that he and his fellow protesters were taking over the base. They intended to open a school where Indian children could learn in an atmosphere that respected Indian culture. Suddenly, dozens of cheering men, women, and children began climbing over the six-foot-high chain-link fence that surrounded the air station. They broke open the gate and rushed onto the grounds.

The protesters claimed that the land belonged to them now. But did it?

On May 17, 1971, American Indians climbed over the fence at the Twin Cities Naval Air Station to begin their occupation of the base.

Dennis Banks and most of the other Indians who participated in the take-over were members of a new organization called the American Indian Movement (AIM). AIM had been founded three years earlier to help urban Indians in Minneapolis. Banks believed that Indians were ready, as he was, to fight for their rights. "I want to fight and live for my people," he said. "I want to live and fight for my struggle so that I myself can enjoy some of the benefits, so that I myself can see an end to…discrimination."

At first, AIM focused on the problems facing Indians in the Twin Cities area. It formed citizen patrols to monitor police and make sure they didn't harass Indians. It found lawyers for those who had been arrested. It helped out-of-work Indians find jobs. But soon AIM started shifting its focus. It turned itself into a national movement with national goals. And it did this by confronting the federal government and trying to force it to live up to promises made in its treaties with Indian tribes. This was what the takeover of the naval air station was all about.

Later, after the occupation of the Twin Cities Naval Air Station had ended, the leaders of the American Indian Movement held a news conference with U.S. Senator Walter Mondale (right). Dennis Banks is at the microphone.

The protesters claimed that the base now belonged to them because of a treaty the Dakota people had signed way back in 1868. The AIM leaders said the treaty gave Indians the right to take back any land that the U.S. government abandoned. They said that's exactly what the naval air station was—abandoned government property.

This wasn't the first time that American Indians had made this kind of claim. A year and a half earlier, a large group of Indians had taken over the abandoned federal prison on Alcatraz Island in California. Like the protesters in Minnesota, they also based their claim on the 1868 Dakota treaty. The protesters at Alcatraz had attracted a lot of attention to their cause. AIM's leaders were hoping to do the same thing with their occupation of the Twin Cities Naval Air Station.

AIM soon discovered that attracting attention was the easy part. The newspapers and television stations reported the group's demands. They explained the 1868 treaty and why the protesters believed they were entitled to the land at the air station.

But AIM also wanted the government to take its demands seriously. That was the hard part. At first, their negotiations with government officials seemed to go well. Everyone they talked to—from the Minneapolis mayor to the base commander—seemed to understand why the protesters had taken over the base. They all agreed that something should be done to make life better for the Indian people. AIM's leaders believed they were making progress through negotiation.

But then things started to go wrong. Just as the protesters were getting ready to leave the air station, the base commander locked them out of the base's main administration building and prevented them from holding a news conference with reporters there. The protesters felt insulted. The commander apologized for what he called an honest mix-up, but it didn't matter. The protesters changed their minds about leaving. They went back to their headquarters in the base's theater and started setting up a school.

AIM's leaders continued trying to negotiate. They even planned a meeting with U.S. Senator Walter Mondale. But on May 21, four days after the takeover began—just five hours before Mondale was supposed to arrive—dozens of federal marshals raided the air station and ordered the Indians to leave. About half of the protesters left voluntarily. The rest were arrested. By the time Mondale got to Minneapolis, no one from AIM was there to negotiate with him.

Even though the protesters were forced to leave, they succeeded in raising public awareness of Indian issues. Suddenly, it wasn't so hard to raise money for the kinds of schools AIM had hoped to open at the air station. In 1972, AIM opened two schools—one in Minneapolis and one in St. Paul. They were called survival schools because they taught Indians how to survive in two worlds at one time—the Indian world and the white person's world.

In the months and years that followed, AIM's national organization continued to attract attention by confronting the government. "We're going to close the doors to the kind of oppression that has been brought forth in this country," Banks said. Within Minnesota, AIM shifted its focus back to where it began—to the day-to-day needs of the people it represented.

In 1980, these students learned a traditional Indian game at the Red School House in St. Paul. This survival school was one of the two AIM opened in the Twin Cities.

The Women's Movement

On a summer day in 1970, a group of women unfurled a banner from the Foshay Tower, the tallest building in Minneapolis. The banner read "WOMEN UNITE!" A month later, the Minnesota chapter of the National Organization for Women (NOW) was born. NOW was not the only women's organization in Minnesota. Groups such as the American Association of University Women and the Federation of Business and Professional Women's Clubs had been around ever since women won the right to vote in 1920. But NOW was different. It was interested in one thing—**women's rights.** It was an idea whose time had come—for women and for girls, as well.

IN THE SWIM

Only 12 years old, Kathy Striebel hadn't planned on becoming a crusader for women's rights in Minnesota. She just wanted to swim.

Kathy had been swimming with an Amateur Athletic Union (AAU) team since she was seven years old. She enjoyed the sport and she was good at it. In the fall of 1971, she was an eighth-grader at Murray Junior High School in St. Paul. She wanted to swim for her school. But there was a problem.

Murray didn't have a girls' swim team, and it had no plans to start one.

But Kathy didn't let that get her down. The boys at Murray had a swim team. Why not join them? She went to the swimming coach and the principal and told them what she wanted to do. They both gave her the same answer: No way.

"They said they wouldn't let me because I was a girl," Kathy told the newspapers. "They thought if I beat some of the boys it would ruin their egos."

Kathy's mother, Charlotte Striebel, was angry. She knew that St. Paul had a law against sex discrimination in the schools. She had learned about it through her work with the local NOW chapter. So she filed a complaint with St. Paul's Human Rights Department accusing the school of sex discrimination.

It didn't take long for Murray Junior High to change its mind about letting Kathy on the swim team. The complaint that Charlotte Striebel filed with the city had the desired effect.

"It worked so quickly, it was breathtaking," Ms. Striebel later recalled. "Within three days she was on the team."

To celebrate Women Power Day on August 27, 1970, women hung a banner from the observation deck of the Foshay Tower.

women's rights: economic, legal, and social rights for women equal to those for men

Many groups used buttons to deliver their messages.

For a while, everything went smoothly for Kathy. She competed in swimming meets with boys and got her picture in the newspaper, holding a trophy that she had won. And not only that—girls at other St. Paul schools were following her lead and joining boys' teams, as well. Things were looking up for young female athletes in the state. But then Kathy found out that not everyone was happy with her victory.

It happened during a swim meet at Irondale High School in New Brighton, a suburb north of St. Paul. Kathy was up on the diving block, waiting for the starting gun to sound, when the Irondale athletic director demanded that Kathy not be allowed to swim. He said that the decision to let Kathy swim was a St. Paul rule. It didn't apply to schools like Irondale, which was outside St. Paul. Kathy was humiliated.

"So they pulled that little girl off the block," Ms. Striebel said later. "The cruelty of what that man did to that little 12-year-old girl! The fact that he could do something that cruel to a child gave me some sense of the depths of the problem."

Kathy Striebel attended her first practice with the boys' swim team in November 1971.

WOMEN'S RIGHTS

MY CONSCIOUSNESS IS FINE... IT'S MY **PAY** THAT NEEDS RAISING!!

A new generation of women's rights activists came of age during the 1960s and 1970s. Like the woman suffrage leaders of the early 1900s, they challenged gender roles by demanding equality with men. Examples of sex discrimination were everywhere. Women were paid less than men. They were rarely hired for the most prestigious jobs. (Many women worked as teachers and nurses, but not as school superintendents or doctors.) Women were even barred from eating lunch at one well-known Minneapolis restaurant unless accompanied by a man.

Thousands of American women—outraged by discrimination and inspired by the civil rights and anti-Vietnam War movements—joined together in the women's movement. They demonstrated for equal pay and equal job opportunities. They picketed for equal access to all-male schools and clubs. They marched in support of an Equal Rights Amendment (ERA) to the U.S. Constitution. Women's rights activists succeeded in creating many new opportunities for women and girls during the 1970s and beyond, but they also suffered occasional setbacks. Though Minnesota ratified the Equal Rights Amendment in 1973, not enough other states did. Eventually, the ERA died in 1982, after failing to gain ratification from the necessary 38 states.

Kathy didn't get to swim that race, but her fight was not in vain. Murray eventually started a girls' swim team. So did other schools around the state. In 1975, Minnesota held its first statewide girls' swimming meet.

The 1970s were important years for women's athletics in Minnesota and throughout the nation. In 1972, a new federal law called Title IX (Roman numeral "nine") made it illegal to discriminate against women and girls in any educational program that received money from the federal government—which meant almost every school in the nation. Almost immediately, schools started adding girls' teams and thousands of girls joined them. In 1976, a judge ordered St. Paul's junior and senior high schools to give girls the same athletic opportunities as boys. That didn't necessarily mean boys and girls on the same teams, but it did mean that all teams should be treated equally—equal budgets, equal practice time, equal use of equipment and facilities. The lawsuit that led to the judge's ruling had been filed by two St. Paul women who weren't about to put up with sex discrimination in the schools. Kathy's mother, Charlotte Striebel, was one of them.

These reform movements proved that there is strength in numbers—that people can change things, especially when they team up with others who share their goals. African Americans, American Indians, and women all organized during this period to fight for justice and equality. In the process, they transformed American society. But even as these activists tried to bring change, many Minnesotans were noticing that the land they called home was, itself, changing in some very big ways.

Kathy Striebel had already won many swimming awards by the time she entered junior high school.

Singing Out for Social Change

Americans have sung protest songs for centuries. Slaves and abolitionists sang songs against slavery. Temperance activists sang songs about the evils of alcohol, and farmers and jobless workers sang the blues during the Great Depression.

These songs helped people express their frustrations and teach others about their problems. To help people learn the song and understand the message, these earlier songwriters used simple, catchy tunes with lots of repeated phrases. Even so, these songs were often known only to people in the protest group.

But in the 1960s, protest songs became a popular way for Minnesotans and other Americans to speak out against issues such as discrimination, violence, and poverty. Students and other activists sang protest songs at marches, sit-ins, and rallies.

Written by professionals, these songs used repeated phrases, plenty of emotional language, and memorable images to help the listener remember the song. With the growth of records and radio, many of the protest songs of the 1960s became nationally known.

The next few pages have lyrics from protest songs that Minnesotans sang between 1960 and 2000. Look for the characteristics that make them protest songs. For each song, think about the following questions: What issue is the songwriter protesting? What do the lyrics mean? What methods does the songwriter use to help listeners learn and remember the song?

After you have analyzed these songs, think about today's social issues. Write your own protest song about one of them. Use your Investigation Guide to help you plan your song. What will your song be about? How will you make your song memorable?

In 1972, these University of Minnesota students gathered to protest the Vietnam War. **In what ways do you think this event is similar to the one pictured on page 280? How do these protests differ?**

BOB DYLAN

Bob Dylan was named Robert Zimmerman when he was born in Duluth in 1941. He grew up in Hibbing and, as a teenager, he learned to play piano, guitar, and harmonica. In 1960, he moved to New York City to become a full-time musician, and he changed his name to Bob Dylan.

Dylan was just 21 years old when he wrote the song "Blowin' in the Wind" in 1962. The song was immensely popular, and Dylan became nationally known. It is now known as one of the most famous protest songs of the 1960s.

Message: What is Dylan protesting?

Lyrics: What does the white dove represent in the first verse?

Methods: How does Dylan help the listener learn and remember this song?

Blowin' in the Wind

1. How many roads must a man walk down
Before you call him a man?
Yes, 'n' how many seas must a white dove sail
Before she sleeps in the sand?
Yes, 'n' how many times must the cannon balls fly
Before they're forever banned?

Chorus: The answer, my friend, is blowin' in the wind,
The answer is blowin' in the wind.

2. How many times must a man look up
Before he can see the sky?
Yes, 'n' how many ears must one man have
Before he can hear people cry?
Yes, 'n' how many deaths will it take till he knows
That too many people have died?

Chorus: The answer, my friend, is blowin' in the wind,
The answer is blowin' in the wind.

3. How many years can a mountain exist
Before it's washed to the sea?
Yes, 'n' how many years can some people exist
Before they're allowed to be free?
Yes, 'n' how many times can a man turn his head,
Pretending he just doesn't see?

Chorus: The answer, my friend, is blowin' in the wind,
The answer is blowin' in the wind.

Pope County Blues

1. From my pa I got this farm,
He got it from my grandpa
What can a poor man do?
Well, it ain't much but five hundred acres,
Lots of beets and potaters
Giving me them Pope County Blues

. . . 3. Now with each year that passes,
You know up and up goes my taxes
What can a poor man do?
Now they come along with a good old plan,
They want to survey my own land
Giving me them Pope County Blues

4. They want to build a power line from North Dakota
Straight through my farm here in Minnesota
What can a poor man do?
So I told them they better hit the road,
Because this farm of mine is all I own
Giving me them Pope County Blues

. . . 6. Now the president talks about the common man
While meeting with the big corporation heads
What can a poor man do?
Says he's gonna boost up our economy
Get a job for you and me
Giving me them Pope County Blues

7. But I got a feeling what's on his mind:
Corporate farms and power lines
What can a poor man do?
But if that drought keeps coming just you wait
The trouble is it might be too late
Giving me them Pope County Blues

8. 'Cause that farmer out there grows the food
That feeds both me and you
What can a poor man do?
So I looked at my watch, read a quarter to nine,
Stole the quarter and saved some time
Giving me them Pope County Blues

LARRY LONG

Larry Long was eight years old when his family moved to Minneapolis in 1959. A few years later, when Long's father died, supportive family and friends taught him that "the people who have the least are often the most generous." As an adult, Long became a troubadour—a traveling musician—living with various people and writing songs about their problems.

In 1977, Long wrote "Pope County Blues" after reading about a power-line debate in local papers. The song was a hit with farmers in western Minnesota, and he recorded it as his first single.

Message: What is Long protesting?

Lyrics: What problems does the farmer face in verses 3 and 4?

Methods: How does Long help the listener learn and remember this song?

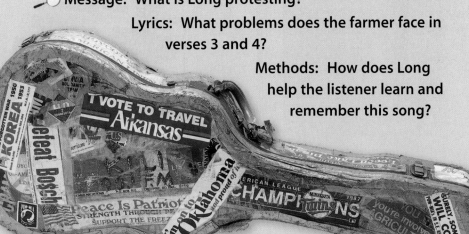

Paper Doll

1. When I close my eyes I see the dresses and the gowns
The paper dolls and the Barbie dolls
The pretty bows that tied me down
Then I see my face looking down at my shiny shoes
They took me to a place where they gave me pink instead of blue
I pressed my face against the glass that kept me safe
Wanting to throw the sticks and stones
To break the bones that God had gave me

Chorus: I will move without moving at all
I will be
Does it feel real
Does it feel real

2. I see the way I'm supposed to be in the magazine
Cover me up with your make-up and such
I'll get married and be a beauty queen . . .
I press my face against the glass that keeps me safe
From those wanting to throw the sticks and stones
To break the bones that God had gave me

Chorus: I will speak without speaking at all
I will be
Does it feel real
Does it feel real

3. I've been branded and [called bad names]
I've been hated and felt my fate
It's the weight that keeps me here
It's the weight that keeps me here

Chorus: I will be without being at all
I will be
Does it feel real
Does it feel real

TINA SCHLIESKE

Christina Schlieske was born in 1966 and grew up in Apple Valley, a suburb south of the Twin Cities. She began playing guitar and writing songs when she was 13. Soon after high school, she formed the band Tina and the B-Side Movement. As the lead singer and songwriter, Schlieske wrote and sang about the pressures she faced as a young woman.

In 1994, Schlieske wrote "Paper Doll." Later, she explained why: "At the time, there weren't a whole lot of female songwriters writing about what it was like to be a woman. The issue of self-esteem in young girls is a big concern of mine. I wanted to write a song that projected strength no matter what box they put you in."

Message: What is Schlieske protesting?

Lyrics: What pressures does Schlieske feel about her appearance in verse 2?

Methods: How does Schlieske help the listener learn and remember this song?

ANNIE HUMPHREY

Annie Humphrey grew up on the Leech Lake Reservation in northern Minnesota. In 1973, when she was in first grade, Humphrey taught herself to play the guitar. Later, she also taught herself to play the piano and the Ojibwe wooden flute. After her time in the Marines and at college, Humphrey returned to the reservation and began recording her songs.

In 2000, Humphrey wrote "500 Years," a song about the injustices American Indians have faced since Christopher Columbus came to America. She hopes the song "will inspire some people to pay more attention to our past," and notes, "Awareness is so important in fighting prejudice. At the end of the song I sing about the red oak, the one tree that holds its leaves all winter. Like the red oak leaves, we will always be here."

Message: What is Humphrey protesting?

Lyrics: What types of careless words bother Annie in verse 7?

Methods: How does Humphrey help the listener learn and remember this song?

500 Years

Introduction: In the smoke of the sacred fires
Lifted up like holy hands
Understand there's something wrong
There's trouble on the land . . .

Chorus: Our relatives are watching
Our spirit helpers near
Five hundred years of genocide
Who's left to hear
Who's left to hear

. . . 5. The Indian Removal Act
Stolen land, the bitter fact
The Trail of Tears, the Cherokees
Cold and hunger, grief, disease
The Creeks, Chickasaw, Choctaws
Miami, Shawnees and Ottowa
The Delaware, the Wendat Nation
All were torn by relocation

. . . 7. Sticks and stones that break our bones
Careless words that mock our own
Chippewa Water, Crazy Horse Liquor
Indian givers who take back quicker
The Red Skins, Braves, The Fighting Sioux
Eskimo Pies and Red Man Tobacco
A billion insults, do the math
When we object, we're on the warpath

8. Struggles with racist laws and violence
From Wounded Knee to Alcatraz Island
Marching the trail of broken treaties
Fishing rights and police beatings
Destroy the land and you will pay
AIM reinvents the warrior way
Native heroes refused parole
Stop and search by state patrol
Release our dead, return their bones
Let us live, return our homes

Conclusion: Some things haven't changed at all
Resistance standing strong and tall
Like the red oak leaves we will remain
To snap the links that form our chain

Skyscrapers rise above open spaces, showing the dramatic changes in Minnesota's landscape in the decades following World War II.

1946
Orrin Thompson builds his first three homes near the Minneapolis–St. Paul International Airport.

1948
Levittown, the first suburb of mass-produced housing, is built on Long Island in New York.

1950
Minnesota's population reaches 2,982,483. For the first time, more than half of all Minnesotans live in urban areas.

1956
Southdale, the world's first indoor shopping mall, opens in Edina.

1961
The Housing Act of 1961 offers cities federal money for public transportation and housing.

1962
The first skyway in downtown Minneapolis opens.

The Metropolitan Building is torn down as part of an urban renewal project for Minneapolis.

1967
Nicollet Mall opens in downtown Minneapolis, creating a street reserved for pedestrians and public transit vehicles.

For centuries, Minnesotans—from the earliest mound builders to the latest urban planners—have shaped the land to fit their needs. But by the 1950s, the state's landscape was changing in ways that most earlier Minnesotans could never have imagined. Cities were spreading out and new communities were multiplying. Remote wilderness areas were turning into popular recreation spots. The 160-acre homestead of the late 1800s was giving way to the 1,000-acre farm of the late 1900s.

Some Minnesotans worried about these changes. They believed that the demands of modern life were threatening the state's remaining natural treasures—its forests, prairies, lakes, rivers, and streams. But many other Minnesotans were excited to see how the landscape was changing. They called it "progress."

Few people in Minnesota symbolized this faith in progress as much as a young man named Orrin Thompson.

LOOK FOR

- How did Orrin Thompson's ideas change the Minnesota landscape?
- Why did the government want Benny Ambrose to move?
- How did the Tobkin family farm change from the 1960s to the 1990s?
- What land rights belong to Minnesota's Ojibwe?
- How have the inner cities changed in the last 50 years?

KEY TERMS

suburb
GI Bill of Rights
urban renewal
urban sprawl
mixed use

1970	1973	1975	1978	1980	1982	1992
The Environmental Protection Agency established.	The IDS Center becomes the tallest building in Minnesota when it opens in Minneapolis.	Minnesota passes the Clean Indoor Air Act, limiting smoking in public places.	Congress passes a law banning logging and limiting motorboats and snowmobiles to certain areas of the Boundary Waters Canoe Area (BWCA).	Bloomington, a suburb of Minneapolis, grows to become the third-largest city in Minnesota, surpassing Duluth.	The Hubert H. Humphrey Metrodome opens in downtown Minneapolis.	The Mall of America becomes the largest shopping mall in the United States when it opens in Bloomington.

The Suburb Builder: Orrin Thompson

Orrin Thompson was a farm boy at heart. He grew up on the family farm near Barrett, in western Minnesota. He later told people he probably would have become a farmer himself if it hadn't been for the Great Depression. Instead, he left the farm, looking for work. He became an electrician and found jobs in several Midwestern factories during World War II. When the war ended, Thompson started thinking about another line of work, building homes.

Minnesota—like the rest of the country—faced a major housing shortage as thousands of war veterans returned home with plans to start new families. Many Americans made do by moving in with friends or relatives. Others settled for tin Quonset (KWAHN-seht) huts or even the bodies of unused airplanes. Thompson saw an opportunity. "I got intrigued," he said. "People were just looking for shelter, for a roof over their heads."

Thompson decided to build houses, but not just any houses. They had to be affordable and plentiful. Thompson's plan was simple: He would keep prices low by building his houses on cheap land outside the cities, and by using the same designs over and over again. With this system, he could build dozens of houses in a matter of months.

Thompson built his first homes in South Minneapolis, near the site of the Minneapolis–St. Paul International Airport. At that time, the area was more country than city. One day, a young couple came to look at a home that Thompson had built and joked about how far from the city it was. "Do you get a cow with the house?" they asked.

Soon Thompson's company was buying up large pieces of land even farther away from the Twin Cities and building entire neighborhoods on them. People called these communities **suburbs.** Each house looked almost identical to the one next door. In the words of one company official, Orrin Thompson homes came in three colors: "white, white, or white."

suburb: community built in an area surrounding a city

In 1978, Orrin Thompson visited the first three houses he built in Minneapolis decades earlier.

In Richfield in 1954, cows and cars competed for space. This suburban housing development sprang up right next to a family farm.

Spreading Out

Soon, the suburbs were exploding with new homes and new neighborhoods. **The GI Bill of Rights** was one of the most important factors behind this boom. This government act rewarded veterans who served in World War II by paying for their college education and by helping them get the loans they needed to buy their first homes. Without the GI Bill, many veterans never would have become home owners.

GI Bill of Rights: the U.S. law that assisted veterans with home loans and college tuition

People who previously lived and worked in the cities lined up to buy Thompson's little white houses. They did not seem to mind that Thompson's neighborhoods were miles from downtown—miles, even, from the outermost stops on the old streetcar lines. Thompson had found ways to keep the prices of his homes low. That helped make them enormously popular.

Another major force behind the creation of the suburbs was the automobile. Thanks to the car, Minnesotans no longer were tied to the central city. They could hop in their new Fords, Chevrolets, and Oldsmobiles and drive many miles in the same time it had once taken them to travel just one mile by foot or by streetcar. It wasn't uncommon to see cars lined up for miles outside the many model homes that seemed to be popping up in the middle of nowhere.

Orrin Thompson and other builders like him were building houses so fast that nearby communities had trouble keeping up. Often, entire neighborhoods appeared on the landscape before water and sewer lines could get to them. The few paved roads that existed were often clogged with traffic. Communities struggled to build new schools fast enough for all those new families and young children. Still, the people kept coming. They were willing to put up with the disadvantages of suburban life if they could also enjoy the advantages—their own house, a newfangled kitchen, a yard where the kids could play, and a garage for the car.

Quonset huts housed returning veterans and their families at the University of Minnesota in 1946.

By 1959, Orrin Thompson's company had become the largest home builder in Minnesota and one of the five largest in the nation. Over the years, it became the driving force behind the creation of new suburbs like Coon Rapids, Cottage Grove, and Apple Valley. Later, some people would criticize Orrin Thompson for building his homes so far from the city and for contributing to something called **urban sprawl.** But he was proud of his work. "I feel that I've done a lot of good for a lot of people," he said.

urban sprawl: the rapid spread of a city into the surrounding countryside

urban renewal: the process of improving inner cities in order to attract new businesses and new residents

NEW HOUSING IN COTTAGE GROVE, 1961

URBAN RENEWAL

Between 1950 and 1960, the number of Minnesotans who lived in the suburbs nearly tripled, while the population in the central cities began to shrink. As people moved away from the cities, businesses followed, and downtown areas began to deteriorate. Many of the old department stores either went out of business or moved to the suburban shopping malls. Specialty shops, professional offices, churches, and movie theaters soon followed. Low-income residents who had little money to spend on home improvements moved into older neighborhoods. New interstate highways split apart established communities like St. Paul's Summit-University neighborhood. Minnesota's urban areas were facing serious problems.

But during the 1960s, city leaders got serious about **urban renewal.** They began to look for ways to renew, or rebuild, the strong downtowns and neighborhoods they once had. They gave businesses financial incentives to set up shop in the central cities. Slowly things began to change. Old buildings were torn down to make way for new office buildings and hotels. Old warehouses were turned into shops, restaurants, and housing. As the 1900s came to a close, many of Minnesota's cities seemed more alive than they had in decades.

As the twenty-first century began, Minnesotans disagreed about how to keep their cities vital. Many problems remained. Traffic congestion had worsened and some people wanted more housing closer to the core cities. Others defended their decision to live far from the inner cities and their places of work. Leaders in Minnesota greeted the new century searching for policies that would improve life for both urban and suburban Minnesotans.

Caught in the Middle: Benny Ambrose

On a cold day in January 1965, 69-year-old Benny Ambrose answered a knock at the door of his little cabin on Ottertrack Lake near Minnesota's border with Canada. There, standing in front of him, were the very people he least wanted to see—a small group of foresters from the U.S. Forest Service. Ambrose had a pretty good idea what the foresters wanted, but he invited them inside anyway.

Ambrose had lived on Ottertrack Lake for more than 30 years. He was a legend of sorts in Minnesota's Boundary Waters Canoe Area (BWCA). People knew Ambrose as a prospector, trapper, and wilderness guide who seemed to know the lakes and woods better than anybody. He loved his home in the woods and planned to live there the rest of his life. But the government had other ideas.

Motorboats and nonmotorized boats shared Saganaga Lake in the Superior National Forest around 1960.

The Boundary Waters Canoe Area, 2002

Beginning in 1926, a large part of the Superior National Forest was set aside as a wilderness area called the Boundary Waters Canoe Area (BWCA). For decades afterward, Minnesotans disagreed about how wild the BWCA should be.

Seaplanes, like this one shown in 1945, flew tourists to remote lakes in the Boundary Waters area.

Under a 1964 federal law, all private homes were now illegal in wilderness areas. This included Ambrose's year-round cabin. That's why the foresters had come to visit. They handed Ambrose some papers that said the federal government was buying his property. He had no choice in the matter.

Ambrose glanced at the papers, gazed out the window, and sighed. He turned back to the foresters and announced that he didn't care what the papers said. He intended to stay. He told the foresters to leave and not come back.

At that moment, Benny Ambrose became a symbol of sorts—a man caught in the middle of a bitter struggle over the use of the land. In the end, he also became a symbol of something else: compromise.

Wilderness or Not?

People had been fighting over the BWCA for decades by the time Benny Ambrose became part of the story. The BWCA had been set aside in 1926 as part of the Superior National Forest. From the beginning, Minnesotans had used the word "wilderness" to describe the BWCA. A federal wilderness area was supposed to be free of permanent buildings and was meant to be "protected and managed to preserve its natural condition." But the BWCA had not been completely wild for a long time. Roads cut through its forests. Logging companies harvested its trees. Vacationers traveled through it on motorboats and snowmobiles. A few people, like Benny Ambrose, even lived there. So was the BWCA a wilderness or not?

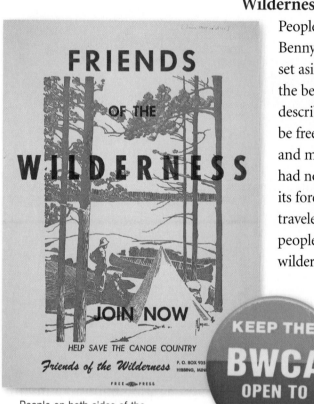

People on both sides of the wilderness debate tried to influence public opinion.

mixed use: managing lands to allow for many different uses

On one side of the issue were environmentalists, from northern Minnesota and elsewhere. They believed that the BWCA should be a wilderness. They wanted to make it as natural as possible—no logging, no motorboats, no snowmobiles. They also wanted more limits on the number of people who could visit the area.

On the other side of the issue were many local residents, business people, and sports enthusiasts, who all argued for **mixed use.** They believed that logging and tourism in the BWCA were important to the region's economy. Some were afraid they would lose their jobs if the BWCA were closed to logging, motorboats, and snowmobiles. They argued that the strict rules would keep out the elderly and people with disabilities. Many others considered the environmentalists outsiders who had no right to decide what the people of northern Minnesota could and could not do.

In the mid-1960s—at about the time the government was trying to force Benny Ambrose to sell his cabin—the struggle over the BWCA intensified. Minnesotans on both sides of the issue found new ways to promote their views. Environmentalists set up tents in the middle of roads to stop logging trucks from getting through. Those in favor of mixed use set up blockades to keep canoeists off the lakes. Tensions rose. Arguments turned nasty. Finally, in 1978, the federal government passed a new law meant to resolve the disagreements over the area that the law renamed the Boundary Waters Canoe Area Wilderness (BWCAW). The law banned logging in the area while continuing to allow motorboats and snowmobiles under certain conditions. Neither side got everything it wanted. Neither side was completely happy. The law was a classic compromise.

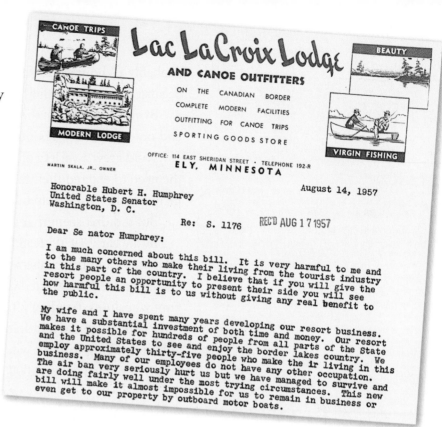

A lodge owner wrote this letter to U.S. Senator Hubert Humphrey protesting a wilderness bill.

In the end, Benny Ambrose and the federal government compromised, too. Ambrose sold his property on Ottertrack Lake, but at the same time the government let him stay in his cabin as a "volunteer." He kept an eye on things for the forest service and provided emergency assistance to campers. Over the years, as the struggle to determine the future of the BWCAW continued, Ambrose got to be good friends with many of the foresters in the area.

Benny Ambrose died of a heart attack in August 1982. A few days later, the forest service bent the rules one last time on his behalf. Motorboats were allowed into the protected waters of the BWCAW so that Ambrose's friends and relatives could say good-bye at a memorial service on Ottertrack Lake.

The Large-Scale Farmer: Ron Tobkin

Ron Tobkin grew up during the 1950s and early 1960s on his family's farm near Perham in west central Minnesota. He learned at an early age that living on a farm was a lot of work. Wake up at four in morning. Feed the cows. Get them ready for milking. Take a bath. Eat breakfast. Go to school. Come back from school and get all your chores done before supper. Do your homework, get some sleep, and start all over again. The family stayed busy. "We worked seven days a week and

THE TOBKIN FAMILY

305

Perham

probably 12 hours a day," he recalled years later. "But you enjoyed it because it was a good living."

By most standards, the Tobkin farm in the 1960s was not too big and not too small—about 160 acres. The family kept about 45 milk cows and grew a variety of crops. Ron's mother and father never felt the need to expand their farm much beyond that. With 11 kids— including Ron—to help out, the farm seemed to be just the right size.

But it didn't seem that way for long.

In the early 1970s, Ron graduated from college and returned to the Perham area to begin his career as a farmer. With his parents' help and encouragement, he started buying his own land and adding it to the family business. Gradually, the Tobkin family farm grew. A hundred acres here. A couple hundred acres there. By the late 1990s, Ron Tobkin—along with his wife and several other members of the family—owned about 4,000 acres of land and 1,400 dairy cows. The Tobkins' Little Pine Dairy was one of the biggest dairy operations in the state. "We had to expand to get more efficient," he said. "We had to do things that allowed us to get the most bang out of our dollar."

Bigger Farms, Fewer Farms

The expansion of the Tobkin family farm reflected a trend in Minnesota agriculture during the late 1900s: farms were getting bigger. In 1964, when Ron Tobkin was still a teenager, the average Minnesota farm was 235 acres. By 1997, it was half again as big—354 acres. And many farms were much larger.

But as farms grew bigger and large-scale farmers bought out small-scale ones, the number of farms dwindled. Minnesota had seen its peak year for the number of farms in the state back in 1935, when there were 205,000 of them. Between 1964 and 1997, the number of farms in Minnesota dropped 44 percent— from 131,000 to 73,000.

Many Minnesotans believed that the trend toward bigger and fewer farms was a good thing. As they saw it, large farming operations were more efficient. But many other Minnesotans worried that large farms were crowding out small family farms—the traditional anchors of rural life. With larger farms and fewer farmers, churches

In the 1990s, Little Pine Dairy milked 1,180 cows three times a day.

and schools closed, and local towns suffered. Ron Tobkin worried about the loss of small farms and the decline of rural towns. "There are people dropping out of the industry every day," he said. "Some of them end up working for me or for our family, but it's a sad deal."

By the late 1900s, Ron Tobkin was looking forward to the day when he could hand over the daily operations of the Little Pine Dairy to his two sons. Maybe they would continue to expand the family farm. Or then again, maybe they would be content with 4,000 acres. It was hard to predict. One thing Tobkin knew for sure: the bigger a farm gets, the more staff and overseeing it requires. It was enough to make one farmer wish for the days when farms were not so big. "I'd rather be smaller," Tobkin said with a tinge of regret in his voice. "Oh, absolutely."

Minnesota's landscape changed in all sorts of ways during the final decades of the 1900s. Its cities stretched out to make room for more people. Its wilderness areas attracted thousands upon thousands of visitors—many of whom disagreed about what a wilderness should be. More and more of its small farms vanished as large farms expanded. But the landscape was not the only thing that changed during this period. Waves of newcomers arrived at about the same time and—like earlier immigrants—changed the face of Minnesota.

TREATY RIGHTS AND INDIAN LAND USE

For more than a century, the Dakota and Ojibwe had struggled with limited economic opportunities—and poverty—in their communities. Tribal governments had looked for ways to help, but with little success. In 1988, a new federal law cleared the way for tribal governments to operate casinos on Indian land. By the year 2000, 11 bands were operating 17 casinos in Minnesota. Some casinos generated massive wealth; others were only modestly successful. But virtually overnight, many Indian communities had money to build schools and community centers. Some bought back land that had been lost during allotment in the 1880s. Others paid out the money to tribal members. By the beginning of the twenty-first century, one thing seemed clear: income from casinos was making a big difference

to many Indian communities.

Another important victory for Minnesota's Indian communities came in the legal battle over treaty rights. During the 1990s, the Mille Lacs Band of Ojibwe went to court in what became a bitter fight over hunting and fishing rights. They based their case on the 1837 treaty under which their ancestors had given up all their land between the St. Croix and Mississippi Rivers. The Mille Lacs Ojibwe believed that the treaty gave them the right to hunt and fish as they wished on Mille Lacs and other lands that their ancestors had given up. The state, as well as many resort owners and fishing and hunting enthusiasts, argued that the treaty was no longer valid. They believed that some Ojibwe fishing methods—including the traditional practice of

gillnetting—would decrease the size of the fish population. Local resort owners feared that they would lose money if fewer people took fishing trips to their resorts.

In 1999, the U.S. Supreme Court ruled in favor of the Mille Lacs Band. It said that the 1837 treaty did, in fact, guarantee hunting and fishing rights to the Ojibwe. The Mille Lacs Band and the Department of Natural Resources then agreed to a plan to control the number of fish that anyone—both Ojibwe and others—could catch.

Confirming that the 1837 treaty was still valid established a very important legal principle for the Mille Lacs Ojibwe—that the promises the U.S. government made 162 years ago could still be enforced.

The Transformation of Duluth's Canal Park

Imagine a broad vista of sparkling sunlight on waves, the sound of water lapping at the shore, the smell of pinesap and a wood fire in the air. Now imagine the bellow of a ship's horn, the thick smells from a restaurant's kitchen, and the sight of a huge cargo ship sliding through a canal.

If you could picture these two scenes, then you have imagined the site of Duluth at two very different points in history. In the last 200 years, Duluth has changed from a quiet, pine-shaded Ojibwe camp to an international industrial port. In the scope of history, this is the blink of an eye, yet the changes are dramatic. In this Investigation, you will explore the changes that have occurred on Canal Park, a section of Minnesota Point, the narrow strip of land that extends into Lake Superior near Duluth.

Duluth and the Surrounding Area

Before the canal was built, ships entered Superior Bay through the natural harbor opening and docked at Superior, Wisconsin.

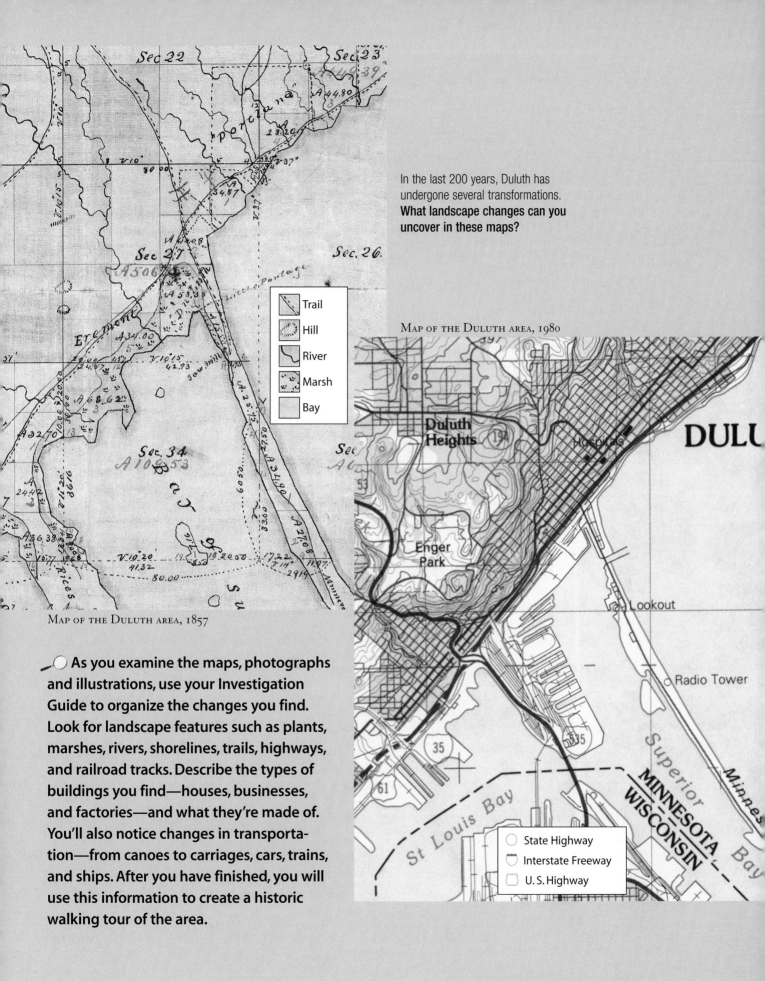

MAP OF THE DULUTH AREA, 1857

	Trail
	Hill
	River
	Marsh
	Bay

In the last 200 years, Duluth has undergone several transformations. **What landscape changes can you uncover in these maps?**

MAP OF THE DULUTH AREA, 1980

Duluth Heights

Enger Park

Lookout

Radio Tower

St Louis Bay

Superior Bay

MINNESOTA
WISCONSIN

	State Highway
	Interstate Freeway
	U. S. Highway

⊙ As you examine the maps, photographs and illustrations, use your Investigation Guide to organize the changes you find. Look for landscape features such as plants, marshes, rivers, shorelines, trails, highways, and railroad tracks. Describe the types of buildings you find—houses, businesses, and factories—and what they're made of. You'll also notice changes in transportation—from canoes to carriages, cars, trains, and ships. After you have finished, you will use this information to create a historic walking tour of the area.

This photo, taken in the late 1860s, looks south down Minnesota Point, from the future site of downtown Duluth.

This view of Minnesota Point in 1870 looks north toward the future downtown of Duluth.

ONIGAMIISING, PRE-1870

In the early 1800s, Minnesota Point and the Duluth area were home to the Ojibwe. They called the area Onigamiising (oh-nih-guh-MEENH-sihng), or Small Portage, in reference to the narrow strip of land they would carry their canoes across to enter the bay. In 1854, a treaty opened the area to fishermen, land developers, and other settlers.

When Duluth became an official city in 1870, the city's first citizens hoped that they could rely on the shipping business to help Duluth grow. Unfortunately, most of the ships sailed through the natural entry to the harbor and docked in Wisconsin. To make a more direct route to Duluth, citizens dug a canal through Minnesota Point in the fall of 1870 and spring of 1871. When the canal was complete, the boats and the business came to Duluth.

What was the area's landscape like before 1870? Its buildings? Its transportation methods?

Duluth's harbor in 1883.

BOOMTOWN, 1871–1919

The new canal and the arrival of the railroad in 1870 turned Duluth into a boomtown. Lumber, iron ore, grain, and livestock poured into the city to be transferred to ships headed east. As boat traffic increased, Duluth made more changes: more wharves, a deeper harbor, a wider canal. Then, in 1905, a permanent canal bridge was built. This aerial bridge carried cars back and forth to the rest of Minnesota Point.

🔍 **What was Duluth's landscape like between 1871 and 1919? Its buildings? Its transportation methods?**

This 1908 postcard looks south down Lake Avenue to Duluth's first aerial bridge.

The Transformation of Duluth's Canal Park **311**

By 1920, Duluth had grown to be an international port. Shipping was the central part of the economy, but Duluth also had many small factories and businesses.

Canal Park was home for many of these small industries and businesses. In 1929, the aerial bridge was changed into a lift bridge, which allowed larger ships to pass. For years, Canal Park was a thriving industrial area, but a series of economic changes caused a decline in business. By the late 1970s, most buildings in Canal Park were shabby and neglected.

What was Duluth's landscape like between 1920 and 1979? Its buildings? Its transportation methods?

This photograph looks south down Lake Avenue to the second aerial bridge in 1931.

Taken from a plane, this photograph shows the harbor and first aerial bridge in 1928.

TOURIST AREA, 1980–PRESENT

In the mid-1980s, Duluth's Canal Park underwent another transformation. Canal Park was made into a tourist destination. Old buildings came down to make way for parking lots. Tourist shops, antique stores, hotels, and chain restaurants moved in. Nearby, a convention center, aquarium, and bandstand were built. Duluth's Canal Park is now the heart of the local tourism business.

What is the modern-day landscape of Canal Park like? Its buildings? Its transportation methods?

Now, create a historic walking tour of Canal Park for tourists. What will you tell them about the changes that have occurred in the area since the early 1800s? Use your Investigation Guide to create a model or illustrations to explain how Duluth's Canal Park has changed.

This view looks south down Lake Avenue to the second aerial bridge in 2002.

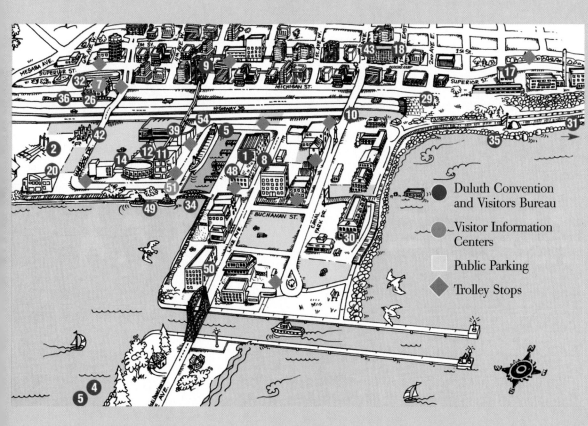

This map was created to guide tourists in 2002. The dark red numbers signify tourist attractions.

● Duluth Convention and Visitors Bureau

◗ Visitor Information Centers

▢ Public Parking

◆ Trolley Stops

Many Hmong storycloths describe the journey the Hmong made to escape from Laos after the Vietnam War.

1973	1975	1976	1980	1986	1987	1989
Minnesota governor Wendell Anderson is featured on the cover of *Time* magazine for a story on the "Good Life" in the state.	U.S. military personnel leave Vietnam. Hmong refugees begin escaping Laos.	Minnesota schools begin offering English as a second language (ESL) classes.	Compact discs (CDs) are invented. Post-It Notes, an invention of 3M chemist Arthur Fry, hit the market.	U.S. government offers legal status to many previously illegal Mexican immigrants.	Minnesota Twins win the World Series for the first time.	Cold War ends as communist governments in Eastern Europe collapse, and the Soviet Union begins to break apart.

In the late 1900s, new waves of migrants and immigrants made Minnesota their home. Russian Jews, Africans, Asians, and Latinos made up an increasing portion of the state's population.

Some of the new arrivals came directly from other countries. Some came from elsewhere in the United States. Like earlier newcomers, they left their old homes for specific reasons, often to escape violence or poverty. And like all earlier newcomers, they came to Minnesota for specific reasons, often to join family and friends or to find new jobs.

The new Minnesotans settled mainly in places like the Twin Cities, Rochester, and Worthington, and helped lead Minnesota into a new century—and, like all immigrants before them, transformed the state with their presence.

LOOK FOR

- Why did many of the Hmong leave Laos?
- What drew Kao Xiong to St. Paul?
- Why did Maria Melendez move to Worthington?
- What did Ali Noor do to get to Rochester?
- How has the experience of immigrating to Minnesota stayed the same?

KEY TERMS

refugee camp
migrant worker
asylum
tolerant

1990	1991–1993	1995	1998	2000	2001	2002
Carlos Mariani from St. Paul is the first Hispanic elected to the Minnesota House of Representatives.	A civil war in the East African country of Somalia causes thousands of refugees to leave.	Digital video discs (DVDs) are invented.	Jesse Ventura, the Reform Party candidate, is elected governor of Minnesota.	Minnesota's population reaches 4,919,479. Over 5 percent—260,463—were born outside the United States.	Terrorists seize four planes and crash them into the World Trade Center, the Pentagon, and a field in Pennsylvania.	Mee Moua from St. Paul is the first Hmong elected to the Minnesota Senate.

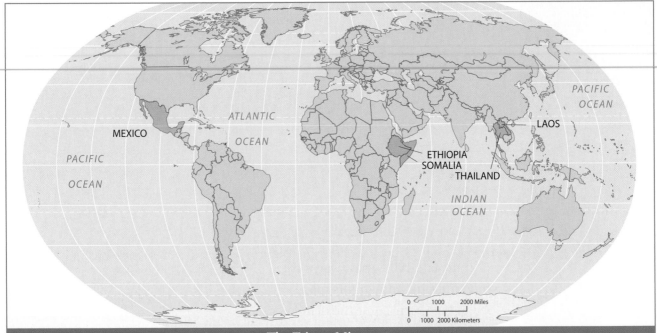

The Trip to Minnesota

The last decades of the twentieth century saw a dramatic increase in the number of Latino, African, and Asian immigrants coming to Minnesota. **Can you follow the routes that Kao Xiong, Maria Melendez, and Ali Noor took to get to Minnesota?**

Leaving Laos

The year was 1979, and 17-year-old Kao Xiong (KOW SHAWNG) was swimming for her life.

Crack! Crack!

Kao knew what that sound was. Gunshots. Soldiers were firing at her, her father, and more than a dozen other people who were trying to swim across the Mekong (may-KAHNG) River, which separates the Southeast Asian countries of Laos (LAH-ohs) and Thailand (TEYE-land). The rest of Kao's family had already made it safely across to Thailand. If Kao and her father could just make it to the other side, they'd be safe, too. They had made triangle-shaped life preservers out of strips of bamboo, but Kao's father's triangle kept breaking.

"The current was very strong," Kao later recalled, "but my father and I knew that if we didn't make it this time, we would be shot. My father prayed to our ancestors and asked them for help. Moments after he prayed, the river seemed gentler. Our group finally made it to the Thai shore, where my mother and the rest of my family were waiting. We had all escaped Laos, and we were finally safe."

Kao is a member of an Asian ethnic group called the Hmong (MUHNG). The Hmong lived and farmed for many years in the mountains of Laos before they were forced to flee

Kao Xiong holds a storycloth.

their homes. Their problems started with the war in neighboring Vietnam during the 1960s and 1970s. The United States was fighting the communists in Vietnam, and the war spilled over into nearby Laos. The United States recruited Hmong men to fight the communists in Laos and had promised to protect the Hmong soldiers and their families. But when the communists won the war in 1975, the Americans left Vietnam. The communists in Laos killed many Hmong because they had helped U.S. soldiers. Some Hmong tried to hide in the mountains. Others, like Kao, decided to flee across the Mekong River to Thailand.

After escaping across the Mekong, Kao and her family made their way to a **refugee camp** in northeastern Thailand. There Kao met a young Hmong man named Toua Vang (TOO-uh VAYNG). They fell in love and got married. Over the next several years, Kao gave birth to three sons and a daughter. As her family grew, so did her desire to leave the camp. "There was no future for our kids in Laos or in the refugee camp," Kao remembered. "We wanted our children to be free to have an education and to have a good life."

In 1986, the U.S. government granted Kao and Toua's request to bring their family to America. Kao, Toua, and the children boarded a plane and made the long journey across the Pacific Ocean. For eight years, they lived in California. But relatives in Minnesota encouraged Kao's family to join them. There were good schools, they said, and plenty of jobs. In 1994, Kao, Toua, and their children left California to begin a new life in St. Paul.

refugee camp: a place that provides protection and care for refugees—people who are fleeing dangerous conditions in their homeland

COMING TO ST. PAUL

Hmong refugees began settling in St. Paul and other Minnesota communities in 1976. Churches and synagogues made special efforts to sponsor Hmong refugees and bring them to Minnesota. Word began to spread among the Hmong people in the United States and in Thailand's refugee camps that Minnesota was a good place to live. Soon, thousands of Hmong were moving to the state. The first arrivals followed Hmong tradition by helping members of their extended families, or clans, move here, as well. The growing Hmong community welcomed the newcomers and helped them feel at home. By 1994, when Kao, Toua, and their family arrived, Minnesota had the second largest Hmong population in the United States.

Still, many Hmong immigrants found it hard to adjust to life in Minnesota. The weather was harsh and unfamiliar. Most Hmong had been farmers in Laos, but, without land, they couldn't become farmers

KAO XIONG, TOUA VANG, AND THEIR FAMILY

317

in Minnesota. The older generation faced overwhelming challenges. Instead of being respected elders as they had been, they were dependent on younger family members who knew English and had adapted more quickly. Male family and clan leaders found their authority challenged by their children. Many immigrants feared crime, especially in the poorer neighborhoods where they first settled. They had to endure name-calling and discrimination. Often their neighbors disapproved of traditional Hmong religious and cultural practices. Most native-born Minnesotans did not know that the Hmong had been loyal allies to the United States during the Vietnam War. They did not seem to care that the United States had promised to protect the Hmong once the war was over.

Because Kao Xiong and her family had lived in California for eight years before coming to Minnesota, they adjusted to life in St. Paul more easily than many of their fellow Hmong immigrants. Soon after arriving in St. Paul, Kao took a job at a telecommunications company. Toua went to work for a Hmong community group. Their children enrolled in the St. Paul public schools. Within a matter of months after their arrival in St. Paul, everyone in the family became U.S. citizens. They were officially Americans. They were Minnesotans. But in their hearts, they also remained Hmong.

"Our goal is to raise our children to be leaders for the next generation of Hmong here in America," said Toua. "We believe getting a good education in the American schools is very important for our children. But we also believe that our children should never forget where they're from."

HMONG
BABY CARRIER

MARIA MELENDEZ

Leaving Texas

At first glance, life seemed to be going pretty well for Maria Melendez (meh-LEHN-dehz) during the early 1990s. She was a beautician in San Antonio, Texas, and she made a good wage. She owned her own home. She had five kids—a teenage son and four adult daughters—whom she loved very much. But there was one problem: crime. She and her neighbors had to put bars on their windows to keep out thieves. Some of her son's friends were joining gangs and carrying guns. Her neighborhood was becoming a dangerous place. She knew she had to do something. "That's why I decided to move out of there," she said. "Because they were going to end up killing my son or he was going to end up in jail, or on drugs."

But where could she go? Melendez had lived in Mexico for several years as a child. For a while she thought about going back, but decided against it. Finally, she made her decision. She would move to Worthington, Minnesota.

Melendez knew something about Worthington. Several years earlier, she had traveled to Minnesota to work in the farm fields near Crookston. She had made a side trip to Worthington after hearing that jobs were available there. It seemed like a nice place where her son would be safe. So in 1992, she packed up her belongings and moved up north. Almost immediately after arriving in Worthington, she got a job at the meat-packing plant owned by Swift and Company.

COMING TO WORTHINGTON

Mexicans and Mexican Americans had been coming to Minnesota for more than a century by the time Maria Melendez arrived. Seasonal **migrant workers** had been coming north for the sugar-beet harvest since 1907. Most early permanent Mexican immigrants had settled in the Twin Cities—not in the rural areas of the state. By the 1980s, that was changing. Thousands of Mexicans and Mexican Americans were settling in small towns such as Willmar, Marshall, and Worthington, where jobs—especially meat-packing jobs—were plentiful.

migrant worker: a worker who travels from place to place to find work, usually picking farm crops

Jobs had not always been plentiful in Worthington. In the mid-1980s, the town suffered when its economy slowed down. Many of the stores on Main Street were boarded up. Farmers went out of business and banks closed. People moved away.

In 1989, things began to change when Swift and Company announced it was expanding its pork production plant and would soon hire hundreds of new workers. At first, this seemed like a dream come true for Worthington. Unfortunately, the new jobs did not pay very much—some paid as little as $7.50 an hour. Since most people in Worthington would not work for such a low wage doing such dangerous, difficult work, Swift had to look elsewhere for workers.

Latinos in Worthington have opened stores offering foods and other goods from Latin America.

It looked south, to Mexico and the border regions of Texas. Swift and Company put commercials on Texas radio stations announcing that good jobs were available in Worthington. Many Mexicans and Mexican Americans heard the radio ads and decided to make the trip north. By 2001, Latinos made up 45 percent of the 1,840 people working at Swift's Worthington plant.

The sleepy town with the struggling Main Street was waking up. Mexican restaurants opened for business. The

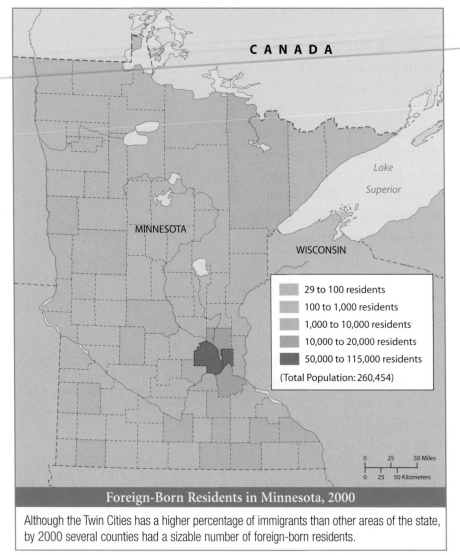

29 to 100 residents
100 to 1,000 residents
1,000 to 10,000 residents
10,000 to 20,000 residents
50,000 to 115,000 residents
(Total Population: 260,454)

0   25   50 Miles
0   25   50 Kilometers

Foreign-Born Residents in Minnesota, 2000

Although the Twin Cities has a higher percentage of immigrants than other areas of the state, by 2000 several counties had a sizable number of foreign-born residents.

local newspaper started publishing a weekly edition in Spanish. But Mexicans and Mexican Americans weren't the only people coming to work in Worthington's meat-packing factories. An Asian grocery store and a Thai restaurant opened to serve a growing community of Asian immigrants. Refugees from Africa were also putting down roots. By 2000, Worthington—with a population of 11,283—was Minnesota's third most racially diverse city, behind only Minneapolis and St. Paul.

As with many other times in Minnesota history, the arrival of newcomers created tension. Some of Worthington's longtime residents were reluctant to accept newcomers with different customs and a different language. They believed that these new workers hurt Worthington's labor force by agreeing to work for such low wages.

Others blamed immigrants when the crime rate started to rise. At the same time, newcomers discovered that life in Minnesota wasn't easy. Each winter, many of them applied for heating assistance because they were unable to pay their bills with the money they made at the factories. With housing in short supply, landlords demanded high rents for homes that often were run-down and infested with cockroaches.

BARBER SHOP IN WORTHINGTON, 2002

But as time passed, new arrivals and established residents seemed to grow more comfortable with each other. The city started holding an annual international festival to celebrate its ethnic diversity. City leaders spoke with pride about how the newcomers had helped Worthington overcome economic hard times.

For Maria Melendez, this was all good news. Worthington was her home now. Her daughters all had good jobs. Her son—the one she had worried so much about in San Antonio—had graduated from high school and was going to college. She was happy to stay. "I'm already used to living here," she said. "I might go for vacation or whatever, but I'll always come back."

Leaving Somalia

By 1992, many people in the East African nation of Somalia (soh-MAH-lee-uh) felt like they were living a nightmare. Ali Noor (AH-lee NOHR), a civil engineer in the capital city of Mogadishu (moh-guh-DEE-shoo), was among them. "You never knew if you were going to make it to the next hour, whether you were going to be all right," he later recalled. "When you went to bed at night, you weren't sure you were going to get up in the morning alive. If you made it to the morning, you never knew you were going to make it to the night. That was life in Mogadishu. Hell."

ALI AND SOPHIA NOOR WITH THEIR CHILDREN

Somalia was a country without a working government. The dictator who had ruled the nation harshly for many years had fled for his life in 1991. He was escaping threats from enemy clans within Somalia who wanted to take over the government. The country quickly fell into chaos and civil war as the different clans struggled for power. No one was safe. Food was scarce. Ali Noor and his wife, Sophia, decided it was time to get out. They gathered their three children and headed for Ethiopia (ee-thee-OH-pee-uh), a more stable African country.

The Noors knew that the trip would be difficult and dangerous. They would have to make much of the journey on foot or, if they were lucky, on camel. Their children were young (ages two to seven), and Sophia was pregnant. Armed fighters and bandits haunted the deserts that lay between Mogadishu and the Ethiopian border. The Noors paid a man who knew the deserts well to guide them. They arrived in Ethiopia safely, but their troubles were not over.

Ethiopia was safer than Somalia, but jobs were hard to come by. For six years, Ali Noor supported his family as best he could by buying and selling goods on the streets. His brother, a doctor who lived in another country, helped by sending money when he could. But life was still hard. Noor wanted something better. He started planning to move his family to the United States.

The Noors brought some items from Somalia when they immigrated to the United States, including this cowhide stool.

A MORTAR AND PESTLE, HEADREST, AND INCENSE BURNER FROM SOMALIA

asylum: protection offered to refugees who would likely be harmed if forced to return to their homeland

Noor had to make a choice. He could apply to the U.S. government for permission to bring his family to America (a process that could take years), or he could enter the United States illegally and apply for permission to stay (a much faster process). Noor decided he couldn't wait. In 1998, with the help of an American relief group, he set off for North America. He went alone, planning to send for his family later. Noor traveled first to Mexico. Then he sneaked across the border into California. There he applied for **asylum,** stating that his life would be in danger if he were forced to return to Somalia. Three months later, the U.S. government granted his request. Noor was now free to live wherever he chose. After thinking it over, he decided to move to Rochester, Minnesota.

COMING TO ROCHESTER

Hardly any Somalis lived in Minnesota in 1990. But as the civil war raged in Somalia during the early 1990s, more and more Somali refugees made their way to the state. By 2000, thousands of Somalis were living in Minnesota. Most lived in Minneapolis, but many others lived in smaller cities such as Marshall, Owatonna, and Rochester. Somalis came because they heard that jobs were plentiful. Some worked in farm-related industries such as meatpacking. Others worked in high-tech fields such as computers. As those first arrivals settled in, they encouraged new refugees to join them. That was how Ali Noor heard about Rochester. "I knew the Somali community was here in Minnesota, and that is one good reason to come to Minnesota," he said.

SOMALI BOOKSTAND FOR SUPPORTING OPEN BOOKS

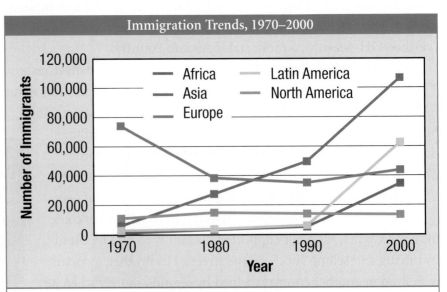

In the 30-year period between 1970 and 2000, more immigrants to Minnesota came from Asia, Latin America, and Africa and fewer came from Europe.

Like many Somalis in Rochester, Noor found work at the local IBM computer assembly plant. He began saving money to bring his family to his new home. In 1999, his children arrived. Two years later, his wife, Sophia, was finally able to join the rest of the family. Nine years after fleeing their home in Mogadishu, the Noors were reunited in a place where they felt safe.

"I love the people where I come to live," Noor said. "Nobody bothers you. Everybody does his own business. When people get out from their car, nobody locks their doors. You can trust people here. They are very calm, generous. You can depend on them. You can trust them. That gives me a lot of confidence."

Like other places with increasing immigrant populations, Rochester experienced growing pains. In 1996, three Somalis were beaten by whites in three highly publicized attacks. City leaders responded with programs, discussions, and advertisements that encouraged Rochester residents to be more understanding and **tolerant** of each other. Despite the occasional outburst of violence or name-calling, Ali Noor still believed that Rochester was a good place to live. "It's human nature," he said of those who aren't tolerant. "You may find bad people and some very good people. But you cannot judge the whole community with two, three bad people. I'm not going to do that."

Samera Mohammad and other Somali women perform a Somali dance in Rochester in 1999.

tolerant: willing to recognize and respect the feelings, ideas, or behaviors of others

Ali Noor, Maria Melendez, and Kao Xiong now share a common bond with you and with the millions of other people who—over the centuries—have called Minnesota home. We can add their names to a long roster of Minnesotans that includes Alexander Ramsey, Harriet Bishop, Taoyateduta, Charles Pillsbury, Nellie Stone Johnson, Hubert Humphrey, and Dennis Banks. The stories of their lives, like the story of your life, are now bundled in that huge package of experiences that we call our shared history.

With each day that passes, Minnesota's shared history grows and evolves. And you are part of that evolution. As you live your life, you will do things that change your home state in countless ways, both small and large. Keep track of what you do. Take pride in your stories and your family's stories. Maybe someday students all over the state will be reading about you.

Welcome to Minnesota

Nearly 150 years separate the stories of the Swedish immigrant Hans Mattson and the Somali immigrant Ali Noor. Both men came to seek opportunity—the chance to earn a living and raise their families in safety and freedom. Both also faced difficulties and disappointments—the harsh realities of Minnesota's winters, the struggle to adjust to a new culture, the intolerance of some native-born Minnesotans. In each case, these immigrants found comfort and support in the welcome of the people who came before them.

While the stories of Hans Mattson and Ali Noor are similar, there is a significant difference: in the years since Hans Mattson came, Minnesota has changed dramatically. Ali Noor moved to a Minnesota where most people live in urban areas, not rural ones. The forests and prairies that Hans Mattson knew are long gone—replaced by large-scale farms and suburbs.

But Minnesota's present is formed by its past. Throughout *Northern Lights*, you have studied a variety of sources that tell our state's history. The artifacts, diaries, letters, contracts, paintings, photographs, maps, scrapbooks, newspapers, buildings, toys, and songs have formed a story of a changing Minnesota and changing Minnesotans. Review these stories. Which ones do you remember the best? Which have had the greatest impact on Minnesota today?

Which stories from Minnesota's past do you think these items illustrate?

Which of these stories would you want to share with a new immigrant to Minnesota? Use your Investigation Guide to plan a gift basket to welcome a newcomer to Minnesota. Include five to ten objects that represent stories from *Northern Lights*. Which stories do you think a new immigrant should know in order to understand our state?

This index will direct you to information about people, places, and ideas. When information appears in a picture or map, the page number will be in *italic* as follows: *p. 155* or *m. 118*. *See* references will point you to alternative terms used in the index. *See also* references will lead to additional information about the topic. If you do not find the term you are looking for, try related words. Example: Instead of "girls," look under "women."

A

Advertising, *p. 101, p. 102, p. 155*, 160, 218, 267–269
African Americans
  civil rights and discrimination, 198–199, 281
  employment, 79, 199, 220–222
  military service, 114, *p. 255*
  population, *p. 108*
  slavery and the Civil War, 107–115
  Somali immigrants, 321–323
Agriculture
  Civil War and, 107–108
  dairy industry, 220, 235, 305–307
  droughts, 238
  economics and, 234–235, 235
  family farms, 141–142, 144, 220–222
  the Grangers, 145, 149
  in American Indian cultures, 13–15, 28, *p. 31*, 126
  land use, *p. 197*, 299, *p. 301*
  large-scale farming, 305–307
  mechanization, 220–222
  migrant workers, 319
  one-crop and diversified farming, 144–145
  protest song, 295
  railroads and, 145
  settlement and, 11–12, *p. 89*, 142–143, 147–148, *p. 155*
  subsistence farming, 141–142, 144
  wheat and flour milling, 145–146, 158–160
  during World War II, 252
Allotments, 200
Ambrose, Benny (wilderness guide), 303–305
American Indians
  American Indian Movement and civil rights, 286–288
  ancestral peoples, 6–15
  civil rights and discrimination, 281, 286–288, 297
  education issues, 50–55, 80, 200–201, 288
  land, relationship with, 78, 79, 84
  military service, 255
  religion and, 125–126
  reservation system, 83, 95
  sovereignty of Indian nations, 76
  warfare among, 77
  see also Dakota and Ojibwe
Anishanaabe. *See* Ojibwe
Annuities, 123, 127
Antilla, Anton (miner, labor activist, and farmer), 164–165, 167
Antitam, Civil War battle, 112
Archeology, 15–23
  Bradbury Brook site, 16–23, 19, *p. 20*
  Bryan site, *p. 13, p. 14*, 15
  Grand Mound site, *p.12*, 12
  Itasca Bison Kill site, 6, 10
Architecture
  American Indian dwellings, 26, 27, *p. 29*, 35, *p. 35*, 42, *p. 87*
  Foshay Tower, 231–232
  settlers' homes, 142–143
  suburban development and urban sprawl, 300–302
  urban growth and, 180–182
  Victorian compared to Prairie School, 186–191
Artifacts, as historical evidence, 4–5, 11, 13, 15, 19–23, 324–325
Assimilation, 125–126, 200–203
Automobiles, 182–184, 221, 301

B

B. P. date system, 21
Banks, Dennis (Ojibwe civil rights activist), 286–288
Beads and beading, 53–54, 59
Beaver, the fur trade and, 45, 60, *p. 62*

"Betty Crocker," 267–269
Big Eagle "Waŋmbditaŋka" (Dakota leader), 126–127
Bircher, William (Civil War solider), 120
Bishop, Harriet (St. Paul teacher), 92–93
Bishop, Judson Wade (Civil War soldier), *p. 119*
Bison, 6, 10, 30, *p. 32*, 37, 49, 86, 89
Black Americans. *See* African Americans
Blue Earth "Makato" (Dakota leader), 126
Bonga, George (African American fur trader and interpreter), 79
Bost, Theodore (Swiss immigrant), 105
Boundary Waters Canoe Area Wilderness (BWCAW), *m. 303*, 303–305
Bradbury Brook archeological site, 16–23
Brass, Maggie "Snana" (Dakota War witness), 134–137
Bremer, Edward (banker), 241–247
Bryan site, *p. 13, p. 14*, 15
Buffalo. *See* Bison
Bull Run, Civil War battle, 112
Businesses. *See* Industries

C

Cahokia, 13
Cannon River, Bryan archeological site, 13–15
Catalogs, 223
Chequamegon Bay, Ojibwe settlement of, 42
Children
  farm work and, 220–222
  in American Indian cultures, 32, 33, 38, 50–55
  settlers and, 143, 144

see also Toys and games
Chippewa. *See* Ojibwe
Cities. *See* Urban life
Civil Defense, 272–273
Civil rights and discrimination
    civil rights movements, 281–291
    discrimination against German-
       Americans, 200–201
    discrimination against immi-
       grants, 179, 320–321
    Dr. Martin Luther King, Jr., 282,
       283
    music as protest, 291–297
    racial discrimination, 109,
       198–199, 281, 282–288
    sex discrimination, 281, 289–291,
       296
    suffrage (voting rights),
       p. 192–193, 194–195
Civil War, 110–114, 115–121
    Missionary Ridge, Battle of,
       m. 118
The Cold War, 266
The "Common Good," 193–194
Communism, 265, 273
Conservation, 196–197, 303–305
Crime, 180, 194, 233–234, 240–247
Cuban Missile Crisis, 172–173
Cummings, William (World War II
    soldier), 251, 252, 253, 254, 256
Curot, Michel (fur trade clerk),
    63–65
The Cutover, 196–197

Dairy industry, 220, 235, 305–307
Dakota
    agriculture and, 28–29, *p. 31*, 126
    assimilation, 126–127
    children in Dakota culture, 32, 33,
       38
    Dakota War, 122–140
    fur trade and, 48–49, 64, 77
    Ojibwe and, 40–41, 47–49, 77
    oral tradition and storytelling,
       25–27, 31–32
    territory of, *m. 33*, 41
    traditional lifestyle, 25–39, 126

    treaties and, 76, 78, 79, 81–83,
       86–89, 123
Dakota War, 122–140
Discrimination. *See* Civil rights and
    discrimination
Diseases
    American Indians exposed to, 45
    public health issues, 184, 198,
       204–211
    urban growth and, 180
Donahower, Jeremiah C. (Civil War
    soldier), *p. 116*
Dred Scott Decision, 110
Duluth, 185, 308–313
Dylan, Bob "Robert Zimmerman"
    (musician), 294

Eastman, Charles "Ohiyesa" (doctor,
    author), 26, 27–28, 37
Eastman, Mary Henderson
    (author), 88
Eastman, Seth, paintings by, *p. 29,*
    p. 36, p. 37
Economics
    agriculture and, 234–235
    capitalism, 265
    the Cold War and, 266–271
    communism, 265, 273
    conservation and, 304
    consumer goods, availability of,
       213–214, 253–254
    GI Bill of Rights, 301
    Great Depression, 232, 233–239
    New Deal programs, 237–239
    wages and prices, 66, 164, 291
    welfare programs, 236
    World War II and, 250
    see also Industries
Education
    civil rights issues, 283–285
    Harriet Bishop, St. Paul teacher,
       92–93
    Indian education and schools, 80,
       200–201, 288
    see also Oral tradition and story
       telling

Electrical power, 214, *p. 215,*
    215–216, 220, 295
Ellestad, Gerhard and family (of
    Lanesboro), 217–219
The Emancipation Proclamation,
    114
Employment
    in flour milling, 160
    in fur trade, 60–62, 66–73
    joblessness during Great
       Depression, 236–237
    labor unions and, 164–165, 166,
       167
    in lumber industry, 160–161
    the middle class and, 213
    in mining industry, 164–166
    wages, 66, 164, 291
    of women, 92–93, 258–263,
       267–268, 291
Environmentalism. *See*
    Conservation
Evidence, history and, 4–5, 10
Explorers, 48–49, 58, 69, 76
Extended Tail Feathers
    "Upiyahideya" (Dakota elder),
       81–82, 87

Fallout shelters, 271–272
Farmers Holiday Association, 235
Finnish immigrants, 164–165, 167
Flags, Civil War era, 119
Food and diet
    "Betty Crocker," 267–269
    famine and, 270
    of American Indian cultures,
       10–11, 27–31, 37, 44, 52
    Multi-Purpose Food, 270–271
    safety and quality of, 198
    soda fountains, 219
    victory gardens, 254
    of voyageurs, 69
Foreclosures, 235
Forest fires, 197
Forest Mills, 150
Fort Ridgley, *p. 130*
Fort Snelling, 76–77, *p. 77, p. 132*
Fort William, 68

Foshay, Wilbur (businessman), 231–232
Frank, Melvin and family (of Minneapolis), 214–217
Freeman, Rose Mary (civil rights activist), 282–285
Fritsche, Louis A. (politician), 203
Fur trade
    Dakota and, 64
    employment in, 60–62, 66–73
    European traders, 48–49, 58–65
    Fort Snelling and, 76–77
    interpreters, 62
    Métis and, 64
    Ojibwe and, 45–46, 47, 48–49, 57–58
    portages, 63, 72
    rendezvous, 65, 71
    trade goods and trade economics, 58–60
    trade routes and trading posts, *p. 61, p. 63*
    treaties and, 80, 83
    United States and, 65
    voyageurs, 60–65, 66–73

Galbraith, Thomas (Indian agent), 124–125, 127
Gangsters, 234, 240–247
German immigrants, 89, 98–99, 104, 129–130, 137, 179, 202–203
Gettysburg, Civil War battle, 113
Ghost towns, 150
GI Bill of Rights, 301
Giishkiman "Sharpened Stone" (Ojibwe elder), 62–63
Glenn, Horace (logger and lawyer), 160–161, 163
Goddard, Charley (Civil War soldier), 111–114, 115
Gonsior, Leroy (archeologist), 16–23
Goodhue, James (journalist), 88
Good Star Woman "Wicaŋḣpiwaśtewiŋ" (Dakota witness of fur trade), 127
Government. *See* Politics and government
Grand Portage, 56, 68

The Grange, 145, 149
Great Depression, 232, 233–239
Greek immigrants, 79

Hawley, 176–177
Ḣdaiŋyaŋka "Ran with the Sound of a Rattle" (Dakota), 132
Health, public health issues, 180, 184, 198, 204–211
Hennepin, Louis (missionary), 58
Hickman, Richard (freed slave), 114–115
Hill, James J. (railroad developer), 149
Hinman, Samuel (missionary), 125
History
    Dakota perspective on, 32
    evidence and, 4–5, 10
    photographs as sources, 168–173
    point of view and, 4
    primary sources, 2, 4–5, 84–85
    shared history, 3
    see also Archeology; Oral tradition and storytelling
Hmong immigrants, 316–318
Homestead Act, 142–143, 147
Hope, Virginia Mae (World War II pilot), 258–263
Houses. *See* Architecture
Howe, Oscar, painting by, *p. 24–25*
Humphrey, Annie (Ojibwe musician), 297
Humphrey, David W. (settler), 104
Humphrey, Hubert H. (politician), 285
Huntley, Horace (civil rights activist), *p. 282*
Hurd, Alomina Hamm (Dakota War witness), 138

Immigration
    asylum, 322
    discrimination against immigrants, 179, 320–321
    land availability and, 89, 95–96
    letters of immigrants, 103–105
    motives for immigration, 89, 315, 316, 321

    recruiting settlers, 98–99, 100–103
    settlement houses, 184–185
    to towns and cities, 96–97, 178–179, 317–318
    women and, 104, 105
Indians. *See* American Indians
Industries
    economic development and, 156–166
    flour milling, 156–160
    lumber industry, 78, 94, 160–164, 196–197, 253
    manufacturing, 252
    meat packing, 319–320
    mining, 164–166
    progressivism and, 196–197
    see also Agriculture
Iŋyaŋgmani "Running Walker" (Dakota elder), 79, 84
Irish immigrants, 98, 199
Iron Range, 164–167, *m. 166*
Iśtaḣba "Sleepy Eyes" (Dakota elder), 81–82
Italian immigrants, 79
Itasca Bison Kill Site, 6, 10

Jazz Age, 232–233
Jeffers, petroglyph ridge, *p. 6–7*
Johnson, Nellie Stone and family (African American farmers), 220–222

Kaposia, 78
Kegg, Maude (Ojibwe storyteller), 50–55
Kelly, Oliver H. (farmer), 145
Kienholz, Foster, memory book of, 226–227

Labor unions, 164–165, 166, 167
Land
    American Indian relationship with, 78, 79, 84
    Dawes Act, 200
    European land claims, 41, 75
    land speculators, 147
    settlement and, 89, 95–96
    see also Treaties

Lanesboro, 217–219
Language
    interpreters, 62, 79
    Ojibwe language, 47, 50, 201
Laotian immigrants, 316–318
Lawrence, Elden (Dakota elder), 32
Lawrence, Lorenzo (Dakota farmer), 139
Lea, Luke (politician), 89
Le Duc, William G. (politician), 89
Leisure time, 213–214, 219, 224–229
    see also Toys and games
Lewis, T. H. 15
Lifestyle, defined, 183
Little Crow "Taoyateduta" (Dakota leader), 86, 87, 126, 128
Long, Frank (World War II soldier), 251, 256
Long, Hildred Shelland (government employee), 251, 253–254, 257
Long, Larry (musician), 295
Lumber industry, 78, 94, 160–164, 196–197, 253
Lyles, Amanda and Thomas (African American business operators and activists), 199

Magner, Mike (archaeologist), 16–18
Makato "Blue Earth" (Dakota leader), 126
Maple sugaring, 27–28, 50–51
Mattson, Hans (Swedish immigrant), 96–97
May, Sebastian (German farmer), 89
Mayer, Frank, drawings by, p. 81–82
Melendez, Maria (beautician, factory worker), 318–321
Mendota, 77, 83
Merritt, Leonidas and Alfred, 165
Métis, 64, 74, 92
Metropolitan areas, 175–176
Mexican Americans, 318–321
Migrant workers, 319
Migrations, 10, 41–44, m. 43, m. 46
Milling industry, 156–160, 266–271
Mining industry, 164–166, 253

Minneapolis, 175–176, 214–217
Minnesota Territory, m. 79, 79–83, 94–95
Missionaries, 36–37, 58
    Dakota War and, 125–127, 131
    treaties and, 80, 83
Missionary Ridge, Civil War battle, 116–121
Mondale, Walter (politician), p. 287, 288
Morrill Hall civil rights protest, 284–285
Mound builder culture, 11–15
Multi-Purpose Food (MPF), 270–271
Music
    Jazz Age, 232–233
    protest songs, 291–297
    voyageur's song, 68
Myrick, Andrew (trader), 125, 128

Natural resources
    conservation and, 303–305
    industries and, 157
    lumber industry, 162
    mining, 165–166
    settlement and, 77, 150
Nelson, George (fur trade clerk), 71
New Deal programs, 237–239
Noor, Ali and family (Somali immigrants), 321–323
Northwest Ordinance, 94
Norwegian immigrants, 98–99

Ohiyesa "Charles Eastman" (doctor, author), 26, 27–28, 37
Ojibwe
    alliances with Europeans, 46–47
    assimilation programs, 200–201
    beadwork, 53–54
    children, education of, 50–55
    Dakota and, 47–49, 77
    fur trade and, 45, 57–58, 62–64, p. 71, 77
    land use issues, 95, 307
    language, 47, 50, 201
    migration of, 41–44, m. 43, m. 46

oral tradition of, 43–44, 50–55
    traditional lifestyle, 53–54
    treaty of 1837, 78
Olson, Floyd (governor), 235
Oral tradition and storytelling
    Dakota culture, 24–27, 31–32
    education through, 50–55
    Ojibwe culture, 40–41, 43–44, 50–55

Parks, p. 212–213, 216–217, 308–313, m. 338
Perrault, Jean (fur trader), 70
Petroglyphs, 7, 15
Photography, as historical source, 168–173
Pike, Zebulon (soldier and explorer), treaty negotiated by, 76
Pillsbury, Charles (industrialist), 158–160
Place names, origins of, 47, 99
Platting, planning towns, 152–153
Plumbing, 215
Polish immigrants, 79
Politics and government
    civil rights, activism, and protest movements, 282–291
    Dakota decision making and governance, 32, 83
    environmental issues, 303–305
    the Grange and, 145, 149
    progressivism, 194–195
    railroad regulation, 149
    sovereignty of Indian nations, 76
    statehood, 99, 107
    Territorial government, 80
    woman suffrage (voting rights), p. 192–193, 194–195
Pond, Peter (explorer and trader), 69
Pond, Samuel (missionary), 36–37
Population, 91, p. 108, 177–179, 286, p. 336
Portages and portaging, 63, 72
Poverty, 180, 200, 281
Prehistory. See Archeology; Oral tradition and storytelling
Primary sources, 2, 4–5, 84–85

Progressivism
   civil rights, 198–199
   government and, 194–195
   public health issues, 198, 208–211
Prohibition, 93, 233–234, 240

R

Race and discrimination, 109, 198–199, 281, 282–288
Radiocarbon dating, 21
Railroads, 92, 145–149, *m. 148*, 152, 159, *m. 166*, 196
Ramsey, Alexander (politician), 80, *p. 80*, 81–82, 89, 95
Rationing, 253–254
Red Banner "Wapahaśa" (Dakota leader), *p. 86*, 86, 126
Red River area, *m. 151*
Red Wing, immigration and settlement of, 96–97
Refugees, 316–318
Religion
   missionaries, 25, 36–37, 41, 56, 58, 80, 82
   mound builder culture, 11–12
   St. Anne's Church, 69
   temperance movement and, 93
Rendezvous, fur trade gatherings, 65, 71
Reservation system, 83, 95, 124
Riggs, Stephen (missionary), 80, 82, 125, 131
Rochester, 322–323
Rogers, John "Wekwaa-giizhig" (Ojibwe boarding school student), 201
Roosevelt, Franklin D. (president), 237
Rowberg, Leland (World War II soldier), 257
Running Walker "Iŋyaŋgmani" (Dakota elder), 79, 84
Ran with the Sound of a Rattle "Ḣdaiŋyaŋka" (Dakota), 132

S

St. Croix river, 62, 78
St. Paul, 78, *p. 88*, 93, *p. 174–175*, *p. 177*, 317–318
Sanders-Dotter, Guri (Norwegian settler), 105

Savoyard, Toussaint (fur trade voyageur), 63–65
Sayer, John (fur trader), 63–65
Schlieske, Christina "Tina" (musician), 296
Schmitz, Friedrich (settler), 104
Schools. *See* Education
Schwandt, Mary (Dakota War witness), 129–130, 134–137
Scott, Dred and Harriet (freed slaves), 110
Scrapbooks, 224–229
Segregation, 282–283
Settlement houses, 184–185
Settlers and settlement
   agriculture and, 11–12, *p. 89*, 142–143, 147–148, *p. 155*
   children's roles, 143, 144
   Homestead Act, 142–143, 147
   houses constructed by, 142–143
   importance of land to, 89
   New England and, 93–94, 104
   population growth and, 91
   recruiting settlers, 98–99, 100–103, 153–155
   towns, location and planning of, 150–155
   westward expansion and, 75–76
Sharpened Stone "Giishkiman" (Ojibwe elder), 62–63
Sibley, Henry (fur trader and politician), 80, 82, 95, 99, 131
Sioux. *See* Dakota
Slavery, 107–111
Sleepy Eyes "Iśtaḣba" (Dakota elder), 81–82
Smallpox, *p. 211*
Smith, William (Civil War soldier), 112
Snana "Maggie Brass" (Dakota War witness), 134–137
Somali immigrants, 321–323
Sovereignty of Indian nations, 76
Sports, 217, 289–291
Star Boy (Dakota oral tradition), 31–32
Star Face "Wicaŋḣpiitetoŋwaŋ" (Dakota elder), 81–83

Statehood, 99, 107
Stereotypes of Minnesotans, 2
Stillwater, *p. 10*
Stillwater convention, 94–95
Stories and storytelling. *See* Oral tradition and storytelling
Striebel, Kathy (athlete and activist), 289–291
Strikes, 164–165
Swedish immigrants, 96–97, 98–99, 179
Sweeney, Robert, drawing by, *p. 29*
Swiss immigrants, 105

T

Tainter, John and Sarah (Lincoln County settlers), 142–143, 147–148
Taliaferro, Lawrence (Indian agent), 77
Taopi "Wounded Man" (Dakota farmer), 126, 128–129
Taoyateduta "Little Crow" (Dakota leader), 86, 87, 126, 128
Technology and tools, *p. 219*
   agriculture, 220–222, 305–307
   cameras and photography, 168–173, *p. 224*
   Dakota tools, *p. 37*, *p. 30*, 34–39, *p. 46*
   electrical power and appliances, 214, *p. 215*, 215–216, 220, 295
   flour milling, 159–160
   lumber industry, 161, 162
   machines and industries, 157
   mining and, 166
   plumbing, 215
   stone age tools and technology, 7, 8, 11, 14, 19, 20, 22
   telephones, 218
   as trade goods, 45
   see also Transportation
Temperance movement, 93
Territorial period, *m. 79*, 79–83, 94–95
Thompson, Orrin (land developer), 300–302
Thunderbird and Water Spirit (Dakota oral tradition), 26–27

Tobkin, Ron and family (farmers), 305–307

Toso, Conrad and Elizabeth (farmers), 233, 234, 235

Towns. *See* Urban life

Toys and games, 32, 33, *p. 52*, 143, 216–217, *p. 218*, 274–279, *p.288*

Traders, 70
  Dakota War and, 125, 127, 128
  see also Fur trade

Transportation, 221
  American Indian transportation methods, *p. 29*, 36, *p. 73*
  automobiles, 182–184, 221, 301
  canoes, 42, *p. 48*, 49, *p. 56–57*, 63, 72
  Duluth and, 308–313
  immigration and, 96
  portages, 63
  railroads, 92, 145–149
  Red River oxcarts, 74
  on rivers, *p. 90–91*, 162
  settlement and, 92
  streetcars, 182–183
  suburban growth and, 301
  urban growth and, *p. 181*

Treaties
  American Indian claims and protests, 286–288, 307
  American Indians' relationship with land, 78, 79
  changes in, 83
  defined, 76
  missionaries and, 80, 83
  negotiation of, 81–82
  Pike's treaty, 76
  reasons for seeking, 79–80
  sovereignty and, 76
  Traverse des Sioux and Mendota treaties, 81–82, 86–89, 123
  Treaty of 1837, 78

Turtle Island (Ojibwe oral tradition), 43–44

Typhoid Fever, 204–211

Ueland, Clara (suffrage leader), 195

Upiyahideya "Extended Tail Feathers" (Dakota elder), 81–82, 87

Urban life
  location and planning of towns, 150–155
  lumber industry and, 162
  political and social changes, 193–194
  problems of, 180
  suburban development and urban sprawl, 300–302
  the Twin Cities metropolitan area, 175–178
  urban planning, 299–302
  urban renewal, 302

Vang family (Hmong immigrants), 316–318

Van Sant, Samuel (politician), *p. 196*

Vietnam War, 273

Volk, Douglas, painting by, *p. 116–117*

Voyageurs, 60–61, 63–73

Walton, Dorothy, memory book of, 228–229

Waŋmbditaŋka "Big Eagle" (Dakota leader), 126–127

Wapahaśa "Red Banner" (Dakota leader), *p. 86*, 86, 126

Warmington, Carl (musician and relief worker), 232–233, 236–237

Warren, William (Ojibwe historian), 49, *p. 49*

Wars
  among American Indians, 47–49, 77
  Civil War, 110–121
  Dakota War, 123–140
  as immigration motive, 316, 321
  Vietnam War, 273
  World War I, 200–201
  World War II, 249–263

Wefald, Knud (politician), 176–177, 184, 185

Wekwaa-giizhig "John Rogers" (Ojibwe boarding school student), 201

Westward expansion, 75–76

Weyerhauser, Frederick (lumberman), 163

Wheat, 145–146, 158–160

Whipple, Henry (missionary), 131

Wicaŋħpiitetoŋwaŋ "Star Face" (Dakota elder), 81–83

Wicaŋħpiwaśtewiŋ "Good Star Woman" (Dakota witness of fur trade), 127

Wild rice, *p. 29*, 29–30, 44, 52

Willard, S. I. (settler), 97

Williamson, John (missionary), 125

Winston, Eliza (freed slave), 109–110

Women
  Civil War activities of, *p. 113*, 115
  discrimination against, 281, 289–291, 296
  employment of, 92–93, *p. 253*, 258–263, 267–268, 291
  in fur trade, 62, 63, 71
  immigration and, 104, 105
  in American Indian cultures, 14, 32–33, 36
  Jazz Age and, *p. 233*
  sports and, 183, 289–291
  suffrage (voting rights), *p. 192–193*, 194–195
  as teachers, 92–93
  temperance movement and, 93

World War I, 200–201

World War II, 249–263
  economic impacts of, 252–254
  home front experiences, 251–255
  soldiers' experiences, 255–257
  women's roles during, 258–263

Worthington, 319–321

Wounded Man "Taopi" (Dakota farmer), 126, 128–129

Xiong, Kao and family (Hmong immigrants), 316–318

Zimmerman, Robert "Bob Dylan" (musician), 294

Illustration Credits

All images reproduced in this book that are not listed here or identified as to source are owned by the Minnesota Historical Society. Dates and photographers are listed when known.

Cover: *Fiery Sunset over the Island River*, Raymond Gehman, 1996.

Chapter 1: Opening spread State symbol photos by Kent Kaiser. **4-5** Objects courtesy of Kathryn and Dan Wackman, photos by Jerry Mathiason.

Chapter 2: 9 Copyright © 2002 Publishers Resource Group, Inc. **14** John Koepke, *Bryan Site*, 1993. Courtesy of the Goodhue County Historical Society, Red Wing, Minnesota, photo by Phil Revoir. **22** Scottsbluff Point courtesy of Leo Pettipas, Manitoba Archaeological Society; Alberta Point courtesy of the Oklahoma Anthropological Society, Bell 1960.

Chapter 3: 24 *Dakota Teaching*, c. 1951, Oscar Howe, Yankton Sioux, 1915-1983. Gouache on paper, Museum purchase, The Philbrook Museum of Art, Tulsa, Oklahoma, 1951.8. **27** Seth Eastman, *Indians Spearing Muskrats in Winter*. Courtesy of W. Duncan and Nivin Macmillan and Afton Historical Society Press. **28** Seth Eastman, *Indian Sugar Camp*. Courtesy of W. Duncan and Nivin Macmillan and Afton Historical Society Press. **29** Robert Sweeney, *Dakota Summer Camp;* Seth Eastman, *Gathering Wild Rice*. Courtesy of W. Duncan and Nivin Macmillan and Afton Historical Society Press. **31** Seth Eastman, *Guarding the Corn*. Courtesy of W. Duncan and Nivin Macmillan and Afton Historical Society Press. **35** Photo from *Daily Life in a Plains Indian Village 1868*, by Michael Bad Hand Terry. Copyright © 1999 by Breslich & Foss Ltd. Reprinted by permission of Clarion Books, a Division of Houghton Mifflin Company. All rights reserved. **36** Seth Eastman, *Indian Mode of Traveling*, 1869. Courtesy of Architect of the Capitol. **39** Woman making parfleche photo by John A. Anderson, 1900. Courtesy of Nebraska State Historical Society, RG2969:2-226. **37** Seth Eastman, *Hunting Buffalo in Winter*. Photo courtesy of Edward E. Ayer Collection, The Newberry Library, Chicago.

Chapter 4: 40 Carl Gawboy, *Ojibwe Storyteller*. **48** Francis Lee Jacques, *Daniel Greysolon Sieur Dulhut at the Head of the Lakes— 1679*, ca. 1922. **50** Courtesy of the Kalk family, photos by Bonnie Johnson. **51** Sugaring photo courtesy of Loretta Kegg Kalk, photo by Bonnie Johnson. **52** Dolls courtesy of John D. Nichols, photos by Eric Mortenson. **53** Bandolier bag courtesy of Lost and Found Traditions Collection, Anthropology Section, Natural History Museum of Los Angeles County. **54** Pendant courtesy of John D. Nichols, photo by Eric Mortenson. **55** Courtesy of Betty Kegg.

Chapter 5: 56 Frances Ann Hopkins, *Shooting the Rapids, Quebec*, 1879. National Archives of Canada, Ottawa. C-002774. **60** Frances Ann Hopkins, *Canoes in a Fog, Lake Superior*, 1869. Collection of Glenbow Museum, Calgary, Canada. **62** Copyright © State of Minnesota, Department of Natural Resources. **63** Frank Earle Schoonover, *Dickering with the Factor*, 1912. Glenbow Collection, Calgary, Canada. [59.35.1]. Reprinted by permission of Louise Schoonover Smith, granddaughter of Frank E. Schoonover. **65** Franklin Arbuckle, *Spring Brigade Leaves Montreal for the West*, 1948. Hudson's Bay Company Archives, PAM, P-412. **67** *The Annual Cycle* from *The Illustrated Voyageur* by Howard Sivertson, Grand Marais, Minnesota.

68–69 Illustration by David Christofferson. **69** Frances Ann Hopkins, *Voyageurs at Dawn*, 1871. National Archives of Canada, Ottawa. C-002773. **71** Eastman Johnson, *Ojibwe Women*, 1857. Permanent Collection of St. Louis County Historical Society, Duluth, Minnesota. **72** William Henry Bartlett, *Burial Place of the Voyageurs*, 1840. National Archives of Canada, Ottawa. C002336. **73** William Cary, *En Route to Winter Camp*. Collection of Gilcrease Museum, Tulsa, Oklahoma.

Chapter 6: 74 Francis Millett, *Treaty of Traverse des Sioux*, 1905. **77** John Casper Wild, *Fort Snelling*, 1844; Anonymous, *Lawrence Taliaferro*, ca. 1830. **78** John Schmitt, *Chapel of St. Paul*, ca. 1845. **79** Photo by Charles A. Zimmerman. **81** Frank Mayer, *Sioux Evening Meal*. Photo courtesy of Edward E. Ayer Collection, The Newberry Library, Chicago, Illinois. **82** Frank Mayer, *Winona*. Photo courtesy of Edward E. Ayer Collection, The Newberry Library, Chicago, Illinois; Frank Mayer, *Traverse des Sioux-Camp*. Photo courtesy of Edward E. Ayer Collection, The Newberry Library, Chicago, Illinois. **84** Franz Holzhuber, *A Burial Place of the Sioux Indians in Minnesota*, 1856-60. Collection of the Glenbow Museum, Calgary, Canada. [65.39.125]. **85** Dakota woman and child photo courtesy of Ramsey County Historical Society; Frank Mayer, *Good Thunder*. Courtesy of Edward E. Ayer Collection, The Newberry Library, Chicago, Illinois; Henry Sibley and Joseph R. Brown photo by Mathew Brady Studio. **86** Photo by Charles Fredericks; Lithograph by George Catlin. **87** Seth Eastman, *Dakota Encampment*. Courtesy of W. Duncan and Nivin Macmillan and Afton Historical Society Press; Taoyateduta photo by A.Z. Shindler-Washington, D.C. 1858. Courtesy of the National Anthropological Archives, Smithsonian Institution. **88** St. Paul photo by Benjamin F. Upton.

Chapter 7: 90 Ferdinand Reichardt, *View on the Mississippi River*, 1857. **93** Andrew Falkenshield, *Harriet E. McConkey Bishop*, 1880. **96** *Harper's Weekly*, June 26, 1858. **105** Photo from Ralph H. Bowen, ed. and trans., *A Frontier Family: Letters of Theodore and Sophie Bost 1851-1920*. University of Minnesota Press, 1981.

Chapter 8: 106 Rufus Zogbaum, *The Battle of Gettysburg*, 1906. **109** *St. Anthony Evening News*, Aug. 23, 1860. **113** Eastman Johnson, *The Letter Home*, 1867. The Minneapolis Institute of Arts. **116** Photo by Hiram Jacoby. **117** Douglas Volk, *The Battle of Missionary Ridge*, 1906. **119** Photo by Palmquist & Jurgens.

Chapter 9: 122 Alexander Schwendinger, *The Battle of New Ulm*, 1891, photo by Eric Mortenson. Brown County Historical Society, New Ulm, Minnesota. **125** Andrew Myrick photo by Steve Cushman. Courtesy of Chippewa County Historical Society, Montevideo, Minnesota. **127** Photo by Whitney Gallery. **128** Wambditanka photo by Simon and Shepherd. **129** Taopi photo by Martin's Gallery; Refugees on the prairie photo by Adrian J. Ebell. **130** James McGrew, *Battle of Fort Ridgely*, 1890. **131** Photos by Whitney Gallery. **132** Photo by B. F. Upton. **135** Photo by Shepherd Studio. **138** Seth Eastman, *Prairie Back of Fort Snelling*.

Chapter 10: 140 Joseph Meeker, *Minnesota Harvest Field*, 1877. **143** Photo by Hugh Chalmers. **145** Grange meeting photo by E. N. James; Oliver Kelley photo by Burgess & Co. **146** Photo by Alexander Gardner. **149** Photo by Pach Bros. **151** J.W. Trygg Historical Collections.

Chapter 11: 156 Courtesy of General Mills Archives. **159** Milling district photo by Henry Farr; Grinding wheat photo by Keystone View Co. **160** Photo by A.A. Richardson. **162** Taylors Falls log jam photo by John Runk; Log sled photo by Burkhart.

Chapter 12: 174 Nicholas Richard Brewer, *View of St. Paul (Wabasha Streetscape),* 1908. **177** St. Paul photo by Charles P. Gibson. **179** Photo by George E. Luxton. **181** Streetcar photo by Eclipse View Co. **186** Prairie School glass mosaic photo courtesy of Jerry Mathiason. **187** Elsinger house photo by Thomas Lutz; Beebe house photo from William Gray Purcell Papers, Northwest Architectural Archives, University of Minnesota Libraries, Minneapolis, Minnesota. **188** William Gray Purcell Papers, Northwest Architectural Archives, University of Minnesota Libraries, Minneapolis, Minnesota. **189** Clarence H. Johnston Papers, Northwest Architectural Archives, University of Minnesota Libraries, Minneapolis, Minnesota. **190** William Gray Purcell Papers, Northwest Architectural Archives, University of Minnesota Libraries, Minneapolis, Minnesota. **191** Clarence H. Johnston Papers, Northwest Architectural Archives, University of Minnesota Libraries, Minneapolis, Minnesota.

Chapter 13: 192 *Minneapolis Journal,* May 3, 1914, p. 14. **196** Herbert Conner, *Samuel R. Van Sant,* 1905. **206** Collections of Library of Congress, 314804. **208** Cartoon from *St. Paul Pioneer Press,* July 17, 1909.

Chapter 14: 214 Store photo courtesy of Marshall Field's. **217** Photo by Gilbert B. Ellestad. **220** Photo courtesy of Nellie Stone Johnson. **223** The 1913 catalog is reprinted by arrangement with Sears, Roebuck and Co. and is protected under copyright. No duplication is permitted.

Chapter 15: 230 Edwin Nooleen, *Unemployed Men in Minneapolis,* 1933. **232** Photo by Charles J. Hibbard. **235** Toso photo courtesy of the Otter Tail County Historical Society. **238** Woman listening to radio photo by Monroe Killy. **245** Ma Barker photo courtesy of the Minneapolis Public Library, Minneapolis Collection. **247** AP/Wide World Photos.

Chapter 16: 253 Women workers photo from *Minneapolis Star Journal;* Ration books courtesy of Dominic Abram, photo by Eric Mortenson. **255** Photo courtesy of Mr. James Lawson. **259** Horse photo courtesy of the Hope family. **261** Telegram information is given by the U.S. Office of Personnel Management. **263** Logo on jacket, Disney character © Disney Enterprises, Inc. Used by permission from Disney Enterprises, Inc.

Chapter 17: 264 Courtesy of Xcel Energy Corporation. **267** *Minneapolis Star Tribune.* **268–269** Courtesy of General Mills Archives. **270** Appliances photo by Kenneth M. Wright. **274** Rocket toy courtesy of Tim Talbot, photo by Eric Mortenson. **275** Disney characters © Disney Enterprises, Inc. Used by permission from Disney Enterprises, Inc. **276** Game and toy courtesy of Thomond and Alvina O'Brien, photos by Eric Mortenson. **277** Toy gun courtesy of Tim Talbot, photo by Eric Mortenson. **278** Toy gun courtesy of Tim Talbot, photo by Eric Mortenson. **279** Montgomery Ward catalog page courtesy of GE Capital.

Chapter 18: 280 Photo by Jon Walstrom. **282** Antiwar protest photo from *St. Paul Pioneer Press;* Freeman and Huntley photo from *Minneapolis Tribune.* **283** *St. Paul Pioneer Press* photo. **284** *Minneapolis Tribune* photos. **286** *Minneapolis Star* photo. **287** *Minneapolis Tribune* photo. **289** *Minneapolis Star* photo. **290** *St. Paul Pioneer Press* photo. **291** *St. Paul Pioneer Press* photo; Protest button courtesy of Maureen Otwell, photo by Eric Mortenson. **293** *Minneapolis Tribune* photo. **294** Bob Dylan photo © Daniel Kramer; "The Freewheelin' Bob Dylan" courtesy of Columbia Records; "Bob Dylan" courtesy of Columbia Records; "The Times They Are A' Changin'" courtesy of

Columbia Records. **295** Photo by unknown University of Minnesota student. Courtesy of Larry Long; Guitar case courtesy of Larry Long, photo by Eric Mortenson. **296** Photo by Michael Crouser; Ticket stub courtesy of Tina Schlieske, photo by Eric Mortenson. **297** Photo by Joseph Allen, 2001; Guitar and case courtesy of Annie Humphrey, photo by Eric Mortenson.

Chapter 19: 298 *The Long View,* Copyright © Larry Kanfer. **300** © 2002 *Star Tribune*/Minneapolis-St. Paul. **305** Tobkin family photo courtesy of Ron Tobkin. **306** Photo courtesy of Ron Tobkin. **309** From U.S. Geological Survey 1:100,000 Scale Map, 1980. **310** Top photo courtesy of Northeast Minnesota Historical Center, Duluth, Minnesota, Gaylord, vol. #1, image #21, photo by Paul Gaylord. **311** Front view of aerial lift bridge Northeast Minnesota Historical Center, Duluth, Minnesota "Looking South on Lake Avenue" S2386, Box 37, folder 3; Northeast Minnesota Historical Center, Duluth, Minnesota "View of Duluth, Minnesota 1883." Drawn by H. Wellge. Lithographers Beck & Paul, Milwaukee, Wisconsin. Publisher J.J. Stoner, Madison, Wisconsin. Detail, digitally enhanced. **313** Photo by Grandmaison Photographic Studios, Duluth, Minnesota; Map courtesy of Duluth Convention and Visitors Bureau.

Chapter 20: 314 Storycloth courtesy of Laura A. O'Brien, photo by Eric Mortenson. **316** Photo courtesy of Peter S. Ford. **317** Photo courtesy of Peter S. Ford. **318** Baby carrier photo courtesy of Peter S. Ford; Photo courtesy of Maria Melendez. **319** Photo by Juan Montoya. **320** Photo by Juan Montoya. **321** Photo courtesy of Ali Noor and family, copyright © *Rochester Post-Bulletin;* Stool courtesy of Ali Noor and family, photo by Eric Mortenson. **322** Bookrest courtesy of Ali Noor and family, photo by Eric Mortenson; Objects courtesy of Ali Noor and family, photo by Eric Mortenson. **323** Photo courtesy of Samera Mohamed, copyright © *Rochester Post-Bulletin.*

Other Credits

Chapter 4: 50-54 Reprinted with permission from *Portage Lake: Memories of an Ojibwe Childhood* by Maude Kegg, edited and transcribed by John Nichols, Edmonton: The University of Alberta Press and Minneapolis: The University of Minnesota Press, 1993, pp. 16-17, 20-21, 92-93, 132-33, and 150-51. **55** Maude Kegg quote "Advice to Young People" reprinted with permission from *Against the Tide of American History: The Story of the Mille Lacs Band of Ojibwe.*

Chapter 16: 260 Excerpt used with permission of Lyle Schmidt.

Chapter 18: 294 "Blowin' in the Wind" Copyright © 1962 by Warner Bros. Inc. © Renewed 1990 by Special Rider Music. All rights reserved. International copyright secured. Reprinted by permission. **295** Lyrics and music by Larry Long; Quotation courtesy of Larry Long. **296** Lyrics by Tina Schlieske; Quotation courtesy of Tina Schlieske. **297** Lyrics written by Anne M. Dunn, Carson Gardner, and Annie Humphrey; Quotation courtesy of Annie Humphrey.

Chapter 20: 316-318 Quotations from *A Hmong Family* by Nora Murphy, photographs by Peter Ford, copyright © 1997 by Lerner Publications Company, a division of Lerner Publishing Group. Used with permission. All rights reserved.

Every department at the Minnesota Historical Society contributed time and expertise essential to the creation of this book. The *Northern Lights* team extends heartfelt gratitude to all our colleagues who contributed.

Special thanks to the following people for their generous advice:

Carolyn Anderson, Kent Bakken, Barbara Bezat, Clifford Canku, Brenda Child, Katie Dishman, Leroy Gonsior, William Green, Roger Grant, Dr. Jennifer Gunn, Thomas Harvey, Annie Humphrey, Loretta Kegg Kalk, Patty Kakac, Betty Kegg, Dave Larson, Paul Larson, Dr. Elden Lawrence, Bryan Lean, Larry Long, Donna Lundquist, Paul Maccabee, Ed Mahowald, Mike Magner, Rose Freeman Massey, Patricia Maus, Maria Melendez, Karen McDonald, Larry Millet, Juan Montoya, Dr. John D. Nichols, Ali Noor, Thomas Saylor, Christina Schlieske, Ron Spencer, Valerie Tanner, Vicki Tobin, Ron Tobkin, Gaylord Torrence, Vernell Wabasha, Bruce White, Joe Williams, Rebecca Williams, Tina Williams, Vernon Zacher

Special thanks to the following teachers for testing chapters in their classrooms:

Jan Anderson, Chad Atherton, Bill Beckman, Linda Bonde, Bob Bowden, Laurine Braukmann, Matthew Busch, Gloria Collyard, Steve Decker, Tom DeGree, Kari Dietrich, Ginnie Donner, Nicole Fettig, Joan Frost, Lynn Genter, Robert Graef, Greg Hadley, Mona Hanson, Patricia Humphrey, Lea Iverson, Charlie Johnson, Lance Johnson, Cheryl Keenan, Jon Klocker, Dan Kuball, Sharon Marshall, Kara Pavlisich, Molly Ring, Nora Sandstad, Patricia Schmidt, Joan Schwarz, Elizabeth Simmer, Bridgitte Smisek, Krista Stadther, Diane Strandberg, Marilyn Stroble, Sheri Tinklenberg, Angie Ulseth

A book like *Northern Lights* doesn't just happen. It takes years of hard work by a team of people, each with different interests and talents. All of the people who worked together to create this book have some important things in common. They share a long-time love of history, Minnesota history in particular. They care deeply about Minnesota's young people and their future. Most of all, they share a conviction that knowledge of Minnesota's past is the best preparation for participation in its future.

Left side, clockwise from bottom: Sara Schroeder Yaeger, Gretchen Bratvold, Mindy Keskinen, Hillary Wackman, Dave Kenney.
Right side, clockwise from bottom: Suzanne Hunn, Carol Schreider, Maureen Otwell, Dominic Abram, Will Thiede, Nancy O'Brien Wagner, Margaret Lee.

The people who created Northern Lights: The Stories of Minnesota's Past, Second Edition

- ◆ Dave Kenney was the author of the student edition.
- ◆ Hillary Wackman and Nancy O'Brien Wagner wrote the Investigations, the teacher's edition, and the student workbook.
- ◆ Dominic Abram was the historian who researched the stories and images.
- ◆ Sara Schroeder Yaeger was the project manager.
- ◆ Suzanne Hunn was the production editor.
- ◆ Gretchen Bratvold was the copyeditor.
- ◆ Mindy Keskinen was the proofreader.
- ◆ Margaret Lee and Mollie Igo assisted with research and copyediting.
- ◆ Will Thiede and Alice Thiede created the maps.
- ◆ Carol Schreider and Maureen Otwell directed the project and reviewed all components.
- ◆ Publishers Resource Group, Inc. designed and composed the pages and coordinated the *Northern Lights* production schedules.

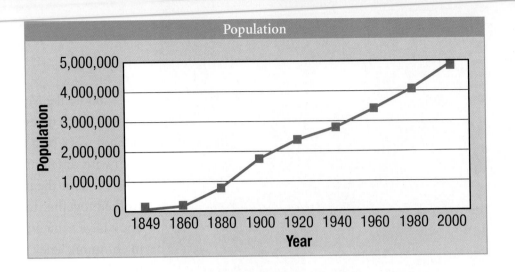

Population

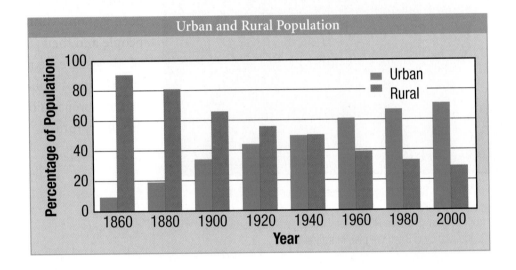

Urban and Rural Population

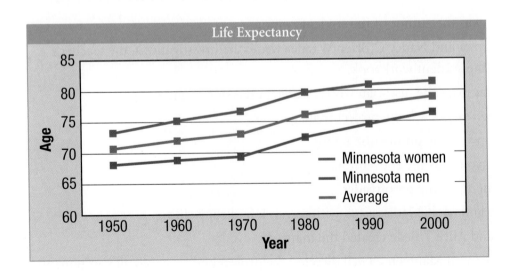

Life Expectancy

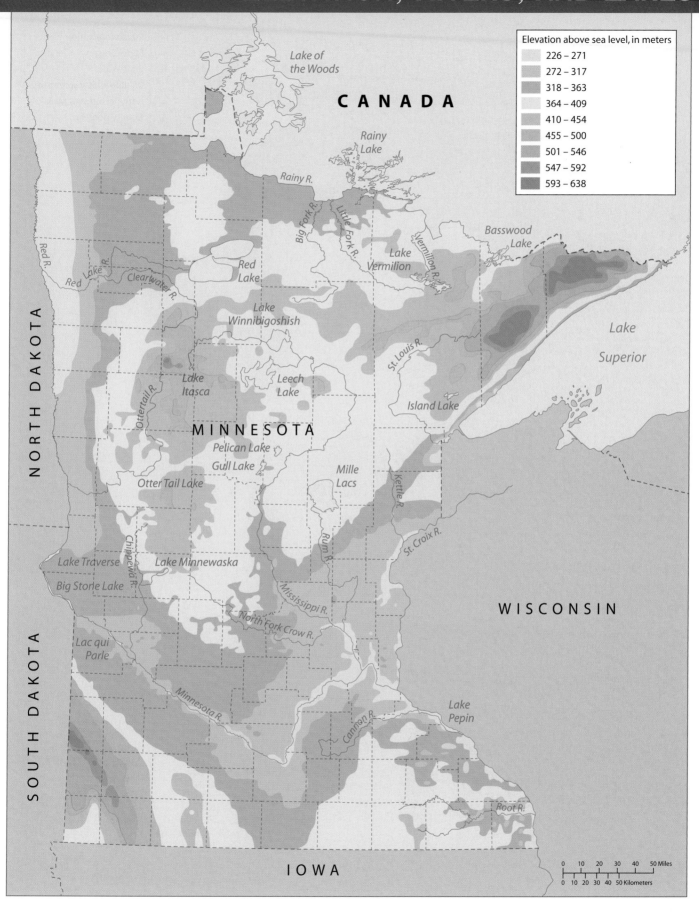

CANADA

Lake of
the Woods

Rainy
Lake

Rainy R.

Basswood
Lake

Big Fork R.

Little Fork R.

Vermilion R.

Lake
Vermilion

Red R.

Red Lake R.

Clearwater R.

Red
Lake

St. Louis R.

Lake
Superior

Lake
Winnibigoshish

NORTH DAKOTA

Ottertail R.

Lake
Itasca

Leech
Lake

Island Lake

MINNESOTA

Pelican Lake

Gull Lake

Mille
Lacs

Kettle R.

Otter Tail Lake

Chippewa R.

Lake Traverse

Lake Minnewaska

Rum R.

St. Croix R.

WISCONSIN

Big Stone Lake

Mississippi R.

North Fork Crow R.

SOUTH DAKOTA

Lac qui
Parle

Minnesota R.

Cannon R.

Lake
Pepin

Root R.

IOWA

Elevation above sea level, in meters

226 – 271
272 – 317
318 – 363
364 – 409
410 – 454
455 – 500
501 – 546
547 – 592
593 – 638

0   10   20   30   40   50 Miles

0   10   20   30   40   50 Kilometers

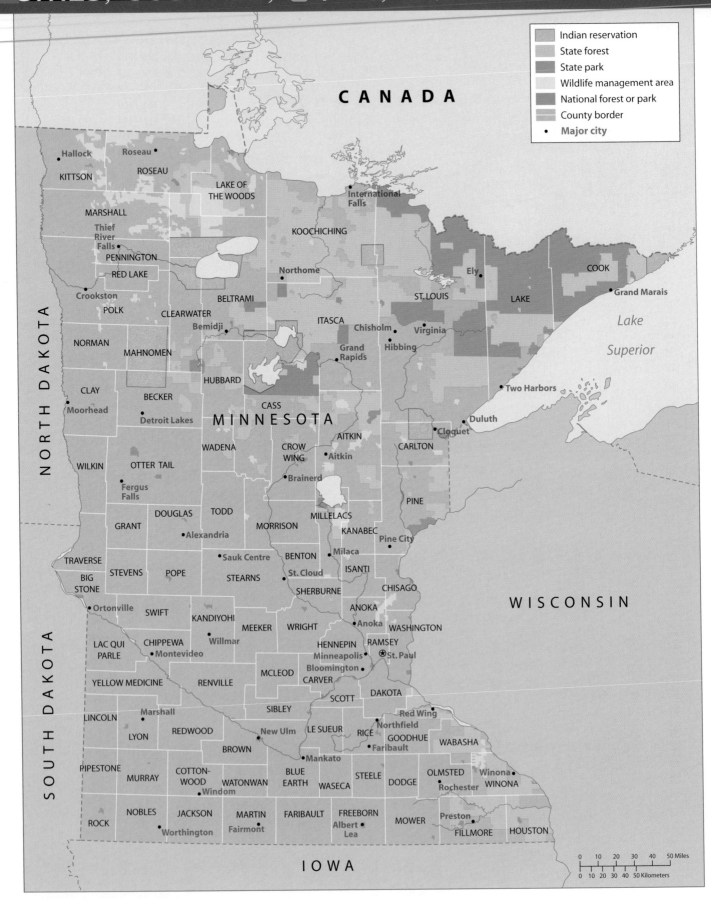

Indian reservation
State forest
State park
Wildlife management area
National forest or park
County border
• Major city

CANADA

Hallock
KITTSON
Roseau
ROSEAU
LAKE OF
THE WOODS
International
Falls
KOOCHICHING
Ely
COOK
LAKE
Grand Marais
MARSHALL
Thief
River
Falls
PENNINGTON
RED LAKE
Crookston
POLK
NORMAN
MAHNOMEN
BELTRAMI
Northome
ITASCA
Chisholm
Virginia
ST. LOUIS
Hibbing
Grand
Rapids
Lake
Superior
Bemidji
CLEARWATER
HUBBARD
CLAY
Moorhead
BECKER
Detroit Lakes
MINNESOTA
CASS
Two Harbors
Duluth
Cloquet
CARLTON
AITKIN
WADENA
CROW
WING
Aitkin
PINE
WILKIN
OTTER TAIL
Fergus
Falls
DOUGLAS
TODD
MORRISON
MILLELACS
KANABEC
Pine City
GRANT
MORRISON
BENTON
Milaca
Alexandria
Sauk Centre
St. Cloud
ISANTI
STEARNS
SHERBURNE
CHISAGO
TRAVERSE
STEVENS
POPE
BIG
STONE
Ortonville
SWIFT
KANDIYOHI
MEEKER
WRIGHT
ANOKA
Anoka
WASHINGTON
RAMSEY
WISCONSIN
LAC QUI
PARLE
CHIPPEWA
Montevideo
Willmar
HENNEPIN
Minneapolis
St. Paul
YELLOW MEDICINE
RENVILLE
MCLEOD
CARVER
Bloomington
SCOTT
DAKOTA
LINCOLN
Marshall
LYON
REDWOOD
SIBLEY
New Ulm
LE SUEUR
RICE
Red Wing
Northfield
GOODHUE
Faribault
WABASHA
BROWN
Mankato
PIPESTONE
MURRAY
COTTON-
WOOD
WATONWAN
Windom
BLUE
EARTH
WASECA
STEELE
DODGE
OLMSTED
Rochester
Winona
WINONA
ROCK
NOBLES
JACKSON
MARTIN
Fairmont
FARIBAULT
FREEBORN
Albert
Lea
MOWER
Preston
FILLMORE
HOUSTON
Worthington

NORTH DAKOTA
SOUTH DAKOTA

IOWA

0 10 20 30 40 50 Miles
0 10 20 30 40 50 Kilometers

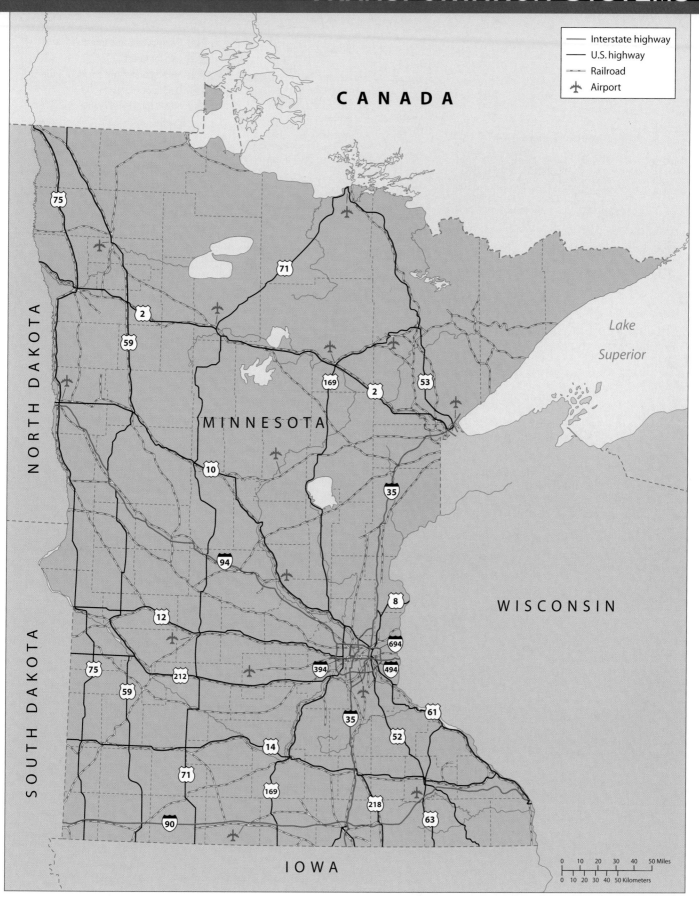

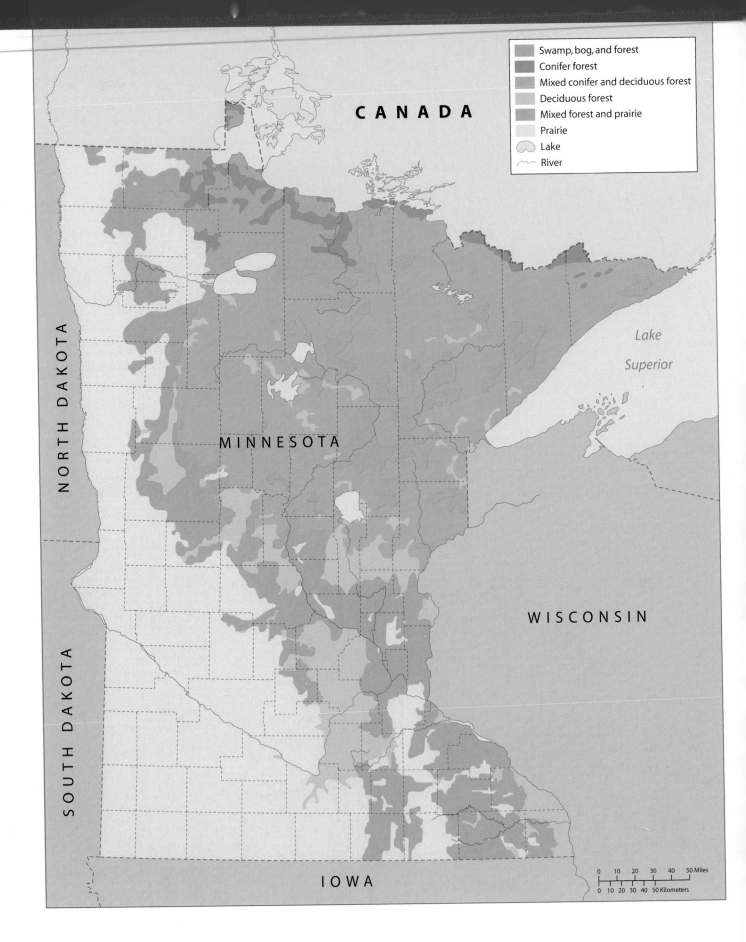

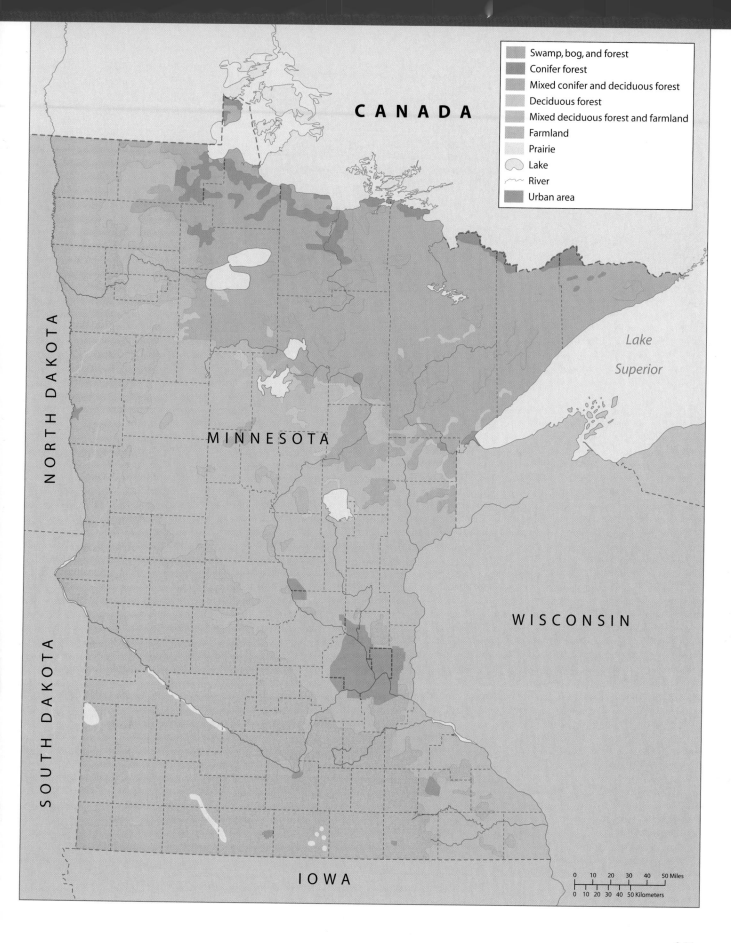

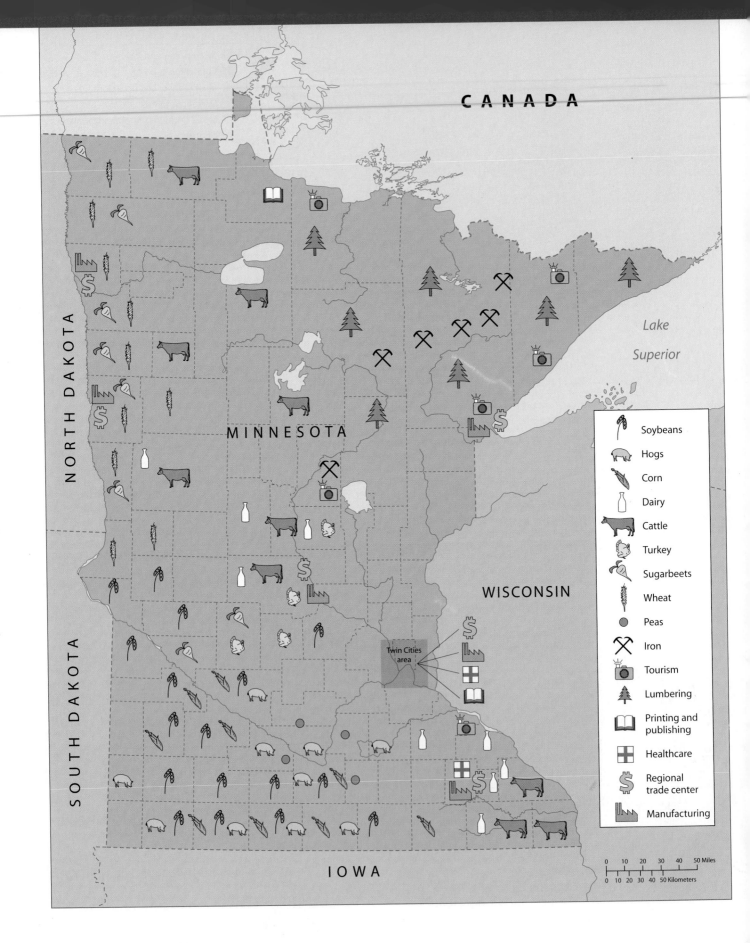

CANADA

NORTH DAKOTA

SOUTH DAKOTA

MINNESOTA

WISCONSIN

Lake Superior

Twin Cities area

IOWA

	Soybeans
	Hogs
	Corn
	Dairy
	Cattle
	Turkey
	Sugarbeets
	Wheat
	Peas
	Iron
	Tourism
	Lumbering
	Printing and publishing
	Healthcare
	Regional trade center
	Manufacturing

0 10 20 30 40   50 Miles

0 10 20 30 40 50 Kilometers